H
C
C
S

Harvard Contemporary China Series, 10

The Harvard Contempory China Series, now under the
editorial direction of Harvard University Press, is designed
to present new research that deals with present-day issues
against the background of Chinese history and society.
The focus is on interdisciplinary research intended to
convey the significance of the rapidly changing Chinese
scene.

Engendering China

Women, Culture, and the State

Edited by

Christina K. Gilmartin

Gail Hershatter

Lisa Rofel

Tyrene White

Harvard University Press

Cambridge, Massachusetts

London, England 1994

Library of Congress Cataloging-in-Publication Data
Engendering China: women, culture, and the state / edited by
   Christina K. Gilmartin . . . [et al.].
      p.   cm.—(Harvard contemporary China series)
   Includes bibliographical references.
   ISBN 0-674-25331-0 (cloth).—ISBN 0-674-25332-9 (paper)
   1. Women—China—Social conditions—Congresses.   2. Sex role—
China—Congresses.   I. Gilmartin, Christina K.   II Series.
HQ1767.E52   1994
305.42'0951—dc20   93-39866
                                                            CIP

To the women, both here and in China, who have led the way in the study of Chinese women, and to our students, who have much work to do

Contents

Acknowledgments   xi

Introduction   1
Christina K. Gilmartin, Gail Hershatter,
Lisa Rofel, Tyrene White

I Beyond Family, Household, and Kinship

1. Learned Women in the Eighteenth Century   27
   Susan Mann

2. From Daughter to Daughter-in-Law in the
   Women's Script of Southern Hunan   47
   Cathy Silber

3. Out of the Traditional Halls of Academe:
   Exploring New Avenues for Research on Women   69
   Chen Yiyun
   Translated by S. Katherine Campbell

4. China's Modernization and Changes in the
   Social Status of Rural Women   80
   Gao Xiaoxian
   Translated by S. Katherine Campbell

II Sex and the Social Order

5. Desire, Danger, and the Body: Stories of Women's
Virtue in Late Ming China 101
Katherine Carlitz

6. Rethinking Van Gulik: Sexuality and Reproduction
in Traditional Chinese Medicine 125
Charlotte Furth

7. Modernizing Sex, Sexing Modernity: Prostitution
in Early Twentieth-Century Shanghai 147
Gail Hershatter

8. Male Suffering and Male Desire: The Politics
of Reading *Half of Man Is Woman*
by Zhang Xianliang 175
Zhong Xueping

III Where Liberation Lies

9. Gender, Political Culture, and Women's
Mobilization in the Chinese Nationalist
Revolution, 1924–1927 195
Christina K. Gilmartin

10. Liberation Nostalgia and a Yearning
for Modernity 226
Lisa Rofel

11. The Origins of China's Birth Planning Policy 250
Tyrene White

12. Chinese Women Workers: The Delicate
Balance between Protection and Equality 279
Margaret Y. K. Woo

IV Becoming Women in the Post-Mao Era

13. Women's Consciousness and Women's Writing 299
Li Ziyun
Translated by Zhu Hong

14. Women, Illness, and Hospitalization: Images
of Women in Contemporary Chinese Fiction   318
Zhu Hong

15. Politics and Protocols of *Funü:*
(Un)Making National Woman   339
Tani E. Barlow

16. Economic Reform and the Awakening of
Chinese Women's Collective Consciousness   360
Li Xiaojiang
Translated by S. Katherine Campbell

Notes   385

Contributors   451

Acknowledgments

We have accumulated many debts in preparing this volume and planning the conference out of which it grew. First thanks go to Merle Goldman, who decided that a conference should took place, organized us to organize it, and put all her fund-raising and lobbying skill at our disposal. "Engendering China: Women, Culture, and the State" was held at Harvard University, Wellesley College, and MIT February 7–10, 1992. We acknowledge the generous financial support given by the John King Fairbank Center for East Asian Research at Harvard University, Wellesley College, the Mayling Soong Foundation, the Ford Foundation, the Center for Cultural Studies at the Massachusetts Institute of Technology, the East Asian Legal Studies Center at Harvard Law School, and Northeastern University.

At each of these institutions, individuals went out of their way to make the conference a success. Mary Ann Burris and Peter Harris at the Ford Foundation made it possible for the conference to be truly international. The Fairbank Center's Director, Roderick MacFarquhar, Betty Burch, Paul Cohen, the late Patrick Maddox, Hue-tam Ho Tai, James Watson, and Rubie Watson provided financial, logistical, and moral support. For heroic staff support at the Fairbank Center, we thank Antoinette Colbert, Anne Denna, Fuji Lozada, Brett Rubel, and James Selman. Nannerl Keohane, Paul Cohen, William Joseph, and Kim Roberts funded and coordinated our day at Wellesley. Sigrid Bergenstein and Pam Kubbins provided memorable food. Helen Dunstan, Peter Perdue, and Ruth Perry at MIT helped arrange a supplementary day of panels involving the conference participants. Sun Lantao of the PRC Consulate and Laura Frader of Northeastern University also rendered important assistance. Students who provided crucial logistical help include Jacqueline Armijo-Hussein (rapporteur), Maris Gillette, Alison Groppe, Kenneth Hammond, Lyn Jeffrey, Lida Junghans, Matthew Kohrman, Grace Moy, Greta Niu, Michelle Sie, and Emma Jinhua Teng. Guo Xiaolin, He Hongfei, Carma Hinton, Kang Hongjin, Ma Yuanxi, Yue Mei, and Zhu Hong contributed to making all conference conversations as bilingual as possible.

The essays in this volume are the result of the work not only of the individual authors but of all who were engaged in the conference, including Marilyn Young, who provided a historically informed and witty opening statement, Bao Xiaolan, Laurel Bossen, Flora Botton, Chang Chueh, Elisabeth J. Croll, Dai Qing, Delia Davin, Dong Xiuyu, Du Fangqin, Harriet Evans, Christine Gailey, Susan Greenhalgh, Yukiko Hanawa, Kathleen Hartford, Gail Henderson, Emily Honig, Hsiung Ping-chen, Joan Kaufman, Lydia Liu, Luo Yuzheng, Ma Jingheng, Susan Naquin, Heather Peters, Qi Wenying, Susan Reverby, Nancy Riley, Paul Ropp, Vivienne Shue, Richard Smith, Su Hongjun, Hue-tam Ho Tai, Tan Lin, Tan Shen, Ann Waltner, Wang Qihui, Wang Xingjuan, Ellen Widmer, Elizabeth Wood, Yang Jin, Ye Weili, Zhao Xiyan, Zhou Xiao, and Rubie Watson, who provided a fine closing summation.

The volume was immeasurably improved as a result of criticisms and suggestions by Rubie Watson and Marilyn Young. Any remaining flaws are our responsibility. Elizabeth Suttell at Harvard University Press has been efficient and enthusiastic about shepherding the book through the publication process. Amanda Heller provided superb copyediting. Patricia Sanders and Lisa Morgan of Merrill College Faculty Services, University of California at Santa Cruz, helped keep the contributors in touch with one another. Each contributor labored mightily to meet the draconian deadlines we set. Finally, we are grateful to one another for the multiple pleasures of collaborative work.

Engendering China

CHRISTINA K. GILMARTIN
GAIL HERSHATTER
LISA ROFEL
TYRENE WHITE

Introduction

The authors whose essays are included in this volume are of different generations, hold citizenship in different nations, and were trained in different disciplines. Nevertheless, the essays have a common intellectual concern: gender relations in China.

The book's title, *Engendering China*, is meant to invoke two aspects of that common project. First, it defines gender as an ensemble of social and cultural practices; analyzing those practices is central to our understanding of human societies. Gender signifies that the categories female and male—the meanings assigned to them, the behaviors expected of them, the sense of self associated with them, and the relations among and between those female and male selves—are cultural constructions.[1] Gender is relational; femininity and masculinity make sense only in relation to each other, and behaviors that are thought to transgress gender boundaries can be understood only if we know how a particular society has mapped those boundaries. Gendered identity and relationships are not merely an individual or personal matter; they are enforced (and sometimes undermined) by family, religion, medicine, state authority, and a variety of other institutions. In turn, gender provides some of the language and categories through which family, state, and other social arrangements are articulated and justified. Gender is not just an updated or academically sanitized word for "women." Attention to gender illuminates women's lives, but more fundamentally, it addresses the very operation of social life.

Second, the word *engendering* conveys the sense that new knowledge is being created. In using it we mean to suggest that adding women to the social and historical picture, and highlighting gender as a category of analysis, changes the whole. China viewed through the lens of gender is not just more inclusive; it is different. By proposing to "engender China," we make the claim that research on women and gender does not rest in a corner of sinological endeavors, but revises the most basic categories through which we strive to apprehend Chinese social relations, institutions, and cultural productions.

From the sixteenth century to the present, China has faced a series of dilemmas that intensified under western pressure in the nineteenth century and continued throughout the revolutionary upheavals of the twentieth. In the process, the entire ethical and cultural system was called into question by Chinese and foreign critics with a multitude of agendas. By the late nineteenth century, Chinese elites, whose political and scholarly commitments were intertwined, had come to define China's central problem as one of building the nation under hostile circumstances. In the twentieth century, Chinese thinkers and western scholars as well have viewed the dynamic of events in China as propelled by the need to accommodate "tradition" to the demands of "modernity." Neither conceptualization gives gender a prominent place in historical and cultural change. In fact, much of the writing about China makes women invisible. A closer look at recent Chinese history, however, suggests that the language of gender has been crucial to the way Chinese people have defined their own modernity.

In the writings of late imperial and early republican reformers and revolutionaries, for example, raising the status of women and strengthening the nation were presented as inseparable projects. Both the Nationalists and the Communists promised women status as equal citizens as a marker of China's arrival at modernity. For complex reasons, neither party managed to keep this promise fully. Major political transformations, such as the founding of the People's Republic in 1949, exhibit both dramatic change and striking areas of continuity when the effects and limits of state policy on gender relations are examined. In the post-Mao era, gender has exploded as an arena for the expression of popular discontent, conflicts with state power, and deeply felt longings for prosperity, stability, and, once again, "modernity." Arguing that historical and contemporary China cannot be understood without examining these conflicts, each of the essays in this volume dislodges the paradigms through which scholars have interpreted China by asking what happens when we regard gender as a central issue.

If gender is the book's common project, it is also the source of diversity among the essays. The authors come from different disciplines, received different types of academic training, and have different relationships to the Chinese revolution, the state it created, and the history assembled under the imprimatur of that state. We did not all grow up with or absorb the same knowledge; our "common sense" is not held in common. We all speak *to* the shared project of making women visible and taking power-laden gender relationships as a legitimate object of inquiry. Yet each essay also speaks *against* some received wisdom. Our voices share an oppositional tone but take aim at different targets of opposition. Because each author's intentions, like the concerns of the subjects we portray, are historically contingent and culturally specific, we do not all sound alike, and sometimes we talk past one another, or find ourselves engaged in direct argument about just how to "engender" China, and to what end. In introducing these essays, then, we have to ask: What claims is each of us making, and whose claims are being challenged?

The overlapping but diverse agendas of the contributors were apparent at the conference that gave rise to this volume. The conference drew scholars of anthropology, Asian American studies, economics, history, law, literature, politics, public health, and sociology. In three days of panels, forty-nine scholars presented original research, spoke at a roundtable discussion, and provided formal commentaries. Participants came from the United States, Canada, England, the People's Republic of China, and Taiwan. Eight scholars from institutions in the People's Republic attended, as well as a significant number currently in graduate programs, faculty positions, or visiting scholar posts in the United States. Guests from the United States, the PRC, Mexico, Germany, and Austria also contributed to the discussions, among them "Family, Household, and Kinship," "The Social Construction of Sexuality," "Aesthetic Representations of Gender," "Gender and Work," "Women's Status and Gendered Relations," "Gender and the State," "Women's Health and Reproductive Issues," and "Multiple Perspectives on Feminism."

The concerns and intellectual commitments of these scholars are not easily classified; they do not divide along a "West"/"China" axis. Chinese scholars, for instance, have a range of opinions about the usefulness of western feminist theory. It became clear in three days of intensive conversations that the papers were informed by diverse disciplinary approaches and experiences in China. The concerns of the authors can be partially situated by looking at the issues that prompted four American scholars of China to organize the conference and assemble the present volume, as well as the environment in China that has produced a new body of women's studies research since the mid-1980s.

In imagining and shaping the conference and this volume, the editors have worked within four contexts: the development of feminist research inside and outside the academy over the last two decades; the emphasis on "difference" among postcolonial feminists and women of color writing about the United States; new conditions of research in the PRC; and, at a moment of social flux, the broader question of what China will become and represent, both to those who live in China and to those who look on from other places.

Feminist research within the academy has always been linked, if at times indirectly, with feminist activism outside the academy. As the second wave of the women's movement gained momentum in the United States and Europe in the 1970s, western feminists engaged in a concerted effort to understand not just their own systems of gender hierarchy but also the experiences of women elsewhere in the world. The goals were several: to uncover commonalities and universals that might point to the sources of women's secondary status; to envisage alternative paths for social change presented by the record of cross-cultural variation; to find those factors that, when they intersected with gender, produced fundamental transformations in women's lives (socialist revolutions, with their stated commitment to women's liberation, attracted a great deal of attention); and to build an international women's movement.

Research on women outside Europe and the United States initially took two approaches. The first concerned the development of women's status, with particular attention to education, labor, and the impact of technology. Some argued that women had been left behind in the development process. Women, they said, needed to be offered the skills that would enable them to extricate themselves from the traditional sectors of the economy. The second approach attempted a unified analysis of women's oppression. Feminist scholars used the concept of patriarchy or focused on a symbolic, cross-cultural division between domestic and public spheres to explore male domination in the family, the workplace, and politics. All of this research, dedicated to making women visible, generated an enormous quantity of new knowledge about women. The results were transformative rather than merely additive. They altered disciplinary knowledge and provided new ways to think about women in multilayered contexts. Margery Wolf's ground-breaking ethnography on women and the family in Taiwan, for instance, irrevocably altered conceptions of "the Chinese family" as a harmonious group experienced in the same way by each of its members. Marilyn Young's edited volume *Women in China* illustrated the tremendous range of historical questions that could not be understood without reference to women.[2]

Building on these earlier studies, a new round of feminist scholarship in the 1980s laid emphasis on women's agency and resistance, gendered divisions of labor, and critiques of development under colonialism and neocolonialism. Rather than exclusively delineate the contours of women's oppression, feminist scholars began to argue for the complex ways women are caught up in relations of power. They no longer viewed "patriarchal" relations, for example, as static, ahistorical configurations, but saw them instead as contingent social arrangements that were always being contested and, in turn, required a great deal of cultural and political force to keep in place. Studies also expanded the concept of gender to include the symbolic meanings of femininity and masculinity that shape the way power is represented in a given society. Thus, they linked divisions of labor found in the development process to larger frames of meaning through which tasks are gendered. They placed development itself in the context of European and American global power since the Second World War. They argued that socialist revolutions have conceived of power in masculinist ways. Trenchant critiques of China's revolution, for example, were developed by Kay Ann Johnson, Judith Stacey, and Phyllis Andors.[3] These scholars found that although the revolution had improved women's lives, it had not addressed the full range of gender inequalities. Finally, feminists argued that "woman," previously assumed to be a transhistorical, transcultural category, was not a unified identity and did not mean the same thing in all contexts.

Feminist scholars in the 1980s made the issue of "difference" a vital problematic in theorizing gender. Their concerns ranged from postcoloniality to minority discourse to psychoanalytic theory. A number of postcolonial writers in particular[4] argued that feminists based in the United States and Europe too often establish a unitary standard for what constitutes a feminist agenda elsewhere in the world. Universalist needs, desires, and social circumstances are then extrapolated from this agenda, which is often rooted in western experiences, and used to measure women's status. The result is an effacement of the diversity of women's lives and their agency in constructing specific gender relations and meanings.

Placed in the context of a universalist feminist agenda, the problems Chinese women face are often attributed to differences that seem unalterably "other" to the West. Here the West remains the unmarked standard against which difference is measured. The subordination of Chinese women, for example, is explained by reference to overarching frameworks of "socialism" or "Chinese culture" without sufficient recognition of the historically contingent quality of these broad categories.[5] Too often Chinese women come up short when compared to women living in the West. They are made to seem not only oppressed but unaware of the true nature of their oppression.

The conference and the resulting volume grew directly out of our concerns with the univocal nature of this theorizing. We sought to bring together women and men from a variety of social, cultural, and intellectual positions in order to create a dialogue that would challenge the dichotomy between Europeans and Americans as theory makers and Chinese women as objects of theory. The point, however, is not to create a unification of perspectives or goals.[6] Our hope is to begin to forge alliances across differing feminist agendas.

At the same time, it is critical for those of us in the United States who do research on gender in China not to adopt wholesale the theoretical insights of postcolonial feminism and merely superimpose them onto the local Chinese case. China, after all, was not colonized outright, nor is its relationship to postcolonialism a simple one. Rather than universalize yet another particular story, this one developed by intellectuals in the postcolonial world, we need to attend to the ways in which Chinese women and men assign meaning to their own recent history. We must listen to how Chinese women's studies scholars frame their struggles—paying close attention, for instance, to their evolving critique of state power, state-sponsored feminism, and the multiple effects of economic reforms on gender hierarchy. We must also reflect on how we interpret these issues in light of our own political and scholarly concerns.

We hope, then, that this volume will make a unique contribution to the enterprise of decentering western women as the standard from which to analyze other women's lives. One of the tendencies against which contributors from the United States have struggled is the still prevalent feminist direction here and in Europe toward developing universal theories about the meanings of femininity and masculinity, theories that in fact derive their generalizations from those specific places. The attention given in this volume to the state's involvement in constructing the category "woman"; to the relationship of feminist and socialist strands in the early communist movement; to the uses of officially sponsored feminism in a socialist state; to the historical production of writings by female literati; to cultural specificity in the meanings of sexuality, prostitution, work, political participation and bodies (especially through birth control policies) should challenge recent feminist theorizing in "the West."

Part of the excitement of the conference and the essays in this volume is that they address the nascent yet already productive alliances between Chinese and western women's studies scholars. In the early 1970s Margery Wolf and Roxane Witke organized the last United States–based conference on women in China. At that time they noted that "the gravest handicap in the study of women in Chinese society is the inadequacy of data on the attitudes and opinions of ordinary women."[7] New conditions in the PRC have begun to remedy that handicap, making possible much of the work presented in this volume. These transformations in ethnographic, survey, and archival research do not simply mean that improved access leads to a more complete picture. Rather, the production of new knowledge about China takes place in a multivocal environment, one that involves a proliferation of research agendas, an expansion of conversations, and an enhanced attention to the diversity of Chinese women's experiences.

If the authors in this volume hope to offer a more vital cross-cultural perspective to women's studies here "at home," they have a precedent for doing so. Feminist theorists in the United States and Europe turned their attention to China in the 1970s, hoping to learn from the vast social experiments undertaken there. The answers that came back were sometimes unexpected, but the effort led to a deepened appreciation of the complexity of gender, and spurred much of the current theorizing. China is once again undergoing fundamental transformations as it moves away from socialism. Anyone concerned with the possibilities and constraints of gender arrangements will need to grasp the implications of these changes, for the end of socialism has global reverberations.

The contributors to this volume also bring a renewed attention to the links among gender, power, and knowledge in the field of Chinese studies. We find ourselves situated both within and between feminist studies and sinology, and we look forward to producing intellectual sparks from these multiple positions. As sinologists who study gender, we share with other sinologists the excitement in these problematic times of figuring out what China means for us, always needing to consider what China also represents in wider public discussions in the United States. This is a moment of flux, when older stories about a communist China have faded but new frameworks are still elusive. It is challenging enough to explain the introduction of a market-based economy in China and the divergent popular responses to it. Add to that the destabilizing collapse of socialism in eastern Europe and the former Soviet Union, and we see a situation in which the U.S. government, media, business, and academic worlds have not developed a dominant narrative about what China is and should be for the United States. In this situation, sinologists face the challenge of identifying, interpreting, and reshaping the multiple narratives that circulate about China.

For Chinese scholars working in China, as well as for those in diaspora who write with a Chinese audience in mind, the 1980s produced a crucial change in the centrality of gender questions to ongoing social debate. This period has seen the development of women's studies programs at a number of Chinese universities, and the publication of research on women by people working for a variety of government and nongovernment agencies, including the national and provincial Women's Federations, provincial family planning research bureaus, and women's counseling and research centers.

This surge in publishing activity represents a rupture with the recent past. Since its founding, the Chinese Communist party has used women's liberation as one of the key categories through which it justified its revolutionary promise. Nevertheless, since 1949 gender has not been a tool with which people in China could analyze persistent social inequalities, since these inequalities were assumed to be "nonantagonistic contradictions" which would gradually diminish as socialism flourished under the leadership of the party. The party/state created categories of identity exclusively through class, and many women certainly developed their sense of themselves by way of class relations. For years new gender problems emerging under socialism went unarticulated, by state authorities or anyone else.

In the late 1970s, with the rejection of Maoist class labels (though certainly not the disappearance of class), people began to describe their experiences using the language of other categories, including gender. Gender became visible, audible, and full of controversy. In both popular and academic circles, attentiveness to gender came to stand for many things: rejection of the Cultural Revolution, support for as well as criticism of the policies of economic reform, and a critique of the way socialist politics had constructed sameness between women and men and failed to recognize the specific circumstances of women's lives.

Over the years of reform, new issues in gender relations have become the subject of public controversy: hiring policies toward women workers, job and marriage prospects of women college graduates, a proliferation of extramarital affairs (or at least public discussion of those affairs), the decision of many work units to provide extended maternity leave for working women (sometimes for a period of years), and the resurgence of prostitution.

Everyone involved in debates on these issues emphasizes gender difference. For instance, some Chinese women excoriate the state for having tried to suppress women's "natural" femininity. They demand that this difference be recognized and reflected both in state policy and in literary production. The post-Mao state, in turn, has laid claim to a recognition of gender difference as a means of distinguishing itself from its predecessor and legitimizing the whole reform enterprise. Whether this state attention to difference is protective, discriminatory, or adequately developed is a matter of argument between Chinese gender activists and the Chinese state. These women insist that recognition of difference should be a means toward achieving greater equality rather than an indication of women's special disabilities. Echoes of that argument are audible in many of the essays by Chinese scholars in this volume. The treatment of gender by Chinese writers in the early 1990s is best understood as part of a larger Chinese conversation: What kind of society do we want to have? What does the good life look like? What are the costs of achieving it?

Gender research now being conducted in China is animated by a variety of concerns. One involves the multiple effects of reform, and whether reform policies have had good, bad, or mixed results for women. Researchers look at women's income, job opportunities and rate of work force participation, access to education, and an intensification of the gendered division of labor. Some scholars have begun to analyze the particular situation of rural women: their movement into nonagricultural pursuits and sometimes into cities, as well as their changing contribution to the household economy. Second, with respect to women's reproductive labor, these scholars look at a range of issues: reproductive health, birth control, abortion, maternity leave, child care facilities, and division of labor in the home. Third, legal scholars have turned their attention to the legal basis for women's rights, in particular the comprehensive law for the protection of women's rights passed in 1992 (but without detailed provisions for implementation). Fourth, also evident is an effort to restore women to Chinese history, for the writing of that history since 1949 has been dominated by Maoist class categories, and to explore gendered writing strategies in literature. Fifth, the boundary between women's studies scholarship and activism is a permeable one; scholars have been active in establishing call-in hot lines for women, opening marriage counseling practices, and issuing position papers on a variety of legal and social issues. Writing on gender in China today does not always involve a rejection of socialism or every aspect of state gender policy; it does, however, involve a challenge to old state paradigms and an attempt to help shape new ones.

Although the essays in this volume span the time period from the sixteenth century to the present, and include contributions from a variety of disciplines, they speak to one another through four shared themes. One is the issue of representation, that is, in what times, places, and contexts people write about Chinese women. Many of the essays study the process by which Chinese and Westerners, usually but not always male, as individuals as well as in complex entities such as the state, have framed a category called "Chinese women." In all the historical periods covered in this volume, including the present, these voices have talked for and about Chinese women, but they have also talked through them to express concerns about society, the nation, and politics. The essays on twentieth-century China, for example, demonstrate that gender is one of the key categories through which China has conceived of itself in relation to the rest of the world, but especially in relation to the West. As one essay demonstrates, prostitution was a particularly sensitive issue in this regard. "Engendering" China means bringing these processes of representation to the fore.

A second theme is the effort to complicate the category "Chinese women." These essays are attuned to the multiplicity of identities, voices, locations, and moments hidden when that general category is invoked. The category "women workers" in socialist China, for example, covers a range of women who differ by generation, by class aspirations, and by the moment when they entered the local political economy of particular industries. Attention to these differences brings out a much richer picture, demonstrating that not much about "Chinese women" is easily generalizable.

A third theme is the search for women's agency—the manner in which different groups of Chinese women, in different times and places, have taken up and responded to the powerful social forces shaping their lives. Many of the essays detail women's voices and actions in places where women often have not been visible—in high literati circles, in a special women's phonetic language circulated among "illiterate" peasant women, and in the contemporary literary strategy of portraying women as ill or hospitalized in order, para-doxically, to open up new ways of presenting an awareness of women's lives. These essays do much to dispel the notion of women as victims of overwhelming social structures, an approach that char-acterized an earlier decade of gender research. Instead, they trace a range of women's actions—accommodation, negotiation, resis-tance—complicating any portrait of Chinese women as the uncritical embodiment of official virtue.

A final theme is the centrality of gender to questions of state formation and state policy-making. State authorities, both national and local, have enormous power to shape concepts of "woman." Many of the essays concern themselves with the question of how institutional structures define women and affect their daily lives in specific and practical ways. Conversely, gender and its effects are felt at every level of the policy process, whether or not policymakers analyze and acknowledge those effects. The family planning pro-gram and its unintended consequences are a good example of both these processes.

The volume is divided into four sections. The first, "Beyond Family, Household, and Kinship," acknowledges that these are the venues in which Chinese women conventionally have been located and studied. Aside from a small number of empresses, courtesans, intellectuals, and revolutionaries, it is primarily in their roles as daughters, wives, and mothers that Chinese women have been encountered in the historical record. In fact, family and kinship networks have been presented in much anthropological scholarship not only as the predominant environment for women but also as the essence of Chinese society. Without discounting the importance of these institutions, the four essays in this section suggest that women were and are involved in other networks as well: poetry societies, formally recognized extrafamilial friendships, and work relationships, to name a few. Furthermore, these essays indicate that family and kinship networks do not move through history in a hermetically sealed social structure. They are profoundly intertwined with state policy, intellectual movements, economic trends, and a variety of other factors. In turn, family and kinship arrangements may stymie or facilitate state policy, nurture or limit the effects of intellectual change, stimulate or stall particular kinds of economic developments. Serious attention to these interactions calls into question our very notion of what family and kinship are, and how women are situated within them.

Susan Mann's "Learned Women in the Eighteenth Century" examines the production of poetry by a group of educated elite women in the late imperial period. The poet Yuan Mei admired their artistic talent and characterized them as rebels against social convention. By contrast, the Confucian scholar Zhang Xuecheng condemned their poetry making, counseling women to return to the "separate sphere" of specifically feminine learning and practice. As Mann points out, Yuan and Zhang shared the assumption that women should be educated; they differed on what the content of appropriate female education—and behavior—should be. But Mann is not content to let an account of women poets' lives and work remain enmeshed in a debate between learned men. Instead, she turns to the texts in which these women most directly represented their own concerns and emotions: their poems. There she finds a multiplicity of voices, from child prodigies through scholarly poet brides to older women mourning the loss of children and other loved ones. Many of these poets, she argues, explicitly embraced classical morality and family attachments; they were not the rebels whom Yuan Mei praised and Zhang Xuecheng repudiated. Yet if theirs are not voices of resistance, she suggests, neither are they the obedient murmurings of complicit victims. Many of the poems are highly personal, passionate, often anguished ruminations on individual lives; in Mann's words, they "command our respectful attention" as both literary work and historical source.

Cathy Silber's "From Daughter to Daughter-in-Law in the Women's Script of Southern Hunan" examines the creation of *nüshu* (literally, "women's writing") in the first half of the twentieth century. Through a highly formalized syllabic script, young unmarried women wrote to others of similar age and socioeconomic background to form "couples" marked by expectations of exclusivity and long-term commitment in a relationship metaphorically cast as analogous to marriage. Women also wrote in this script to mourn the loss of friends through marriage and to express profound antipathy toward that institution. Silber contends that these non-kin peer group friendships were as meaningful to the women of southern Hunan as kinship ties. The female social networks they established long before marriage, far from being marginal to a patriarchal society, played a vital part in local social life. The writing and circulation of *nüshu*, Silber suggests, indicates that women were not merely subservient to male-dominated kinship; they had agency and room to maneuver as unwed daughters even while situated in a patriarchal society. But Silber cautions us not to romanticize the women's script as a discourse of resistance. *Nüshu* created a way for women to express anguish over life transitions, but it also formalized a socially induced disposition against marriage. The women's script, and the relations established through it, highlighted the dilemmas of womanhood in an asymmetrical world; they were a contained, nondisruptive means of negotiating those dilemmas.

Chen Yiyun, a leading sociologist at the Chinese Academy of Social Sciences, has pioneered the development of research on women during the reform period. Her essay, "Out of the Traditional Halls of Academe: Exploring New Avenues for Research on Women," asks what the best methodologies are for exploring the complexities of women's lives under economic reform. After languishing in disgrace for several decades, sociology in China has been partially rehabilitated as an academic discipline. With it have come legions of western and Chinese researchers armed with questionnaires and computers, eager to collect data on marriage and family life. Chen offers a series of reflections on the inadequacy of western social science methods as they have been practiced in China. Scholars beware, warns Chen; your subjects will tell you what they are socially expected to feel rather than how they do feel or act. They will all say that they married for love, and eschew any concern with material considerations; their answers will be brief, bland, and not particularly useful. Chen argues that research on marriage and the family requires the development of new, socially engaged research methods. She describes her own move into less orthodox strategies: her decision to talk about marriage and family life on radio and television; her careful perusal of the gunnysacks of mail her programs elicited from troubled listeners and viewers; her growing practice in marriage and family therapy; her methods of conducting in-depth interviews across many regions and occupations; and her development of sustained friendships with those whose lives she seeks to understand. In investigating the effects of economic reforms on popular attitudes and practices, she warns that scholars are tracking a moving, even volatile, target, and she offers four suggestions: attentiveness to difference in Chinese women's experience across region and class; respect for the beneficial effects of several decades of the state-run women's movement; development of a socially engaged feminist methodology that draws on anthropology; and promotion of international exchange among women's studies scholars.

Gao Xiaoxian is among the minority of women's studies scholars who have turned their attention to the majority of Chinese women: rural residents. Her essay, "China's Modernization and Changes in the Social Status of Rural Women," analyzes the gendered effects of past and present Chinese development policy. She begins with a reevaluation of the major political movements in the People's Republic by asking how each of them affected the status of rural women. Judged by this criterion, an event such as the Cultural Revolution does not loom large (as it might if we focused on intellectuals or students of both sexes), whereas the collectivization process of the 1950s and particularly the Great Leap Forward emerge as events of signal importance. Gao does not retrospectively idealize the process of socialist construction, however, noting that it added to women's work burden and did not further rural economic modernization. When she turns to the effects of more recent reform, she finds women earning increased income in township and village enterprises as well as household commodity production. A sizable group has migrated from the villages to work in township factories, take jobs in coastal export-processing zones, or perform paid domestic labor for urban families. Gao finds some signs that the status of wives and daughters in the family, and their own self-evaluation, has risen accordingly, particularly in the areas where rural industrialization has proceeded most quickly. Yet she also notes that opportunities and income for men have improved even more rapidly, and that some new employment opportunities for women (such as export processing) track them into the lowest-paid and least secure new jobs. At the same time, the reforms have left rural practices of virilocality, patrilineality, and patriarchy unchanged, perpetuating the preference for sons. Concluding that "modernization in and of itself will not spontaneously liberate women" (just as socialism did not), Gao calls for intensive educational efforts aimed at rural women, as well as government promotion of what amounts to affirmative action for women in the course of economic development. Women scholars and women's organizations, she suggests, will have to take the lead in formulating such initiatives and pressuring the government to adopt them.

The book's second section, "Sex and the Social Order," explores the ways in which sexed bodies, usually but not always female, have signified both desirable and despised social attributes. The late Ming woman martyr, the connubial Qing couple, the twentieth-century urban prostitute, the fictional impotent prisoner in a Maoist labor camp: each literally embodies a social message, which in turn helps to frame the ways that bodies and sexual or reproductive acts are given historically specific meanings. Sex and sexual acts cannot be reduced to a series of physical positions and motions; they are cul- turally interpreted, even by the most immediate participants, and the context in which they are understood is always being trans- formed. Each of the four essays in this section examines a different moment in that transformation.

Katherine Carlitz, in "Desire, Danger, and the Body: Stories of Women's Virtue in Late Ming China," takes up the stories of (mostly young and beautiful) women who sacrificed parts of their bodies, or even their lives, in order to demonstrate the Confucian virtues of filiality, chastity, and loyalty. She argues that the tales of such acts should not be seen as a contrast to what Mark Elvin has called the "robust sensuality" of the late Ming. Rather, in their loving attention to the gory details of sacrifice, and their intense focus on the physi- cal dimension of women's ordeals, the stories themselves participate in a robust sensuality—one that made female exemplars "simultane- ously icons of virtue and objects of sensuous connoisseurship." The stories were meant to excite *qing*, or intense emotion, but the *qing* they inspired came to include romantic love and sexual desire as well as canonically correct political loyalty. Carlitz carefully analyzes the language used to describe such virtuous women, and explores the institutional networks that collected and promulgated their stories. Although the notion that women's virtue was a pillar of the Confu- cian political order has long been a truism among scholars, she urges us to go further and attend to the ways in which "the Empire was imagined through the bodies of women."

Charlotte Furth's "Rethinking Van Gulik: Sexuality and Reproduc- tion in Traditional Chinese Medicine" reworks the categories and meanings of sexuality in China during both the late Han and the Ming-Qing periods. She provides a provocative challenge to the work of Robert Van Gulik, which has stood as the classic account of Chinese sexual life in western sinology. Furth argues that Van Gulik's interpretation of the late Han bedchamber manuals as exemplary of libertarian sexuality is based in twentieth-century western sexology research, with its assumptions of natural drives and the need to "liberate" one's sexual desires. Such an interpretation assumes Euro- centric constructions of both sex and the "Orient." Furth's essay concentrates instead on contemporary meanings of sexuality in the context of prolonging life and generativity. She challenges us not to constitute sexuality as a freestanding realm marked by struggles of repression and liberation, but rather to situate it historically.

Gail Hershatter's "Modernizing Sex, Sexing Modernity: Prostitution in Early Twentieth-Century Shanghai" examines the changing ways in which urban elites represented prostitution. Over a forty-year period, the urbane, cultured, witty, scheming, and duplicitous courtesan was displaced in their writings by the figure of the streetwalker, "a victimized, disorderly, dangerous embodiment of social trouble." New forms of sex work proliferated during this period. At the same time, and inseparable from these social changes, the eye of the beholder (literatus, journalist, legislator, reformer, women's rights activist, Christian, communist, social scientist) was changing, too; it was, in fact, a roving and inconstant eye. Nostalgically remembered or energetically denounced, prostitution provided a realm for these shifting elites to articulate their concerns about Chinese modernity and map the kind of sexual and gender arrangements that would either signal that modernity or disqualify China from participating in it.

Zhong Xueping directs her essay to a contemporary humanist position voiced by male Chinese intellectuals who express political opposition within China and in diaspora. Humanism has become a focal point for much intellectual dissent against the state, whose actions are taken to be intrusions on the autonomy of the individual. In "Male Suffering and Male Desire: The Politics of Reading *Half of Man Is Woman* by Zhang Xianliang," Zhong Xueping engenders—or rather discerns the already engendered nature of—this discourse as exemplified in Zhang's popular and controversial novel. In the novel Zhang asserts that the state has emasculated its male citizens; physical emasculation is made to stand for loss of political virility. Yet Zhong Xueping argues that the "human nature" represented in the novel as suppressed by the state is a masculine human nature, whose fulfillment depends on making women its object. Zhong contends that the oppositional political subject has been constructed as male and formed over the bodies of women. Although Zhang's male protagonist may be a victim in relation to the state, his desire for political power includes a reinscription of patriarchal relations.

The book's third section, "Where Liberation Lies," explores the imbrication of state-making and gender construction in twentieth-century China. "The state" in China and elsewhere has often been studied as a gender-neutral domain of power. The essays in this section challenge this assumption. As a group, they trace how gender has been essential in shaping the contours of China's socialist state. They lead us to consider two linked questions: How has the modern state constructed itself as an imagined vision through its representations of women? And how, conversely, have women's issues, womanhood, fertility, and feminism been established through the state?

The conventional story pervasive in western scholarship about the Chinese Communist party's gender policy goes something like this: early CCP leaders initially embraced a May Fourth feminism that espoused free-choice marriage and divorce, and an end to polygamy and prostitution. They then quickly abandoned the more potentially divisive parts of this program (notably free marriage and divorce) when faced with the horrified reactions of male peasants. In its place, the party developed a more orthodox Marxist approach to women's liberation which focused on bringing women into socially productive labor. Pursuit of this goal was subordinated to economic exigencies and competing political goals in such a way that women were never truly liberated by the revolution. Rather, they were more tightly subjected to state domination, as exemplified most strikingly by China's birth planning policies. Scholarly reaction to the promulgation of reforms has been ambivalent. Some argue that the initiation of legal reform in the post-Mao period provides women with the promise of more neutral guarantees of equality, while others warn darkly that the reforms will reverse the gains of the socialist period while compounding its errors.

Each of the essays in this section challenges previous representations about socialist state power. Christina K. Gilmartin's "Gender, Political Culture, and Women's Mobilization in the Chinese Nationalist Revolution, 1924–1927" argues that early CCP mobilization campaigns paradoxically demonstrate both more commitment and more ambivalence toward feminism than previously assumed. Gilmartin reevaluates this complex stance for the often overlooked

National Revolution period (1924–1927), when Nationalists and Communists formed a brief and fragile alliance. Gilmartin finds that the women's mobilization campaigns in Guangdong, the center of revolutionary activity, motivated untold numbers of women to join the revolutionary cause through their prominent emphasis on women's emancipation. Moreover, Peng Pai, one of the foremost peasant organizers, initially lent his active support for women's participation in the peasant movement. Yet genuine commitment to women's emancipation contained its own set of contradictions. Tensions arose over whether to stress nationalism or gender oppression in the mobilization of women. Male radical leaders such as Peng Pai, though they thought of themselves as progressive on women's issues, were ultimately influenced by their own uninterrogated assumption of male privilege, as well as by their peasant organizing, toward more patriarchal values.

Lisa Rofel, in "Liberation Nostalgia and a Yearning for Modernity," argues that the insistence of women who came of age in the 1950s that they were liberated by the revolution must be interpreted with close attention to a particular generation's cultural and historical context. She urges us to reconsider the argument that the socialist revolution primarily reconstituted gender inequality in a new form, by recognizing the historicity of various feminisms—Chinese and Euro-American—and the heterogeneity among Chinese women, not only by class but by generation. For the generation of women already working in urban factories at the moment of revolution, the Marxist discourse on women and labor introduced by the CCP replaced a sociospatial construction of female gender identity, based on an opposition of "inside" and "outside," with a functional dichotomy between the enslavement of domestic dependency and the liberation of "work." This Marxist representation was empowering for these women, as it enabled them to shift the terms of pride and shame, moving from the social bottom to the place of vanguard, liberated woman. If this generation currently engages in nostalgia for that moment when they figured as heroes, says Rofel, and if the youngest generation of workers yearns for a modernity that entails a rejection of the Marxist liberated woman, one should not allow these structured sentiments to obscure an earlier meaning of liberation.

Tyrene White, in "The Origins of China's Birth Planning Policy," ventures into the controversial realm of China's birth planning program. More than any other Chinese state activity, the family planning program has been represented in the United States, especially during the Reagan-Bush era, as the quintessence of communist oppression. Many who would under no circumstance call themselves feminist have denounced the subjection of Chinese women to compulsory birth control. American feminists, by contrast, find themselves caught in a painful dilemma. The support for women's control over their own bodies exists simultaneously with a wariness toward New Right attacks on abortion in China and the unwillingness to see women used as signs of another country's "backwardness" in relation to the United States. White enters this political debate by stepping back from contemporary policies, examining instead the origins of the family planning program in the early 1950s. Only then do we discover a complex historical process in which women first gained then lost the capacity to influence state policy toward their preferences. Women cadres challenged the dual forces of state-sanctioned pronatalism and medical cum moral opposition to birth control. They insisted on the importance of access to birth control as a fundamental part of women's liberation. Their early success was mixed, however, causing advocates of birth control to search for a political rationale capable of protecting the policy. The theory they embraced—that of socialist birth planning—paradoxically became the instrument that justified a new and equally invasive form of state-mandated contraception and limits on childbearing. White concludes that women were more than simply objects of state policy; they were accomplices to its creation.

In "Chinese Women Workers: The Delicate Balance between Protection and Equality," Margaret Woo challenges the presumption that legal reform in post-Mao China necessarily spells progress or more equitable treatment for women. The 1982 Constitution restates China's commitment to equality between women and men, but more recent legislation has turned toward measures that seek to "protect" women's special biological differences, particularly their reproductive capacities. Woo argues that the myriad of rules explicitly structured around women's reproductive cycles contribute to a "biologization" of women that partially contradicts population control policies, which exhort women to limit the exercise of those capacities and have only one child. Woo points out that this protective legislation provides benefits for pregnant women and women with children, but more autonomous employers have failed to implement these benefits. Even where implemented, the legislation leads to discriminatory hiring, occupational sex segregation, and unemployment among women. Woo discusses the striking case of the special economic zones, where women constitute the majority of the labor force and yet protective legislation is nonexistent, to highlight the fact that protective legislation is not simply a matter of women's interests but is foremost an effect of the state's economic development goals. She proposes several strategies Chinese women might pursue to ensure gender equality in the workplace through legal means.

The essays in the fourth section, "Becoming Women in the Post-Mao Era," comment on and take part in the ferment that has brought new visions of womanhood into existence. The explosion of writings by and about women represents a creative attempt to wrest the power to define "woman" away from the state in both its Maoist and its reform incarnations. Women writers and theorists have exposed the problems that women face under reform. Through novels, short stories, social tracts, political treatises, and autobiographies, these critics have rejected the national revolutionary female subject of Maoist socialism, questioned state demands on women justified in the name of economic privatization, and condemned what Li Ziyun calls "the facade of sexual equality in contemporary Chinese society." They have told stories about a growing awareness of themselves as women, overt and covert discrimination and harassment, and restrictive definitions of female sexuality. To varying degrees, they have embraced a sense of essential differences between women and men as one of the most powerful ways to challenge socialist versions of women's liberation.

Li Ziyun's essay, "Women's Consciousness and Women's Writing," is engaged in a revisionist and recuperative literary history: revisionist because she sees the portrayal of women in post-1949 stories as a relentless silencing of women's actual concerns rather than as a record of liberation and equality; recuperative because she seeks to carve out a space beyond the reach of the state where women can express such concerns. Li applauds the strategies women writers have adopted to dismantle the "nonrecognition of gender issues" that persisted in the Maoist period. These begin with giving voice to women's emotions, including love, then move on to fictional portrayals of women facing conflicts between love and work, and finally to explorations of female sexuality. For Li, the major achievement of contemporary women's writing—and the major task before it—is to give voice to authentic female experience. Unlike many of the western or western-educated writers included in this volume, she is less concerned with the cultural construction or specificity of gendered experience than she is with making sure that *any* female voices can be heard over the drone of the state.

Zhu Hong's "Women, Illness, and Hospitalization: Images of Women in Contemporary Chinese Fiction" takes up a phenomenon that has perplexed many western readers of contemporary Chinese women's fiction. If, as Li Ziyun tells us, these short stories and novellas represent a new and bold emergence of "women's consciousness," then why does this newfound women's voice so often emanate from sickly, incapacitated, or dying female protagonists? Zhu resists the most obvious explanations—that a romantic fascination with sickliness is part of the re-creation of delicate "femininity," or that illness serves as a metaphor for the ills of society. Rather, she argues that women authors have spied liberatory possibilities in the hospital bed and the condition of being sick. Relieved of the necessity to be the women others expect them to be, these fictional protagonists "repossess their own bodies" and create new voices for themselves, which they use to speak uncomfortable truths.

In "Politics and Protocols of *Funü:* (Un)Making National Woman," Tani Barlow theorizes the debate over gender politics through an analysis of female subject positions in discourse. Taking the poststructuralist position that language does not merely reflect reality but constructs its meaning, she traces the history of the terms *funü, nüren,* and *nüxing.* All of these terms could be translated as "women," but if they were to be so translated, they would lose the political signification in their various usages. Barlow argues that *funü* signifies the Maoist national woman who fights in the name of the proletariat, a female subject the Women's Federation has tried to resurrect. Federation efforts to monopolize the representation of women have been challenged by oppositional discourses that use *nüxing* to posit essential differences between women and men, and *nüren* to develop a "woman's theory" of women's oppression in society.

Li Xiaojiang's "Economic Reform and the Awakening of Chinese Women's Collective Consciousness" turns a critical eye toward the social and political contradictions women face as a result of economic reform. Women, she contends, have been a cornerstone in the development of China's modernity under reform. They have been used to resolve problems of surplus labor and production efficiency, industrialization, and the use of educated personnel. This situation has been treated not as a significant social issue, however, but as a dilemma women face as individuals. Li readily admits that the road China is pursuing toward modernity makes (at least one kind of) economic sense, but she argues that it leads in exactly the opposite direction from the road women ought to be traveling. If reform holds the promise of promoting China's economic development, it says nothing of women's needs for their own development. Arguing that women's liberation is not the same thing as class liberation or equality with men, Li calls for women to awaken their collective consciousness in order to pursue their freedom as human beings, to possess a sense of self-worth, and to affirm the positive qualities of what has been denigrated as "femininity."

These essays take their place in a volatile and expanding field. Even while this volume has been in preparation, new scholarship has appeared and new conferences have been held or planned, in China and abroad, that contribute to the larger project of "engendering China." We have no doubt that this writing and thinking will augment, challenge, and eventually supersede the classificatory frameworks devised herein. We look forward to conversations with Chinese and western scholars of gender, with comparativists, with scholars from many disciplines who produce knowledge about China, with Chinese from many walks of life, and with all those who have been drawn to the possibilities of respecting difference and challenging gender inequality.

I | Beyond Family, Household, and Kinship

1 | Learned Women in the Eighteenth Century

Authoritative studies of modern China present a uniform picture of women in premodern times. They stress the low status of women in traditional Chinese society, and they emphasize the marginalization women experienced in the patriarchal, patrilocal, and patrilineal kinship system.[1] At worst, women appear as victims;[2] at best, they become strategists forced to achieve their ends by manipulating men, especially their sons.[3] They seem to act as their own oppressors, binding their daughters' feet and tyrannizing their daughters-in-law. As historical actors, they are portrayed as agents of a larger process, their individual identity forever obscured.

Two shifts in recent scholarship have opened new windows on female consciousness in premodern China. The first insists on the importance of historical change, pointing to rising female literacy rates and expanding female economic roles after the sixteenth century.[4] The second identifies a female voice in written sources from the late imperial period, analyzing that voice for new evidence of female perspectives and female consciousness.[5]

This chapter follows these new leads. The moment of historical change it examines is the late eighteenth century, a time when learned women had become so prominent that they provoked a debate about "women's learning" (fu xue).[6] Few parties to the debate disputed the idea that women ought to be educated. The argument focused rather on the question of what, precisely, women ought to learn, and why. This in turn called attention not only to learned women but also to deep-seated moral and philosophical conflicts within the scholarly community. In many of these conflicts women played a symbolic role, serving as emblems of one set of values or another. For obvious reasons, then, the phrase "women's learning" is best seen as one idiom in a larger eighteenth-century debate about art and morality. Such a debate may shed little light on learned women themselves. Nonetheless, because learned women were so prominent and so prolific during this period, a great corpus of their work survives. The debate marks an optimal moment, then, to locate a female voice in the historical record.

A brief account of the debate will show how the range of women's erudition animated bitter arguments between a Confucian philosopher, Zhang Xuecheng, and an iconoclastic poet, Yuan Mei.[7] Then, relying in part on Yuan Mei's observations about his "female disciples" *(nü dizi)* and on the memories preserved in poems and memoirs by and about women, I shall try to see beyond men's debates about women's learning to reveal learned women as literary subjects constructing an identity on their own terms.

The Eighteenth-Century Debate about Women's Learning

The most systematic statement of the issues in the debate appears in an essay titled "Women's Learning" *(Fu xue)* written in 1797/98 by the philosopher Zhang Xuecheng (1738–1801).[8] In this essay, Zhang sets forth his own views, stressing that the proper sphere of women's learning ought to be rigorous classical education, including not only rote memorization but also actual practice of the moral conduct prescribed for women in classical texts. Zhang developed this conception of "women's learning" as a critique of the literary judgments and even the life-style of another proponent of a different kind of women's learning, his contemporary, the poet Yuan Mei (1716–1798).

Yuan Mei flouted Confucian norms of propriety (Zhang's vaunted rituals) by publicly associating himself with young married women poets, more than a dozen of whom he numbered among his "female entourage" *(nü dizi)*. Yuan's appreciation for women's poetry, which smacked to Zhang of courtesan-style entertainments, was based on his conviction that the best poetry was intuitive and spontaneous, and that women were more likely than men to produce it. Yuan once wrote, for example, that an illiterate village woman could utter a phrase so beautiful that it would shame China's greatest male poets.[9] Whereas Zhang bitterly attacked Yuan for his gross misinterpretations of seemingly lewd poems in the classic *Book of Odes,* Yuan praised the pure, spontaneous voice of female desire that he detected in the bawdier *Guofeng* (Songs of the States).

Zhang's *Fu xue* was written at the height of China's great age of classical revival, when scholarly writers were particularly self-conscious about knowing and being faithful to the past. Reflecting this obsession with classical learning, Zhang's essay sets out to prove that women's learning in China had deep roots in antiquity. It begins with a survey of the earliest evidence of learned women in the Chinese historical record: descriptions of female officials in the ancient ritual records of the Zhou court. Zhou rituals were important for Confucian scholars of the eighteenth century because Confucius had revered the rites of the early Zhou state (ca. 1045–771 B.C.E.) as the ideal model for China's kingly government. Citing passages from the classic *Zhou li* (The Rites of Zhou), Zhang wrote:

> The term "women's learning" [*fu xue*] can be found in the references to women's posts in the Ministry of State during the Zhou period. There it refers to "virtue, speech, comportment, and handwork" [*de, yan, rong, gong*], terms which are extremely broad. This definition of women's learning bears no resemblance to the use of the term in later times, when it has been used to refer to literary arts alone.[10]

And:

> The subjects of women's learning are virtue, comportment, speech, and handwork. The commentary says that "speech" refers to rhetoric. It follows that unless a woman is well versed in classical ritual and accomplished in letters, she cannot be considered learned.

Thus we know that in the recitation of poetry and mastery of the rites, the learning of a woman of ancient times was nearly like [lüe ya] that of a man. Although the writings of women after the ancient period have tended slightly toward elegance and richness, it is fitting that women know their original heritage.[11]

Zhang noted that Zhou rituals also supplied the language of the first complete text devoted to women's learning, written by the female scholar Ban Zhao (ca. 49–120). In accordance with the Zhou rites, her *Instructions for Women (Nü jie)* explained and gave examples of learning appropriate to women—womanly virtue, speech, comportment, and handwork—for the edification of the ladies of the Han court. According to Zhang, Ban Zhao had many successors, great women writers who carried on the classical women's canon. The last surviving proponents of classical women's learning, however, died before the end of the Tang dynasty in the tenth century.[12] In Zhang's view, with their passing, classical women's learning disappeared. Instead of turning back to the classical models, even the most admirable women writers began to write books for women based on male, not female, models of learning. Famous Confucian didactic works for women, the *Analects for Women (Nü lun yu)* and the *Women's Classic of Filial Piety (Nü xiao jing)*, both written by female scholars, were merely imitations of men's writing with no relevance to women's learning. Zhang wrote: "Wishing to write instructions for women, they [the female authors Song Ruohua and Lady Zheng] did not know enough to study Ban Zhao's *Nü jie* model; instead they mistakenly tried to imitate the sages' classics."[13]

Zhang had no use for such Confucian moral tracts for women, which were popular in his day, but he was even more disturbed by the fact that learned women had come to prefer poetry above every other form of writing. Their preoccupation with poetry, he charged, had replaced the study and mastery of ritual, the necessary foundation of women's true classical learning. Worse, women were encouraged to think that poetry was their métier because they wrote poetry for men such as Yuan Mei, who praised women's poems for the wrong reasons. Men who admired women's poetry, Zhang said, were merely entranced by women's sensuality[14] and therefore incapable of judging women's talent as writers. As far as Zhang was concerned, in fact, women ought not to write poetry at all; their proper sphere of learning was ritual practice. Once seduced by the praise of male mentors, Zhang suggested, women poets were corrupted twice over. Their reputations were scarred because they associated with men outside the home; and their pure learning as women was corrupted by the quest for fame that had already destroyed men's classical learning:

> In my opinion, wherever official honors are proffered, the wise and the talented will vie for them. In that sense, the scholar pursues learning for the same reason that the farmer tills his fields, and there is nothing at all unusual about it. But a woman's writing is not her vocation. Therefore, when a woman happens to excel as a result of her own natural endowment, she need not compete over style, nor be stirred by the promise of fame and reputation.[15]

The origins of the corruption of women's learning dated, in Zhang's view, from the late Tang period (the ninth century), when women's learning was reduced (in his words) to mere "short verses about spring love and autumn loneliness" *(chun gui qiu yuan)*.[16] After that, what passed for women's learning—apart from the moral tracts he dismissed as imitations—became little more than entertainment. Whether in the palace or in pleasure boats, whether at courier outposts or in the heart of the court, women's talents were mainly devoted to singing and dancing, all to please men.

Zhang's argument suggests that he imagined a pristine sphere of learning reserved by and for women. He refers to men's words as "public vessels" *(gong qi)*. By contrast, he invokes the classical phrase *jing nü* to describe the place of the ideal learned woman: "A woman who is beautiful is called a *jing nü* [a maid at rest]. To be at rest is very near to learning. But the women we now call 'talented women' [*cai nü*]—how they move about! What a dreadful racket they make!"[17]

In this debate about women's learning, we find two models, both articulated by men. Zhang Xuecheng's model required strict classical training developed through disciplined ritual practice, and the strict confinement within the domestic roles of the family that such training inevitably required. Yuan Mei's model advocated spontaneous poetic license and the pursuit of desire and pure emotional expression, which could best be developed in the company of other poets, male and female, outside the domestic sphere. But what sorts of models for learning do women writers offer in their own work?

Women Poets of the Eighteenth Century

Through her own writings, we can observe the learned woman's development as a child, her maturation as a writer, and her finely honed ability to make public her innermost feelings. At times we can glimpse a quest for spiritual autonomy. True, a portion of women's writings in this period hints at entertainment (as Zhang would have it), or at spontaneous desire (Yuan's ideal). Many of the great poems of this period, however, place women's emotional center in the family, confounding both Yuan's and Zhang's views. And desire for a man seems among the least of the profound emotions that women poured into the tightly controlled cadence of their poetry.

Early Fame: The Child Prodigy and the Brilliant Young Wife

Young women developed a sense of themselves as writers while they were very young. Often, if we may judge from stories told by doting friends and relatives, they were responding to an environment in which they were put on display as precocious darlings. Learned young women cultivated literary personas—a sense of the dramatic, a flair for performance. They savored the turn of a phrase or the dash of a line. They dazzled stuffy visitors.

Child prodigy stories became part of the aura surrounding women poets admired by Yuan Mei. One example illustrates the little tests such girls were expected to pass, and the ways in which their performance became a matter of public record. Yuan Mei, in his *Poetry Talks*, recalled a story about Sun Yunfeng, who in her adult years was part of his entourage. A precocious reader "of great critical intelligence," at the age of eight *sui* Yunfeng was presented to a guest visiting her father. The guest, thinking to test her prowess, challenged her with the first line of the *Shi jing:* "Guan guan ju jiu"

("Guan guan! cries the osprey").[18] No doubt he expected to hear the second line in return. Instead, little Yunfeng shot back: "Yong yong ming yan" ("Honk honk! cries the goose").[19]

The line Yunfeng chose to recite was *not* the second line in the *Shi jing* but a parallel phrase from a different *Shi jing* poem. Yunfeng signaled her precocity by not simply choosing a parallel line. She was quick enough to select a line in which the bird-call metaphor was identical—both *guan guan* and *yong yong* symbolize the husband calling to his wife—and she also knew that *guan* and *yong* are harmonic *(he)* rhymes. Her reply, then, was a perfect linguistic, aesthetic, and moral mimesis. Observed Yuan Mei, recounting this story long after the fact: "Her father was amazed." The point of Yunfeng's story, however, is not the amazement of the father but the reputation of the daughter, which quickly spread beyond her household with the departing guest.[20]

Though Yuan Mei admired Yunfeng for her poetic precocity, his story also reveals that a young woman schooled in the *Book of Odes* learned carefully the moral significance of the wife's role in a marital relationship. Art and morality were linked more closely than either Yuan or Zhang realized. As a very young girl, Sun Yunfeng already knew that a wife served as the beloved moral preceptor of her spouse, and she was able to demonstrate her knowledge by comparing two lines from disparate poems with the same wifely image.

Fame of the sort Sun Yunfeng enjoyed—which in her case hardly appears corrupting—began early for many learned young women. Visitors and family members were fond of telling stories about precocious young girls such as Wang Biyun (Wang Qiong) of Dantu, who "could write poetry before her hair-pinning ceremony" (before she turned 15 *sui*). At that age, Biyun composed a poem for her elder brother which included these lines:

> Fallen chrysanthemums in circles of three fly about with
> indolence.
> Maple leaves in a whirl of red cover the moss in heaps.
> I was on the verge of calling the maid to sweep them
> away,
> When—who would have thought?—the wind came up
> and whisked them off for me.[21]

Young prodigies heard of one another's work across the miles. The young girl Yan Jing of Wuxing, a skilled calligrapher and bamboo painter at the age of barely nine *sui*, received this colophon on one of her paintings from a fourteen-year-old girl admirer from Putian: "Who would know that the one in the golden carriage [the poet] is not yet ten years old?"[22]

Admirers of precocious young women enhanced their fame by comparing them to young men who were more visible. As a poet, Wang Qiong was said to be "as famous" *(qi ming)* as her elder brother Yu.[23] Yuan Mei's favored "female disciple" Xi Peilan was such a gifted poet, he wrote, that he first suspected her husband of writing her poems for her.[24] Women themselves sometimes mockingly referred to the putative difference between men's and women's learning. Xie Daocheng,[25] an early Kangxi official, recalled his mother's words in a poem titled "Remembering My Mother Urging Me to Study" *(Yi mu quan xue shi):*

> "Son, come here. How many years has it been since Yao?"
> "Son, you must remember. From Yao to the present, how
>   many emperors have reigned?"
> As a boy, whenever I showed the slightest hesitation in
>   my reply,
> My mother's face changed color and flared up in anger:
> "To spread out a book with a humble heart, this is a
>   student's responsibility;
> "In studying the ancient ways, are you no better than a
>   woman?"[26]

Other comparisons between male and female writers stress the irony of inverted hierarchies. Yuan Mei wrote about female poets who corrected and improved on the poems of their spouses, and about brothers who were known to plagiarize their sisters' work.[27]

As female prodigy stories show, one's "fame" might spread beyond the home, but learning for women began there. Learned women who were "respectable"—that is, learned women not trained as courtesans—hailed from privileged backgrounds where families had the resources and the motivation to educate their daughters. We still do not know how common it was for women in elite families to receive rigorous classical training, but the women who did receive such training were from the upper classes. According to Yuan Mei, "All respectable women poets [*guixiu shiren*] come from great families."[28] Anecdotal evidence suggests how much daughters benefited from nurturing family ties. Each of Zhang Qi's four daughters, reared by a poet mother, had an illustrious reputation as a writer; one had four poet daughters of her own.[29] The literary patron and official Bi Yuan headed a houseful of talented women: his mother, his wife, and his eldest daughter were all accomplished poets.[30] Ruan Yuan's (1764–1849) second wife, Kong Luhua (1777–1833), published her own collected verse, and Ruan himself published a book of one of his daughter's verses after her death.[31] Longer literary genealogies have been identified, linking not only husbands and wives, fathers and daughters, but also fathers-in-law and daughters-in-law.[32] Yuan Mei mentions the two cousins of Xu Shanmin, Xiufang and Caijia, who married into the Li family and became sisters-in-law, "exchanging poems with each other every day."[33]

Even within the proper confines of the family, of course, a woman writer might gain not fame but infamy, as the subject of a scandal. In one case described by Yuan Mei, Lady Xue, "a seductive and passionate person," composed a poem that she presented to her husband's younger brother, and her husband sued for divorce on the grounds that she had violated the rules of propriety. Eventually the cognizant magistrate threw the case out when it was revealed, through a clever poem submitted to the court by the lady herself, that she was the victim of a scheme by her husband's brothers to gain control of his property.[34]

Stories about "famous" women writers reveal how talented young women coped with the transition to wifehood. A bride might bring her writing directly into the nuptial bedchamber, as did Bao Zhihui, of whom Yuan Mei wrote: "If she didn't have a pen and inkstone in her boudoir for even a single day, she was disconsolate." A new bride could stack the wedding trousseau so that even an obtuse husband would know at once that he had married a serious writer; the poet Jin Yi brought her inkstone and brushes into her marriage as part of her dowry and "within a few days turned the bedroom into a study."[35]

A new husband might accommodate a writer bride with appreciation. Jin Yi herself was delighted by her marriage to a man with whom she could exchange poetry. But some talented young women never adjusted to married life, escaping instead into their books: "When Miss Lu married Cao Huangmen, at the age of 17, she had already styled herself with a literary name (The Person from Elegantly Wooded Hills). Her dowry was full of books on literature and history. She was especially fond of the *Chu ci* [Elegies of Chu], and when she was not doing her embroidery, she would always recite them." Miss Lu's maids gossiped about the fact that their mistress was so fond of these tragic poems, and even her husband became alarmed and cautioned her not to read them. Yuan Mei comments ominously that this seemed a forewarning, because she died soon afterward. Elsewhere, he remarked, "These days respectable women with a talent for poetry are never happily married."[36] Yuan preserved a scrap of poetry left by one unhappy daughter who burned her work before she died, unwed, at a young age. The poem attests to the girl's dark view of a married future she never lived to experience:

> *Palace Song*
> The eunuchs proclaim the imperial will that the new
>   woman play on the *zheng*.
> Her jade-white fingers lightly pluck sounds of sorrowful
>   separation.
> Just then the sounds scatter on a breath of spring wind.
> The lords and princes outside, suddenly hearing, don't
>   understand.[37]

Although he rarely mentions it, we know that Yuan Mei was well acquainted with the dark side of learned women's experience. His gifted fourth younger sister, who died in childbirth, left poems betraying her loneliness. And the mother-in-law of his aunt, who served several wealthy families as a governess, once witnessed the murder by poison of two of her talented charges.[38] Yuan Mei's reluctance to dwell on this aspect of learned women's lives may explain his relish for the love stories he recounted with so much pleasure, and his impatience with melancholia. Momentarily saddened by Jin Yi's death of illness at the age of twenty-five, he set out at once to find her bereaved husband another poet bride.[39]

The subject of death—in childbirth, from illness, by suicide—recurs in writings by and about young women in the eighteenth century. This poem reveals the agony of one young person whose very mastery of the moral lessons in her classical studies drove her to kill herself:

Farewell, Mother
Though your daughter's body is very weak,
Her spirit is strong as iron.
Though the books she has read are few,
She grasps their meaning with clarity and determination.
Before a woman is betrothed,
Her body is pure like snow.
After she is betrothed, her commitment cannot be
    scorned.
If she is lucky, she will sleep with her husband all her life,
In keeping with the proper roles for husband and wife.
If she is unlucky, her husband will die when he is young,
And she will vow to keep her chastity forever.
Sadder yet am I, who never saw her future husband.
His fate grieves me each time I see the waning moon.
I am still called "one who is not yet dead,"
But now I am as good as buried with him.
I do not die from the pain of grief;
For three years I have waited to lay aside mourning.
Once I stopped, I began to fast,
But passion is strong and the rites are hard to violate.
To destroy my life will violate my mother's heart,
My heart too is pained beyond measure.
As I follow my betrothed to the Yellow Springs,
Human bonds, moral bonds, none will split apart.[40]

The human and moral bonds trapping this young poet formed the confining matrix within which most women wrote. A few, as we have seen, achieved a rare integration of literary talent and family roles. Others turned to writing as a solitary act expressing the isolation they felt during the transition to married life. Either way, young women writers defied the stereotypes entertained by Zhang Xuecheng and Yuan Mei. "Fame" did not impede their understanding of ritual obligation; pleasing men was not an obsession of their writing; and spontaneity is hard to find in the disciplined, often anguished language of their poems.

Mature Writers: Testing Convention

Yuan Mei reserved his most effulgent praise for female poets who mastered poetic conventions and turned them to new and original uses. Women writers tested their skill at conventional themes ("Arising from My Sickbed," "Seventh Night," "Poem to My Sojourning Husband") by carefully placing a word or a phrase to make readers catch their breath and to draw attention to their own individual talent. Mature women writers deployed conventional poetic topics to plumb emotions born of empty marriages and cloistered lives.

Consider the range of poems on the "Double Seven" (Qi xi) festival, one of the most popular themes in Qing poetry, and one frequently singled out for special attention by Yuan Mei.[41] Double Seven—with its literary tropes of the lonely weaving maid and the eager cowherd, their eternal separation in the heavens, and their single yearly tryst on the seventh night of the seventh lunar month, the earthly casting of needles to test for the embroidery skills that foretell a woman's marriageability—gave women writers a vocabulary for writing about loss, loneliness, and desire.[42]

Here are some examples (a few drawn from a collection of Ming poems by women):

> *Seventh Night*
> The autumn night obscures the misty shore.
> The crane carriage waits by the Heavenly River.
> The bridge complete, we thank the ravens and magpies;
> As our delight rises, feelings of separation flood in.
> The young girls gathered can now test for skill.
> But they don't dwell on the songs among the clouds,
> They think only of the nights to come
> When a lone shadow will lift the golden shuttle.[43]

Seventh Night

On the green gleaming mossy steps the rain has spun
    silk,
Insects cry *jiji* announcing the approach of autumn.
We humans are the ones burdened by the passions and
    feelings of the sensual world;
How could heavenly creatures be moved by the sorrow of
    parting?
In her empty pavilion she rolls up the blinds;
the moon is like a fishhook.
On the flowery wall pure fragrance;
the dark of the night is deep.
Each new phrase sighs and sings ever more languidly,
As the little maiden makes her way up the lofty tower.[44]

A Record of Light Refreshment Taken in the Moon Tower on
Seventh Night

The tower is high, the shadows of the trees are deep
    green.
The bamboo leaves unroll as the heat of the day recedes.
A solitary soul envies the peace of this quiet night,
As a faint trace of movement reflects across the
    jade-screened window.[45]

Seventh Night

Vast, boundless, thin clouds send off the setting sun.
People say that on this night she will meet the cowherd.
The first rays of moonlight glow, a reflection in the river,
The magpie carriage hastens anew, a jewel on the water.
Now that she has reached this happy state, does she yet
    feel resentment?
At once she will be told to leave again, her passions
    stirred still more.
How many humans are fated to pass long years apart!
Do not despise the star raft for being so ephemeral.[46]

Seventh Night

Heaven has sent down its instructions; thoughts of
    separation flood over them,

> They face each other, east to west—what can they be
>   thinking?
> She must regret that she is the cowherd's lady,
> Alone waiting every year for one river crossing.[47]

These poems, conventional though they are, express profound desire, extricating the poet from family bonds and re-presenting her as a lover.[48] It was this poetry of desire that drew Yuan Mei's special attention. He celebrated the relationship between desire and poetry, judging poetry to lie at the heart of passion and, in his poetics, linking desire, literary talent, and sensual female beauty. He once compared the talent of the poet to the beauty of a woman, and he conflated poetry with sensual pleasure ("I love poetry the way I love sex [se]—when I hear a beautiful phrase, I can never forget it," he wrote.)[49] Although there is no reason to believe that Yuan Mei had sexual relations with his female disciples—they were, after all, respectable ladies (guixiu)—his recollections of various meetings with them, and their own poems about those meetings, reveal relationships in which gentle teasing and flirting were the norm. In one passage, Yuan Mei regrets that he was unable to take a planned trip to West Lake with the poet Luo Qilan; in another, he describes a meeting on West Lake with seven of the young women in his self-styled entourage.[50] Once while traveling he stayed for a short time at the home of his pupil Luo Peixiang; on another occasion when they planned to meet and missed each other, she sent him a poem expressing the wish that he had come to her "cold apartments" to "raise a glass."[51]

These mature women poets testing convention resemble the learned woman of Zhang Xuecheng's fears and Yuan Mei's fantasies. They enter the male poet's world and write on themes male poets favor. They are suspended—so it seems—from the bonds of wifehood and family obligation which Zhang believed were all-important and Yuan preferred to ignore. A woman's poems on conventional themes exposed her readily to the male gaze, offering—in Zhang's view—mere entertainment. But as Zhang himself recognized, they were also dangerous poems, plumbing emotions denied expression in women's ritually sanctioned roles of wife and mother. The conflicts between personal passion and ritual obligation, between human emotion and family hierarchies, were explored in other kinds of poems that moved beyond conventional themes to personal experience.

Technologies of the Self: Writing Personal Experience

As they mastered poetic convention, learned women came to use their brushes and inkstones as "technologies of the self."[52] They found ways to externalize personal, particular experiences through classical poetry writing and its tools: inkstone, brush, and paper. In poetry, their emotions entered the disciplined forms imposed by printed words and erudite readers, claiming recognition. Countless poems by women in Yuan Mei's entourage, and other stories from his circle, reveal a deeper personal voice that Double Seven poems barely capture. Many grieve, voicing the unspeakable:

> *On Giving Birth to Another Girl Just as the Soul of My*
> *Second Daughter, Dead of Smallpox, Returned*
> I summoned her soul and she happened to come
> Just as my new daughter was born.
> From this I know that life returns from the dead,
> That reincarnation is possible.
> She could see my old gold bracelets and recognize her
> mother.
> As the jade swallow settled in my breast,[53]
> I thought still more of my dead child.
> Your coming again confirms the dream
> That your former life seemed to be.
> I called you back as if you were still
> In that liminal state from which the dead may return.
> I strained to hear the baby's cries,
> And see the handkerchief hung to right of the door[54]
> Half to console myself, half to cherish my grief.[55]

> *Weeping for My Elder Brother*
> A death notice comes; sudden shock
> I fight to hold back the flood of tears.

What use is it to take up official seals
If in the end you will leave this ephemeral life?

News from afar might be mistaken—
I still remember your face so clearly—
But now comes a letter from Dalei.
As I reach into the bamboo satchel, the sharp pain
    doubles.[56]

A mother who had guided her adolescent son through the competition for fame so despised by Zhang Xuecheng wrote a poem
about the day he left to join the army. It begins:

To My Son Yongji on His Journey Far Away
My son, the grandson of a man honored by the emperor
    as a "pure official,"[57]
Proved slow in his own studies, and failed to win a
    position.
At the age of thirty, fame still eluding him,
He returned to his old home, empty-handed.
Threats from the outside returned,
Distress within the land continued;[58]
Suddenly he set off to join the army.
He threw on his clothes and went away.
It was the middle of the night,
The bright stars shone in the sky,
The river flowed to the top of its banks,
The moving clouds came and went,
But my traveling son stopped for nothing.
Grasping at his streaming face,
He left his parents' home.
His long journey began here.[59]

Poems of grief and loss belie Zhang Xuecheng's claim that poetry
pulled women away from family bonds and led them to trivialize
their ritual obligations. Measured against the depth of emotion in
these poems, conventional pieces on the Double Seven appear shallow, their expressive possibilities far surpassed by a woman's unique
rendering of a moment that belongs to her alone.

Some learned women withdrew from the family altogether, seeking a private meditative space. Some turned to Buddhist texts for respite from their wifely and maternal responsibilities; a few even embraced religion in lieu of marriage. Personal accounts of this spiritual side of women's lives are rare, but a few survive.

Lady Zhang, the mother of the eminent Qing official Tian Wen (1635–1704), was widowed in 1654 when her husband died while serving as a magistrate, but she saw a son take the *jinshi* degree ten years later, and two of her three boys later won high office at court. In memoirs of her life, her children recalled her years of widowhood, when she reeled thread in her chambers while tutoring her sons in the classics. On her seventieth birthday, Lady Zhang's friends and relatives decided to throw a party in her honor. When she received news of the plan, however, Lady Zhang reached for her brush and composed a scathing rebuke a thousand characters long, quoting the classics and the histories on proper behavior for widows. She presented it to her sons, and they canceled the party.

This poem, one of Lady Zhang's few surviving writings, may have been composed at about the same time:

> *Shown to My Children*
> A copy of the *Surangama sutra;* my door is barred by day.
> The wooden fish, the bamboo staff[60] lean against the
> folding screen.
> This old person[61] decides for herself to keep a vegetarian
> diet.
> I don't recite Buddhist sutras for *your* benefit.[62]

Most accounts of Buddhist piety involve mature married women like Lady Zhang. Yun Zhu (1771–1833), compiler of a major anthology of women's poetry of the early nineteenth century, mentions in her preface that during the busiest years of her married life, one of the few books on her desk was the slim *Surangama sutra (Lengyan jing).*[63] In a Ming memoir of their mother, Lady Li, Yuan Biao (1533–1606) and his brothers recorded her entrepreneurial skills, including her ability to wring savings out of the family's spartan budget and keep the patriline out of debt. Asked how she could manage everything so ably, their mother told them that she kept her mind clear with Buddhist meditation.[64]

We hear of a few young girls who convinced their parents of their religious beliefs and seceded from the family altogether, in the manner of the young Ming mystic Tanyangzi.[65] Yuan Mei describes one child who "liked to dress in Buddhist robes and recite rosaries and pray six times a day." Her parents observed this behavior with growing resignation as she matured. They finally built a convent to house her when, still unwed, she turned thirty.[66]

Learned women had access to a Buddhist avenue of retreat from all human emotional bonds. But this was not perceived as a threat posed by women's learning, perhaps because few young women chose to follow it. Instead, the focus of the controversy over "learned women" was the problematic relationship between learned young women and learned men. Yet women's writing shows that relationships of passion or romance were not the dominant inspiration for their poems. In that respect, both Yuan's and Zhang's views of women's learning seem narrow and limited by their own concerns.

How are we to read these complex women poets? Were they engaged in a kind of resistance to Confucian moralism, giving voice to emotions that social convention repressed? Reading women's Double Seven poetry as resistance, one sees why Zhang Xuecheng found learned women's activities—their noise and motion—disturbing. It is equally easy to understand Yuan Mei's admiration for women poets who flouted conventional human relationships.

Yet the evidence in women's writings will not permit us to read them as documents of resistance. Many women—perhaps most—did not see their writing as an expression of alienation, dissent, resistance, or even autonomy. The young suicidal "widow," Miss Ye, found herself unable to resist; her determination to follow an unbearably difficult moral standard is the subject of her poem. In less impassioned statements about writing by women of this period, we find similar views solidly grounded in the tradition of classical moralism. The best example is Yun Zhu's own preface to her collection of nearly 1,700 women's poems from the late Ming and early Qing periods, in which she wrote:

Long ago when Confucius edited the *Book of Odes*, he did not eliminate writings from the women's quarters. In later times, parochial scholars have said that the task of wives and daughters should be limited to taking charge of making wine and drawing water, sewing clothes and embroidering. They are not aware of prescriptions for women's learning . . . described in the *Book of Rites*. These prescriptions begin with "womanly virtue," followed by "womanly speech" [*yan*]. To be sure, the word speech does not refer explicitly to essays and written phrases, but surely these are implied by it. This being the case, what harm has there ever been in women studying or writing poetry?[67]

Invited to write the second preface to this collection, Wang Pan Suxin (a former member of Yuan Mei's entourage) insisted: "Of the three hundred poems in the *Book of Odes,* more than half were written by women. The first two chapters begin with the poem *Guan ju,* showing how the Way of Correct Beginnings, which is the foundation for kingly transformation, transforms all under heaven even while it regulates the women's apartments."[68] Far from resisting the injunctions of Confucian moralism, these women were able to *invoke* them, in *support* of an authorial voice.[69]

More important for our own understanding of women's consciousness in this period is the passion and the skill with which women writers used the poem as a medium for expressing their most personal feelings. The range and intimacy of their writings defy Zhang's and Yuan's attempts to gloss "women's learning," and they show us how much we must learn from women's own voices before we can begin to locate them in the historical record. At the same time, we see that Zhang was overreacting to Yuan's fantasies about these women. Most of the women in Yuan's entourage were truly learned and practiced in the rituals he revered. None belittled their responsibilities as wives and mothers, and many suffered great pain precisely because of them. On the whole they seem, in their sentiments and their moral sensibilities, nearer to Zhang's ideal than to Yuan's.

Zhang was also wrong about women's debt to classical learning. To classical learning they owed their poetic voice, and to classical learning we owe this chance to see past the male gaze and hear women's voices in eighteenth-century China. As marginalized members of a patriarchal system, these women hold little interest; as victims of false consciousness, they inspire only pity. As writers, they command our respectful attention, long overdue.

CATHY SILBER

2 | From Daughter to Daughter-in-Law in the Women's Script of Southern Hunan

Another instance of women's culture snatched from the maw of oblivion, *nüshu*, the writing system used solely by women in one small part of rural Hunan, dramatically contravenes conventional wisdom about women's lives in China. Although it was strictly a local practice, confined to Shangjiangxu township in Jiangyong county and neighboring villages in Dao county, the generic nature of its name, women's writing, lends itself to resonance with the hopes and dreams of many women engaged in their own struggles against oppression. The temptation becomes great indeed to romanticize *nüshu* as a discourse of resistance and enshrine its writers as heroines in a national (or global) struggle against gender oppression.[1] But the main underground aspect to *nüshu* is the fact that, until recently, it was unknown to the outside world; for the women of Shangjiangxu it was no more clandestine an activity than embroidery, and though men could not read it, they could understand it if they heard it sung aloud. Though *nüshu* texts unmistakably voice resistance, what *nüshu* as a local sociotextual phenomenon may say to our received view of Chinese culture and what *nüshu* discourses may reveal about the situated knowledge and practices of girls and women in local systems of power need to be heard as two separate conversations.

This essay, a preliminary report on social and textual

practices involving the transition from daughter to daughter-in-law in the *nüshu* culture area in roughly the first half of this century, inevitably engages both conversations, first nodding to the former, then exploring the latter in some detail.[2] The practices I discuss add to an ever lengthening list of sinological surprises that contest the validity of Confucian elite models of marriage and social structure in rural China, and expand our understanding of women's lives to encompass their roles as producers of culture.[3] In the *nüshu* area, the customary form of marriage even today is *buluo fujia* (not going to [literally, "falling into"] the husband's home), or what one writer has termed "delayed patrivirilocal marriage";[4] and highly formalized non-kin ties among girls and women, for which the term *sisterhoods* only partially suffices, were an integral part of social life.[5]

Many questions about these formalized non-kin social arrangements await further research; but evidence to date suggests that, as an integral aspect of local society, they could be just as important to those who participated in them as family ties. The fact that nonhierarchical and/or non-kin social arrangements lack prominence in Confucian social ideology merely indicates a need to see through this ideology, especially where those who have the least to gain from it are concerned. Furthermore, the fact that social arrangements such as sworn sisterhood and (better known) brotherhood are already recognized for many and diverse times and places in China, and that marriage practices entailing a woman's prolonged residence in, or enduring ties to, her natal home are now known to occur in Shandong, Guangdong, Guangxi, Guizhou, Fujian (Huian), Hainan, and Hunan, indicate that it is time to stop looking at these as isolated exceptions, even when they are identified as non-Han practices.[6] The fact that some Han social arrangements bear marked resemblance to some non-Han practices in South China, rather than explaining them away, raises a host of productive questions about ideologies of gender and kinship vis-à-vis ethnicity and the sinicization of the south, not the least of which is, what is Han anyway? Undoubtedly, practices in the *nüshu* culture area fit into such broader pictures, but I cannot pursue the matter further here.[7]

Toward such ends, however, I do explore the social world of girls and recently married women in the early part of this century by examining *nüshu* representations of their social relationships and marriages. I describe the two kinds of formalized non-kin relationships they practiced (the girl couples called *laotong* and *jiebaizimei*, or "sworn sisters"),[8] and the ways these relationships, alongside kin ties, shaped peer groups of girls who faced their marriages as a group. I read the *nüshu* texts produced by these relationships—among them the letters that formed *laotong* matches and writings to brides *(sanzhaoshu)*—for the conceptions they proffer of girlhood peer group relationships and village exogamous marriage. I situate a girlhood discourse of antipathy toward marriage in the context of discourses about marriage and relationships other than kin and affinal. I suggest that, at least for the *nüshu* culture area, a reading of village exogamous marriage solely in terms of the way it changes a bride's relationship to her natal family slights the importance of non-kin social arrangements. Although changes on marriage to a bride's relationships with both kin and non-kin alike merit further study, evidence so far suggests that women could continue to rely on natal kin after marriage (a matter I mention only peripherally), but they may have had a harder time maintaining their formalized non-kin girlhood ties once they had settled in their married home.

Research to date indicates that formalized non-kin relationships were (and to some degree still are) customary for both males and females in the *nüshu* culture area. Xie Zhimin provides the broadest definition of these relationships: "Whoever hits it off, regardless of surname, generation, or age (generally not over twenty or so), can become [*jiewei*] sworn sisters or sworn brothers [*yizimei, yixiongdi*]. Sworn sisters or brothers are called *tongnian* [same year], also *laotong* or *laogeng*."[9] His list of appellations for these relationships, though it cannot speak to their meanings in practice, provides strong evidence that they are seen locally as an integral part of "social structure." He documents seven terms of address, each prefaced with *tongnian,* for the age mate of an elder brother, younger brother, elder sister, and younger sister, as well as the wife of an elder brother's age mate, and the husband of an elder or younger sister's age mate. Other kin terms prefaced with *tongnian* appear in *nüshu* texts to describe particular relationships.[10] Zhao Liming also conflates *laotong* and sworn sisterhood,[11] and groups letters that established both kinds of relationships under the *laotong* rubric.

In his description of "ritual siblinghood," William Chiang appreciates a distinction between *tongnian* and *jiebai zimei* and *xiongdi*. He describes the ideal *tongnian* relationship as a voluntary bond between people (usually of the same gender, "although people claim that such a bond can be contracted between a man and a woman as well"), "born in the same year and if possible, even the same month and same date." He describes *jiebai zimei* and *xiongdi* as "an alternative type of ritual siblinghood," "short of the ideal," "formed between people not born in the same year but . . . of the same generation." He notes that the *laotong* "relationship may be initiated by the parents even before the participants are born," and that "it is said that it was once required for the contracting parties to exchange their 'eight characters,' as in marriages."[12]

Yi Nianhua (1906–1991), one of the last and most prolific writers of *nüshu*, made an emphatic distinction between *laotong* (literally, "old same"—as in "old friend") and *jiebaizimei* (sworn sister) relationships when she described them to me in late 1988 and 1989. (She did not use the term *tongnian* very much, if at all, in conversation with me, though it appears in her writing.) According to Yi (speaking of female relationships), *laotong* was a match made between two (and only two) same-age girls by exchanging small gifts and letters of invitation and reply written in *nüshu* on fans whose top border was adorned with a row of flowers. *Jiebaizimei* could include any number of members (ideally seven),[13] contracted at any time from girlhood through old age (and not necessarily all at once), with or without letters in *nüshu*. Judging from *nüshu* texts and an argument I witnessed between Yi Nianhua and Gao Yinxian and Tang Baozhen in August 1988 over just who were and were not members of their sworn sisterhood,[14] *jiebaizimei* seems the looser of these two kinds of social arrangements. Some of the writings to brides suggest that *jiebaizimei* could include a pair of *laotong* among their members.

In actual practice by real people, the *laotong* match no doubt admitted the same ad hoc flexibility and inventiveness found among sworn sisters, or, for that matter, in most human relationships. But the ideal match, as Yi Nianhua took great delight in telling it, joined two girls of the same age and different villages. They came from families of similar social and economic standing, preferably with the same number and sex distribution of elder and younger siblings, in the same birth order. Ideally, the two girls had the same height and the same size feet, and one was no prettier than the other. Yi told me of a song about a girl with a pockmarked face and big feet who was rejected as *laotong* material on these grounds. Yi said, "The good ones matched with the good ones, the ugly with the ugly, the smart ones with the smart ones, just like husband and wife."

Yi continued her normative account by describing how the making of this match was facilitated by an older female intermediary, who, like the marriage matchmaker, was often a woman who had married into the village of one prospective "same" from the village of the other. (In an earlier conversation, Yi told me that when, in cases of *in utero* marriage engagements, both babies turned out to be of the same sex, they would become *laotong* instead of spouses.) When a girl was eight or nine years old, a woman in her village might recommend to her a prospective same from her own natal village. If the first girl liked the idea, and generally she did, she would write (or get someone to write for her) a fan to her prospective same, asking her to make the match. If the recipient was willing, she would write (or have written) her reply on a fan and send it to her same. This exchange of fans, along with gifts of a pair of shoes, candy, and tobacco, took place in the fifth or sixth lunar month, after agreement to the match was reached by word of mouth. When the match was set, the girls would arrange to meet, perhaps at a temple fair or a Dragon Boat festival celebration, and one would spend a few days in the home of the other, the first of many such visits back and forth. Sames slept in the same bed on these visits. They brought no change of clothes with them; they wore each other's.

Although Yi Nianhua first described *laotong* to me by saying, "Back then, everybody did it," she later told me that she had not, because her grandfather would not let her. Around 1919, the story goes, a girl was raped while visiting her same, by her same's older brother and his schoolmates. After that, parents in Shangjiangxu put a stop to their daughters' overnight visits, and this is the explanation Yi gave for her grandfather's refusal to let her make a *laotong* match at all. The reply she received to the *laotong* invitation letter she wrote on the sly reads at first glance like a wholehearted acceptance, but is actually a reluctant refusal to make the match. This girl wrote that she had to obey her parents, who, Yi explained, had forbidden her to make the match.[15] Roughly four years later Yi wrote a *laotong* letter for an illiterate girl who wanted to make a match, so it appears that this crackdown did not wipe out the practice entirely. This *laotong* proposition letter[16] seems to be addressed to a daughter of its writer's mother's brother; whether this indicates an accommodation of *laotong* matching practices to parental concerns over their daughters' safety or that *laotong* relationships customarily reinforced matrilateral ties is impossible at this point to say. (Worth noting in the latter regard, however, is the fact that this letter mentions frequent visits by its sender and her widowed mother to her mother's sister's home.)

While *nüshu* representations of the *laotong* match may have far more to say about its ideals than any actual lived relationship, these representations did shape the meanings of *laotong* for both the women who taught girls how invitation and reply letters ought to be written and the girls themselves. Moreover, since little is known about *laotong* matching practices that did not require literacy (for I suspect there must have been some), it is interesting to consider how these texts in particular discursively produced their speaking subjects as participants in a social relationship they had yet to experience personally.[17] Like all *nüshu*, these letters are written in highly formulaic verse; meaning is less literal than conventional, born of shared knowledge within this specific community of writers and readers.[18]

Based on an examination of nine letters written to establish a *laotong* relationship, I offer here a composite description. These letters (not always, it seems, on fans), consistently conceive the *laotong* relationship as an exclusive couple through repeated use of pair metaphors and both implicit and explicit analogies to marriage. They portray this relationship as long-lasting and intimate and fun, based in fidelity, great emotional attachment, and mutual high regard. They speak of pleasure taken in whispering and embroidering together upstairs. And, full of high praise for their intended and often descriptions of both sender's and recipient's family composition, these letters portray the relationship as one that meets parental approval and confers social worth on girls lucky enough to have made such a good match, envied by all. Some of these letters contain Buddhist associations and references.[19] (Later in this essay I list the various expressions that convey these conceptions in order to explore them further; see the appendix for one complete *laotong* letter in translation).[20]

One of the most common metaphors used to describe the *laotong* relationship in these letters is *yidui yuanyang* (a pair of mandarin ducks), which, in Han culture, connotes a happily married couple. Other creatures, mostly birds, appear frolicking in the sky or treetops or water, virtually always in pairs, as, for example, in the passage

A pair of mandarin ducks quacks in the same tree
a phoenix pair flies across the sea,
flapping their wings and singing, up into the sky
all around they're envied for such carefree joy,
a pair of phoenix flies together in a pair
swearing a good dear, a pair's a pair.[21]

While this (Zhuangzian) sense of freedom and frolic which accompanies most references to paired and coupled creatures was not, to say the least, commonly associated with marriage for rural Chinese women, the point for now is the multitude of pair images. Other associations with marriage include the sense of a match made in heaven, destined in a former life, as in lines such as, "It was fated in a former life that we swear a bond, it is fated in this life that we match into a couple,"[22] and "The heavenly spirits matched the two of us."[23] One letter includes the couplet, "I don't know your birthday, don't know the day or time,"[24] supporting the notion that the matching of "eight characters" was considered necessary (as in marriage), or at least salient. Kinship is sometimes invoked to describe these relationships in a way more reminiscent of marriage than siblinghood (though this is arguable), in lines such as, "We make our bond on the basis of *qin*,"[25] and "Make the bond of one family."[26] The notion of the absolute exclusivity of the match appears in lines such as, "Unless you, girl, have already done this [matched with somebody else]"[27] and "Just one star accompanies one moon, you can't have any old star going with the moon."[28] While these letters cast the *laotong* relationship as a match by enlisting the applicable aspects of a marriage match, they also bear out the sameness between the two so privileged in Yi Nianhua's normative account, as in lines employing mirror images, such as, "Crossing the bridge, mirrored in the water, two people the same height," and "Combing and dressing [before] the mirror propped high, reflecting girls, a pair facing a pair."[29]

Reminiscent of social expectations of marriage, many expressions of lifelong togetherness appear in these letters, sometimes linked with expressions of deep attachment and inseparability. The most common of these are, "Going for a long time, for a long time not stopping,"[30] and "Long years of a lifetime, for a long time not stopping."[31] Other lines convey an even stronger notion metaphorically by recasting the tropes of female as plant or flower and marriage as transplant so common in the *nüshu* corpus, as in the passage

> Hyacinth bean and papaya:
> long vines, deep roots.
> Palm trees inside the garden walls,
> with deep roots, stand a thousand years.[32]

No uprooting and replanting here. Bridges, rivers, and sea also commonly represent the strength and length and depth of the *laotong* relationship, as in lines such as, "A bridge over the long river, we'll walk [to and fro] forever, as ever flowing as the river, as deep as the sea."[33] One couplet joins these images: "For a thousand *li*, like [two] streams flowing into one river, for ten thousand *li* like flowers in the same garden."[34]

Letters indicate that fidelity and commitment were prerequisites for the match, in questions such as, "Same, are you true?,"[35] replies such as, "My heart is true to go with you,"[36] and the question that appears in some letters, "Are you backing out or not?"[37] Linked with this sense of fidelity and commitment is the expectation of the longevity of the match, discussed earlier, also expressed in lines such as, "[We of] good affection do not break off feeling," and "[We of] good affection do not sever the bond."[38]

The great sense of intimacy conveyed in these letters is presented as an already established fact, often linked with the notion of inseparability, as in lines such as, "The two of us as a couple, not a step apart," "[We of] good affection, not a step apart," and "Day after day [we] can't bear to part."[39] Every letter characterizes the relationship as entailing time spent together upstairs in embroidery and conversation, in lines such as, "The two of us sit upstairs, threading needles, matching colors complete,"[40] in which phrases such as "asking each other" and "talking it over together" are substituted for "matching colors complete." Conversational intimacy is conveyed in lines such as, "Speaking in whispers, [we] give over affection,"[41] and "In the whispering voices of flowers [girls] we talk it over."[42] One letter, following a line about sitting together and whispering and a line about never arguing, further expresses the notion of intimacy with the line "When washing our hands, the two of us use the same basin of water."[43]

All the letters (even the reluctant refusal) convey a sense of how glad their writers are to make the match and how much pleasure they expect it to bring: "My heart's red hot to swear this bond together," "Same, our hearts are glad," and "The two of us happy and carefree, [like] the immortals playing chess."[44] Some lines indicate that the letters brought great joy to their recipients: "Everything you wrote makes my heart beautiful," and "I read it over and over, day after day."[45]

These letters teem with effusive praise for their recipient, in both positive and self-deprecatory comparative terms. In addition to prizing qualities of intelligence, literacy, and beauty in a same, these letters make frequent mention of the reputation of her family. Common expressions are, "Of the intelligent, you count as one,"[46] and "I've heard from afar of the girl who can write in your worthy home; all along, a proper family, educated people."[47] Writers frequently substitute specifics such as my home/family (jia), my coarse writing (cuwen), and my protocol (liyi) into the common comparative formula, "Everything about me hardly compares with you." Such praise for a same helps attest to the value of the match being made, which every letter describes as enviable, in lines such as, "People all around look on in envy."[48]

Most letters refer to their writer's parents, indicating that they too are pleased with the match: "[Our] parents are really glad," and "[Our] parents' rules are good."[49] Near the end of some letters comes mention of the family composition of both sender and recipient, noting the death of a parent or a dearth of brothers in terms of worry and woe at home. Some letters explicitly address their recipient's mother, asking her not to make fun of the writer's effort. Particularly valued are mothers described as *"fangshangnü,"* mothers who enjoyed having a same when they were girls.[50] One letter, whose sender's mother was widowed, ends with the line, "[I'll] have you come here and make my mother happy."[51]

As a couple relationship, a predestined, long-term match made between two members of different families, *laotong* is clearly far more structurally similar to marriage than it is to siblinghood. These letters suggest that participation in a *laotong* relationship conferred social worth on a girl and prestige on her family in the same way that the making of a marriage match can be seen as a negotiation of social value and prestige. The *laotong* relationship, like marriage, established ties between two families, particularly between the women. Sames became like a daughter to each other's mother, or so other textual representations claim. The *laotong* relationship entailed mutual favors and obligations between families. The exchange of gifts and the hosting and visiting over a period of years meant the extension of family material resources and labor—food, drinking and bathing water, laundry—to a non–family member. And while a guest same probably did not directly contribute labor to her host family, she certainly helped by keeping her same company over the needlework they both had to do, making it a shared activity involving consultation and comparison. (Gao Yinxian, for one, gleefully recounted how much she had hated needlework as a girl, how she had gone to great lengths to escape it.) Despite these structural similarities between the *laotong* match and the marriage match, the conceptual similarities can be misleading. After all, even though the marriage match and the *laotong* match may relate metaphorically (in context- and genre-specific discourses), as we shall soon see, the rosy ideals inherent in these invocations of the marriage match seldom figure in the discourses about marriage produced by these girlhood relationships.

I fear it is only because relatively little is as yet known about social life in the *nüshu* culture area (especially in the early part of this century, but also even today) that accounts like this one end up presenting lived relationships as abstractions of social structure. In my attempts to reconcile the distinctions Yi Nianhua made between *laotong* and *jiebaizimei* relationships with the ways some scholars have tended to conflate them, I have wondered whether there is a tendency nowadays for people in Shangjiangxu to refer loosely to all such practices as *laotong;* in any event, William Chiang, Benedikta Dorer, and I all agree that there is a meaningful distinction between these practices.[52] Dorer reports that while the *laotong* relationship was exclusive in the sense that it involved only two people ("usually of the same sex"), "one could have more than one *laotong* at the same time; one woman told me she had five."[53] Although *laotong* relationships may have entailed deeper family obligations than girlhood *jiebaizimei*, there is no evidence to suggest that *laotong* attachments were the stronger of the two, and inquiring minds may never know whether any of these relationships were sexual. None of the extant *jiebaizimei*-formation letters were written by unmarried girls; all were written by older, married women. It seems girls generally swore sisterhood with those in their own or perhaps neighboring villages, without letters. In fact, Dorer reports that

> quite a few women told me about their *jiebaizimei* relationship, where the only condition was to bring a certain amount (up to fifty catties) of rice. When you brought your share you were a member of the sisterhood. Some of them would rent it out and earn interest on it (up to fifty percent). When one of them got married her share was sold and the others would buy presents for her with that money. When the last share was sold the sisterhood was dissolved. One woman told me that they had the same custom without becoming sworn sisters (although sworn sisters were common in her village).[54]

Even though it seems that girlhood sworn sisterhoods were not formed with writing, writings to a sworn sister on the occasion of her marriage nonetheless use many of the same expressions of intimacy and long-term attachment found in the *laotong* letters. In his entry on "seven sisters" *(qizimei),* Xie Zhimin describes sworn sisterhood as possible between anyone who hit it off, "regardless of surname, generation, age, [or] marital status, generally of seven members, and thus called 'seven sisters,'" and notes that people took whether or not a girl was part of a seven-sisterhood as a measure of her intelligence and character; the failure of a girl to achieve a seven-sisterhood, Xie reports, brought heavy concern to her parents in arranging her marriage, lowered her in the eyes of her husband, and lessened the face of her parents-in-law.[55] By all accounts seven was the ideal, yet of the dozens of extant *sanzhaoshu* written by sworn sisters, hardly a one describes a sisterhood of seven; most common in these texts are sisterhoods of four, five, or six members.[56]

Thus we begin to get an idea of how literate and nonliterate practices coexisted and interrelated in Shangjiangxu, and it may not be rash to conclude that we can see in these social formations the coexistence of practices whose origins probably lie in Han *(jiebaizimei)* and non-Han *(laotong)* traditions. But regardless of their ideal forms or the distinctions between them, *laotong* and *jiebaizimei* relationships were not formed in isolation from each other or other kinds of social relationships, kin and non-kin alike. These formalized non-kin relationships were voluntary, and a girl growing up in one of these households in one of these villages had no lack of peers from whom to choose her companions or of ways to formalize her non-kin relationships. We can expect that groups of girls spending time together would include various combinations of biological sisters, cousins, sworn sisters (from the same or a nearby village) and, from time to time, somebody's *laotong* on a visit, and that emotional attachments within these social circles had more to do with the real people involved than with dicta abstracted from normative accounts of these relationships or the texts produced by them.

Village exogamous marriage, even when tempered by delayed virilocal residence, would disrupt these peer group relationships, and so it is not surprising that they would produce a discourse of profound antipathy toward marriage. (This focus on peer groups by no means denies the disruption to parent-child and other kin ties, but merely locates these peer groups of daughters as the primary production site of this discourse.) The practice of delayed virilocal residence customary in the *nüshu* culture area entailed a bride's return to her natal home on the third day after the wedding and residence there until sometime into her first pregnancy, but for no more than three years, with requisite visits to her marital home during that time on four or five specified occasions a year. It was mandatory that she give birth in her marital home.[57] For peer groups of girls, then, this meant a long span of years marked by repeated departures and returns of close companions, a roller coaster ride of loss and reunion. As Andrea Sankar and Janice Stockard have demonstrated for the Pearl River delta, this customary marriage residence pattern did not in itself constitute marriage resistance; rather, as the standard form of marriage, it is precisely what girls were resisting when they balked at marriage.[58]

For an unabashed feminist like me, who delights in scathing critiques of patriarchal institutions, the temptation is nearly irresistible to write these *nüshu* critiques of marriage into a romance of resistance; doing so, however, would depend on the unwarranted assumption that this resistant discourse could somehow exist completely outside the relations of power it critiques, independent of all the other discourses produced by those relations.[59] I isolate just one—a startling one, perhaps, because we do not often hear it—from a veritable din of competing and overlapping discourses surrounding marriage. Mothers and mothers-in-law produced the same critiques of marriage when they were girls.[60] None of this denies the heartfelt unwillingness to marry so adamantly expressed in the discourses produced by girls' peer relationships. Yet the fact remains that it was socially unacceptable for a girl to express a willingness to marry, and the *nüshu* "bizarre incident" tales of the foolish girl who, tired of waiting, dolls herself up and brazenly marches off all by herself in search of her betrothed were a source of great hilarity for their readers.[61] A girl on the brink of village exogamous marriage in a patriarchal, patrilineal society found herself subject to diverse and competing social claims on her person; among others, the structurally embedded conflict between filiality and fertility playing itself out on her body was bound to engage a morass of conflicting desires and resentments.[62]

It is with this in mind that I now turn to the texts produced by the peer relationships discussed earlier to explore their representations of these relationships and marriage. *Sanzhaoshu* (literally, "third day books"), predominantly cloth-bound volumes but also fans and cloth written by a bride's close peers (*laotong*, sworn sisters, sisters, cousins) and female relatives (mother, sisters-in-law, and in one case mother's sister) and delivered to her in her marital home on the third day after the wedding, constitute just one of many ritualized wedding practices that negotiated the conflicts engendered by village exogamous marriage.[63] These books, among the most highly conventionalized of *nüshu* writing, would be sung aloud among women of the bride's marital home and village, and some of them include a few pleas for leniency and compassion addressed to her mother-in-law. Yet the writers of these texts, the vast majority of whom were members of the bride's peer group, focus far more on their own loss and what the bride has lost and left behind than what lies ahead for her. For their wider audience, these expressions of great loss can be read as a testament to the bride's social value, perhaps of some use in facilitating new relationships in the family and community of strangers she would come to join, and perhaps even tacitly warning against whatever abuses her mother-in-law might be inclined to inflict upon her. For the bride and her girlhood companions, however, these writings represent anguished attempts to come to terms with the disruption wreaked on their relationships, kin and non-kin alike, the durability of which is suddenly very much at stake.

Because *sanzhaoshu* are so highly conventionalized, reading and rereading nearly a hundred of them leaves one with the impression that they all say the same things, the same impression, I imagine, one would get from an anthology of all the wedding cards received in a small American town over several decades. (See the appendix for one *sanzhaoshu* in translation.) These texts have also been called *hesanzhaoshu* (third day congratulations books), yet all of them predominantly express their writers' pain and anger over losing the bride to marriage, reading far more like laments and condolences; large numbers of them contain no congratulations whatsoever.[64] Taken as a genre, these texts do read one just like the next, yet it turns out that the presence or absence of certain sentiments (including congratulations) in these texts can be attributed to the different relationships between writers and recipients. Significantly, these relationships are sometimes surprisingly difficult to determine. Relationships such as mother and sister-in-law are easy enough to recognize in this writing, but peer group relationships such as those of biological sisters and cousins, on the one hand, and those of the formalized non-kin relationships *laotong* and *jiebaizimei*, on the other, are sometimes nearly impossible to distinguish. Part of the difficulty lies in the fact that many of the texts from peers were group efforts, written in turns; these writers usually identify themselves, but it is sometimes difficult to tell where one stops and another begins.[65] The truly significant difficulty, however, lies in the fact that dialect modifiers and measure words for siblings are used for both kin and formalized non-kin relationships in these writings,[66] and many of the expressions of intimacy, attachment, and inseparability found in the *laotong* letters are used not only by both *laotong* and *jiebaizimei* but also by sisters and cousins, giving the distinct impression that sisters and cousins came to appropriate some of the discourse produced by these non-kin relationships to bolster their own "real" biological ties.

Based on a survey of about forty *sanzhaoshu* in which the relationship between writer and recipient can be decisively determined to be either kin or non-kin, the pattern of the presence or absence of certain expressions that emerges as a function of this relationship turns out to center on issues of face for the bride's natal family, issues which, not surprisingly, would be of little, if any, immediate concern to non-kin members of a bride's peer group. While it cannot be said that non-kin writers never express congratulations, these sentiments are found far more often in texts from kin, and only extremely rarely in texts from non-kin. Apologies and excuses for dowry insufficiencies (intended just as much for affines as for the bride herself, for whom dowry represents both a public and a personal statement of her worth to her natal family) appear only in writing from kin. Kin almost never fail to include direct address to the mother-in-law in their writings, whereas non-kin writers are far more likely to omit this nicety than they are to include it. Explicit recognition of the hardships a bride would face as a daughter-in-law (as opposed to the hardships of separation) is often articulated in exhortations to the bride to serve and obey her in-laws without expressing too much misery. (Kin tend to amplify this warning by reminding the bride that her excessive lamentations of misery will give people cause to make fun of her and her natal family.) These exhortations can be found in writing by both kin and non-kin, only slightly more often in writing by kin. But when we look at the texts that omit them entirely, all but one turn out to have been written by non-kin.

Aside from differences attributable to whether or not a writer had any vested interest in the reputation of the bride's natal family, all *sanzhaoshu* have in common repeated expressions of pain, sorrow, and anger over losing the bride—flowing tears, knives in the heart, sleepless nights of sorrow. Virtually all these texts cast the wedding as the end of *nüri*, a term that, although properly rendered "daughter days," I translate "girlhood days," as a way of gaining distance from the notion that village exogamous marriage is fundamentally about a daughter's loss of membership in her natal family and only incidentally about the disruption of non-kin ties, as a reminder that daughterhood means more than being a daughter. All these writers represent the end of girlhood days as the disruption of girlhood ties. Close companions, kin and non-kin alike, profess an expectation that their relationships, often described in terms of time spent together upstairs embroidering, "never a step apart," "never a harsh word between us," would last forever, as in lines such as, "I thought the four of us would have long days, who knew that this year two would leave," and "Forever, year after year, not separated and distant."[67] These texts contain frequent reminders to the bride not to forget her close companions, to know how miserable they are without her. One married elder sister with two children wrote to her younger sister, "People of the same father separated and distanced, I just hope younger sister will forgive me, already gone to the other place—in a word, it's hard." A same wrote, "I ask, are you stopping or not? It's like a boat sinking to the bottom; in deep water, it's hard to turn around and come back."[68]

These texts are often fraught with expressions of anger and resentment over the disruption of these relationships. Attempts to rationalize village exogamous marriage and its disastrous effects frequently blame the emperor or the court or the Jade Emperor, while lamenting how "useless" it is to be born female. Many remark that if they had any say in the matter, they would stay together for a lifetime, not be torn apart after "half a lifetime" *(banshi)*. Common expressions of such sentiments include, "Don't be mad your girlhood days upstairs have ended, it's that the court has set up the wrong rules [of protocol]"; "If the world ran according to our say so, we'd be together for a lifetime, and not live apart"; "It's that we shouldn't have been born wrong, [as] two red flowers [girls], useless people"; and "Don't blame your parents for marrying you too soon, just blame the Jade Emperor for setting up the wrong rules [of protocol]."[69] Many of these statements are followed up with expressions of how oppressive the world is, how girls are not free to do anything but follow protocol.[70] An abundant variety of such expressions is found in the *sanzhaoshu* corpus, just as likely to be voiced by a mother as by kin and non-kin peers.[71]

Although the vast majority of women in the *nüshu* culture area did marry, however willingly or unwillingly, it seems that some did seek alternatives, about which little is known,[72] and that strong peer group ties played some role for these women. For instance, one *nüshu* song alludes to a pact made by two *laotong* never to marry or have children; this song reflects the grief and sense of betrayal felt by the one who kept the pact toward the one who did not and died shortly after childbirth. Tang Baozhen, a sworn sister of Yi Nianhua and Gao Yinxian, insisted that Yi transcribe this song for me in *nüshu*, and Yi argued with her a long time before relenting. When I read it with her later, she was reluctant to talk about it, but did provide the foregoing explanation before cutting off further discussion by snapping, "Oh, everybody gets married." I cannot discount the truth of that claim. At the time, I attributed Yi's obvious discomfort with my knowing this text to having to explain a breach of the status quo, which she frequently defended. Though this text can say nothing about whether such pacts were common or if they were ever kept, the fact that the song survives indicates that it must have been meaningful in some way. (See the appendix for a translation.)[73] At the very least, unwillingness to marry, in one case anyway, gave rise to a vivid fantasy of having the gods kill off an entire family of affines in response to the prayer of a girl who did not want to part with her sworn sister.[74]

My impression is that peer pressure among close companions reinforced both an unwillingness to marry and the social unacceptability of any willingness to marry. But in a very real sense, the issue of willingness is quite beside the point in a society where "everybody gets married," a society that did not squelch the many conflicts engendered by its patriarchal institutions, but accommodated resistant discourses as an institutionalized part of village exogamous marriage. As the material I have presented here makes clear, the social institutions oppressive to women, though dominant and pervasive and seemingly permanent, were not so monolithic as to render women utterly passive victims with no room to maneuver. The more important issue, I think, in these peer group discourses about marriage is the durability of girlhood relationships after marriage. Another text, written by a recently married woman to her same on the day of her wedding, reminds her of their closeness and chastises her for betraying their bond by treating her coldly after she returned to her natal home. Her message: even after marriage "we'll be together just the same."[75] Many researchers have wondered how successfully these girlhood ties were maintained after marriage in the *nüshu* culture area, imagining how beneficial they could have been to a daughter-in-law taking up residence in a home and village (primarily but perhaps not always entirely) of strangers. Benedikta Dorer reports that "most of my informants told me they lost contact with their sworn sisters and *laotongs* after they moved in with their husbands."[76] We may yet learn more about this, but it is clear that, at the very least, daughters-in-law had had years of experience forming and participating in female social networks by the time they began married life. Although social hierarchy in Shangjiangxu allowed women very limited range for movement upward over the course of a lifetime, the material I have presented here shows a much wider range for lateral movement, in the form of social ties that could provide a source of emotional and sometimes economic support for women in times of trouble. These lateral social arrangements stood in line with, but also in tension with, vested patriarchal interests.

APPENDIX

Laotong Reply
Fine brush in hand, I write
To answer, girl: truly you have heart.
Two days ago I received your gift;
All along, proper people, an educated family.
When I received your worthy letter, opened it and read,
Every line had cause, meaning most profound.
I return a coarse missive to your worthy home,
Offered to you who knows my heart to fan herself.
You are the daughter of a worthy home,
The fan you did makes my heart beautiful.
I've taken your fan in hand and read it many times,
Every moment I recite it in my heart, in my mouth.
We'll join together, join,
Join good sympathy, our hearts happy.
Same like a pearl by Mother's side,
Of the born intelligent, you are one.
I just hope you won't mind,
We'll match good dears, our hearts glad.
People everywhere will envy our good match,
We each have one elder brother, one younger.
Today I send a letter to receive you,
I ask you, girl, to come to my home.
But our lowly gate hardly compares with yours,
I've a coarse heart, I'm careless.
I'll have you come and stay a few days,
We'll speak in whispers, exchange affection.
You asked me first if I was true,
My heart is true to go with you.
We'll embroider flowers together upstairs,
Choose our colors, thread our needles, talk it over.
Your mother was a girl like us,
Born of an educated family, proper people.
When you open to read my coarse writing, don't laugh,
I just hope the two of you will be lenient.

Sanzhaoshu
Taking speech, offering words, a poem,
A book sent to their worthy home
To see Elder Sister
In her fine abode, every step higher.
Father gave away his precious daughter,
On a glorious day, into a worthy home.
The day before yesterday, we sent you out in rush and
    flurry,
Parting on the road, tears flowed.
The flowered palanquin went like wind to a place far
    away,
I watched it go, starting, leaving, turning, going,
So hard to lose you, standing there watching.
Not seeing you, Elder Sister, where are you?
Turning back, going in, cold as water,
My hands can't do anything.
Remember before, upstairs,
Mother and daughters together we saw no sorrow.
Father and Mother had the five of us,
Three elder brothers, two flowers.
And a *fangshang* sister-in-law,
Who treated our parents with care.
We had some good luck,
To get a wise sister-in-law who knew right.
Having the good fortune to get a good, wise woman,
Father and Mother were known all around.
It shouldn't have been that we came in this life wrong as
    girls,
Red plums on the tree, a useless branch.
If we had been sons,
We could be together, not torn apart.
Sister, everyone went by so fast,
But I can't stop crying.
And I'm mad I have no one to keep me company
    upstairs,
My hands take to tasks without knowing at all.

I'm young, in Mother's house,
When I embroider, whom can I ask?
How long, days, years, without you to depend on?
With you upstairs, I had you to teach me.
If only I could persuade that worthy family:
No, not yet, wait a few years before taking her.
A year goes by as blown by the wind,
Wait a few years, let her teach me to roll floss.
Sister has gone to him like a seabird,[77]
Two days ago, a whole day of glory.
Gone into the dragon gate, without care or woe,
The phoenix mates the golden hen, a match made in
    heaven.
A flower planted by the pond, five colors, green,
Transplanted to the garden, transplanted affections.
The worthy home, rejoicing,
Rich, resplendent, above all others.
Also, worthy family, please be lenient,
The dowry wasn't complete, please don't mention it.
Two days ago my father gave her to you,
The dowry, everything, was far from complete.
My poor sister has gone to another home
With a dowry so scant even the top layer is plain.
Third day writings, said like this,
Sister, in that other home, be at peace.
In that fine home, be calm of heart, please,
Don't take everything to heart.
Smooth your anxious brow, living in that other place,
Take the long view, attend the six relations.
Don't let sobbing sorrow build in your heart,
And cause people to laugh at us ill-mannered folk.
Daughters are like the swallow,
Feathers barely grown, they fly their separate ways.
Just blame the court for making the wrong rules.
The world presses her to marry, not free, just follow the rules.
Being there is hard to compare with being upstairs,
In everything, just follow the rules . . .[78]

(Contract Song)
On red paper, I write a letter,
I'll have my say.
Today you who know my heart haven't gotten out of bed,
Though the sun shines in the room, over the mountains.
I told you to avoid it and you didn't,
Now you're ill and it's too late for regret.
A cold or a headache is easy to cure,
But you did it too soon after childbirth and died.
Two days ago at dawn, then broad daylight:
"You who know my heart, please be the aunt,
Won't you be the aunt?"
I made the hat, made the bauble,
The hat was made, the bauble done.
I was a proper aunt.
We agreed before the stove god,
But your words didn't match your heart, and you've died
    young.
We spoke true words,
And if you'd kept them, you'd still be worth something.
We went to the street and bought red paper,
We bought red paper and made a contract.
We made a contract and said those words,
Just like buying a field of rice seedlings.

CHEN YIYUN

Translated by S. Katherine Campbell

3 | Out of the Traditional Halls of Academe: Exploring New Avenues for Research on Women

In recent years I have been researching changes and problems in marriage and the family in urban China. After the Chinese government instituted a policy of economic reform and opened to the West at the end of the 1970s, rapid structural shifts and a fast-paced modernization of urban society resulted. My principal interest is in understanding the effect of these changes on people's attitudes toward marriage and the family, as well as on their behavior and styles of family life. In what conditions do women find themselves in the midst of such changes? What roles do they play? What kind of pressures and consequences do they suffer? What experiences have they had? All of these questions are naturally of interest to me.

Whether one traces back through China's history and traditional culture or investigates the social realities of contemporary China, one discovers that the fate of Chinese women is always tied to their marital and family circumstances. From start to finish, the home has been the focus of women's world. Until now it has been rare in China to see women who are willing to give up the union of the two sexes through marriage and choose a life of solitude, or to see women who can accept "love between women."[1] This is perhaps different from the current situation in Europe and the United States. Research on the issues of marriage and family life thus remains the most feasible means to study the lives and destinies of women; those issues remain a basic link to all women's issues. Close attention to the ranks of current Chinese women's studies scholars reveals that many of them are sociologists, legal workers, demographers, or social workers who originally studied or were concerned with marriage and the family.

Research Methodologies in the Chinese Context

As a sociologist, I have long worried over problems of method. The foundation of sociology in old China was weak, and after the founding of New China, this discipline was nearly eliminated. The field of sociology was rehabilitated and reestablished in the 1980s, taking advantage of both the comprehensive opening of Chinese society and initiatives in the academic world to "invite foreign elements in." Whether Chinese scholars go to the West on a "pilgrimage for scriptures," or European and American scholars come to China to "deliver treasures,"[2] encounters with the whole range of western sociological theory and methods have very quickly created an almost mystical effect on China's young and inexperienced sociological world. The precise science of quantitative methods often used in western sociology has been especially fetishized by young scholars. Computers have become popular in China's marketplace in recent years, further encouraging the preference of sociologists for technology and statistics. Scholars then pick and choose among questionnaire data entered into computers to write their scholarly works. Certain foreign colleagues are even more ingenious: if only they can get hold of a floppy disk of data, they can stuff China's numbers into a theoretical framework, and thus complete a "sinological" treatise. Chinese scholars are not accustomed to reviewing their colleagues' results, however, and are even more awed by thick books in foreign languages. Explanations with many absurd figures and farfetched analogies are thus unimpeded in their distribution. Some studies pass on erroneous information, others lead young people astray, still others do not care even to ask about certain issues. Are those results? Is that wealth? Or is it rubbish; is it a waste product? And who will make an effort to distinguish between the two?

When I use questionnaires to collect data or want to draw support from the "database" of Chinese colleagues, concern over the reliability of data is unavoidable. I discovered that, when dealing with flesh-and-blood topics relating to marriage and the family, information from questionnaires is often contradictory or is based on incorrect suppositions. Careful examination reveals two crucial reasons for this. First, marriage and the family are the most concealed part of social life, and for many it is difficult to be open about them with outsiders. Openness is hindered not only by courtyard gateways and walls, but also by all the ingrained characteristics of conservatism, shyness, self-respect, vanity, and family reputation. To elicit the true situation is especially difficult.

Second, in the realm of marriage, people's actual behavior is almost always at odds with written and oral declarations. For example, there are some husbands whose thinking and behavior is "male chauvinist," but when answering questions about male-female equality, they select socially acceptable answers and do not express their own true opinion. When questions touch on marriage prices and motives for marriage and divorce, insincere answers on questionnaires are even easier to spot. When most people fill out questionnaires, they do not consider the requirements of science, but apply their own personal standards, trying not to leave an "unhealthy record" on the questionnaire. For example, social morality places a high value on love in modern marriage. When people answer questions about motives for marriage, they all conform to stereotype and give love as the first answer. In reality, who is willing to admit that they themselves married for money, or a house, or a household registration,[3] motives that are not socially approved?

In western sociology, statistical questionnaires or other precise scientific quantitative methods are used in the context of a developed industrial society. In such a society the level of social conformity is relatively high; most people are highly educated and open-minded, and express themselves freely. Privacy in these societies is protected by law and morality, as well as professional regulations concerning confidentiality. These are all social preconditions for pursuing research by means of questionnaires. But in Chinese society at present, these preconditions have not yet been established. If one looks back to the despotic rule endured by common people in Chinese history, if one remembers the political instability, the disasters, and the harsh realities suffered by innumerable households from the 1950s to the 1970s, it is even easier to understand why people in China lack the consciousness and habit of free expression.

Anonymity and confidentiality are, after all, new concepts that have been publicized only in the last few years. Chinese people have lingering fears and only half believe those promises. The closed-minded attitude reflected in the phrases "The family is a forbidden zone, outsiders not admitted" and "Don't wash the family's dirty linen in public" is both a remnant of previous traditional culture and a mark left by past government and society. The use of questionnaires copied mechanically from foreigners will leave Chinese people feeling dubious about the method. Even if people sometimes go through the motions and complete a questionnaire for the sake of appearances or to fulfill an obligation, how can such answers be believed? The sociological world has mechanically followed the precise scientific quantitative trend, with grave consequences for the study of women's issues.

Given this situation, I resolved to blaze my own trail. I remembered that five years earlier, after a sampling investigation failed, I simply went from door to door gathering information from the households that had originally completed the questionnaire. I discovered that most people were obviously answering my questions in a perfunctory manner, and some heads of household even politely refused me at the door. (No wonder that some questionnaire investigations are quickly completed by an investigator sitting alone under a big tree.) I later had an opportunity to give a lecture about marriage issues on the People's Central Broadcasting radio station. Because of that previous experience of failure, I made an effort to avoid an academic manner and tried to select topics that could appeal to listeners. As I expected, after the program was broadcast, listeners from every part of the country wrote to engage me in dialogue, and I answered their questions on the air. Following that, the Central Television Station also invited me to do a program, and afterward I received even more letters. I began a magazine column for letters from readers and also took charge of a special newspaper column.

What excited me most was not how much publicity I had received, but the trust that listeners, viewers, and readers conveyed in their letters. It gave me confidence in subsequent investigative research. Ninety percent of those who wrote were people from urban areas, who have a certain level of education and an ability to express themselves. Women made up more than 80 percent of these respondents. The problems they recounted in their letters fell roughly into three categories: dissatisfaction with their husbands or worries brought on by desperate household situations; confusion about love and choice of marriage partners; and complaints about children or parents. I first responded to the letters of the Beijing residents, and invited a portion of them to talk with me in person. Probably because it gave them psychological reassurance, most were willing to come to my home to talk rather than to my office. My fifteen-square-meter bedroom henceforth doubled as a "consultation room." I also responded to a few letters from other parts of the country, to induce those writers to tell me their stories in a little more detail. After a year I had accumulated two full gunnysacks of mail.

In order to make sure my study was not limited to the "problem households" of the people who wrote me letters, I made full use of my opportunities to lecture. I pursued individual interviews with people of different occupations, ages, educational levels, and economic circumstances. I went into households to talk and held informal group discussions; from this I came to understand the lives, experiences, and feelings of my informants. At the same time, I enthusiastically participated in all kinds of social activities and social work related to my research. These activities included the "good husband" contest jointly sponsored by Beijing Television and the Women's Federation, official and unofficial psychological advice "hot lines," collective weddings organized by the Communist Youth League, introductions to potential spouses, discussions at singles clubs, volunteer consulting and legal advising in parks and on the streets, and so on. I also participated in pioneering work at marriage consultation centers in Beijing and Shenzhen. Currently, I write a special column in a magazine called *Marriage and Family,* and publish articles in several influential Chinese publications. I often have men and women arrive seeking help at my home and at my office. I have installed two phone lines at home in order to be available to talk with "concerned parties" at any time. I use all these opportunities to conduct investigations and collect individual case material for my research.

What I find most gratifying is that, unlike the situation where people routinely fill out questionnaires, those who write and visit, especially the women, trust in me completely. They candidly open their hearts and pour out their private troubles. They voluntarily give me private letters, diaries, and other written materials, such as published writings, certificates of awards, written divorce judgments, and so on which might help explain their experiences. Of course, I keep these materials strictly confidential. Some people even invite me to their homes as a guest, giving me an opportunity to have contact with their family, relatives, neighbors, and friends. From this I gather even more information. The number of research subjects and the amount of consultation work I have has thus snowballed. With these people I have an exchange almost like that between old friends, and not one like the simple relationship between a researcher and her subject. They are not awkward in my presence; there are times when they do not mind that I take notes or make recordings; and I am relatively confident of the veracity of the situations they describe.

My lectures, consulting work, and research together have allowed me to conduct interviews in many different regions of China. The subjects of my work range from young prostitutes in Guangdong to peasants in suburban Beijing, from petty entrepreneurs in Shandong to folk artists in Guizhou, from women cadres of the Zhuang national minority in Guangxi to college students in the northeast, from writers in Jiangsu to scientists in Shaanxi. This group includes professional women and leading women cadres.[4]

Chinese society is in the midst of rapid change, and I am just beginning to get a sense of the effects on marriage and the family, and the reactions of women. There are some trends that are still unclear, and some established views of former times seem now to be negated by reality. Continued observation gives me new insights, and keeps me continually revising my previous understandings. There are those who label me a "traditional sociologist"; I would rather consider myself an anthropologist or an ordinary social worker.

Current Issues

Although for the moment I have not generated any comprehensive research results, I have a few simple insights from the impressions I have gathered that I would like to share with those who study women's issues. These include the increasing differentiation of Chinese society, the effects of the state-sponsored women's movement, the particular characteristics of women's studies, and the importance of international academic exchange.

First, after the founding of New China in 1949, through top-down economic reform and ideological revolution, Chinese society began to centralize and move toward a greater uniformity. At least within the two strata of rural and urban dwellers, differences were essentially eliminated. Everyone ate the same food, wore the same clothes, read the same books, even thought about the same issues, so that to take any group of people, any issue, any category of phenomena and crown it with the word *Chinese* was the logical thing to do. No wonder that the Westerners who came to China from the 1950s through the 1970s went back home and one after the other wrote major works titled "China's . . ." In the period since reforms began in the late 1970s, however, a rapid process of differentiation has appeared in China's cities and countryside. Not only are regional differences more apparent, but even the proliferation of administrative levels among the people is dizzying. Mao Zedong's "Analysis of the Classes in Chinese Society" is already useless to explain Chinese social structure and the existing state of social divisions; the western three-part class division of upper, middle, lower seems even more simplistic and unsuitable. Guangdong's Shenzhen and Gansu's Dingxi,[5] the directors of transnational corporations and the peasants of mountainous border villages, inhabit two separate worlds, and are like citizens of two different countries.

If you go deep into the heart of a "modern social district" such as Shenzhen, you will discover that squeezed around the edges of the city in corrugated tin shanties are "guerrilla above-quota birth groups,"[6] while "unmarried aristocrats" live in sumptuous apartments. These two groups have no interests in common. Traveling scholars who come to China and get a superficial understanding through cursory observation, returning home to write sinological tracts, are not the only ones who now dare not use the phrase "China's . . ." Even those old, experienced experts at sampling in Chinese sociology feel that "the true face of Lushan is beyond the ken of one deep in the heart of the mountain."[7] When foreign reporters bring up questions such as, "What new progress has there been in Chinese women's liberation?" "What changes have there been in Chinese people's sense of family, or Chinese people's lifestyles?" I feel quite embarrassed, and often I can only say, "No comment."

Second, after New China was established, a top-down marriage reform and liberation of women definitely occurred. This was a real revolution, attacking customs and habits of the feudal patriarchal system which had stretched back hundreds and thousands of years. On the macro levels of law and morality, these reforms achieved results that attracted worldwide attention. Circumstances in the wake of this revolution are very different from what they would have been had it not taken place. Comparing the achievements of two hundred years of the western women's movement with a few decades of liberation for Chinese women, one can see the efficacy of the revolutionary process.

The revolutionary act of liberation for women in New China brought benefits to several generations of women, and the depth and breadth of its influence should not be underestimated. Recently, both outside and within China, some people are saying that Chinese women's liberation was merely a favor bestowed by government authorities. Without a foundation in women's self-consciousness, it was a gift that is in danger of being withdrawn. Therefore some hold that China should start a grass roots women's movement on the western model in order to achieve the right of female self-determination, incorporating enlightenment through education as well as a refusal to marry or bear children. These ideas and suggestions are absurd. It is well known that the U.S. women's movement has wrestled with the liberal notion of enlightenment through education and the radical notion of destroying family structure for two centuries. But to date, elementary questions such as whether men should do housework and care for children or whether women should receive equal pay for equal work are still topics of public discussion and debate. According to the author of the feminist book *Backlash,* since the 1980s women in the United States have been on a downhill path; certain gains of women's liberation are in the process of being lost.[8]

How can this sort of phenomenon be explained? I believe we still need to examine Marx's exposure of the character of capitalist economy and society. If the means of production are concentrated in the hands of an exploitative minority, and the goal of economic activities is to obtain the greatest possible extent of industrial profit and private wealth, women will not even be able to imagine equality with men. Because industry cannot acknowledge women's reproductive and household labor or calculate it as valuable social labor, women act only as consumers and become "the second sex." Those roles are much more important than women's participation in society and government. Examine the recent phenomenon of certain administrative levels in Chinese society also taking "a downhill path," and it is likewise clear that the cause lies in the ill effects brought by capitalist market economies.

In the situations of "single proprietors" in the open coastal zones and women workers at transnational corporations inland, there is indeed cause for worry. In Chinese society, whoever wants the high production of a market economy and also wants to protect women's rights and interests and the socialist equality between men and women faces a difficult dilemma. A "market economy under socialist conditions" constitutes a new problem in theory and practice. Scholars of women's studies need to examine the contradictions generated in the course of China's social reform and opening up to the world. European and American capitalist companies push on China a model of inequality in employment between men and women; they do in China things they cannot do under the restrictions in their home countries. They thus erode the rights Chinese women already have. Under these circumstances, alert Chinese women's studies scholars should realize that the socialist women's liberation movement, with its struggle against inequality between men and women under capitalism, has become a joint historical mission of Chinese and foreign women. In this respect Chinese women have their own superior theoretical base and practical experience. There is no reason to belittle ourselves inappropriately.

Third, women's studies is a new discipline which is always interconnected with the demand for women's liberation. Because women themselves study women, the research is for the sake of women, and the results will be used by women. This obviously differs from the scholasticism of the halls of traditional sociology, where scholars pay attention only to publishing articles and piling up endless theoretical arguments, activities that have very little to do with people's real lives. In other words, the birth and development of women's studies itself is a kind of "revolution" against traditional scholasticism. Consequently, women's studies scholars should use their own unique methods and styles of research to make a contribution toward this discipline. Women's sensitivity, sympathetic nature, and excellence at listening attentively to others' opinions, their desire to avoid and resolve conflict as well as their intuition about and experience in the world, the ease with which women connect with one another, their courage in earnestly practicing what they advocate all bring a special vigor to women's studies.

From my own experiences over the last few years, I think that contemporary western sociology, with its advocacy of precise science and technology and dry mathematics, can offer scant help to women's studies. Anthropology, by contrast, with its attention to cultural difference, its in-depth inquiry into the rich and varied lives of different peoples, and its simple and unadorned theory, methods, and results, is worthy of study and use by Chinese women's studies scholars. If we scholars who ourselves come from the collectivity of women use anthropology's method of participant observation to investigate every stratum of women, we will be able to apprehend our own position and develop the proper range of expression.

Fourth, Chinese women's studies is in its initial phase; opportunities for international academic exchange have been very rare. I feel that Chinese and western scholars cannot at present form significant links; language and culture are the main barriers. Both sides have many accomplished scholars who have difficulty expressing themselves in a foreign language. I honestly hope that western scholars who are interested in doing in-depth research on Chinese women, and Chinese scholars who have the responsibility of introducing foreign colleagues to the true state of Chinese women's studies, as well as those who study the results of western women's studies scholarship, will all put effort into improving their foreign language proficiency. Aside from this, the content, forms, and methods of the issues under discussion by eastern and western scholars are still often at odds with one another; this is perhaps partially due to cultural difference. Nevertheless, at recent women's studies conferences I have met many western scholars who could speak Chinese, use language we Chinese can understand, have an attitude of respect and value toward Chinese culture, and earnestly discuss with us issues of Chinese women's history, literature, marriage, and social situation. Further scholarly exchange of this kind will definitely enhance the cultural understanding, links, and closeness between Chinese and western women scholars.

GAO XIAOXIAN

Translated by S. Katherine Campbell

4 | China's Modernization and Changes in the Social Status of Rural Women

The significant gap between the status of rural women and urban women is well known. Rural women still make up the majority of Chinese women. This alone confirms that if there are no significant improvements in the situation of rural women, then liberation for the entirety of Chinese women will be impossible. China today is in the midst of modernization; thus, modernization's potential influence on the status of peasant women naturally becomes a focal point for women's studies scholars. Modernization of society has a specific connotation: it is a process that moves people to use modern science and technology to transform comprehensively the material and spiritual conditions of their lives.

Before 1949 China's course of modernization was mostly limited to urban areas. Women's liberation barely touched the rural areas. Most rural women (except in the base areas under Communist control) remained in the midst of traditional society characterized by a patriarchal structure and culture. Its central features such as a sexual division of labor whereby "men are primarily outside the home, women are primarily inside the home,"[1] the practice of women moving from their father's household to their husband's, with the male always as head, and the pervasiveness of consciousness and values that respect men and despise women all in one way or another remained intact.

Rural Women and Socialist Modernization

The founding of the People's Republic of China in 1949, and along with it the establishment of a unified nation with a centralized government, laid the foundation for China's modernization and the fundamental transformations in rural women's lives. After 1949 reform and experiments in social engineering were of unprecedented scope. The common characteristic of these reforms was a high level of centralization in the process of economic and political transformation. While this kind of top-down social transformation, created through the use of political and ideological power, was essentially externally induced, the large-scale mass movements used to promote social change nevertheless did have a profound effect on common people.

From the perspective of changes in rural women's status, none has had a greater effect than the cooperative movement (1952–1956) and the communization movement (1956–1958), which gradually established a basis for rural women's economic identity. Historically, women in most of China's rural areas had not taken part in agricultural labor. After New China was established, however, because of the need for agricultural labor, and as an effort to improve women's economic and political status, the government promoted and encouraged women to participate in field labor. It continued to do so throughout the process of the transformation to cooperatives. In 1950, in newly liberated areas, only 20 to 40 percent of the female labor force participated in farm work; by 1957, 70 percent of adult rural women were engaged in field work.[2]

Rural women's achievement of an economic identity influenced their social status in four ways. First, it changed the traditional division between the two sexes. Women participated in social production as independent laborers, so their independent status as persons gradually became socially recognized. Second, those who had been provided for became providers, which increased their importance within the household. Third, collective labor broadened women's views and enlarged their scope of interaction, furthering the dissemination and acceptance of new perspectives. Fourth, the government encouraged and trained a group of women as model workers and activists, some of whom were promoted to administrative departments at all levels. They became models of the transformation in rural women's status and had an exemplary effect in rural areas.

Generally speaking there are at least two preconditions for the large-scale participation of women in social production: one is the use of modern technology, since using large machinery ensures that differences in physical strength will no longer have fundamental importance in production; the other is the replacement of household labor through the popularization of social services such as cafeterias, child care centers, tailor shops, and so on. Lacking these preconditions, how was mass participation in social labor realized by China's rural women in the 1950s? Three factors were important. One was China's earlier self-sufficient, small-scale peasant economy, with its tradition of seasonal participation by women in farm activities. A second was the gradual elimination of profits from land and other means of production. The amount of a household's income was then directly determined by the amount of labor it contributed. This kind of distribution structure compelled all able-bodied household members to earn work points,[3] including women and students who were not yet of age. Third, cooperativization led to the creation of an administrative system founded on production teams, which intensified the effect of using public pressure to establish women's place in social labor. As a result of these conditions, rural women were able to complete the process of moving from the home into wider society in a very short period of time. But the use of external force (as opposed to women organizing themselves) had pronounced side effects: rural women held mostly low-level (i.e., unskilled) or part-time (i.e., seasonal or temporary) positions. With externally induced change, backlash or "reversal" can occur.

The emergence of cooperatives weakened the social function of the lineage and the family, and also weakened lineage authority and patriarchal authority over women. Even though the leaders of the new rural political organizations were still peasants, they were spokespersons of government at the village level, and did a great deal of work implementing government orders and policy and discouraging traditional customs. But the majority of cadres at the village level were peasants with a low level of education who had only recently received government training. Thus, their traditional consciousness emerged in the course of their work, strengthening feudal consciousness in others because it appeared to be the official viewpoint.

The movement to organize people's communes in 1958 constitutes a unique chapter in the history of women's liberation. With the ideological goal to "leap forward into communism,"[4] the people's communes became infused with a militaristic discipline in organization, production, and daily life. Overnight, public cafeterias spread throughout rural areas; child care centers, sewing collectives, laundries, hair salons, shoemaking shops, knitting shops, and so on appeared. For the first time, women could forgo household chores and throw themselves into social production. For the generations of women who had been tied to the kitchen, this was an extraordinary transformation. At the same time, a great deal of male labor was drawn off to smelt steel and iron and build irrigation works, thus creating a shortage of labor in agriculture and other industries. In accord with the slogan "Release men and substitute women,"[5] women assumed the great burden of agricultural production, and also held nonagricultural positions such as drivers, storekeepers, and animal breeders. This was the first time in history that rural women were participating in all aspects of social production. In 1958–59, 90 percent of women participated in field labor, averaging about 250 days of labor per year, equivalent to approximately three quarters of the annual labor of a male worker.[6]

The 1958 endeavor to accelerate both the development of productive capacity and the liberation of peasant consciousness was, however, only a utopia. Soon after, following economic adjustments and the dismantling of public cafeterias, rural women returned to their previous position, once again assuming the burden of household labor.

In the early socialist period, the government relied on the extraction of agricultural surplus in order to achieve industrial accumulation. Rural migration to urban areas was strictly limited, thus effectively sealing off rural areas. This made China's historical rural-urban divide even more pronounced. Peasants who had for generations lived in their ancestral villages continued the same longstanding traditions. Even though footbinding, child brides, concubinage, and other vile habits and customs were rooted out, there were few significant changes in traditional family structure. Patrilocal and patrilineal marriage practices continued as before. With the household as the unit of distribution, the continuation of patriarchy meant that women who had already participated in social production had not achieved real economic independence. Even though the government and society advocated male-female equality, in the peasant subculture men continued to be considered superior to women.

A comprehensive look at the changes in Chinese villages in the 1950s and 1960s reveals that social and political reform produced great achievements, but they did not lead to rural economic modernization. Nearly all villages outside the coastal areas had almost no industry, had poorly developed agricultural production methods, and had a very low level of mechanization. Labor methods that depended on human and animal strength intrinsically limited women's participation. Women were merely helping hands, playing supporting roles. An undeveloped commodity economy led to a continuation of household self-sufficiency. Women naturally took up all the traditional chores: cooking, weaving, mending, raising children, taking care of the elderly, raising pigs and chickens, milling flour, and so on. During collectivization, then, in addition to the burden of household labor, women also had to take part in earning work points in collective production. Adding the burden of social production to traditional tasks made their lives all the more heavy.

Post-1978 Rural Reform

Extensive and substantial rural modernization began in the late 1970s, with the household responsibility system[7] as its central feature. The pressures of social reform led to changes in the overall situation of rural women that surpassed those of any earlier period. These changes were the result of further industrialization efforts in rural areas, the introduction of a market economy, urbanization, changes in the concept of the individual, and the modernization of family relations.

The first ten years of reform (1978–1988) were in essence a process in which the rise of town and township enterprises led to the industrialization of the countryside. Rural productive capacity increased at a rapid pace. By 1989 the total output value of such town and township enterprises was already 58 percent of total rural social output value. The rise of small-town industry also increased the social status of rural areas and broadened rural occupational choices. For some rural women it facilitated a change in economic status; they became "rural workers" who left the soil but not the countryside. By 1987 female workers made up 35 percent of the total labor force in rural enterprises.[8] These female workers were concentrated in the textile, clothing, electronics, papermaking, printing, plastics, and food processing industries. Most of the coastal and export-oriented enterprises were engaged in processing, so the proportion of women workers was somewhat higher. In 1987 the two provinces of Fujian and Jiangsu had a proportion of female workers in rural industry of 48.7 percent and 43.2 percent, respectively.[9]

These women workers still live in rural areas, retain rural residency, and do not receive state grain discounts or any other state subsidies.[10] But their work styles and life-styles differ from those of peasants, and more nearly resemble those of urban workers. This group of workers thus occupies a middle ground between the two other groups. When we compare them to traditional peasant women, two marked changes are evident. First, owing to the demands of large-scale mechanized production, these women have developed a strong sense of discipline, a broad outlook, and an ability to accept new things quickly. Second, they receive fixed wages by the day, so this group of contemporary rural women has truly realized financial independence. They have lessened their dependence on the household and their husband, and increased their autonomy. This is especially true of female industrialists, who, despite the fact that they do not yet constitute a large group, have won the recognition of society and especially of men through their knowledge, competence, and daring. They are the heroines in the transformation of rural women's status. If it can be said that industrialization provides a path to rural modernization, then this group of women represents the direction the transformation of rural women's economic status will take.

Another major change in rural reform has been the introduction of market mechanisms, accelerating the specialization, commodification, and modernization of the rural economy. Most rural women have seized this historic opportunity to turn products of their household labor into commodities, including such formerly nonmarket "sidelines" as weaving, embroidery, sewing, knitting, and raising chickens and sheep. They have also followed the imperatives of market mechanisms to develop them into large-scale and specialized businesses. Some discriminating women enthusiastically produce new items according to the demands of the market; they develop processing, knitting, planting, and breeding enterprises, and even directly enter the realms of distribution, marketing, trading, and service provision.

The household-based commodity economy has obscured the separate contributions of men and women. Generally speaking, the man's range of activity is broader, he has more information, and most policymakers and managers are male, whereas most women are concentrated in production. Yet market mechanisms have provided a relatively equal competitive arena, compelling some women to rely on their own ability, courage, and insight to become policymakers and managers. I conducted a survey of one hundred rural households in the Guanzhong prefecture of Shaanxi province in 1987. Of the women who took part in commodity production, 42 percent started the business on their own initiative, 19 percent purchased the equipment and materials themselves, and 15 percent took the responsibility of marketing their goods.[11] In 1988 the number of rural, privately run commercial and industrial households headed by women[12] made up 25 percent of the national total.[13] Moreover, owing to the links between a commodity economy and market mechanisms, diversified producers must be more competitive and more willing to take risks. This no doubt inspires self-improvement in rural women and the modification of traditional attitudes.

Urbanization is a necessary consequence of industrialization. In China throughout the 1980s the process of urbanization has accelerated, with the nonagricultural population increasing from 16.6 percent of the total population in 1979 to 21 percent in 1990.[14] This rapid increase is due in large part to the development of small towns.

In Chinese history, towns emerged as centers of commodity exchange and areas for the accumulation and dispersal of agricultural by-products. In most rural areas today, towns have become centers for industrial collection, commodity transfer, transportation, and information transmittal. They have played an irreplaceable role in industrialization.

Because of a lack of statistical information, it is difficult to determine how many rural women moved into towns in the ten-year period between 1978 and 1988. Calculations based on research data from a sample of 1 percent of the population in 1987 indicate that in the five years between 1982 and 1987, 6.76 million women moved to towns, making up 55.9 percent of the total migration into towns in that period. Of those, 41.1 percent came from rural areas.[15] Women make up the majority of the migrant population because a large proportion move for reasons of marriage or to accompany others, but a significant number of women also move to engage in business or to study.

The reforms have already begun to undermine the household registration system that limits mobility. The demands of urban lifestyles have also attracted labor migration from rural to urban areas, so that the movement of rural labor into towns and cities has become an inexorable trend. Those entering urban areas are mostly unmarried young women who perform jobs many city dwellers are unwilling to do. There are, for instance, "rotating seasonal workers"[16] recruited from rural areas to work in the textile industries in cities that cannot recruit enough urban textile workers; "working sisters"[17] of the industrial processing districts of new and developing coastal cities (Shenzhen alone has 250,000 temporary female workers from rural areas); and the crowd of "nannies"[18] individually hired in every major city in recent years (in 1989 there were more than 3 million rural women working as nannies in urban areas).[19]

These people's wages are both low and undependable. When there is an economic slump, they are the first to be laid off. But the significant gap between urban and rural areas means that these women view their participation in urban industry as clearly superior to agricultural work, whether from a financial or a life-style point of view. Rural youth can at least learn some new skills and see the world. Urban areas thus hold a great deal of fascination for them. Most of these women return to their rural home after earning some money, but some stay on to marry and settle down, or work on a long-term basis. These women are the only ones to leave both the land and the countryside. The changes in their life-style and attitudes are relatively thorough.

Modernization of the individual[20] and societal modernization are interrelated. Yet changes in conceptions of gender in rural China over the last decade or so, which might indicate greater female development and male-female equality, are rarely studied. According to my observations in rural areas, compared with the peasants of the 1970s, today's peasants are more willing to accept women working (including outside the home). Male peasants recognize women's competence and authority in the home, discuss important issues with their wives, subsidize their daughters' school attendance, and are beginning to help with household chores. The degree of male-female equality has clearly changed.

With industrialization and a commodity economy, people are privileged because of their skills, not because of their sex. Business-women, female entrepreneurs, and the other successful women who have emerged during reform have used their celebrated accomplishments to change attitudes toward women. Another reason for change is the popularization and use of media for public dissemination. Following reform, increased rural income has made radio, television, and newspapers much more widely accessible than before. In 1989 in rural China there were 108 million radios and 65.58 million television sets,[21] and the rate of popularization of television had already reached 38 percent.[22] The widespread appeal of radio and television has played a large role in initiating change in peasant attitudes and values.

A third reason for the shift in gender relations is the improvement in education. This is the result of many years' accumulation of education in rural areas. In 1987, out of every 100 rural workers, 0.06 had post-secondary education, 0.37 had technical post-secondary education, 6.79 had senior middle school education, 29.39 had junior middle school education, 38.4 had primary education, and 24.99 were semiliterate or illiterate. In 1988 alone there were 640,000 rural senior middle school graduates, 7.5 million junior middle school graduates, more than 300,000 agricultural-vocational school graduates, as well as 5 million peasants engaged in other forms of adult education—radio courses, correspondence courses, or night school.[23] Improvement in peasants' cultural literacy is a key factor in the modernization of peasant values.

Changes in peasant concepts of gender also include changes in women's sense of self-worth. As an example, in my study of one hundred households in Guanzhong prefecture, Shaanxi province, 72 percent of my informants believed that when choosing a marriage partner young people should "make their own decision, and ask for their parents' agreement." Regarding childbearing, it was commonly thought that to have two children is best, with one male and one female as the ideal combination. As far as the investment in children's education and their career expectations, the differences between boys and girls were not very large. As for women's estimation of their self-worth, 30 percent of the women indicated a desire "to achieve some success through work." When asked if there was merit in the opinion that "if a husband earns enough for the whole family to be well off, then the wife does not need to work, and can just stay home and care for her husband," 74 percent of women responded that "there is no merit in it."[24] The awakening of women's self-consciousness has been an intrinsic driving force in the changes in women's status. Its effect should not be underestimated.

The strength of tradition in rural cultural practice has made it difficult to link family life with modernization. Here the term modernization is used to mean only the process of moving from tradition to modernity. Yet rural economic reform has effected structural change in the household in two ways. First, the rural responsibility system returned the task of production to the household. Because of production's intrinsic labor needs, it created a trend toward family unity. Second, the commodity economy and the processes of industrialization and urbanization have led to decreased family size. Nuclear families are more common, already constituting more than 60 percent of the families in Shaanxi's Guanzhong prefecture. The trend toward nuclear families has eroded the base of the traditional patriarchal system. The relationship between husband and wife has become primary; women's status in the family has risen accordingly.

Changes in the level of household consumption have also propelled changes in women's status. Peasant cash income has increased since reform, and has for the most part enabled peasant households to break from traditional self-sufficiency. In 1980 commodity consumption accounted for 50.4 percent of total consumption; by 1989 it had increased to 68.8 percent. The proportion of food products that were commodities in 1980 was 31.1 percent; in 1989 that figure had increased to 52.3 percent.[25] Now that burdensome traditional roles have been relaxed for rural women, they have more time to take part in social production, and to seek self-development.

Until now, there has been a lack of specialized research and measured analysis of the improvement in rural women's familial status. But every person who lives in the countryside or maintains close relations with those who do can see that these changes are real.

The Uneven Impact of Reform

To summarize, rural Chinese women have experienced a great deal of change during the years of reform. But China covers a vast territory; the external circumstances and the specific policies which each locale confronts in the course of industrialization and the introduction of market mechanisms vary. Consequently, regions have developed unevenly: eastern coastal districts have developed faster because of geographic advantage and preferential policies; remote western mountain districts and those adjoining minority areas are lagging behind somewhat. Relatively speaking, changes for women in districts with developed industry are greater; in backward areas many women still live amidst tradition. This shows that the transformation of rural women's status depends on the process of modernization. But can the improvement of rural women's status just wait for the onset of modernization? This brings up a theoretical question: Does modernization intrinsically bring about the improvement of women's status?

The point of departure as well as the immediate goal for modernization is to develop the economy, not to improve women's status. While modernization has positive effects on women, it also has negative ones. Moreover, women's status is relative, and is often defined in comparison with that of men. Consequently, to analyze the transformation in rural women's status, one cannot merely compare women in the present with women in the past. In the context of modernization, it is even more important to continually compare women with men. Differences in occupation and income are crucial factors here.

In the face of the increasing quantity of jobs created by industrialization, striking differences in the redistribution of men and women into those jobs are evident. First, numerically there are more men than women. By 1989 town and township industry already employed close to 100 million laborers. Accurate statistics on the actual number of women workers are lacking. Nonetheless, the Rural Development Research Institute at the Chinese Academy of Science did a multitiered study of 222 villages, 59 counties, and 11 provinces, autonomous regions, and independent municipalities.[26] In 1986 women made up only 25 percent of the transferred labor. The less developed the area, the smaller that percentage was. If these provinces are divided geographically into eastern, central, and western categories, the proportion of women making up the flow of labor is 36.4 percent, 20.8 percent, and 13.6 percent, respectively.[27] The proportion in the eastern developed districts is thus slightly more than a third.

The second difference is that men occupy higher administrative levels and women lower ones. Women workers in town and township enterprises are concentrated in labor-intensive, low-skill jobs. These industries also have poor working conditions and low wages. The more highly skilled jobs are usually held by men. There are very few women in the kinds of jobs—enterprise manager, technician, salesperson, accountant—that peasants consider highly prestigious.

The third difference is that women receive lower wages than men. Even though at present there are no reliable statistics, the research of several prefectural Women's Federation branches shows that many town and township enterprises do not implement standards of equal pay for equal work. Some enterprises are still using the distribution system from collective agriculture when men's labor earned ten points to women's eight,[28] so there is an obvious disparity in salary.

Several phenomena that have emerged in the course of China's rural industrialization deserve special mention, such as "women returning to the home," best characterized by Tianjin's Daqiu village, and the large-scale use of young rural female labor, or "working sisters," in industrial districts such as Shenzhen. How can we account for these phenomena? What is their effect on Chinese women themselves?

Let us first consider Daqiu village. Daqiu village is in a suburban county outside Tianjin. Industrialization came early to the village, and it quickly grew wealthy. Daqiu village attracted national attention not only because of its success, but also because during that process it forced all the women in the village to "return to the home."

I conducted research in Daqiu village in 1985, and consider this phenomenon to be the result of three interrelated factors. One is that Daqiu village chose heavy industries such as steel rolling mills, foundries, and so on in the start-up period of industrialization. These heavy industries exclude women. Another factor is that industrialization linked to the production of heavy machinery needs a corresponding structure of social service institutions. In order to minimize investment not oriented toward industrial production, Daqiu village relied on the sacrifice of women, sending them back to the home to do full-time housework to compensate for a lack of service industries. The third factor is that, as I mentioned previously, women's large-scale participation in production during the collective period was not their own conscious choice but was based on subsistence needs and administrative initiative. Thus, after basic needs were met and administrative preference reversed, women themselves were willing to "return to the home."

This phenomenon exists to varying degrees in newly prosperous rural households in every region. The situation of Daqiu village women is still much better than that of women in impoverished areas where even the problems of food and shelter have not been resolved. Nonetheless, it is clearly not advantageous to women's development. It repeats the historical pattern of women sacrificing individual development in exchange for men's realization of their greatest social value.

Now let us turn to the case of Shenzhen. The phenomenon of "working sisters" appeared in tandem with China's opening to the outside and the transformation of coastal districts into export-processing zones. The products of these zones are mostly those of light industry: clothes, electronics, toys, and so on. Such industries prefer female labor. Of Shenzhen's temporary workers from rural areas, the ratio of women to men is about 2 to 1, sometimes even higher. In some industries, such as in a plastic handbag processing factory, the ratio of women to men is 50 to 1. These industries have already been markedly "feminized."[29] These occupations do not demand much skill; technical training is rarely needed, and most of the women employed are young and unmarried.

Compared with women workers in towns and cities, these women offer many advantages for management. One is that the price of their labor is cheap: wages are low, benefits are poor, and factory management can avoid the expense of constructing day care centers, family housing, and other facilities not directly related to production. Another advantage for management is that rural residency status makes long tenure for temporary workers in the processing zones difficult. By taking advantage of this rotating labor system, the factory can increase the use-value of labor. A third advantage is that in response to changes in the market, the factories can recruit and fire their workers at will. This is very convenient, enabling factories to reduce labor costs when operating at less than capacity. The processing zone's partiality for young rural women laborers is thus certainly not a means of improving women's status. Exactly the opposite: it is proof of the disadvantaged position of rural women in the labor market. I will not deny that "working" itself can initiate changes for rural women. But what influence it has on their social and household status still awaits more detailed research.

Rural reform was directly manifest in increased peasant incomes. As occupations became differentiated, there was an obvious widening of the income gap between peasants. Although to date there are no specific statistics on women's income, salary is always linked to one's job. Generally speaking, those with the highest rural incomes are private enterprise owners, town and township enterprise managers, salespersons, individual households, specialized households, and so on. The income of agricultural households, by contrast, is relatively low. Differences in occupations among women also affect income. In 1987 I used a 102-household sample to extract data on women's income from their records of daily expenditures. The sample was generated by the Provincial Rural Research Team from the two Shaanxi counties of Changan and Jingyang. In 1979 the women's average per capita income was 129.8 yuan,[30] of which the highest was 450 yuan and the lowest was 0. By 1986 their average per capita income was 807.9 yuan,[31] with the highest at 2,087 yuan, and the lowest still at 0. Women's income made up only 27.7 percent of total household income.[32] Women's income has thus dramatically increased during the years of reform, but a large disparity in income among women has also resulted. Some women's income has caught up to or surpassed men's. But there is still a large gap between most women's income and most men's, a gap that tends to become larger in the process of modernization.

The process of urbanization has not necessarily favored women, either. The sex ratio has been consistently high in the small towns and cities that have developed so quickly in recent years. Jiangsu is one province in China that has had comparatively rapid recent development. Studies of cities in seven counties by the Jiangsu Provincial Academy of Social Sciences found an average sex ratio that reached 133 to 100 (male to female) and a sex ratio in the labor force of 148 to 100.[33] Because they are burdened by household chores and limits in their personal development, women appear a passive force in urban migration, often waiting for their husbands to establish themselves before moving to join them. In some more economically developed areas, signals of a trend toward rural feminization have emerged, arousing anxiety among sociologists.

Both the promise and the unpredictability of a market economy have created another serious problem. Rural middle and elementary school students have increasingly discontinued their studies. Nationally between 1980 and 1988 at least 40 million middle and elementary school students left school prematurely to work;[34] most were in rural areas, and more were female than male. In 1988, 83 percent of school-age children not enrolled in school and 70 percent of the

3 million who left school were female.[35] This just exacerbates an already unfortunate trend toward low levels of female education. In the fourth national census,[36] the illiteracy rate was 15.88 percent; one out of every six adults was illiterate. Among women, one out of every 4.5 was illiterate.

The strength of tradition in rural areas is another significant factor limiting the improvement of women's status. Patrilocal marriage and patrilineal inheritance are important symbols of the structure of patriarchal society that have not changed in the course of economic transformation. Even though marriage and inheritance in China are legislated to give daughters and sons equal privileges as heirs, patrilineal inheritance has continued to be practiced in rural areas. Rural residences, for example, have consistently been passed on to sons, not daughters.

Patrilocal residence is closely linked to patrilineal inheritance. Cooperativization abolished private ownership of land, but it did not affect patrilocal residence patterns. Following the implementation of the birth planning policy, the number of single-daughter households[37] has gradually increased. The government advocates men moving to their wives' home at marriage, but there are very few instances of this in rural areas. It is not just a problem of values; it is also linked to the policies of land distribution for agriculture and residential use. China's rural villages are usually made up of several large single-surname lineages. Because land is limited, villages restrict outsiders' moving in. Peasants see women who move in to marry as conceptually of their own lineage, and all their descendants are welcomed as part of the lineage. Men who move in to marry are seen as outside the lineage and are excluded because all their descendants will belong to a differently surnamed lineage. The great majority of rural Chinese women must marry, or they will have no home of their own. Nor do they have the privilege of choosing to remain in their natal home, because their village will not be willing to distribute any land or residence to their husbands and children. Daughters, destined to marry, can bring no benefit to their natal families, whereas a son, aside from having his own land, will also bring in another portion when he takes a wife.[38] And because he remains near his parents, a son will be able to care for them in their old age. Consequently, peasants usually value sons more than daughters.

Beyond the Modernization Process

From the foregoing analysis we can see that all the central features of rural modernization—such as industrialization, urbanization, market mechanisms, and a commodity economy—create, to a varying extent, new problems for women. While some problems will be gradually solved as modernization proceeds, some will not. Social modernization will not in itself automatically liberate women. In the face of all the problems rural Chinese women must confront, then, what should be done? This question needs detailed discussion in a separate essay. Here I can only make two suggestions.

The first is to improve resolutely the level of rural women's knowledge. Modernization first and foremost requires cultural and technical skills. Compared to traditional society, modernization provides a competitive arena that is relatively fair. Competent women can rely on their own knowledge and abilities to change their status. Women's present disadvantage in the context of competition can be attributed to their gender, but it actually has more to do with their low level of education. Consequently, the government and the Women's Federation must use every method at their disposal to improve rural women's level of education. They must particularly encourage girls and young women to go to school, where they will master cultural and scientific skills to improve their individual status as well as the situation of all rural women.

Second, women's development should be an important goal of modernization. We should focus on those aspects of modernization that benefit women. The effect of industrialization on social differentiation will vary with the method of industrialization. There are usually two ways to achieve industrialization. One way is to use market ideals as basic mechanisms of change, so that members of society can freely move into new social positions created through industrialization, and so naturally generate social differentiation. Another way is to use organizational methods to reallocate new social positions, with differentiation resulting from deliberate intervention. These models have existed simultaneously in China's process of rural industrialization. Strengthened administrative control creates a relatively strong leveling force. Whether from the point of view of participation, occupational differentiation, or income disparity, in all ways it is obviously superior to the first model. Choosing different models of industrialization, then, is important for improving women's status.

As we continue to modernize in China, theorists of women's issues and women's organizations must intensify both macro- and micro-level research on women's issues and on women's development. We must especially increase policy research, not hesitate to propose as many resolutions as possible for women's problems, and urge the government to incorporate our suggestions into national and local development programs. We must use the strength of society to push ahead the progress of all rural women.

II | Sex and the Social Order

5 | Desire, Danger, and the Body: Stories of Women's Virtue in Late Ming China

In the fifteenth-century Chinese play *Five Relationships Complete and Perfected (Wu lun quan bei)*, a concubine traveling to join her master is captured by an invader who demands her in marriage. Her mother, accompanying her as chaperone, exclaims that no Chinese can marry a barbarian. The girl bites her finger, drawing blood so she can write a poem of fidelity, and drowns herself.[1]

In the slightly later but equally didactic play *Loyalty Redoubled (Shuang zhong ji)*, a besieged general's concubine has herself cooked and fed to his starving troops.[2] The scene recalls two other heroines from the past whom Ming didactic writers liked to hold up to the present: Liu Cuige of the Yuan, who offered herself to be cooked by marauding bandits, and the wife of the Tang dynasty merchant Zhou Di, who sold herself to a dealer in human flesh in besieged and famine-ridden Yangzhou. Both women sacrificed themselves so that their husbands could go free to care for aged parents and carry on the family line.[3]

What do these stories mean? We see in them the woman's body dedicated to husband and patriline, and feeding or symbolizing all of China. Although these are very public gestures, Ming memoirs and local histories also abound in stories of private ordeals dedicated to the same ends: young widows swallowing poison in secret or seizing a moment of privacy to hang themselves, all to avoid remarriage out of the husband's family. But the fact that the stories were repeated endlessly in local histories meant that the private ordeals were firmly planted in the public record. Talking about women's virtue in the state-sponsored Confucian tradition never really meant talking about a realm of private experience. The very point of publicizing the private ordeals was to knit the private to the public in a seamless web of idealized loyalties that defined what it meant to be Chinese. The barbarians in *Five Relationships,* witnesses first to the concubine's fidelity and then to the brotherly devotion of the two heroes, are so impressed that they vow to serve the Chinese state.

Stories like these could be found in many Ming dynasty (1368–1644) sources: local history, dynastic history, memoirs of literati, illustrated compendiums of exemplary lives, fiction, and drama. The stories formed a recognizable genre whose heroine was young, dedicated to Confucian virtues, and prepared to undergo horrific ordeals in their defense. This Ming genre set the pattern for the Qing, so the broad outlines of the discourse on female virtue changed little over the last half millennium of imperial Chinese rule.

These stories of fidelity, suicide, and resistance to rape were intimately related to things we know about Ming social life: Ming legal changes tying the wife more closely to her husband's lineage; an increase in recorded suicides of women; and the universal fact of rape in wartime. Scholars have addressed some of these issues: Jennifer Holmgren has explored the influence of Ming law on the ideal of chastity;[4] Susan Mann has studied the place of Qing dynasty widows in their communities, examining cultural pressures for and against suicide;[5] and Jerry Dennerline has pointed out that lineages wealthy enough to establish charitable estates might actually protect their widows against such pressures.[6] Mark Elvin has surveyed the state sponsorship of female virtue from the Han through the Qing,[7] and T'ien Ju-k'ang has amassed invaluable statistics on the numbers and distribution of lifelong widows and widow suicides in Ming local histories, showing that the "cult of fidelity" dates only from the middle of the sixteenth century.[8] But what remains to be addressed are broad questions of ideology. Mark Elvin and Susan Mann have noted new themes and historical shifts in emphasis in the norms of women's virtue, and T'ien Ju-k'ang has related the enthusiasm of Ming literati for the suicide narrative to the intolerable pressures of the examination system. But it still remains to look at the actual language that encouraged and reflected widow suicide and widow chastity. How did that language mesh with other Confucian norms in the examination-dominated Ming environment, where social advancement depended on knowing the texts of the Confucian canon? What were the major aims of the Ming discourse on female virtue, and could they be realized?

To answer, one must ask how these stories were integrated into the whole of Ming culture. Elvin suggests that Ming stories of virtue were elaborated against a background of "robust sensuality," to which they "defined themselves in contrast,"[9] but the detail and enthusiasm with which physical ordeals are narrated (bandits who squeeze a woman's hand around the blades between her fingers, a father who tries to patch his daughter's torn throat with chicken skin) raise questions about how complete that contrast really is.[10] The vast reservoir of stories (from the near and the distant past) available to Ming readers have a heightened sensuality of their own, and the stories were eventually integrated into the "robust sensuality" of late Ming culture in a way that had been true of no previous dynasty. Gazetteer editors and preface writers tell us we are reading about the embodiment of principle, but what we actually find are stories of stealth and guile, as young widows deceive everyone around them to find the opportunity for suicide;[11] or stories of ungovernable lust, as young women dress in rags or daub their faces with mud to conceal their beauty and so protect themselves, but are abducted nevertheless. The endless stories of resistance to rape keep the reader's attention riveted on the unconsummated sexual act. As we shall see, Ming law and lineage organization ensured a focus on young and vulnerable widows. At the same time, the constraints of the examination system were producing generations of restless writers who developed the cult of intense emotion, or *qing*, as an outlet for their frustrations,[12] and a verbal battle ensued between those who saw fidelity as an expression of standards meant to uphold strict sexual segregation and those who saw fidelity—or even political loyalty—as valid only when animated by *qing*. This naturally allowed tales of fidelity to shade over into tales of romantic love (or romantic death). I have noted elsewhere that the beautiful images in late Ming editions of the Han dynasty classic *Biographies of Notable Women (Lienü zhuan)* let women appear simultaneously as icons of virtue and objects of sensuous connoisseurship;[13] here I will examine that phenomenon in more detail.

In the stories with which I began, woman's body is a site or theater used by the imperium to constitute itself, asserting the impenetrability of its borders, undergirding the idealized Chinese pyramid of loyalties. But I will argue that foregrounding women's bodies in this way ensured that the stories would break out of their exemplary frames. The frame was about controlling or constraining the desire *for* women; but by the end of the dynasty, there is a noticeable shift in texts containing stories of virtuous women from desire conceived as negative to intense emotion (including sexual desire) conceived as positive. But at the same time, we see woman reduced to some extent from powerful emblem of loyalty to object of connoisseurship. In the discussion that follows, I briefly survey the Ming cult of women's virtue, examine sources, and turn to the evolution in the stories themselves. Finally, I look for a synthesis that can explain this evolution.

The Ming Cult of Women's Virtue

By the beginning of the Ming dynasty, Chinese rulers had been rewarding filial sons, faithful wives, and undivided multigenerational households for nearly a millennium and a half, with the avowed aim of transforming popular morals and customs. The earliest Ming emperors, eager to resinicize China after two and a half centuries of Tartar and Mongol rule (the Jin and Yuan dynasties), continued the tradition, awarding gifts, insignia of recognition, and exemptions from the state service levy.[14] The founding Ming emperor's proclamation of 1393 detailed the channels whereby reports of virtue should reach the court. In 1402 an expanded version of *Biographies of Notable Women* was commissioned for the second Ming empress, and in 1405 a Confucian conduct book for women (with detailed instructions on self-immolation) was brought out under her name.

The court was committed to women's virtue; thirty-eight concubines committed suicide on the death of the founding emperor.[15]

Earlier dynasties had prepared the way for the Ming categories of women's virtue. There are widows who resist remarriage in the Wei and Tang histories, for example, though they do not dominate the field as they would do in the Ming. Song dynasty (993–1126) and Southern Song (1127–1280) neo-Confucian thinkers established the theoretical underpinnings for the Ming cult by working out in detail the abstract homologies between the traditional Five Relationships, those of ruler and minister, father and son, husband and wife, elder brother and younger brother, and the bonds of male friendship modeled on the fraternal relationship. This Five Relationships language was the vehicle for integrating private and public, as the fidelity of wife to husband (or, more properly, to her husband's family line) was made explicitly parallel to the loyalty of minister to ruler. And by elevating Mencius as a principal Confucian sage, they paved the way for Ming moralists who turned Mencius' statement that "the hands of man and woman do not touch" into a blanket prohibition against the mixing of the sexes. In the years leading up to publication of the Song dynastic history in 1345, ethnic Chinese scholars at the Yuan court (following standard practice by compiling the history of the previous dynasty) selected almost exclusively stories of resistance to rape when they compiled the section on virtuous women.[16] By the middle of the fifteenth century, Ming scholars put the topoi of fidelity and resistance to rape together in the Yuan history, listing twice as many virtuous women as in any previous dynastic history.

By the mid-fifteenth century, then, the Ming categories of Confucian praise for female virtue were well established. In place of the Song dynasty's idealized and abstract analysis of the Five Relationships (which were carefully worked out from the top, describing venerable ritual prescriptions for the emperor's choice of consorts and ministers in matching sets),[17] the Ming honored faithful wives from the common people,[18] exalting the ideals of lifelong widowhood and widow suicide. The venerable language of self-sacrificing filial sons and daughters (filial daughters had been a major topos in the Tang and Song) was redirected toward service to the *husband's* parents. By the twelfth Ming emperor Jiajing's reign period (1522–1576), chapters on virtuous women were appearing in every local history. The Qing dynasty compilation *Gu jin tu shuo ji cheng* (Imperial Collection of Books of All Ages) lists staggering numbers of virtuous women in Ming local histories: a total of nearly thirty-six thousand, a third of whom commit suicide or are murdered while resisting rape.[19] T'ien Ju-k'ang points out that the geographic distribution of these cases is wildly uneven,[20] but for our purposes what matters is that they were described in language that remained uniform throughout the empire. The Shandong playwright and retired official Li Kaixian (1501–1568) describes widow suicide in the same terms as the Zhejiang essayist Gui Youguang (1507–1571).

What were the institutional factors behind the spread of this empirewide language? Briefly, one can identify four: the system of state awards, the culture of the civil service examinations (which included a well-developed tradition of stories of male martyrs to Confucian principle), the standardization of gazetteers, and Ming law and lineage organization. The four are interrelated, with the examination culture perhaps the most pervasive: a system of education and socialization that made examination aspirants throughout the empire far more like one another in their patterns of thought than like anyone outside the system, even as many of them criticized that system.[21] Li Kaixian and Gui Youguang had both experienced this education and socialization, and they were the sort of men who prepared petitions for awards to virtuous widows. The culture of the examinations encouraged the standardization of gazetteers, which became remarkably uniform in format by mid-dynasty; and with curriculum and schooling standardized, the way scholars wrote about and praised their own regions was also standardized.[22] Faithful women and filial sons—even in regions with nothing like the hundreds of faithful widows written up in Shexian or Fujian—became conventional badges of "community honor."[23]

These factors account for the empirewide uniformity of language describing virtuous women, but there is more to the story: the decidedly nonsensuous provisions of the state award system and Ming inheritance law also played a central role in the way women's virtue was integrated into the "robust sensuality" mentioned earlier. The cultural pivot of the typical widow story, the element seized on by fiction, drama, and woodcut illustration, is that the heroine is young and vulnerable—to sale by her relatives, to pressures from her husband's relatives avid for the property she controls. Ming law and social organization practically ensured the creation of this kind of heroine. The state system of awards was the original motor behind the collection of accounts of virtuous women, and Ming law stated that a widow must lose her husband before the age of thirty and remain unmarried until at least age sixty before her case could be considered for official recognition.[24] In the highly centralized Ming, with its focus on political loyalty, this thirty years' duration was intended to dramatize the widow's refusal to switch allegiance. In practice, this meant that attention was focused on *young* widows, rich in dramatic (and erotic) possibilities.

The system of awards by the state thus kept the exemplary widow young, and property and inheritance law conspired to keep her vulnerable. As Jennifer Holmgren has shown, Ming legal and family structures (like the self-conscious promotion of lineage solidarity) made the pressure to remarry very real. Under Ming law, the dead husband's family kept the widow's dowry, the heir, and the husband's share of family property if she remarried. A widow controlled her husband's property in trust for their children, but many are the Ming accounts of women extolled precisely for their "unselfishness" in turning that property over to other members of the husband's family. Susan Mann and Dorothy Ko have both described the Ming and Qing market for young women, which guaranteed that a young widow's parents-in-law or even her own parents could readily find buyers for her.[25] Ming law and institutions thus made inevitable the promotion of a young, vulnerable heroine who in opposing remarriage is opposing opportunism. And while various regulations and proclamations show that the state always preferred duration of widowhood to suicide as proof of sincere loyalty, virtuous suicides were nonetheless often officially commended (and their families excused from the service levy), thus legitimizing suicide as a principled stand against opportunism. The dramatic power of the suicide story, its resonances with centuries of stories of male martyrs to political principle, made it a runaway favorite.

Sources

Ming stories of women's virtue are found in dynastic histories, local histories, literati essays, illustrated collections of exemplary lives, and fiction and drama—more venues than had been the case in any preceding dynasty. Each of these sources had its own work to do in the world, and each context added to the range of connotation of the virtuous woman archetype.

In dynastic histories, the sheer number of stories invokes the sweep of history and focuses our attention as much on China as on any individual heroine. Whereas dynastic history biographies of men can be detailed records of careers, women are generally written up for one glorious deed (and that quite briefly). But since most Chinese dynastic histories include chapters on virtuous women, looking at dynastic histories one after another gives us, almost at a glance, a sense of shifts in emphasis in the discourse on women's virtue. Since later scholars compiled these histories from materials gathered earlier—Yuan scholars making use of the Song dynasty Veritable Records, for example—they give us a dual perspective on their subject: the records of one dynasty and the choices and commentary of another. I draw here on the *Ming History (Ming shi)* and the Ming-authored *Yuan History (Yuan shi)*.

Local histories (gazetteers) by the mid-Ming were composed on a fairly standard pattern of prefaces, treatises, charts of examination degree holders and officials, and reams of biography. As in dynastic histories, these biographies were detailed for the big careers and formulaic for those badges of community honor, virtuous women and filial sons. But also as in dynastic history, the formulas could be very vivid, with much weeping and fainting, and many dramatic gestures of refusal. These gestures are often recounted at greater length in the chapters of poetry and prose that close many a gazetteer.

Gazetteer entries are frequently compressions of the essays written by literati in support of official commendation. These essays glorify fidelity and suicide in the empirewide language of female virtue, and they set the tone even for essays that may not have been destined for official channels. The rhetoric is intended to be persuasive: a little maid watches as her mistress's corpse floats in a pond in the moon-light; a young wife hurls imprecations at the invaders who hold her captive. There were literati who balked at one or another excess of the tradition, but there were few real iconoclasts; even those who objected to the suicides of bereaved fiancées, for example, seem mainly to have wanted to reserve recognition for women whose marriages were ritually complete and whose loyalties were thus un-ambiguous. The archetypal Ming virtuous woman, steadfast in the face of her ordeals, was too useful and potent a symbol for male self-description to be given up.

By the last decades of the dynasty, the thriving trade in books and the pervasive culture of the examinations made collections of model lives an attractive product for publishers. Virtuous women now ap-peared in compendiums of their own, each story typically preceded by a full-page woodblock illustration and followed by the compiler's commentary. The popular "past and present" expansions of Liu Xiang's (80–9 B.C.) Han dynasty classic *Biographies of Notable Women* brought together heroines of all eras, their differences smoothed over by the uniform style of the illustrations and tone of the com-mentary. I treat these stories from all ages that appear in these Ming collections as they were no doubt experienced—as Ming stories (certainly they are given Ming interpretations by the compiler-com-mentators). I draw on two of the best known: Lü Kun's (1536–1618) *Female Exemplars (Gui fan)*, and an early seventeenth-century collec-tion reprinted in the Qing under the title *Illustrated Biographies of Notable Women (Hui tu lienü zhuan)*; and another luxury publication devoted to male and female virtues of all kinds, the *Bright Autumn Mirror for Mankind (Ren jing yang qiu)* of the wealthy and cultivated Wang Tingna (fl. 1573–1622).[26] I also draw illustrations from late Ming and early Qing vernacular fiction and drama, especially since vernacular stories and plays were well established as literati genres, which could be produced by men of examination-oriented educa-tion, by the second half of the dynasty.

But for fiction I draw primarily on anthologies in classical Chinese (the language of essays and examinations), such as Feng Menglong's (1574–1646) *Anatomy of Love (Qing shi)* and the roughly contempo-raneous *Women Scholars of the Green Window (Lü chuang nü shi)*.[27] Ming

literati produced a vast amount of travel literature, notes on interesting phenomena, and collections of anecdotes meant to be edify-
ing or merely curious, all in the format of short classical-language
entries, sometimes newly composed and sometimes anthologized
with commentary. This flexible format was used by authors such as
Feng Menglong to talk about women and desire by the first decades
of the seventeenth century, and it is in these collections that we meet
the partisans of *qing*.

Desire, Danger, and the Body: Ming Stories of Women's Virtue

Virtue in Ming Confucian tales of exemplary women is enacted not
through spiritual struggle but through physical ordeals. The body
was a powerful presence in traditional rhetoric: the influential Fan
Zhongyan (989–1052) of the Song dynasty spoke of the people as
the body of the Sage (the Sage protects them as he would his own
body).[28] The eloquent Gui Youguang, writing from the perspective
of someone out of power, describes the evils of the age as so many
slings and arrows directed at the Sage's defenseless body.[29] In the
didactic literature there are no abstractions: Mencius' injunction
against contact between the sexes finds expression in the Five Dynasties story of Wang Ning's wife, who cut off her hand when an inn-
keeper touched it as he pushed her out the door.[30] A late Ming wife
bites off and spits out the flesh of her arm after a bandit has touched
it.[31] These stories support an enormous complex of metaphor, but
the actual, physical body is where virtue is acted out. This profoundly
physical expression of virtue bespeaks a concept of relationship very
different from our modern western sense of ourselves as individuals.
In the vast Chinese literature of filial piety, the young feed their own
flesh to their elders: one's body belongs to the family, not to oneself.
And by the logic of the Five Relationships, the body belonged to the
imperium as well: the dedicated body was the arena for men *and*
women to display loyalty at any cost.

Women's ordeals of loyalty and fidelity thus do not set them apart
from men (quite the reverse is true), but the characteristics of the
female body gave it unique possibilities as a theater for the drama of
virtue. Women's breasts, providing essential nourishment, could be

offered in filial service. Penetrable, woman's body was a site where the drama of resistance to invasion could be acted out. Weaker, it could shame men unwilling to rise to the same heights of virtue. Procreative, it was a resource to be sold or controlled. Attractive, it offered opportunities to men to prove their moral worth by exercising self-restraint.

There were four didactic Ming story types that seem to have made an unambiguously correct use of this theater of virtue, curbing dangerous desire and exalting loyalty, hierarchy, and the appropriate separation of the sexes. The four are stories of filial piety, virginity, resistance to remarriage, and resistance to rape.

Throughout Chinese history, exemplary filial sons and daughters had sliced flesh from arms, thighs, or livers to make healing soups for their parents.[32] But though women in all eras were praised for filial devotion to their own parents, the typical Ming story of a "filial wife" shows that her body was now dedicated primarily to her husband's lineage. In a celebrated case from the beginning of the Ming dynasty, the filial wife of Han Taichu, surnamed Liu, repeatedly cured her mother-in-law's illnesses with soup made of blood from her arm. When her mother-in-law became paralyzed, Liu ate the maggots infesting the bedclothes (the maggots never returned). In her final illness, the mother-in-law nibbled Liu's little finger as a signal that she wanted to make her eternal farewell—but Liu, misunderstanding, made a porridge the next morning of her own blood and the little finger. The mother-in-law ate the porridge, revived, and lived on for more than a month.[33]

Women also fed and cured their mothers-in-law in one completely gender-specific way, namely, with their breasts. The *Ming History* lists the filial wives Li and Hong, who cured their mothers-in-law with medicine containing flesh from their breasts. Miracles attended both cures: filial wife Li fainted after cutting off her breast; she had been given up for dead, when a mysterious priest appeared at the door, told her relatives how to revive her, and vanished. Filial wife Hong threw the unused portion of her breast into the pond in order to keep her good deed secret, but when ducks lifted it out of the water several days later, it still dripped blood.[34] (Miracles of uncorrupted flesh were a typical proof of virtue.) Most Ming expansions of *Biographies of Notable Women* also contain the story of Tang *furen*, who breast-fed her toothless mother-in-law. The mother-in-law blessed her with a wish for sons and grandsons as filial as herself.[35] In the Ming illustrations, Tang *furen's* toddler son is protesting the diversion of resources, but that diversion is precisely the point of the story: in the typical hyperbolic rhetoric of the Chinese morality story, even the welfare of longed-for descendants was secondary to the welfare of one's progenitors. The stories about women who offer themselves to be cooked and eaten represent the extreme of this dedication. The fact that they sacrifice themselves in some cases for patriline and in others for China itself underscores the Five Relationships continuum between family and state, private and public.

This continuum is ideally maintained by distinctions, not by mixing; hierarchy, not equality. This is made clear in exemplary stories of virginity. These are not like the virginity stories of Christianity, where virginity signifies renunciation of the world and a precious gift to the savior; Confucianism required procreation, not renunciation. What Chinese virginity stories do is show heroes and heroines maintaining their proper place in the social order, unmoved by hyperbolically improbable temptation. Marriage, the only acceptable way of uniting the genders, is the culmination of the Chinese virginity story.

The archetypal heroine of these stories is Mulan, the Tang dynasty girl who took her father's place in the army at the northern border. Though she served for twelve years, no one ever learned she was a girl, and thus her virginity was preserved.[36] Similarly, a Miss Han of Baoning, fearing for her chastity at the turbulent fall of the Yuan, spent seven years undiscovered in the army;[37] and during the Ming, Huang Shancong of Nanjing kept up her father's route as an incense peddler after he died, traveling with male companions for several years without betraying her identity or her chastity.[38] The dangers once past, Miss Han and Miss Huang were both rewarded with husbands; the point of their stories is that they did *not* operate as women in the man's world, with all the temptations that would have ensued. Forced by circumstances to leave the inner quarters, they camouflaged themselves until they could return to their appropriate roles.

Men are praised in virginity stories not for remaining virgin but for resisting the temptation to debauch women, or for protecting the virginity of women. In a typical example, which appears in both sixteenth- and seventeenth-century sources, the Song dynasty magistrate Zhang Yong accepts a concubine whom local notables purchase for him. When his tour of duty is up, however, he returns her to her parents with enough money for a dowry. She is still a virgin.[39] In a similar anecdote, a scholar does not deflower a young singing girl but instead preserves her virginity and arranges a marriage for her. In another case, the itinerant scholar who saves a boatman's daughter from sale to a merchant reasons that a merchant, who "travels from place to place and has no understanding of righteousness [yi]," would be an unfit custodian for her.[40]

Stories of resistance to remarriage and to rape were universally exalted because they dramatized loyalty. These were stories with villains, and the villains were motivated by desires inimical to the Chinese social order: hierarchy-disrupting lust and greed in the domestic setting, lust and armed invasion at the borders. The heroine's youth and sexual attractiveness are central to stories of resistance to remarriage, which are primarily tales of bereaved young women, coveted by unprincipled men or manipulated by relatives eager to turn their sexual attractiveness into cash. In story after story, the widow is presented as possessing "resolve" (zhi) that parents, parents-in-law, or wealthy men who covet her all want to "steal" (duo). How does she foil their schemes?

Since the typical widow in these stories is young and attractive, she can disfigure herself. Here the Ming widow could follow a tradition that went back to Liu Xiang's Han dynasty *Lienü zhuan*, where the widow Gao Xing of Liang (whose story was repeated in all Ming editions and expansions) refused not only the nobles but even the king, since to remarry would be both unchaste (bu zhen) and a breach of faith (bu xin). Reasoning in the typical levelheaded tone of the Han text ("The king wants me for my beauty; therefore I will destroy my beauty"), she cuts off her nose.[41] When Liu Changqing of Pei dies during the Han dynasty, his widow "forestalls suspicion" by cutting off her ear and refusing to visit her parents.[42] The Toba Wei dynasty story of Huai Pu's widow shows that the widow of Liu Changqing was prudent in staying away from home: when Huai Pu died, his wife cut off her ear and put it into her husband's coffin, explaining to her startled mother-in-law that otherwise her parents might not "understand her resolve [zhi]." When she did visit her parents, her suspicions turned out to be well founded: her brother chased her back to her mother-in-law's home, trying to force her to remarry.[43]

The widows who disfigure themselves usually have their purpose respected; they live on in their families of marriage. More dramatically satisfying, however, were the stories of widows who could resist remarriage only by dying. In the gazetteers I have examined, the *Gu jin tu shu ji cheng*'s 1 to 3 ratio of suicides to lifelong widows generally holds true, but it is the stories of suicide or murder that are told at length and in affecting detail.

The young widow's own parents figure prominently in these stories. They may be presented as compassionate, like the parents of Wang Su, who "pitied [min] their daughter's early widowhood"; or they may try to force (qiang) her, like the parents of Hu Shuning. As the 1576 Kunshan gazetteer tells the stories, both sets of parents surreptitiously plotted second marriages for their daughters, but both girls divined (jie) the plan and killed themselves.[44] Often the parents *and* the parents-in-law both stand to benefit from the widow's remarriage: among the many such cases in the *Ming History* are the suicides of Tang Huixin, whose parents-in-law wanted her dwelling back,[45] and of the glorious widow Huang (Huang *liefu*), whose mother wanted a second round of betrothal gifts.[46] In the case of Zhang You's wife, Hong *shi* of Huizhou, her parents and her mother-in-law split the betrothal presents from the wealthy man who wanted her.[47]

A widow might be presented as vulnerable even to her husband's murderer. *Illustrated Biographies* contains the Western Jin dynasty (265–317) case of Liang Wei's beautiful wife, Xin, coveted by the powerful Liu Yao, who had caused the death of her husband. Xin fell to the ground, weeping, and asked Liu how he could possibly want a widow who would disgrace herself by remarrying. (This bit of guile impressed Liu Yao, and he allowed her to commit suicide.)[48] And beautiful widows who lived alone were natural prey to men of wealth, as we see from the case of the glorious widow Gong in the

Ming History. She was too poor to bury her husband, so a rich neighbor offered to supply the coffin. Aware of his true intent, and also knowing that she had no way to withstand him, she left her children with her mother, set her house afire, and died in the blaze with her arms around her husband's body.[49]

The typical rape story in these sources is a rebel/robber/invader story, despite what court case literature shows about rape by neighbors, acquaintances, even fathers-in-law.[50] The rape stories have obvious affinities with the stories of resistance to remarriage: there, the woman is pressured to transfer her sexual services and procreative powers to a man outside the lineage; here, to a man of another race (or to Chinese opposing everything it means to be Chinese). Gui Youguang liked to conflate the topoi: he prefaces more than one story of a virtuous widow with a tale of a young woman fleeing the Japanese pirates.[51] Wang Tingna introduced his chapter on women's fidelity in *Bright Autumn Mirror* by evoking their sexuality and their loyalty in the same breath: "They die to distance suspicion," a phrase that always connotes the inevitability of sexual pressure, "or to ward off violation. When the state is in danger [*guo nan*], they dare to raise martial banners; when they meet personal foes they are brave in wielding the knife [to disfigure themselves]."[52] Rebels, robbers, and invaders are essentially the same in these stories: they are indiscriminately called *zei*, "bandit," and their violent arrival and brutal threats ("Submit to me and live, resist and die!") are identical. These are not typically stories of virgins (what is being disturbed is the social order, emblematized by the family), though some of the famous heroines, such as the Tang dynasty Dou sisters, are unmarried girls. (The beautiful and chaste Dou sisters, eulogized by Zhu Xi and thus prominent in neo-Confucian mythology, leaped from a cliff to escape a robber band during the Tang Yongtai [765–766] reign period. They appear in most Ming expansions of *Biographies of Notable Women.*)[53] The vast majority of the heroines who die resisting rape in Ming texts are young wives, often fleeing with their families. But whereas stories of resistance to remarriage are most often characterized by pathos, these heroines are allowed to be angry. In story after story they revile their captors, often flinging all of Chinese literati culture ("I'm from a family that studies the *Rites* and *Odes!* How could I submit to the likes of you?") in the invaders' teeth.

The *Song History,* compiled by the ethnic Chinese historians at the Mongol Yuan court (that is to say, by men particularly sensitive to the issue of invasion), is the first dynastic history to contain substantial numbers of these stories. Typical is the story of Ouyang Xiwen's wife, Miou, who fled with Ouyang Xiwen and his mother into the mountains during the Baizhan rebellion of the early Southern Song. When soldiers caught up with them, Miou shielded her mother-in-law with her body until her husband and mother-in-law could escape. The rebels saw that she would never submit to them, so they cut off her ear and arm; undeterred, she shouted at them ("Even if you kill me, how long can your butchering go on?") until she fell to the ground and died.[54]

The period of Yuan military conquest produced similar cases. Yu Shiyuan's wife, Tong, refused to submit to marauding soldiers, all the while shielding her mother-in-law with her body. She cursed the soldiers as they cut off first one of her arms and then the other, finally flaying her face and leaving her to die the next day.[55] When rebels captured the beautiful wife Mao of the Zhou family and offered her gold if she would submit to them, she told them they could cut her heart out first; and when they menaced her with a knife, she shouted that if *they* were dismembered, the pieces would stink, but if *she* were dismembered, her body would be fragrant. The soldiers disemboweled her and left.[56]

This rhetoric could be turned against Han Chinese government soldiers when they acted like ordinary bandits. Chinese troops, fleeing Jin forces at the fall of the Northern Song, went marauding through Hezhou, where they tried to rape Xu, the wife of Zhang Bi. She reviled them for failing to protect the populace and for expecting her to submit. They stabbed her and threw her in the river.[57] Even young neighborhood thugs who resorted to rape were assimilated to this story type: *Illustrated Biographies* contains the case of a Song dynasty commoner woman surnamed Zhang, mortally wounded by a young hooligan whose advances she has refused. She uses her last ounce of strength to drag him by the hair and denounce him to the neighbors.[58]

The stories recounted so far—stories of filial piety, widowhood, and resistance to rape (recall that some stories mixed all three)—exalt archetypal behavior universally praised by Ming writers. Many a young widow promises her dying husband that "a minister never serves two rulers," and then commits suicide to foil the lust of her neighbors and the greed of her relatives. She thus—with narrative economy—supports loyalty and opposes dangerous, destabilizing desire at the same time. For most Ming writers there was nothing ambiguous about these heroines; men used them as emblems for themselves, as when generals fighting the advancing Qing armies called themselves "faithful wives" to the Ming.

But from our historical vantage point, knowing as we do that virtuous widows and faithful prostitutes would be found between the covers of the same books by the end of the dynasty, we can see elements even in these supposedly unambiguous stories that tend to undermine their exemplary agenda. No one is supposed to desire the young widow's body, but the focus is unremittingly *on* her body. (Widow Xie, realizing at the end of the Yuan that her beauty made her an inevitable target for the advancing rebels, built a fire and jumped into it.[59] Chen Lin's wife, Gu Amei, was carried off by the Japanese pirates because she was "young and beautiful"; the rest of the village women were simply robbed.[60]) And what is required of the young widow is hyperbolic dedication, an insistence on remaining faithful, whatever the cost. This physical beauty and intense dedication are the elements that blur the boundaries between stories of principle and stories of romantic love. Even in stories centered on the canonical topos of widowhood, an emphasis on emotion, seen as positive, started to displace the emphasis on the control of dangerous emotion.

Two story types newly prominent in the Ming put the woman's passionate dedication at the very center of the story: young widows who die of grief and fiancées who insist on being treated as widows. Lü Kun, perhaps the most orthodox and articulate of Ming writers on women, mistrusted both. Of widows who commit suicide simply to follow their husbands in death, he wrote that they were dying not for righteousness (*yi*) but for passion (*qing*). Lü assimilated this to what he saw as a dangerous new idea within Confucianism itself, namely, the teaching that the untutored, unrestrained "childlike heart" *(tong xin)* could lead one in the right direction.[61] Lü Kun was at one here with the puritanical Song dynasty neo-Confucians, who saw *qing* or passion within marriage as dangerously disruptive. He was not alone; another representative statement is that of Zheng Xuan (who passed the *jinshi* examination in 1631) to the effect that feeling *qing* for one's wife and child is unfilial to one's parents.[62]

But indignation like Lü Kun's had no effect at all on the editors of local histories; the 1605 Jiading local history, for example, in a completely representative entry, praised the wife of Shen Sidao when she swore to follow her husband with her own body:

> When Sidao was placed in the coffin, Sun took a knife and stabbed herself, but did not perish. Family members guarded her day and night. Surreptitiously she swallowed a needle and took poison, trying a hundred different schemes to kill herself. After a year, she managed to find a moment when she was not being watched, and she hanged herself. The year was Jiading 19 [1541].[63]

And the Huizhou compilers of *Illustrated Biographies* sympathized fully with Wang Liang's wife, whom we see in an exquisite woodblock illustration floating faceup in the pond where she has drowned herself because her husband was about to die.[64]

To Lü Kun, these women embodied no principle and resisted no dangers, and must therefore have been governed by sexual love. But men like Lü Kun and Zheng Xuan were voices in the wilderness: six of the eleven suicides in the 1576 *Kunshan xianzhi* are for the purpose of following a husband in death, as are five of the ten in the 1605 *Jiading xianzhi*. Two of these Kunshan suicides were commended by the court!

The exaltation of emotion is even more evident in stories of bereaved fiancées. Their ritually incomplete marriages made emotional display essential, since they had to convince disbelieving parents and parents-in-law of their right to be treated as widows. Their passionate commitment made them particularly powerful and affecting emblems for some Ming writers—and particularly distasteful to others, who felt that passion was being emphasized over commitment. The case of sixteen-year-old Zhuang Ba'er of Huangzhou is typical: she presented offerings of food to her dead fiancé's spirit tablet, weeping and fainting until his parents became so annoyed (*yan*) that they tried to marry her off to someone else. Thereupon she made oracular pronouncements to the wives of her fiancé's brothers, mysteriously gave away all her ornaments, and hanged herself.[65] And Miss Xiong, betrothed to Liu Kang of Linzhong, wore mourning at the age of eleven when Liu's father died, made soup from the flesh of her arm when Liu became ill (he rallied briefly), insisted on attending his funeral, collapsed on his spirit tablet and almost died, ate ashes at his grave, was saved from her first attempt to hang herself, and then died after insisting that her fiancé's mother establish an heir.[66]

As Lü Kun saw it, these frantic girls had no right to the title of widow, and he accused them of excess and of sexual desire. It was out of the question for him that they should serve as role models. That Lü Kun was not alone in his suspicions can be gleaned from a story told by Wang Kaokun (1525–1593) about a bereaved fiancée within his own prominent Huizhou merchant-scholar lineage. Orphaned young, the girl was betrothed to Wang's cousin and was taken into the cousin's family as a child. When Wang's cousin died of a wasting disease, she declared her intention to remain a "widow." Wang seems to feel the need to distance suspicion and deny any hint of sexual attraction when he states that despite their having grown up in the same household, the first time the girl ever saw her fiancé was when she dressed his corpse.[67]

Qing (affection, attraction, passion) between spouses or fiancés was dangerous because it could lead to a relaxation of the rules, undermining the separation of the genders—the spatial and hierarchical segregation that moralists such as Lü Kun saw as absolutely essential to the harmonious functioning of family and society. In his commentary in *Female Exemplars* on a passage from the *Classic of Changes (Yi jing)*, Lü writes, "If household members are not 'fenced in,' and each one lets his fancy run riot . . . they will not stop until they reach disorder and extinction."[68] Moreover, this "fencing in" has to be done with absolute firmness of purpose: "Harsh scolding may breed some resentment, but the worst that will happen is regret over this severity. At least it will keep *qing* from breaking loose! If, on the other hand, the mistress of the house is always smiling, the best that can happen is the absence of resentment. *Qing* will be let loose throughout the household, and even if disaster does not follow, regrets are inevitable."[69]

Lü Kun was not opposed to all connotations of the word *qing;* in his *Groaning Words (Shen yin yü),* a giant prescriptive work directed at the world around him, he states in many passages that a ruler must work with the people's *qing* or feelings if he is to govern effectively. It is *qing* between men and women, with all its sexual connotations, that arouses his anxiety. He would have shuddered to read, several decades later, books such as *Women Scholars of the Green Window* or Feng Menglong's *Anatomy of Love,* which aver that *qing* between men and women is essential for the full expression of Confucian loyalty and fidelity. In a passage from the *Analects (Lun yü)* of Confucius that every schoolboy knew by heart, *ren* (generosity, compassion) is considered essential to *li* (ritual), but *ren* is also impossible to realize without the channeling force of ritual.[70] The *Anatomy of Love* takes a very different tack, stating that "she who is without *qing* cannot be a faithful wife to her husband," and moreover that if one tries to achieve loyalty, filial piety, chastity, or heroism for the sake of principle alone, the result will be forced and insincere, whereas if these principles are animated by *qing,* they will be genuine.[71] An almost identical passage can be found in the *Green Window* anthology: "The one word *qing* can kill the living and bring the dead to life. Thus every loyal courtier, filial son, righteous scholar-official, and faithful wife must be richly endowed with *qing.*"[72]

Qing was a polyvalent word that did not always have sexual connotations in Ming discourse, but a look at the whole of *Anatomy of Love* and *Green Window* suggests that Lü Kun's worst fears would have been realized in these two books. The luxurious format of late Ming books about virtue, their illustrations overlapping with those for plays about romantic love, already suggest that the boundaries considered so essential by Lü Kun were seen as less and less important in certain quarters. And with the emphasis on *qing* in books such as *Anatomy* and *Green Window* came an explicit relaxation of traditional rules about sexual conduct. Lü Kun sanctioned widow suicide only as resistance to immorality; the *Anatomy* advises widows to commit suicide immediately upon bereavement, in the full glory of their grief (moreover, they can thus avoid decades of sexual frustration).[73] Whereas Lü Kun had averred that young people who gave way to lust and forgot the rites of marriage would cause harm even to the most distant branches of their family,[74] *The Anatomy of Love* tells with approval a whole series of stories about young people animated by sincere feeling who have sex first and then marry afterward. Feng's heroine of fidelity is more often the courtesan than the wife. And *Green Window* follows the statement that true loyalty and fidelity must be animated by *qing* with the assertion that women and girls who need a vehicle for the expression of their purity (*zhen,* the word applied to women who resist rape in the didactic collections) find it by offering their attractiveness *(se)* to those capable of appreciating it.[75]

Faithful singing girls were not novelties when they appeared in *The Anatomy of Love* and *Green Window;* the dynasty had been acquainted with them since Zhu Youdun's (1379–1439) early Ming *zaju* plays, whose young, principled, and vulnerable singing girls were essentially indistinguishable from the heroines of the literature of virtue.[76] Feng Menglong's story of Feng Aisheng, who dies of grief at being unable to marry a sincere man and so leave the courtesan's life, brings the topos up to date for the late Ming. Aisheng is the life of every party, participating in her world of transient pleasure even as she longs to leave it. But despondency grows, and a wasting illness earns her rejection by the wealthy nobleman to whom her procuress hastily marries her. Feng explicitly denies the distinction between her sphere and his own when he gives her a ritually correct burial by scholars—"people like you and me."[77]

The young couple whose ardent love shames the older generation had also been a beloved topos for centuries; the Yuan play *Romance of the Western Chamber (Xixiang ji)* celebrates such a couple, and it remained wildly popular throughout the Ming. In the *Anatomy,* a young man surnamed Sun is accused by a neighbor woman of seducing her daughter; the daughter is so mortified that she hangs herself. The mother, determined to punish Sun, ties him to the corpse and goes off to fetch the magistrate. Left alone with the corpse, Sun is overcome by her beauty and does indeed make love to her—

whereupon she comes back to life! The magistrate unites them in marriage.[78]

Feng was a literary chameleon. In something of an about-face, he revised in a conventionally moralistic fashion the play *Peony Pavilion (Mudan ting)*, the late Ming's most profound statement about revivifying love and the rejection of sterile Confucian moralizing.[79] But for our purposes what matters is that Feng's stories of Aisheng, Sun, and others like them are told in the same collection with stories of canonically virtuous widows.

But the *Green Window* anthology is perhaps an even more telling piece of cultural evidence than the *Anatomy*, for it is a more casually compiled work and is thus even less concerned with sexual and hierarchical distinctions. *Green Window* simply includes every possible category of good story—faithful widows, woman warriors, heroically filial daughters, faithful prostitutes. Like other casually compiled late Ming compendiums for women, *Green Window* even contains the full texts of *The Four Books for Women*, a famous set of conduct books dating from the Han through the Ming. Virtuous women are simply inserted in huge, conventional chunks, as in Wang Daokun's "Seven Martyrs of the Jiajing Reign Period,"[80] or the entire text of the original Han *Biographies of Notable Women*. The anthologist is completely unconcerned with Lü Kun's sort of consistency: the *Four Books for Women* follow immediately a preface promising the reader Jiangnan's "feather and pearl brigades," capable of "intoxicating even the fragrant wind," and "so agitating the sun that it forgets to set."[81] The sixteen woodblock illustrations that open the text range from depictions of traditional occupations such as weaving, to a beauty lying half uncovered on her springtime couch, to a widow proving her fidelity by snipping off her hair. We see a similarly eclectic connoisseurship in the mid-seventeenth-century *Book of Female Talents (Nü caizi shu).*[82] Introducing the story of the faithful widow Yang Biqiu (after first listing the attributes of desirable courtesans), the compiler observes that her talents and her chastity would not in themselves have been completely satisfying if she had not also suffered in an exemplary fashion. Rare, he says, is this combination of beauty, talent, and suffering virtue—a combination he obviously savors.

This shift in discourse, this blurring of traditional distinctions, was history's resolution of the paradox that tales devoted to the restraint of desires were being elaborated during a period when desires were being stimulated and satisfied by growth in commerce, literacy, and luxury. Similar discursive changes were evident in other "Confucian" arenas: examination prizewinners were packaged in *Stories and Pictures of First-Place Winners (Zhuangyuan tu shuo)*, a book contemporary with *Illustrated Biographies*, which detailed the stellar moral attributes and fantastic experiences (dreams, portents) of its heroes.[83] Wang Tingna's *Mirror* contains a chapter of pictures and stories of men refusing sexual and financial temptation; the stories of these paragons of frugality are lavishly illustrated by the same artist whose work we see in *Illustrated Biographies*. One factor in the changing discourse on women's virtue must have been the late Ming relation of virtue to power: despite the fact that the stories of virtuous women ideologically support the pyramid of loyalties with the emperor at the apex, the central government was probably not the driving force behind the cult of women's virtue during the period when it flourished most. The court did hand out the awards, but by the late sixteenth and early seventeenth centuries, local notables avid for prestige (or magistrates who wanted to make a name for themselves) were the main stimulus for the collection of cases. The Wanli emperor, notoriously negligent of government in general, paid little attention. (During the period of the founding emperor's active sponsorship of women's virtue, few cases were collected.) Trained officials scouted out virtuous widows all over the empire, but no rigid standard was enforced on the discourse about them. And for many men who chafed under the constraints of the examination system, the notion of spontaneous fidelity not compelled by convention was supremely attractive. For these men, the courtesan and the lover could be personal emblems even more satisfying than the faithful widow.

But finally, we must remember that the "connoisseurship" of women's virtue—the savoring of women who united ideal fidelity with ideal pathos—was also related to the status of actual women. Women's bodies may have offered unique possibilities for the expression of the canonical virtues, but they could not escape being *women's* bodies. Even within the cult of women's virtue there are reminders of the marginality of women to actual power. All late Ming and Qing gazetteers have *Lienü zhuan* chapters, but they are always formulaic, relatively short, and appear in back next to stories of Buddhist and Taoist monks and men of miscellaneous occupations. Virtuous widows had their own temples and shrines, but as often as not they were tucked away in the corner of some more important temple. Ming memoirs show us how cruelly young brides might be initiated into the families to whom they then owed exemplary fidelity. Competing cults remind us of women's continuing vulnerability to sexual violation: the sixteenth- and seventeenth-century cult of the god of wealth, Wutong, whose demonic behavior reflected the social fears engendered by the unpredictability of increasing wealth, gave rise to stories of men propitiating the male god by offering him their daughters or wives.[84] And the thriving market for young women continued apace. The dedicated body might be the medium for both men and women to act out exemplary loyalty, but men's and women's bodies carried very different connotations. In a reflection of the subordinate status of women, women's bodies were always available for use—ideological, physical—by men. Nonetheless, the exaltation of women's ordeals assimilated them to a glorious tradition: a woman who died reviling her alien captors was the ideological sister to a Lian Zining, who scribbled his retorts in blood after his tongue was torn out when he refused to serve the usurping Yongle emperor (r. 1403–1425). This kind of cultural valorization must have helped pave the way for certain women to be respected as highly visible loyalists at the fall of the Ming. But this valorization of the less powerful by the more powerful social subject was also just one more objectification, and in the long run even the exaltation of women's virtue operated to keep women in their cultural place.

6 | Rethinking Van Gulik: Sexuality and Reproduction in Traditional Chinese Medicine

Yesterday the red flower bid adieu
This morning is the time for uniting
The orchid field is planted by the white jade
The blessed hour is between midnight and dawn
Days three and five make a cassia elixir [boy]
Days two and four design a white plum [girl]
The jade tide must be shallow and floating
A heavy load will cause her grief
Let yin blood gather first
Let yang essence follow flowing
The blood will open and embrace the jade dew
Smooth the path to immortals' island home
After this the pair must part
The weaving girl and herd boy are separated by
    the Milky Way
In the second month the flower blooms
Then your happiness is known
The blessed news is spread
No more slander or backbiting is heard.

When Wan Quan (1488–1578?), a popular sixteenth-century doctor, wanted to explain what a young man needed to know in preparation for marriage, he quoted and commented on these verses in a little tract handed down in his family of hereditary physicians.[1] This quaint résumé of what passed for sex education in Ming dynasty China suggests something of the questions raised when contemporary American scholars go looking for traditional Chinese discourse on the erotic. We are not surprised to find that in Ming dynasty China, doctors, as experts on body—or embodied—functioning in general, were authorized to articulate orthodox norms of sexual conduct as well. But we must confront an unfamiliar, holistic view of the human body which integrates primary vitalities at work in sexual acts with the overall organic processes of birth, growth, and decay. And we must take account of a social construction that does not privilege erotic pleasure alone over all other possible aspects of the "sexual." In looking for sex within other social discourses such as Wan Quan's on procreation, we find that the boundaries of the "sexual" itself come into question.

Contemporary Anglo-American perspectives on sexual meanings have been contextualized for our own history by feminist scholars such as John D'Emilio and Estelle Freedman. They show how Americans have only recently come to divorce sexuality from reproduction and to understand its purpose in terms of individual happiness and personal intimacy rather than integrating it into the Christian family. They point back to a colonial American discourse on reproductive and marital sex which Wan Quan would have found less strange than the language of pleasure which dominates so much discussion in the United States today.[2] As we follow them in an attempt to locate sexual meanings in time and space in Asia, it becomes important first to develop a critical perspective on the ways in which sinological accounts of the sexuality of the Orient have been shaped by twentieth-century cultural assumptions: by the rise of a "science" of sex embracing Freudianism, by anthropology's relativization of sexual mores, and by rapidly shifting agendas for sexual liberation antedating the late twentieth-century feminist movement. Our resulting modernist understandings of the sexually "natural," when projected onto the gender systems of subaltern Asian peoples as objects in the culture of colonialism, have been a fertile source of Orientalist representations of the East.

R. H. Van Gulik's *Sexual Life in Ancient China*,[3] the benchmark for sinological discussion in English ever since its original publication in

1961, could be called a classic Orientalist work of this kind. Its impressive erudition and range have made it the standard reference, mined for quotations and sources by China scholars even as we may have overlooked or uncritically embraced its views. My review here of its interpretations is designed to show how today's history of Chinese sexuality has been embedded in twentieth-century Eurocentric constructions of both sex and the Orient. At the same time, like many impressive works of scholarship, Van Gulik's book also provides rich resources for readings of his subject at variance with his own. These allow me to take it as a point of departure for my own alternative, though no less external, analysis of this sensitive aspect of China's gender system(s).

Van Gulik's Chinese Ars Erotica

Van Gulik claims that the fundamental "art of the bedchamber" *(fang shu)* in classical Chinese civilization was based on techniques for "returning semen" *(huan jing)* taught in ancient "bedchamber manuals" *(fang shu*)*[4] and transmitted down through most of the imperial era. Bedchamber manuals circulated openly from the later Han through the Tang dynasties (25–905 C.E.), he says. They were viewed seriously as "instruction" (16), not as titillation, and they taught a "Chinese conception of eugenics" (47) and a cosmic symbolism based on yin-yang dualism which lent spiritual dignity to the sex act (45). The goal of these manuals was to serve as aids to health, procreation, and pleasure. They promoted longevity, which was in accord with Daoist goals of self-cultivation; fertility, which served the Confucian family; and erotic pleasure, especially in women, whose sexual satisfaction, Van Gulik thought, was essential to the harmony of the polygamous upper-class household (155–156).

Van Gulik's message to his mid-twentieth-century English-speaking readers was that traditional Chinese sexual norms were healthy, neither "repressed" (50) nor "perverted" (157). Van Gulik's criteria here are those of Freudian discourse: what is repressive is abstinence, while perversions divert libido away from its proper genital outlets or channel it into sadomasochistic cruelties.[5] He praises "the art of the bedchamber" for combining what he calls a generalized distrust of celibacy with an admirable absence of sexual "pathology." He wants readers to envisage a robustly connubial heterosexual marriage bed at the center of Chinese sexual life, and to share his praise of the enlightened nature of an ars erotica which, he argues, places a high valuation on male responsibility for female pleasure.

Woman is presented by Van Gulik as object of desire twice observed, first by the classical Chinese male writers who provided his sources and second by the author himself, who displays her through that same literati repertory—narratives of famous beauties; tales of courtesans and nuns; descriptions of dress; boudoir furnishing, and ornaments; images in love poetry, genre painting, and woodblock prints. Polygamy is presented as a given aspect of upper-class life; footbinding, rather guardedly, as a minor note, an eccentric erotic specialty, possibly an example of "shoe-fetishism" (219).

In light of late twentieth-century western feminist standards, it is easy to recognize Van Gulik's androcentrism, and to see that the reader is being offered a familiar Orientalist fantasy of an exotic, eroticized "other" woman of the East. Of course, the fantasy was not a purely western invention: Chinese men (and a few women) provided the language and observations he drew upon with such impressive learning. But the mark of "otherness" is that its construction reveals the self. Here Van Gulik saw himself as placing his classical Chinese learning at the service of the "sexologist"—the mid-twentieth-century scientific student of sexuality. He claimed to be correcting stereotypes of Chinese sexual mores as "depraved" and "abnormal"—negative Orientalist representations which were the mirror image of his own positive ones, and like them a product of the modern culture of colonialism.

Van Gulik's picture of the sexually liberated Chinese couple easily evoked the Orient as an imaginary realm of freedom and erotic pleasure absent in the West. But the ideal "normal" sex life he imagined for the ancient Chinese boudoir was further shaped by the normality his contemporaries desired at home. In the first half of the twentieth century, sexology represented a novel scholarly investigation of sexual variation in human communities, replacing religious and moral categories with medical and psychological ones. Derivative of biology in its taxonomic organization, and of anthropology in its concern with human diversity, sexology could also be seen as a liberationist enterprise, which aimed to relativize human sexual customs and so dethrone Judeo-Christian morality from a position of unchallenged cultural authority.[6] Furthermore, nineteenth-century science and Freudian psychology both problematized the female orgasm, with the result that mid-twentieth-century scientific experts who shaped advice literature on marriage both exalted the psychological centrality of sexual satisfaction in marriage and identified female frigidity as a major problem—the result of male ignorance and insensitivity.[7] Chinese sexual techniques for stimulating female pleasure while maintaining male control appeared relevant to these problems of modern marital relations. In Van Gulik's account Chinese bedchamber manuals emerge as the marriage manuals of a sexually enlightened Orient, with much to teach the West. In both settings he sees the goal of the union of man and woman as the same: sexual fulfillment defined as mutual orgasm in a heterosexual lovers' bed.

Although Van Gulik recognizes medical, religious, and literary genres among his sources, he imposes on all types and every period the unquestioned assumption that discussions of sexual practices, wherever they may be found, are evidence for the historical presence of a discrete erotic domain: a self-consciously understood cultural sphere for the experience and understanding of sexual pleasure, in and of itself. The presence of such a domain is assumed to be the natural by-product of human instinct, and this universal category of experience leaves its historical traces as ars erotica. The method locates all discourse about sexual acts, whether esoteric and religious, medical and moral, or found in the literature of popular entertainment, on a common plane.[8] When Van Gulik translated all sexually explicit Chinese passages quoted in his book into Latin, he evoked comparative associations with Greco-Roman classical culture, and gave his Oriental ars erotica the patina of ancient civilization and esoteric science all at once.

In keeping with this implicit framework, Van Gulik dramatizes change within tradition in China as a struggle between the positive traditions of healthy sexual hygiene practiced during the early empire (Han-Tang) and the puritanical ideology of neo-Confucianists who sought to suppress teachings about sex. There are obvious parallels here with our mainstream modernist reading of Victorian sexuality and twentieth-century "liberation"—that is, construction of the recent history of sexuality in our own cultural tradition around the "repressive hypothesis."[9] This liberationist project was not a purely western one. Tracing Van Gulik's research path leads us back to late Qing–early republican scholars who could be called China's own pioneering sexologists, particularly Ye Dehui (1864–1927), a culturally conservative yet iconoclastic official and bibliophile from Hunan.[10] By 1900 bedchamber manuals had ceased to circulate publicly in China for more than a thousand years. But several medieval Chinese originals had resurfaced in the mid-nineteenth century, when a tenth-century Japanese anthology of Chinese medical writings, long buried in the Japanese imperial family library, was published.[11] Ye's scholarly reconstruction of "80 to 90 percent" of five original bedchamber manuals (the texts Van Gulik relies on to establish the character of the genre) was based on this find.[12] Ye's plea in 1907 that his work be allowed to circulate was offered in the name of cultural nationalism: "Today," he said, "subtle and detailed writings on diet and sexual relations by western health experts are translated as new learning on reproduction and eugenics and marital health. The ignorant treat them as treasures, not knowing that the descendants of China's ancient sages and scholars discussed this learning beginning four thousand years ago."[13] Resurrected as part of a modernizing project to bring sex into public discourse, China's ancient sexual lore was firmly connected to the serious issue of ensuring the nation's social fitness through reproductive success. In spite of Ye's claim for the moral seriousness of his work, his publication was castigated as obscene, and his scholarly reputation suffered.

In fact, Ye Dehui's modern revival of bedchamber manuals as tools for nation building was closer to the spirit of the originals than either his critics' view of them as pornography or Van Gulik's construction of them as ars erotica. From the very beginning in medieval times, bedchamber arts had been embedded in medical and religious discourses which were not "about" pleasure or women simply as objects of desire, but about what medieval Chinese understood as serious goals of life and death, linking health, spirituality, and social purposes. They were linked to modes of male empowerment which we may define very loosely here as Confucianist or Daoist.[14] The erotic could be seen as a vehicle for social reproduction and the conception of descendants or for individual self-transformation and sagehood. Both of these alternatives required women to serve male goals, but they constructed gender around alternative forms of service: that of the man as an individual or of the family and descent group. It is through these sexual meanings that we can approach the underlying phenomenology of sexual experience described in bedchamber manuals, and learn how the erotic itself was gendered.

The Question of Genre

In the bibliographical section of the imperially authorized history of the Han dynasty (221 B.C.E.–220 C.E.) we find a group of now lost titles listed under the general heading "Within the Bedchamber" (fang zhong).[15] In each case the author is said to have been a legendary sage, a teacher of Laozi or the Yellow Emperor, who specialized in the esoteric arts of the "Way of Yin." The few fragmentary early references available to us suggest that such works celebrated longevity as an attribute of rulership. Dominion over one's own body, the bodies of women, and the body politic came together for realized "true men," who used the method of sexual intercourse to attain longevity as lords and sages. Sexual techniques were clearly dominant in the Way of Yin, but others—diet, exercise, alchemy—are hinted at in early references to these traditions.[16] The Way of Yin was associated with apocryphal sage-kings who lived to extraordinary old age; the texts that taught it were referred to in the Han history as belonging to the "School of Yin and Yang," or "School of (Natural) Regularities and the Five Phases," (presumably those that constructed cosmology and human destiny around temporal patterns in nature), or else to Daoism. Some of these titles were later included in Bao Puzi's catalogue of Daoist longevity texts.

A smaller group of Han-era titles taught the arts of "cultivating yang" or "cultivating life" (yang yang or yang sheng). Here the adept's goal shifted from longevity to posterity, as illustrated by stories of ancient kings who produced dozens or even hundreds of offspring.[17]

In sum, this earliest stratum of Chinese discourse on the subject treated human sexual relations as an aspect of natural philosophy, accepting a view of the human body as a microcosm of the larger universe, so that through generative acts the individual could tap into embodied aspects of primal cosmic creativity.

As a bibliographically defined category, texts discussing sexual intercourse as part of a Way of Yin or Yang disappeared from the historical record after the Han dynasty. Most of the now known bedchamber manuals are presumed to have circulated between the fourth and tenth centuries C.E. In the Sui and Tang dynastic histories they were formally catalogued not under philosophical schools of thought but as medicine. In keeping with this later classification, these texts were attributed to a number of quasi-historical male masters of medical arts, while sage-kings and emperors were portrayed as learning from legendary females: the Primordial Girl *(su nü)*, the Dark Girl *(xuan nü)*. A large group of new titles appeared: *Xu Taishan's Secret Essentials of the Bedchamber (Xu Taishan fang nei mi yao); Primordial Girl's Classic (Su nü jing); Primordial Girl's Pharmacy (Su nü fang); Secret Instructions of the Jade Bedchamber (Yu fang mi jue); Secret Arts of the Bedchamber Introduced by Master Gu (Gu shi xu fang nei mi shu).*[18] Although medicine had replaced cosmology and natural philosophy as the appropriate context within which to understand the powers of sex, all of these works advertised their esoteric character, and remained suffused with the occult aura surrounding the Daoist longevity cult.

By contrast, the discussion of "bedchamber arts" found in the writings of the leading Tang dynasty physician Sun Simo (d. 683 C.E.) offered advice to ordinary males in the specific context of the section of his collected works titled "Cultivating One's Nature" *(yang xing)*, that is, health in old age.[19] In Sun's work as a whole, revered as a medical classic in later centuries, a modified version of the lore of the bedchamber continued to circulate long after specialized bedchamber manuals had disappeared. Nonetheless, even as medicine maintained its position as the legitimate locus for authoritative discourse on sexual matters, later authorities further revised the older interpretations, including those of Sun. In theory sexual practices always were positioned at a point where the embodied powers of longevity and those of generativity intersected, and all discourse understood the lover as one who balanced claims of each. Under the later empire, however, the specialist texts on preventive health and longevity—the "nourishment of life" *(yang sheng)*—were increasingly critical of "bedchamber arts," while positive representations of eros were presented in writings on "begetting sons" *(zhong zi)* or "the multiplication of descendants" *(guang si)*. In this genre of writing, which became increasingly popular in the Ming and Qing, eros was valorized in a context which also encompassed successful conception, healthy gestation and childbirth, and even aspects of pediatrics.

Containment and Loss in the Art of the Bedchamber

Van Gulik has portrayed *coitus reservatus,* the key technique taught by bedchamber manuals,[20] as evidence for a traditional Chinese understanding of sex as the domain of the erotic, with fulfillment of pleasure for men and women as its central, if not sole, purpose. My alternative reading of the art of the bedchamber concludes that pleasure was a means to other ends. In bedchamber manuals natural philosophy continues to frame the discussion of sex as a microcosmic human reenactment of primary creative processes. Sexual fluids—semen and vaginal secretions—are measurable quanta of primordial vitality, whose exchange has the power to augment life or diminish it in either party. For the partners, longevity or early decline, fertility or sterility in the production of descendants, hang in the balance. Playing with the primordial energies governing birth, growth, and decay in human beings and all things is no casual matter. Rhetorically the texts present the teacher of the sexual arts as a sage: Pengzu, the legendary master of the arts of longevity, is a favorite figure. Since the arts are sexual, knowledge of them is also often feminized as the possession of mythical females such as the Primordial Girl, whose name Van Gulik associates with that of an otherwise forgotten archaic fertility goddess. But the implied reader of the text is always a man, never a woman—a lord of the world seeking the life span of an "immortal" and the power of a king.[21] For males, the social powers rhetorically evoked are aristocratic, even princely, and they are taught that women are less important as partners than as servitors.[22]

This is how the matter is put in the *Secret Instructions of the Jade Bedchamber*:

> The Wise Girl asked Pengzu about the techniques for lengthening life. Pengzu said, Spare your essence and nourish your person. If you take the proper medicines you may attain a long life. But if you do not understand the art of sexual intercourse, medicine will not benefit you. Male and female mutually complete [the cycle of human life] just as Heaven and Earth mutually engender [all things]. The Way of Heaven and Earth is to unite and the [life of the world] continues endlessly. Without the Way of sexual union human life is cut off before its time. If one can practice the art of Yin and Yang, one can find the Way to never die . . . Today lords and kings "rule" [*yu*] over all events and govern the world. Yet they are unable to cultivate the Way in all its aspects. Those who frequent the rear chambers [women's quarters] should know the art of sexual intercourse. Most important, one must "rule" [*yu*] young girls but ejaculate infrequently. It will make one's body light and get rid of all illness.[23]

Pengzu's instructions respect the cosmological powers of yin as exactly complementary to those of yang. The saying "Female overcomes male as water extinguishes fire" (633) represents one aspect of the order of things according to the five phases of Han dynasty cosmology. That women might theoretically use "bedchamber arts" to their own advantage is acknowledged in the account of how the legendary Queen Mother of the West coupled with young boys, who sickened while she enjoyed the bloom of youth. But this story also teaches that female vitality is not a yin source of creativity superior to the powers of yang; here it is acquired at the expense of males. In other words, bedchamber manuals did not claim that the primordial vitality of yin essence, as embodied in females, was an inexhaustible reservoir available to nourish the male. In mortal females, as in mortal males, reproductive *qi* is exhausted in use, making those who couple rival powers in an economy of finite resources. Bedchamber manuals, therefore, are the locus classicus for the commonplace Chinese metaphor of sexual intercourse as combat, with its representation of the partners as "enemies" destined for victory or defeat. "'Ruling' a woman is like riding a galloping steed, or like approaching a deep abyss containing knives where there is the danger of falling in" (634).

Accordingly, bedchamber arts are a male monopoly, and the female partner should be carefully controlled. "These arts should not be taught [to women]," Pengzu warned (636), while the Primordial Girl is made to caution the kingly lover against the snares of enchantment: "Regard the 'enemy' as tile or stone; regard yourself as gold or jade" (634). The ideal woman as object of desire, then, is compliant and easily aroused, ignorant, and young. A girl of fourteen to eighteen or nineteen *sui* is best (635–636). She is "responsive, easily excited to feelings of desire, perspires freely, and follows [her partner] in action and repose" (649). She need not be a virgin (it is not mentioned), but it is significant that marks of female maturity—large, developed breasts, thick pubic hair—are undesirable. Above all, women who have given birth are unsuitable.

In sum, female yin essence is represented at its most concentrated and available in the socially immature pubescent girl whose sexual powers have not yet been channeled into reproduction. Her vitality has its limits, however, and this is why the process of sexual nourishment envisioned by the practitioner demands multiple partners. In the bedchamber of the adept's fantasy, eight to ten partners are desirable, and the sexual athlete performs, if he can, many times a night. The discrepancy between the empowerment envisaged for the male and the service role of the female is highlighted by the warning that practice with a single female will be ineffective: "Her yin *qi* will gradually become overconsumed and the benefit will not be great" (635–636). Discrepancy in social power between the sexes is assured, and is also imagined as a discrepancy in the sexual powers thought actually or potentially embodied in them. Sexual difference is constructed not around gendered contrasts in underlying body processes or erotic appetite but around contrasts in powers of control.

The social male behind the fantasy is less an ordinary polygamist than a prince, one whose well-populated inner quarters would be a badge of royal rank. The esoteric nature of the teaching is emphasized (transmitted, according to one account, by the Immortal Lu Xiang to blood brothers under oath, and not to be casually spoken of [644]), encouraging the practitioner to identify himself with a spiritual elite as well. What is evoked is an inflation of all social and physical powers—their augmentation to a level beyond ordinary human reach.

Power and pleasure, of course, cannot be neatly disentangled from each other, and in the art of the bedchamber eros is never entirely absent from the scene. These authors are, after all, busy enumerating positions, describing bodies, and tracing the stages of both male and female arousal. The gravity of intention may be subverted by the proliferation of detail ready to entangle the reader in the very appetites which the adept is being warned he must control. Such texts always say more than they mean, and this is how Van Gulik can lead the modern student into an anachronistic discourse about ars erotica, just as later generations inside China and out have bracketed these writings as the work of Eros' evil twin, pornography. If we define pornography as erotic images or representations that manipulate the reader or viewer into the role of voyeur, bedchamber manuals come close in that they represent the lover himself as an observer. He observes the woman's arousal first of all ("the nine signs"), but also remains acutely self-conscious of his own actions: he should "enter soft and withdraw hard," count strokes ("the nine shallows and the two deeps"), avoid the deepest level of penetration, and at the critical moment "draw in breath, close eyes and mouth, stiffen neck and body, press tongue against palate, and concentrate mind" (644). But this voyeuristic self-monitoring was taught not to augment the lover's arousal (or the reader's), but as essential to ensure his power of control. In the *Secret Instructions of the Jade Bedchamber,* this tension between pleasure and power is addressed directly:

> The Wise Girl asked, the pleasure of intercourse is in the climax. If a man remains closed without release of essence, what pleasure is there? Pengzu replied, when essence is lost, the body becomes fatigued, ears suffer from ringing, eyes suffer from dizziness, throat is dry, and bones and sinews can no longer support one's weight.

Even if one has a momentary thrill, there is no pleasure in the end. But if one can move without releasing, one's *qi* and strength will be abundant, one's body at ease, one's ears and eyes keen. Although one curbs passion and maintains calm, one's resolve in sparing [one's semen] will be weightier. Holding oneself constant without satiety—is there no pleasure in that? (643)

The modern reader who believes that pleasure deferred is pleasure prolonged will be missing the point here. The goal of Pengzu's art is control of the body/self toward the end of transcending the body's ordinary limitations, defeating the entropy of age so as to achieve immortality.

Psychologically, how are we to understand this organization of the erotic around a performance of masculine self-discipline and self-denial? A common theory, based on the way bedchamber manuals symbolize the female "enemy" and her "deep abyss," is that fear of female power is at work here, linked in Freudian terms to male castration anxiety. But it may be that the deepest anxiety lies elsewhere. The female "other" is not a socially threatening or engulfing mother but simply the instrument drawing males to a boundary where the sense of self is lost. The bedchamber texts are stunningly direct in linking the abandon of coital climax with death as the loss of all selfhood. The loss of volition accompanying climax and post-coital lassitude are both described as destabilizing the conscious spirit or "psyche" *(shen)*, which in the phenomenology of the body is the center responsible for the embodied experience of life itself. The loss of semen, then, is experienced metaphorically as death, and associated with disease and decline into age. If the microcosmic body replicates cosmic processes in generative acts, production and destruction are mutually dependent, and the moments of climax, like the critical transitions in the movements of universal change, destroy phenenomena ceaselessly even as they create. In the final analysis, therefore, for males the art of love is transformed into a work of regeneration, toward the production of an immortal, deathless self.

Van Gulik may be right that the "art of the bedchamber" was accepted as medical wisdom throughout the Tang dynasty. As early as the seventh century C.E., however, the approach to the issue of Sun Simo, the most eminent of Tang dynasty court physicians, showed some significant modifications. In his classic *Prescriptions Worth a Thousand,* bedchamber arts were recommended only for men over forty, whose natural passions are declining. Sexual nourishment from multiple youthful partners—"plucking *qi*" is his term for it—was to be combined with regular use of medicines with "replenishing" action. There was no discussion of positions or stages of arousal; rather Sun focused on the hydraulic system of circulating vitalities identified with the bodily discipline of "inner alchemy" *(nei dan).* The lover combines the sexual act with the practice of the art of *dao yin,* or psychophysical exercises facilitating the circulation and augmentation of *qi* vitalities along the bodily channels especially associated with reproduction and regeneration: the *jen mai* and the *du mai.* He is to concentrate on channeling the ascent of *qi* from the generative "cinnabar field" behind the navel to the brain *(niwan),* associated with nirvana. The ascending *qi* is imagined as a point of light or glowing red spot, or alternatively as inner figurations of sun and moon rising in the body's interior landscape and uniting in the center of the head at a point between and behind the eyebrows.[24] Visualization techniques assist in controlling ejaculation, and they also structure understanding of the process whereby sexual vitality is channeled into psychophysical regeneration.[25]

Sun Simo in fact shifted the key techniques of "bedchamber art" from erotic manipulation of the female partner to the internally focused visual meditation techniques of inner alchemy. He also displayed commonsense skepticism about the workability of a sexual script demanding the incessant testing of male self-control. The young man is better off not trying it, for he will be unable to master it and will end up damaging his health; and even among the old, few will achieve the inner detachment needed for true success. In a famous metaphor repeated down the ages, Sun warned that *qi* is finite, like a lamp's supply of oil, which may either flare up and burn out or, through careful conservation and measured use, last a full span of years. Continence, not abstinence or superhuman performance, is the wise man's course.

Sun therefore offered males practical advice on frequency of intercourse adjusted for one's age. Furthermore, the logic of harmonizing the sexual act with processes of nature was extended to a sweeping consideration of proper times and places. *Prescriptions Worth a Thousand* followed the Han dynasty cosmology of the medical classic *The Yellow Emperor's Inner Canon (Huangdi neijing)* in patterning generative activity around the natural rhythms of the seasons: in "nourishing life" *(yang sheng),* human beings, like the rest of nature, give birth and grow in spring, flourish and flower in summer, harvest and gather in autumn, and in winter close off and hibernate.[26] Similarly, within each day the propitious hours for generative efficacy are those when the momentum of yang is most strongly ascendant—between midnight and dawn. Astrology advised one to watch for taboo days marked by conjunctions of baleful astrisms and planets. Buddhist respect for the gods, and for the souls awaiting reincarnation who will descend into the body at conception, suggested one avoid inauspicious locations such as temples, privies, and granaries. Sun invoked respect for all these ever-present larger influences of nature and gods as pieties ensuring the efficacy of human action. In later centuries practical advice of this kind and the reasoning that informed it continued to be standard in the medical repertory and in chapters on health in popular calendars and almanacs.

Eros, Longevity, and Generativity in Late Imperial Medical Discourse

Van Gulik blamed the disappearance of bedchamber manuals from public circulation on a new code of sexual propriety enforced by an ascendant neo-Confucian puritanism in the Song, Ming, and especially the Qing dynasties. This is not the place to explore the complex transformations of social and economic life which went hand in hand with the rise of neo-Confucianism, or to speculate about shifts in the gender system attendant on the eclipse of the elite of old aristocratic families by the new scholar gentry. The intensification of female seclusion and the spread of footbinding appear to confirm the thesis that stricter norms of female sexual honor were spreading in elite families. The evidence from medicine is for an increased concern with women's reproductive health and the health of children, as evidenced by the emergence in the Song of specialized medical writings in relevant areas: *fu ke,* or medicine for reproductive and other disorders deemed special to women; *er ke,* or pediatrics; and smallpox diagnosis and therapy *(dou zhen),* important now that the disease was becoming endemic in China as a childhood killer. People looked for guidance to physicians with specific expertise. Officials worked to popularize these new specialist medical writings, both at court and in the country. In sum, the shift in sexual mores may also have encompassed a rise in paternalistic concern for women and children in the neo-Confucian family.

Aside from these sociological considerations, Van Gulik's critique of neo-Confucianism assumes that the bedchamber manuals expressed a "liberated" sexuality, an optimal libidinal norm which society came to repress. In fact, the issue here is the construction of the normatively "natural" itself. The sexual arts of the Daoist longevity seeker could be construed as a project to overcome and exceed the "natural." If generative energy is not a rebellious force demanding release but a resource to be husbanded, then the mild creed of continence doctors preferred might claim a "natural" superiority, and the neo-Confucian code of silence and discretion that came to surround sexual matters would simply represent the lessening of a discourse of "incitement."[27] Van Gulik in fact supplies some reports from neo-Confucian critics of the arts of the bedchamber, who identified them with the courts of barbarian rulers and castigated what they called the lamentable imperial habit of keeping harems for "medicine" and imitation of this practice by the gentry.[28]

By the Ming dynasty the "bedchamber arts" had become marginalized practices in medical discourse. They were grouped with "external alchemy"—the pursuit of immortality through consumption of toxic "elixirs" based on powerful mineral materia medica. In both cases techniques associated with the medieval Daoist religious goals of longevity and sagehood were now condemned as dangerous to health and an incitement to lust. Daoist monastic sects themselves, particularly in South China, were stereotyped as havens of magic and licentiousness. In the Ming, mineral elixirs were often defined simply as aphrodisiacs for enhancing male potency, and medical suspicion of them extended to a generalized preference for herbal over mineral ingredients in drug therapy. Esoteric longevity techniques, always theoretically linked to generative vitalities, had become aspects of what were now defined as a complex of transgressive sexual practices alluded to in folklore, popular gossip, and scandalous fiction. In a source such as the famous sixteenth-century erotic novel *Golden Lotus,* the lover is portrayed as unworthy of power because he is a slave to his appetites; his lust exposes him to erotic "defeat" in the arms of seductive but malevolent women. Van Gulik uses *Golden Lotus* and other Ming literati writings to argue for the quiet persistence of the old libertarian ars erotica and neglects the later medical literature, which constructed erotic experience as "naturally" serving birth while representing sexual techniques in pursuit of longevity as dangerous delusion.

We may never know to what extent bedchamber arts adapted and survived underground in Ming society or later as libertine or esoteric practice. But the popular verse taught by the sixteenth-century physician Wan Quan, quoted at the beginning of this essay, fused old metaphors with medical understandings of fertility to describe the ideal sexual union in the service of procreation. Side by side with metaphors identical with those of bedchamber manuals (jade tide, orchid field) are phrases suffused with images of female fertility— the menstrual red flower; the flower/child; Penglai, the womb/island of immortality. While an emphasis on male control is maintained, the poem's technical lore concerning timing and method instruct in the successful conception of a son, a reward in which the woman shares.

As a physician, Wan Quan was particularly renowned for writings in the specialties that supported the health of women and children. He also dealt directly with the issue of longevity and the bedchamber arts in his pamphlet on "nourishing life," making clear the extent to which mainstream medical authorities now distanced themselves from such practices:

Today many gentlemen think that the art of long life consists of "ruling the female" and the warfare of nine [shallows] and one [deep]. They call it "stealing *qi* to return to the origin" or "returning essence to replenish the brain." They don't know that when *qi* and essence well up to an extreme, they must release, like an arrow from a taut bow. Who can "rule" it? If one cannot control one's own essence, how can one expect to "pluck" the essence of another? They may say, "My spirit [*shen*] is not moved, and so I am able to 'pluck' another's *qi*." But they don't realize that those who ignorantly embark on such a road risk becoming leaky vessels. They may say that on the verge of release one "closes off" and "makes the Yellow River reverse course," calling it "yoking the white ox." But they don't know the [proper] place for braking the animal and give themselves hernias and swellings. This is not to nourish life but to harm life.[29]

For Wan Quan, pursuing longevity through sexual performance, like pursuing it through the consumption of dangerous drugs, was an abuse of nature manifest in its debilitating consequences. The proper context for the discussion of erotic experience was not the discourse on "nourishing life" but rather that on fertility: "multiplying descendants" *(guang si)*, or "begetting children" *(zhong zi)*. The balance between longevity and generativity was tipped in the latter direction.

Proper preparation for sexual union involved moral, social, and bodily aspects, all to ensure a couple's fruitfulness. Piety toward the gods suggested an attention to one's accumulated merit in the form of good deeds (not, as in Sun Simo's account, by respecting taboos). An understanding of the rhythms of the cosmos supported a regimen of sexual continence after the seasonal patterns taught in the *Yellow Emperor's Inner Canon*. Socially, the ideal partner was imagined as a wife, chosen with proper attention to horoscope, physiognomy and family pedigree, and without undue attention to beauty. The age of marriage should not be too young for either party. In contrast to the preferences of the *fang shu*, Wan recommended that girls be twenty *sui*, or ten years past menarche (i.e., past the years of early adolescent infertility). The prudent male, however, should follow the *Book of Rites* and delay marriage until thirty, when his yang is firm— that is, when the excitabililty of youth has passed.

Here Ming medical authority understood bodily preparation in a way consistent with the earlier emphasis on male control of desire. As Wan Quan put it: "If a male's body is joyous, his *qi* will certainly overflow; if his inclinations are joyous, his psyche [*shen*] will easily be destabilized . . . his essence will be chronically depleted, and he won't be able to attain the fullness [necessary to healthy] drainage."[30] Wan invoked Mencius' aphorism about having "few desires" *(gua yu)*—reminding his male readers that infatuated husbands also disturbed the emotional health and consequently the fertility of their wives ("If she is personally served, her nature will become ever more proud; if she is greatly pleasured, her mind will become ever more envious"[31]); he praised a bridegroom who succeeded because "his medicines were simple, his intercourse was unhurried, his movements correct, and his timing accurate."[32] At a deeper level, this inner control was understood as the product of a proper balance of the three primary energies: psyche *(shen)*, essence *(jing)*, and *qi*—an abstract formulation of the principles of "inner alchemy" according to which *qi* is nourished through the circulation of essence, and the accumulation of essence completes and realizes the conscious activities of the psyche.[33] As in the bedchamber manuals, the embodied consciousness defining life itself is rendered unstable during the energy exchange of sexual union; here, however, the remedy of control is based on the understanding that although "Heaven's yang *qi* is always in surplus, Earth's yin blood is always insufficient."[34] "Yin blood" here figures the finite generative vitalities of human beings, male and female, as against the inexhaustible creativity of heaven. Microcosmic human bodies have been cut off from the macrocosmic cosmos; the Daoist immortality seeker's reach toward eternity is chastened and redirected toward the transmission of life to the next generation. Although control was still understood as primarily a male responsibility, the fruitful woman here was also one able to "calm her mind and steady her purpose," overcoming the natural female propensity for emotional extremes.[35]

Thus tempered by ritual purpose and trained in bodily wisdom, the procreative couple was deemed ready to apply the teachings of the Primordial Girl. For Wan Quan her words were "too improper for formal recording," but he excused his frankness because "they are also about the beginning of people's life and the origin and transformation of all things."[36] The man's three and the woman's five signs of arousal were important to ensure a fruitful union, since an encounter of "solitary yang and solitary yin," where the partners' desires were not in harmony, would not succeed. The male's responsibility for female pleasure was in the service of the common goal of successful conception. Female orgasm was assigned positive value as essential to fertility.

Whereas the medieval bedchamber manuals valued women as vessels, brimming or drained, of yin essences in the form of sexual fluids, Ming texts on procreation construed female yin vitalities primarily in their aspect as blood, the woman's contribution to new life. Wan Quan, like most others, envisaged a male readership for his manual on "multiplying descendants," but wrote at length about the requirements of female health as well, from menstrual regulation to tonics for replenishing blood and remedies for successful pregnancy and postpartum recovery. Like the bedchamber manuals, Wan Quan's writing portrayed male and female generative vitalities as homologous, and construed sexual difference in terms of women's greater emotionality and diminished capacity for self-control. But where bedchamber manuals encouraged a woman's desire at the risk of its being the source of her undoing, Wan encouraged women, like men, to strive for continence and self-mastery, and offered both the reward of erotic fulfillment through the begetting of children. Traces of the old adversarial model of the erotic encounter survived in the belief that the sex of the child would be that of the partner who reached climax last, making this socially critical outcome a test of their respective powers to control orgasm. But Wan Quan and other Ming physicians vocally disapproved of the metaphors of sexual combat and cautioned husbands to be considerate of their partners' feelings and careful not to damage their health.[37]

From early in the imperial era, medicine has played an important role in the social construction of Chinese sexuality because it has been the orthodox discourse empowered to speak of such things. Medical understandings of body processes shaped theories of sexual function and its place in the natural order; medical moralizations of health articulated a rationale for establishing the normal and the abnormal, the proper and the improper, and for delineating the boundaries of the "sexual" itself. This discussion has focused on erotic experience in keeping with contemporary western constructions of the "sexual" around the privately shared bodily pleasures called sexual acts. But orthodox Chinese medical discourse did not understand such pleasures as constituting an independent domain of "sexuality," but rather positioned the erotic at the fulcrum of body experiences implicating human longevity and even spiritual regeneration on one side and generativity and reproduction on the other. Sexual vitalities were understood as at work not just in acts of organismic arousal and release, but also in those which husbanded essence *(jing)*, *qi*, and psyche *(shen)*, controlling their deployment in order to assist in prolonging individual life as well as transmitting it to the next generation. Since self-cultivation for longevity was constructed around male sexual roles, the ideal "man" became a person not easily moved by women, and whose self-control was manifest in a dispassionate inner calm and an outwardly youthful appearance even in old age. "Womanliness," in this male view, was more morally problematic. The lack of emotional self-control which constituted female difference made women either playthings or temptresses unless they were able to redirect their sexuality toward motherhood. Although based on common understanding of the embodied processes at work, medieval medical discussion of "bedchamber arts" and late imperial writings on sex and reproduction show that conflicts developed over the question of what constitutes a "natural" sexual script. At issue for males was the kind of control deemed beneficial, and whether it should be deployed to serve self or society.

In thinking about female gender in China, China scholars are accustomed to portraying Confucian patriarchy as misogynist in its emphasis on ritual hierarchy privileging yang while confining women to subordinate social and domestic roles. Daoism, by contrast, is portrayed as doctrinally inclined to privilege yin and honor the female, and these metaphorical religious figurations of gender are presumed to go hand in hand with a greater social and sexual equalitarianism. Yet the classical bedchamber manuals teaching Daoist secrets of longevity portray an aristocratic and lavishly polygamous society where very young women were exploited as sexual handmaidens—the stereotype of a royal harem. Wan Quan as a representative of Ming medical thought favored organizing eros to serve the neo-Confucian gentry family. His ethos of sexual continence focused on a husband and wife with relatively homologous erotic roles in the context of a social paternalism protective of women as childbearers and mothers. If the Daoist sexual arts were not Van Gulik's libertarian sexuality, they were also not necessarily a means of vesting real women participants with social or religious authority. If Wan Quan's Confucian valorization of sex for reproduction appears to have restricted the deployment of desire, it also advocated common erotic goals for both sexes and supported social respect for women as wives and dependents in the family. Finally, both Confucian and Daoist constructions of eros (like our own "puritan" or "libertarian" ones) are better thought of as constituting a historically contingent experience in itself rather than as either fulfilling or repressing natural instincts.

7 | Modernizing Sex, Sexing Modernity: Prostitution in Early Twentieth-Century Shanghai

In early twentieth-century Shanghai prostitution was variously understood as a source of urbanized pleasures, a profession full of unscrupulous and greedy schemers, a site of moral danger and physical disease, and a marker of national decay. It was also discussed as a painful economic choice on the part of women and their families, since it was sometimes the best or only income-producing activity available to women seeking employment in Shanghai. The categories through which prostitution was understood were not fixed, and tracing them requires attention to questions of urban history, colonial and anticolonial state making, and the intersection of sexuality, particularly female sexuality, with an emerging nationalist discourse. Prostitution is always about the sale of sexual services, but much more can be learned from that transaction: about sexual meanings, about other social relations, about sex as a medium through which people talked about political power and cultural transformation, about nationhood and cultural identity. In some respects China's modern debates about prostitution echoed those of Europe, where scholars such as Judith Walkowitz (England) and Alain Corbin (France) have traced the themes of medicalization and the desire to return prostitutes to an (imagined) safe family environment.[1] In China, prostitution was also invoked in urgent public discussions about what kind of sex and gender relations could help to constitute a modern nation in a threatening semicolonial situation. What it *meant* (to participants and observers) for a woman in Shanghai to sell sexual services to a man changed across the hierarchy and over time, as understandings of prostitution were shaped, contested, renegotiated, and appropriated by many participants: the prostitutes, their madams, their patrons, their lovers and husbands, their natal families, their in-laws, the police, the courts, doctors, the city government, missionaries, social reformers, students, and revolutionaries. Studying prostitution and its changes thus illuminates the thinking and social practices of many strata of Shanghai society. And since the debates about prostitution often took place in regional or national publications, such a study also suggests the contours of conflicts about gender and modernity in twentieth-century Chinese society.

From the mid-nineteenth to the mid-twentieth centuries, Shanghai was a treaty port—a place where Westerners governed part of the city, and where western and Japanese businessmen, sailors, industrialists, and adventurers made their homes and sometimes their fortunes. Shanghai was also China's biggest industrial and commercial city, a magnet for merchants from around the country and for peasants of both sexes seeking work, and the birthplace of the Chinese Communist party. Shanghai embraced populations from various nations, regions, and classes, and harbored political agitators ranging from Christian moral reformers to Marxist revolutionaries, all presided over by three different municipal governments (International Settlement, French Concession, and Chinese city).

Drawn mostly from the daughters and wives of the working poor and déclassé elites, prostitutes in Shanghai were near the bottom of both contemporary and retrospective hierarchies of class and gender. Yet their working and living situations, as well as their individual standing and visibility in Shanghai society, were strikingly diverse. Shanghai's hierarchy of prostitution was structured by the class background of the customers, the native place of both customers and prostitutes, and the appearance and age of the prostitutes. The hierarchy changed dramatically over the first half of the twentieth century, as courtesan houses and streetwalkers alike faced competition from "modern" institutions such as tour guide agencies, massage parlors, and dance halls. Any account of prostitution in this period must track a variety of working situations across classes and over time.

Prostitution was not only a changing site of work for women but also a metaphor, a medium of articulation in which the city's competing elites and emerging middle classes discussed their problems, fears, agendas, and visions. In the late nineteenth century, prostitutes appeared in elite discourse as the embodiment of sophisticated urbanity. By the 1940s, prostitutes served as a marker to distinguish respectable people, particularly the "petty urbanites," from a newly threatening urban disorder. Every social class and gender grouping used prostitution as a different kind of reference point, and depending on where they were situated, it meant something different to them. The shifting and multiple meanings assigned to the prostitute demand that we move beyond transhistorical references to "the world's oldest profession," or dynasty-by-dynasty catalogues of written references to courtesans,[2] and begin instead to historicize and localize sex work.

Across the century I am investigating here, the changing figure of the prostitute performed important ideological work in elite discussions, particularly as she was transformed into a victimized, disorderly, dangerous embodiment of social trouble. This transformation, and the regulatory regimes it generated, had multiple consequences for the daily lives, identities, and actions of Shanghai prostitutes (indeed, even helped to determine who was considered a prostitute). Changes in migration patterns and economic opportunities may have increased the number of prostitutes and the alarm over them. But changes in elite notions about the link between women's status and national strength helped create the language through which a rise in prostitution acquired meaning—even gave it the modern term for prostitute, *jinü* (prostitute female), which displaced the earlier *mingji* (famous prostitute). And the elite shaped the institutions which emerged to classify, reform, or regulate prostitution, all of which in turn became part of the material conditions of prostitutes' lives. Shanghai prostitution is a rich venue in which to explore the interlocking of material and ideological changes, since neither can be regarded alone as determinative in the last instance of the conditions of prostitutes' lives.[3]

Although the sources delineate an elaborate hierarchy of prostitution, two representations of sex workers dominate the written record: the courtesan and the streetwalker. Courtesans appeared in nostalgic memoirs, guidebooks, and gossipy newspapers known as the "mosquito press" as named individuals with specified family origins, brothel affiliations, famous patrons, and career trajectories. This was a literature of pleasure, devoted to the appreciation of beautiful courtesans and the depiction, often in titillating detail, of their romantic liaisons with the city's rich and powerful. This literature also contained warnings about the capacity of courtesans to engage in financial strategizing at the expense of the customer.

Side by side with this literature of appreciation, the local news page of the mainstream dailies and the foreign press carried accounts of the activities of lower-class streetwalkers, who were portrayed as victims of kidnapping, human trafficking, and abuse by madams, as well as disturbers of urban peace and spreaders of venereal disease. Streetwalkers were sometimes identified in the press by name, age, and native place, but they appeared only as transient violators of urban ordinances against soliciting. Initially, the two types of sex workers were seldom mentioned in a single context, although each embodied a set of dangers posed to and by women in an unstable urban environment. During the middle decades of the twentieth century, courtesans and streetwalkers came to share a wider variety of newly created discursive spaces: as shared objects of journalistic investigation, medical examination, reform, and regulation. In the process, the figure of the streetwalker loomed ever larger, supplanting the courtesan as the emblem of the sex trades.

This essay makes six approximations of Shanghai prostitution, drawn from guidebooks and the press in the first four decades of the twentieth century. "Approximations" is meant to suggest two things. First, each of these portraits is rough around the edges, with inconsistencies left in rather than smoothed out, because each is drawn from sources that are being read both with and against the grain. In addition, some of these portraits overlapped and coexisted in time, and it is not only impossible but also undesirable to try to reconcile them and produce a single seamless account of Shanghai prostitution. The dissonances between them are arguably where the most interesting mapping can be done.

First Approximation: The Urbane Courtesan

Among the richest sources on Shanghai prostitution are guidebooks, written by elite authors, devoted either wholly or in substantial part to descriptions of prostitution. The guidebooks have titles such as "Precious Mirror of Shanghai," "A Sixty-Year History of the Shanghai Flower World," "Pictures of the Hundred Beauties of Flowerland," "A History of the Charm of the Gentle Village," and, most colorful of all, "A Complete Look at Shanghai Philandering," by an author who took the pseudonym "Half-Crazy One."[4] The guidebooks offer a wealth of information about the operations of brothels, simultaneously providing clues to the anxieties and aspirations of the authors. They include biographies of famous prostitutes; anecdotes about famous customers; exhaustive glossaries of the specific language of the trade; meticulous descriptions of brothel organization; instructions on the proper behavior required of customers when a prostitute made a formal call, helped host a banquet, or presided over a gambling party; lists of fees, billing procedures, and tips; explanations of festivals and the obligations of a regular customer at each season; accounts of taboos and religious observances; and warnings about various scams run by prostitutes to relieve customers of extra cash. The guidebooks can be read in conjunction with the mosquito press, tabloid newspapers that typically devoted a page or more to gossip about courtesans.

Most guidebooks are engaged in a literature of nostalgia. Guidebooks written in the 1920s locate the golden age of prostitution a quarter to a half century earlier. In fact, several of the main guidebook authors explicitly say in their prefaces that they are recording the definitive historical account of a world about to disappear because of reform movements to abolish prostitution. One author even compares himself to the famous Han dynasty historians Ban Gu and Sima Qian.[5] And, like classical historians of the Han and later, many of these authors reprint almost verbatim material from earlier guide-books. Also like classical Chinese historians, many of these authors compare the current age unfavorably to the past. Just as historians frequently mourned the failure of contemporary rulers to measure up to the sagacious rulers of yore, guidebook authors deplored the decline in entertainment skill, refinement, and classical training of upper-class prostitutes.

This literature of nostalgia emerged in a time when urban China, and Shanghai in particular, was undergoing rapid and disquieting change. As many China historians from Joseph Levenson on have noted, the question "What is Chinese about China?" emerged as a serious and troubling one for members of the elite in the face of the western assault in the nineteenth century.[6] Part of their answer was to glorify vanishing Chinese cultural practices (now coded as relative rather than universal). And a part of that glorification was to expli-cate meticulously the cultivated and refined social practices of cour-tesans. The production of this literature peaked in the years imme-diately after national civil service exams were abolished in 1905—in short, in years when definition of membership in the elite, and the understanding of China's place in the world, were both in flux. Seldom mentioned in this literature, the West is nonetheless a kind of unspoken standard against which these authors produce an ac-count of the world they have lost.

Although nostalgia for times past was a prominent theme in the guidebooks, their authors were not insensitive to the possibilities available in contemporary courtesan houses. Both guidebooks and mosquito newspapers offered catalogues of the pleasure, explicit and implied, to be found in the high-class brothels. Most obvious were the pleasures of the gaze and the ear: looking at and listening to beautiful, cultivated women, showcased in exquisitely appointed settings, who could sing, compose poetry, and converse with wit. One famous prostitute, whose professional name was Lin Daiyu—taken from the name of the heroine of the classical Chinese novel *Dream of the Red Chamber*—was described in an 1892 guidebook as "just like a begonia after the fresh rain . . . she really is very delicate and attractive."[7] Descriptions of individual courtesans stressed their refinement and cultivation: a typical passage from one mosquito newspaper, the *Crystal*, read: "When guests leave, she burns a stick of incense, makes a cup of Longjing tea, and does watercolors."[8] Another woman was described thus: "She reads a lot and writes well, and knows foreign languages and Shakespeare."[9] Here the image of the courtesan looks both ways—to the literature of nostalgia and to the West. The courtesan is not only defined with reference to *Dream of the Red Chamber*, but also draws part of the repertoire of self-presentation—clothing, bodily stance, hobbies, markers of cultivation—from the West. Urgent conversations among Chinese elites about self-definition are refracted in representations of prostitution.

For the cultivated literati who patronized these houses, the pleasures of looking and listening were intimately related to the pleasures of skilled description and repartee among themselves. Many of the early guidebooks feature elegant poems written by customers in appreciation of courtesans.[10] Perhaps the most intricate ritual of describing and judging was a series of elections sponsored by the mosquito press, held irregularly from the 1880s to 1920. Local literati were invited to vote to enter the names of their favorite courtesans on the "flower roll," a list which paralleled that of the successful candidates on the imperial civil service examinations. The woman who received the most votes, like the man whose exam received the highest grade, was called the *zhuangyuan*, and other titles were awarded as well. After the fall of the dynasty in 1911, the nomenclature was modernized, and leading courtesans were awarded titles such as "president," "prime minister," and "general" instead. In the testimonials which accompanied their votes, patrons marshaled their powers of eloquence to extol the virtues of their chosen favorite, in the process exhibiting their authorial skill to their fellow literati. Courtesans were willing to participate in the elections because they brought prestige to them as individuals and business to their houses.[11]

Any discussion of guidebooks and pleasures should point out that the books themselves offered pleasure. In a study of courtesan novels, a related genre, Stephen Cheng argued that readership in the twentieth century shifted from "literati interested in sentimental love stories" to "shopkeepers, merchants, and clerks who either frequent or are surreptitiously interested in the pleasure quarters."[12] I suspect that guidebook readership underwent a similar transformation, and that for the new urban classes part of the pleasure was in vicarious access to the lives of the rich and famous, patrons and courtesans alike, in deliciously gossipy detail. Reading the guidebooks and mosquito press was part of being "in the know" about who and what was important in Shanghai. Reading about courtesans as the epitome of urbanity was an activity that itself conferred urbanity.

The sections that described summoning a prostitute out on a social call, going to the courtesan house for tea, hosting a banquet, and celebrating festivals can be read as a kind of etiquette guide to correct behavior for the uninitiated guest. Correct behavior included but was not limited to the formal fulfillment of the financial duties already mentioned. It also included the ineffable art of self-presentation. A successful customer enjoyed two benefits: he increased his likelihood of winning a courtesan's favor, and, equally important, he avoided ridicule by the group of courtesans who observed him in the brothel. Someone who failed to meet the requirements by not spending enough money or by spending too much money, by dressing inappropriately, by assuming intimacy too quickly—generally, by saying or doing the wrong thing—would be ridiculed, significantly, as a country bumpkin.[13] If the courtesan embodied urban sophistication, then, the new customer went to the brothel not only in search of the pleasures described earlier but also to create and exhibit his own urbanity. In the rapidly changing Shanghai environment, positioning oneself favorably in the urban hierarchy, and being validated by both courtesans and other customers, was not merely a matter of entertainment.

Second Approximation: The Scheming Businesswoman

The guidebooks were also a repository for a vast and varied cautionary literature, in which the dangers enumerated ranged from the annoying to the deadly. Side by side with the loving and admiring descriptions of individual prostitutes were warnings that prostitutes had one purpose only: to relieve customers of their money. To this end, with and without the collusion of the brothel owner, they would perpetrate various scams. A woman might repeatedly claim to be a virgin in order to collect a defloration fee multiple times. Prostitutes of all ranks, customers were warned, were experts at what was called "the axe chop" (kan futou), requesting clothing or jewelry from a frequent customer.[14] They were said to be as skillful in matching their requests to the customer's resources as a doctor writing a prescription of exactly the appropriate strength. The prescription was "flavored" with "rice soup" (a slang term for flattery), tears, "vinegar" (slang for jealousy), and sweet sugar syrup. One of the later guidebooks carries an illustration of a woman reclining under a quilt while a mustachioed man sits next to her on the bed. She is ticking off on her fingers items depicted in a cartoonlike balloon above her head: a fine house, a car, and a diamond ring.[15]

The hospitable and affectionate demeanor of such women, the guidebooks said, was only a cover for their calculating and deceptive nature, which was reflected in the terms by which they classified guests behind their backs. A "bean curd" guest, for instance, was one who would do the woman's bidding. A "walnut" guest needed one hard knock before he would "put out." A "soap" guest or a "stone" guest needed time and energy, but would eventually yield something. The worst were "flea" and "fly" guests, who buzzed around the brothels but vanished as soon as one "swatted" them for contributions.[16]

In efforts to increase her "take," the guidebooks said, a woman might practice the "bitter meat stratagem" (kurou ji) of pretending to be at odds with her madam. She would then beg the customer to buy her out and take her as a concubine.[17] In fact, the whole procedure of buying a beautiful courtesan as a concubine, which one might expect to find in the litany of pleasures, seems to fall almost completely in the "danger" category. The guidebooks and mosquito papers explain that many courtesans aspired to marriage to a powerful man—or more accurately to concubinage. Principal wives were usually acquired for a man by his family on the basis of matched backgrounds and with the aim of enhancing family assets and status, and a courtesan could not contribute much on any of these counts. Concubines, by contrast, were usually picked by the men themselves with an eye to sex, romantic attraction, and good conversation, as well as the production of male heirs. But, surprisingly, women who made such a match did not settle down into a relatively secure life, but often stayed in a relationship just long enough for the suitor/husband to clear their debts, pay them a "body price," and equip them with jewels and other valuables. The process of marrying under these circumstances was called "taking a bath," and one can find stories of famous courtesans, including Lin Daiyu, who "bathed" many times in the course of their long careers.[18] Many of the women, impatient with the confinement and emotional discomfort of being a concubine, left their husbands and used their newly acquired resources to open their own establishments. When they chose sexual partners for love rather than material advantage, they were said to prefer actors or their own drivers to well-heeled literati and merchants. "They please customers for money," wrote a 1917 guidebook, "but what they really like is actors."[19]

The exhaustive attention to scheming courtesans is perhaps best understood as a warning about the dangers of the urban environment, where some women were unconstrained by the financial and social controls of respectable marriage. Each of the schemes described in this literature centers on a moment when the prostitute slips beyond the control of the customer, taking his assets with her. Chinese writings did not always equate fidelity with marriage or disloyalty with prostitutes; novels and memoirs provide numerous accounts of both scheming wives and virtuous courtesans. But in the early twentieth century, the inability of a customer to secure the loyalty of a courtesan, even by becoming a regular patron or making her a concubine, signified an anxiety-provoking dissolution of conventional gender arrangements.

All of these stratagems, of course, can be read against the grain not as dangers, but as possible points of negotiation or resistance on the part of the prostitutes, who tried to maximize both their income and their autonomy vis-à-vis madams as well as customers. "Axe-chop" income, for instance, went into the pocket of the courtesan, not the owner. When a courtesan became a concubine, the madam was usually paid a fee, but so was the woman herself, and she might use marriage as an interim measure to terminate an unsatisfactory relationship with the madam and accumulate financial resources. More broadly, the historian hears another message—although it is perhaps not exactly what the authors intended—that life in the demimonde, for a woman with an established clientele and acute business skills, allowed more space than marriage for a woman to arrange her own time and control her own income, and that women in the profession of prostitution recognized this, valued it, and acted accordingly.

Third Approximation: The Diseased and Oppressed Streetwalker

If we track these same sources—guidebooks, mosquito papers, the newspapers of record—through the 1920s and 1930s, some voices grow louder, others become muted. Although the courtesan does not completely vanish (she appears in the literature of nostalgia and in classificatory lists through the 1940s), she is no longer the emblematic figure of the sex trades. She has been replaced by the disease-carrying, publicly visible, disorderly, and victimized "pheasant."

The deadliest danger to be found in the guidebooks was that of venereal disease. Usually the warning about venereal disease was a code for class; very little disease was said to be found in courtesan houses, and guidebooks that dealt exclusively with high-class establishments sometimes did not mention it at all. But most guidebooks devoted space to a detailed discussion of the lower reaches of the hierarchy as well. Below the courtesan rank, these guidebooks admonished, venereal disease became distressingly common. "[The prostitute's] body today is wanted by Zhang, tomorrow is played with by Li, and this goes on every day, without a night off, so it is impossible to avoid disease," wrote a 1939 author. "If you want to visit prostitutes [*piao*], high-ranking courtesans [*changsan*] are somewhat more reliable."[20] If a customer insisted on frequenting houses below the courtesan rank, a 1932 guidebook advised him, he ought to take a number of precautions: when paying a call, he was told to squeeze the woman's hand and discreetly check whether it was inflamed; in bed, he should first inspect her elbow joint for lumps, and if he found one, he should "pull up short at the overhanging cliff." One of the most explicit passages elaborated, "When the front lines where the two armies connect are tense," the customer could press down on the stomach and lower regions of his opponent. If she cried out in pain, it meant that she had venereal disease, and he must "immediately throw down [his] spear, don't begrudge the funds for the payment of soldiers or continue to press forward with the attack."[21] Insofar as venereal disease warnings remained tied to the class of the prostitute, they could be read as indications that an elite man should seek out only courtesan houses, rather than as a generalized comment on the dangers of frequenting brothels or the wages of sin.

Prostitutes of lower-than-courtesan rank were typically portrayed as victims rather than perpetrators in this type of account—forced by their madams to have repeated sexual relations until and even after they become infected.[22] This note of victimization was amplified daily in the *Shenbao*, Shanghai's earliest Chinese newspaper. In the pages of the *Shenbao* appeared a group of poor, oppressed, exploited, often battered prostitutes. They were not courtesans but were usually the type of streetwalker colloquially known as "pheasants."[23] They were often barely out of childhood, although occasionally they were married women. Stories about them stressed their rural origins and the fact that they had either been kidnapped and sold into prostitution or else had been pawned by destitute parents. (No embodiments of urbanity they.)[24] In either case, the reports emphasized that they did not wish to be prostitutes, a sentiment reinforced for the reader by the repetition of a standard litany of oppression. Pheasants were most often seen in one of two situations: fleeing from a cruel madam and being sent by the municipal authorities to a relief organization; or being hauled in by the police for aggressively soliciting customers, fined five or ten yuan, and released, presumably to ply their trade again. Coverage of their activities lacked the loving detail lavished on courtesans. A typical article might read in its entirety: "Pheasant Dai Ayuan, from Changzhou, was arrested on Nanjing Road by Patrolman #318 from the Laozha police station and fined 5 yuan."[25] Occasionally, corroborating the guidebook accounts, an article might mention that a streetwalker had venereal disease and had been cruelly treated by her madam.[26] The victim status of these women, however, in no way modified their characterization as dangerous to city dwellers who recklessly sought them out.

Warnings about venereal disease were not confined to guidebooks or the daily press; they became a dominant theme in a growing medical literature that treated prostitution as a public health problem.[27] This theme appeared in documents written by foreigners in Shanghai as early as the 1870s, and was common in western sources by 1920, as part of a general colonial concern with the "cultural hygiene" of governed peoples.[28] But by the 1930s and early 1940s it appears frequently in Chinese sources, usually with reference not to courtesans but rather to "pheasants" and other lower-class prostitutes. By 1941, in fact, a series of articles in the *Shenbao* stated that according to local experts, at least half of the Shanghai population was infected with venereal disease; that 90 percent of the disease was first spread by prostitutes; and that 90 percent of the lowest-class Chinese prostitutes and 80 percent of the foreign prostitutes had venereal disease. The new forms of disguised prostitution were said to be no safer: 80 percent of the guides in guide agencies were said to be infected, while masseuses were not only diseased but also clothed in filthy uniforms. Only in a handful of high-class brothels were the Chinese and foreign prostitutes said to "understand hygiene" or stop working if they became infected.[29] Many of the movements for regulation and reform of prostitution attempted by local governments were explicitly linked to the fear of venereal disease. Venereal disease in turn was linked to China's struggle for survival, which was figured in strictly Darwinian terms. As Lin Chongwu put it in 1936: "The harm of prostitution is none other than its being a site of the spread of disease, which has serious consequences for the strength or weakness of the race. The strength of the race depends on the abundance of good elements. According to the laws of heredity, weeds cannot be sprouts."[30] In the race for survival of the fittest, prostitution and venereal disease were seen to diminish the chances of success, and in themselves became markers of China's subaltern status.

Fourth Approximation: Prostitution as a Marker of Backwardness

The idea that prostitution was a national disgrace and a contributory factor in China's national weakness may first have gained currency among Chinese Christian elites. In a 1913 Chinese-language guide to Shanghai which bore the didactic English subtitle "What the Chinese in Shanghai Ought to Know," a Christian, Huang Renjing, commented on the propensity of Chinese men to conduct business and politics with one another in courtesan houses:

> Famous persons from all over the country go to brothels. They are the leaders of our people. When leaders are like this, one can imagine the situation among industrialists and businessmen . . . The development of the West is due to the skill of the craftsmen and the diligence of the merchants. They are not like the degenerates of our country, who make use of brothels to reach their goal [i.e., who entertain business associates and political cronies at parties in brothels]. I hope that our people will learn from the Westerners, not go to brothels, and forbid prostitution. It is possible to catch up with the Westerners. The reason they developed from barbarism to civilization at this speed is that most of them do not go to brothels. They have virtue; we Chinese should learn from them.[31]

Chinese Christians, like their secular May Fourth counterparts, linked prostitution to China's political vulnerability in the international arena. "The amount of money wasted in Shanghai on prostitution in half a year," observed one Chinese Christian acerbically, "is enough to redeem the railroads which have been mortgaged to the Japanese."[32] Another commented that Japan's victory in the Russo-Japanese war, fought mostly on Chinese territory in Manchuria, was attributable to the fact that 80 to 90 percent of the Japanese soldiers had had no contact with prostitutes.[33] Here is a "nesting" of subaltern statuses, where sex work in China is taken as paradigmatic of a social decay which is then invoked to explain China's position vis-à-vis colonizing powers.

Like the foreign missionaries whose categories they adopted, Chinese Christians located the ultimate cause of prostitution in individual moral weakness. Male and female sexual desire, economic need, and social custom were powerful but secondary factors. One Chinese Christian essayist argued that women became prostitutes not only because they were poor but because their parents, preferring money to virtue, were willing to sell them into prostitution. Traffickers preyed on women who were not only economically vulnerable but themselves morally deficient: "Anywhere there are weak, helpless, poor, stupid, or licentious women who might be caught, the agents of prostitution will be ready to go." Commercialized sex was facilitated by all those "local evil elements" who were willing to sacrifice their scruples for the sake of profits: traffickers and madams, certainly, but also "the landlords who ask a high price for the brothel's rent, the doctors who give prostitutes papers to prove that they are healthy, the lawyers who use clever arguments to defend the business, the pharmacy salesmen who sell forbidden drugs to prostitutes, the local officials and policemen who accept bribes, the tax collectors who have the right to reduce their tax, and some other institutions they deal with who are in charge of trade and transportation." In this analysis, men's patronage of brothels could not be explained by reference to ineluctable sexual desire; the essay cited French and American medical authorities who held that men could live perfectly well without sex. Therefore, prostitution could not be justified by arguing that it sacrificed a few women to protect womankind from uncontrollable male sexuality. In this rendering, prostitutes were both victims and morally deficient; customers went to the brothels because of their moral failings and ultimately became victims of both further moral decay and venereal disease.[34]

International practices shaped by the colonizing powers were not generally invoked as causes of prostitution. For missionaries and their Chinese converts, the continued existence of prostitution pointed to weaknesses in Chinese culture, weaknesses which might be ameliorated by preachers of the social gospel but could be cured only by Christian morality, which would improve the climate for individual moral choices. The necessity of Christianity, in turn, helped to make respectable the entire network of missionary presence supported by imperialist state power.

Like the Christian commentators, other Chinese critics often invoked prostitution as emblematic of weaknesses in Chinese culture, but in their case the solution was often linked to nationalism rather than Christianity. This was part of a larger argument in which gender relations were imbricated with national strength, since it was argued that a system which permitted the treatment of women as inferior human beings would inevitably be a weak nation. Chinese elites of the May Fourth generation argued that China, which mistreated "its women," thus figuring China as male, then was treated like a woman by stronger nations: subordinated, humiliated, with pieces of its territory occupied by force, rights to its use bought and sold with impunity. These critics set themselves in opposition to many elements of Chinese culture and politics, sometimes proposing an agenda for radical political transformation, at other times adopting the language of the social purity campaigns taking place in Britain and the United States.

Writing in the *Crystal,* one such Chinese author summarized three common explanations for prostitution. The first was that women lacked other employment opportunities, the second that prostitutes were victims of madams and male brothel keepers, and the third that prostitution was often a route up the social ladder, allowing a poor woman to become a wealthy concubine. Each of these explanations mandated a different solution: more jobs for women in the first case, abolition of madams in the second, and a lifelong ban on marriage for prostitutes in the third. Yet the author concluded that all three approaches shared a common theme: prostitution was a product of the social system, and any measure that tried to eliminate it without larger social change in the status of women was of necessity superficial.[35]

Many May Fourth commentators linked the elimination of prostitution to a complete program of social reform, in which a strengthened Chinese government and socially conscious members of the elite would both play crucial roles. The government was enjoined to revive industry and commerce so that poor people could support themselves without selling their daughters; to forbid gambling, opium smoking, and drinking so that males would not take up these habits and force their wives and daughters into prostitution; and to forbid trafficking. Other measures could conceivably have involved both state and private efforts: sponsoring public lectures about the dangers of prostitution, expanding charitable organizations, promoting vocational education for women. Still others seemed to rely on nonstate initiative: promoting proper amusements, or perfecting the marriage system so that people did not seek prostitutes because of unhappy family situations.[36] Always implicit and sometimes explicit in such ambitious programs was the goal of a new culture that would support a strong state (and vice versa), with the elimination of prostitution helping to mark the move from backwardness to modernity.

Even when it was not cited as a direct cause of national weakness, prostitution was linked to it by analogy or simple proximity. A newspaper article titled "The Evil of Evil Madams" editorialized in 1920:

> In today's China, there are many who induce others to do evil, but each time avoid the consequences of their crime. Military officials induce the troops to harass people, while civil officials induce their underlings to harm the people. As soon as these activities are exposed, the troops and underlings are condemned, but the officials are calm and in fine shape . . . Furthermore, they shield their troops and underlings and cover up in order to avoid being implicated in the crimes themselves . . . To push the argument further, evil madams who induce prostitutes to solicit customers are in the same category. They force prostitutes to do evil, and also cause people to be harmed by their evil.[37]

To read this passage as a simple rhetorical flourish intended to dramatize the "evil of madams" is to miss an important and barely subtextual message. The practices associated with prostitution are here being invoked as part of a sickness in the culture, expressed in the exploitative and self-protective activities of anyone with power. In this rendering, prostitution was not so much causative as constitutive; prostitutes took their place alongside all those harassed by civil and military authorities, and madams became part of a pervasive and nested regime of power that was manifestly bad for "the people" and the nation.

Fifth Approximation: Prostitution as a Marker of Modernity

Throughout the 1920s and 1930s, municipal governments waged intermittent campaigns to ban unlicensed prostitution. Each of these campaigns, too complex to be taken up here, generated furious production of commentary by intellectuals, many of them associated with feminist causes, the communist movement, or both. Although I cannot yet attempt a detailed account of those commentaries, even a preliminary perusal of the 1930s literature turns up a striking shift in the way intellectuals positioned prostitution in China. While still treated as a serious social problem with specific local features, it had moved from a marker of China's cultural failings and national weakness to a sign of China's participation in universal human history.

A 1936 polemic by Mu Hua against licensed prostitution, for instance, began by invoking the standard May Fourth explanations for prostitution: economic difficulties, trafficking, the atrophy of moral values, the marriage system, and the low level of education. But it moved quickly to universalize the problem by juxtaposing Auguste Bebel's statistics on Parisian prostitutes with a survey of prostitutes who applied for licenses in Suzhou. Mu's conclusion to this section emphasized the primacy of economic causes regardless of venue: "'In sum, [the cause is] just poverty!' The door of the brothel is open for the wives and daughters of the poor."[38] In this move, China is not positioned in a world economy or a colonial system—a positioning which might mark China as simultaneously wronged and backward.

This universalizing narrative was rooted in biology and culture as well as economics: "The male of the human species has a sexual desire which is not less extravagant [*wangsheng*, literally, "prosperous"] than that of the beasts, while the biological burden and the capability of the female in sexual intercourse are very different from that of the beasts."[39] Women's difference from beasts is not specified here, as the author races on, invoking Bebel and echoing Engels, to sketch out the establishment of private property, the rise in the status of men and the imposition of restrictions on wives, and the establishment of prostitutes as objects of enjoyment. With marriage and prostitution linked in a single system,[40] it remains for capitalism to create a situation where more and more men cannot afford marriage and turn to prostitutes. Here Mu Hua makes an unmarked move back to particular local Chinese conditions, arguing that

> because of the immaturity of industry and the desolation of commerce, with most households in economic distress, women in in-

dustry and commerce and maids in households make a meager income insufficient to carry the burden of supporting the household, and only by selling sex as a sideline can they supplement their insufficient wages. So the supply of prostitutes matches male sexual needs, leading to even greater inflation in the market in human flesh.[41]

What is striking about this passage, which echoes many standard depression-era descriptions of the Chinese economy, is precisely that it is left geographically unmarked and historically genericized. Coming as it does directly after Bebel and Engels on the universal evolution of marriage systems, it points away from anything that might be designated as specifically Chinese, even as it describes local problems. The insertion of China into a seamless world predicament is completed when Mu, after quoting the selling prices of women and children in various Chinese provinces, declares:

In this capitalist era, prostitutes themselves are a commodity, and because of an oversupply of the commodity, the middlemen have to lower the price, and adopt the approach of selling more when the profit is meager. So flesh is cheap, and a transaction costs a few dimes, while on the other hand new selling techniques are developed . . . If we cannot use foodstuffs to fill their mouths, we cannot devise ways to have them not sell their lower bodies.[42]

Like the earlier May Fourth commentators, Mu Hua indicates that a comprehensive state initiative is needed to remedy this situation, and warns that if the state permits licensed prostitution, it will damage its own prestige.[43] Unlike the May Fourth precursors, however, Mu's narrative strategy puts across the message that Shanghai is just like Paris: both are mired in the problems of capitalism, with China as a full participant in capitalist ills. Prostitution and its attendant problems have become a badge of modernity.

Elite arguments against prostitution in the 1930s were not without cultural specificity. At one point in commentator Lin Chongwu's essay, after he has invoked the case of Solon and the authority of Parent-Duchatelet, Franz Hugel, Flexner, Rousseau, and Lincoln, his argument takes a sudden particularistic turn. He exhorts the state to promote traditional Confucian virtues for women, such as honesty, honor, propriety, and justice, so that women can resist the lure of western ways:

> The European wind assails the East, leading to female vanity, beautiful clothes and makeup, powder and perfume, living in a fool's paradise and coveting pleasures, love of pleasure and fear of labor . . . If one can't be frugal, how can one be honest? . . . Abandoning a sense of chastity and shame . . . as this goes on, it leads to selling sex for a living. "If this is how it is in the higher reaches of society, how much more so in the lower reaches?" So promotion of virtue should start with the families of government officials—giving up pearls and jade, turning away from gold and diamonds, with coarse dress and simple adornment . . . This will promote the cultivation of female virtue.[44]

In spite of the Confucian overtones and undertones, however, Lin's discussion is firmly grounded both in the twentieth century—where China is one nation struggling among many—and in a universal moral discourse, where Rousseau and Lincoln are cited as sources of the belief that human trafficking cannot be permitted in a civilized society. When Confucian imperatives are set literally paragraph by paragraph next to Parent-Duchatelet, Charlemagne, Saint Augustine, and Max Rubner,[45] an invocation of unique cultural values becomes its opposite: an application to join a human march toward a civilized, moral society, in which both prostitution and the intent to eliminate it are credentials for membership.

Sixth Approximation: Prostitute as Object of State Regulation

Prior to 1949, the police and the courts periodically undertook to regulate prostitution, at least at the margins where it involved the sale into prostitution of "women of good families," or street soliciting, which was seen as a threat to public order. Prostitution per se was not illegal in republican China, but trafficking was.[46] Because of the structure of republican laws about prostitution, women could obtain legal protection in exiting a brothel if they asserted that they had been removed from a respectable family and sold into prostitution. When leaving a brothel meant an improvement in a woman's material or emotional situation, then, she had to portray herself as a victim seeking reunification with her family in order to attain that goal. Thus, abduction and sale was a common story told by prostitutes who brought suits for their freedom, in spite of the considerable evidence suggesting that abductions accounted for a minority of trafficking cases, and that most involved the sale or pawning of a woman for the benefit of her family.[47]

Street soliciting was forbidden in Shanghai under municipal ordinances, and at certain points in the republican period, brothels and prostitutes were required to obtain a license.[48] When prostitutes were brought before the courts or questioned by the police for violating these regulations, they commonly made one of two arguments on their own behalf. The first was that they were working as prostitutes against their will. For instance, in 1929 an eighteen-year-old named Tan Youxi was picked up in a sweep by Chinese plain-clothesmen aimed at clearing the streets of prostitutes. Facing a court-imposed fine, she testified that she had been kidnapped in Suzhou two months before and sold into a pheasant brothel. Although the trafficker had long since disappeared, the brothel owner was charged with buying a good woman and forcing her to become a prostitute *(po liang wei chang)*. The owner was detained pending investigation in spite of his argument that Tan had willingly signed a contract and was entitled to half of what she earned.[49] Tan's assertion that she had not entered prostitution of her own free will, which may well have been accurate, was also strategic, serving to shift the court's attention from her to others.

The second argument made by streetwalkers was that they had reluctantly chosen prostitution in order to support dependent relatives. This type of self-representation appears, for instance, in the transcripts of police interrogations of three prostitutes after their unlicensed brothel was raided in 1947. All three women cited dire economic necessity and the need to support dependents as their reasons for taking up sex work. Tang Xiaolong, age thirty-two, who came from Suzhou, told the police: "My mother recently died, my father is old, and we have many debts. Forced by the situation, in February of this year I came to Shanghai, and willingly placed myself [*zitou*] at the above address, the home of Shen and Sun, as a prostitute . . . As soon as I clear my father's debts, I plan to change occupation, either becoming a servant or returning home. The above is the truth." Although Tang apparently had no husband, her co-worker, twenty-five-year-old Zhang Xiuying from Yangzhou, found that marriage was no guarantee of financial security:

> I have an old mother at home and one son. My husband joined the army four years ago and has not returned. I had no means of livelihood, so on January 14 of this year I left home and came to Shanghai, looking for a former companion Zhang Yuehua, and asked her for an introduction to a job. For a while I could find no regular work. The friend, with my agreement, introduced me into this brothel to be a prostitute in order to survive. Fees were split evenly with the madam, and room and board was provided by the brothel owner. I was definitely not tricked or forced into becoming a prostitute, but actually was driven to it by family poverty. The above is the truth. I ask for understanding in your judgment of this case and will feel very lucky.

Twenty-six-year-old Chen Abao, unlike the other two, had previously done other work in Shanghai:

> I was formerly a wet nurse . . . After February I returned home, because my husband in the countryside was very ill. At the end of last year my husband passed away, leaving an old father at home, and a young son and daughter. Life was difficult in the countryside, so I recently came to Shanghai, borrowed a room at 7 Furun *li*, and entered into a system of dividing the profits with the madam [*laobanniang*], becoming a prostitute in order to live. This is the truth.

Reviewing the testimony of the three women, the chief of the morals correction section of the police concluded: "The reason they became unlicensed prostitutes was because all were forced by life circumstances. They were not kidnapped or forced into it by others."[50]

These stories suggest that many women entered prostitution without encountering any traffickers, much less the kidnappers emphasized in so many of the sources. Some were older than the archetypal kidnapping victims; they had filial obligations to marital as well as natal families, and were often the sole support of children or elderly dependents. The decision to take up sex work was sometimes made by the prostitutes themselves, within the context of family as well as individual economic needs, and they often earmarked income for the support of their families. Under arrest, they could have won lenient treatment and constituted themselves as in need of state protection by arguing that they had been abducted. Instead, they situated themselves in a different nexus of respectability, one in which filial obligations required that they temporarily take up a distasteful occupation. The circumstances under which their confessions were made caution us against reading them as unproblematic statements of "fact." But their statements do complicate the portrait of women violently abducted and forced to sell sexual services. And the particular ways in which they formulated their statements suggest that they were not innocent of the craft of representation or its immediate practical uses in deflecting the expansive reach of the state. If they were participants in their own representation, then perhaps elites did not have a monopoly on the discursive construction of events, and we need not accept a single totalizing account as the only available material for "history."

Although the legal records indicate that prostitutes acted resourcefully on their own behalf and for their families, municipal regimes in Shanghai from the 1920s through the 1950s continued to see prostitutes as dangerously adrift from their proper social moorings, both agents and victims of a broader social disorder. Regulation of prostitution was always part of a broader project in which state authorities extended their reach into new realms in urban life. The Nationalist regime and its twentieth-century municipal governments sought to enlarge their domain of regulation to include the family, echoing both their Confucian antecedents and the modernizing regimes of Europe. In their view, encoded in regulations on trafficking and prostitution, women in families were indicative of a well-ordered society. The sundering of family networks through trafficking and sex work bespoke a larger crisis in the social order, one that would entail the reinsertion of women into families as part of its resolution.

This belief about the proper place of women was not challenged in 1949. In its early years the government of the People's Republic of China began a campaign to end prostitution, armed with organizing techniques that enabled it to succeed in extending the reach of the state into realms where earlier municipal governments had failed.[51] In Shanghai this campaign did not get under way until 1951, and continued with decreasing intensity until prostitution was declared eradicated in 1958. A major feature of the campaign was the detention of prostitutes in the Women's Labor Training Institute. Although they were not permitted to leave the institute at will, neither were they prisoners: the explicit strategy of the municipal government was to cure their venereal disease, equip them with job skills, reunite them with their families, and/or find them appropriate husbands. The key to the success of this entire project, in the view of government officials, was teaching the women to think—and to speak—as recently liberated subalterns. To that end they were organized into study sessions, the most important goal of which was to instill a sense of class consciousness. They had to be made to hate the old society and recognize their oppression in it, and they had to recognize that their own past actions were less than glorious, were now in fact illegal, and must not be repeated.[52] In short, their own understanding of their recent past had to be aligned with that of the state by encouraging them to speak that past—not in unison but in harmony with one another—in a language provided by the state. Their words were often published because they were considered to have didactic value for the larger urban population, most of which was engaged, to one degree or another, in a similar reinterpretation of the past.

In the post-Mao years, prostitutes have once again become visible in Shanghai. Although the organization of the contemporary trade bears little resemblance to the world of republican-era brothels, regulatory discourse features many of the same themes that characterized earlier campaigns. Recent state policy toward prostitution centers on the task, in a rapidly changing reform economy, of returning women to stable work and family situations. In this way, the state argues, China can both modernize and resist the disruptions engendered by "bourgeois liberalization." In each of these cases modernity is seen as simultaneously displacing women (who are both victimized and set loose) and requiring that they be resituated (both protected and contained) with the help of strong state authority. At stake is the very control over what modernity looks like and means, as well as what "women" are and should be.

These different approximations of prostitution coexisted in treaty port Shanghai, and some aspects of them can be reconciled. One might, for example, point out that the mosquito press and the guidebooks both describe women at the top of the hierarchy of prostitution, whereas *Shenbao* and other similar newspapers are describing women at the bottom. Both types of women sold sexual services, but there the similarity ended. Streetwalkers, unlike courtesans, worked in miserable and dirty conditions, under duress, for cash, in the process posing a danger both to social order (dealt with by the police) and to public health (as hinted at in the accounts of venereal disease). If we take these wildly differing accounts at face value, we have to question whether the single category "prostitute" assumes a similarity where one should not be assumed, whether in fact we should stop talking about "prostitution" as a unitary occupation and instead use subcategories such as "courtesan" or "streetwalker."

Ultimately, however, I would prefer to abandon attempts at reconciliation and look instead at the dissonance. Prostitution was an extraordinarily flexible signifier for many different kinds of Chinese engaged in many different conversations. The dissonant chorus they produced raises questions about both the contemporary meaning of the category "prostitution" and the concerns of the patrons and the wider urban population. Above all, we must approach with caution the notion that we can retrieve from history a single set of descriptive or explanatory "facts" about prostitutes.

The perpetual reconfiguration of the discourses on Shanghai prostitution certainly reflected the changing occupational structure of Shanghai, where commercial and industrial sectors grew in tandem with a deepening rural crisis, encouraging the migration, both voluntary and coerced, of peasant women and girls. These interlocked phenomena led to a swelling of the lower ranks of prostitution, changing the sexual service structure to one regarded as more disruptive of social order, and more dangerous to social and physical health.

Yet a research strategy that treats discursive construction as the unproblematic reflection of (prediscursive) social change misses something. One must also look at the eye of the beholder, considering the changing self-definition of urban elites, the effect of the May Fourth movement and the growing revolutionary movement, the development of reformist conversations on the position of women in general and prostitutes in particular, and the effect of language and categories drawn from western missionary sources as well as Chinese radical politics. The discourse on prostitution should also be counterposed to parallel and intersecting struggles over the meaning of marriage, barely alluded to in this essay. It is interesting, for instance, that courtesans were initially regarded as social as well as sexual companions, and portrayed as offering a range of companionship and choice not to be found in arranged marriages. In the social ferment that followed the May Fourth movement, however, intellectuals began to articulate, if not to practice, a notion of marriage as a companionate partnership between equals. If marriage was companionate and desired as such, then courtesans were no longer important as educated women with refined skills, as a means to relieve the tedium of an arranged marriage, or as entertainers. All that was left for the world of the prostitute was sex. Simultaneously, prostitution was redefined as an exploitative transaction where the main connection—an oppressive one at that—was between the prostitute and her madam, not the prostitute and her customer. Because of these connections, prostitution must be looked at in conjunction with marriage and marriage customs.

Finally, the study of prostitution raises the problem of how we simultaneously retrieve and create a historical past. Because the sources on prostitution are so thoroughly embedded in discourses of pleasure, reform, and regulation, they cannot be used in any straightforward way to reconstruct the lived experiences of these women. The voices of a variety of men—the patron, the reformer, the lawyer, and the doctor—are far more audible than the voices of the prostitutes. In the writings of female reformers, representations of prostitution were shaped, if not by gender differences, then most assuredly by class. Their writings were rich in the rhetoric of social purity and pity for fallen sisters. Continually obscured in all of this are the voices of the prostitutes themselves—voices which, while they surely would not have been unified, given the variety of arrangements under which women sold sexual services, would certainly sound different from what we are able to hear at a safely historical distance today.

How can the sources, generated in circumstances of intense public argument about the "larger" meanings of prostitution, be read for clues to the lived (and mediated) experiences of prostitutes, a group that was subordinate and relatively silenced on almost any axis the historian can devise? The voices and actions of Shanghai prostitutes are not completely inaudible or invisible in the historical record. Their experience was bounded by legal, medical, moral, and political discourses that must have affected how they saw themselves, what alliances they sought inside and outside the brothel, what options they had. Prostitutes appear to have engaged in everyday practices which helped them negotiate the dominant discourses and improve their own living and working conditions—using concubinage and the courts, for instance, in ways that belied their portrayal as victims or as threats to the regulated social order.

In each of these representations of prostitutes, whether seen through the particular cautionary lens of the guidebooks or through their direct (though certainly mediated) speech to legal authorities, we discover instances of agency, even resistance. A courtesan who works to enlarge her tips and gifts from customers which are not paid to the brothel is challenging the authority of the madam over her income, and in a certain sense over her body. A courtesan who leaves the brothel with an attractive but impoverished young man who cannot pay the requisite fees—or a courtesan who chooses "actors and drivers" as her companions rather than the free-spending merchants the madam would prefer—is doing the same. A streetwalker who represents herself in court as the victim of traffickers resists being classified as a bad woman, a threat to social order, a spreader of disease.

Nevertheless, these are acts that can also be thought of as "working the system," and ultimately legitimating dominant norms. They not only leave unchallenged but actually reinscribe a larger ensemble of social arrangements in which prostitutes are multiply subordinated. In order to collect tips and private gifts, for instance, a courtesan must cultivate the patronage of customers in ways that can perpetuate her dependence on and vulnerability to them. When a prostitute wins release from a brothel on the grounds that she was illegally brought there, she helps to legitimize the court's authority to determine circumstances in which women may be legally placed in brothels, or more generally have claims on their sexual services transferred. Furthermore, in order to leave the brothels, many of these women averred a desire to be returned to patriarchal family authority, a desire they may well not have felt (given their family circumstances) but which represented their best chance of being seen by the courts as victims rather than offenders. It is important that we recognize these instances of women's agency, resist the desire to magnify or romanticize them, and admit, finally, that our readings of them are tentative and are limited by the many silences and irreducible ambiguities in the historical record.

By reading and listening in multiple registers, we can begin to understand the voices and actions of prostitutes *in relation to* those who were more visible and audible. In the process perhaps we can learn where the voices of prostitutes formed a chorus, where a counterpoint, where an important dissonant note in the changing discourses on prostitution. At the same time, we can trace the discursive uses others made of the prostitute. These are most apparent in arguments about the shifting meanings of urbanity, respectability, government, even nationhood, as elites and less exalted city dwellers sought to define for themselves what it meant to be an urban Chinese in the twentieth century.

8 | Male Suffering and Male Desire: The Politics of Reading *Half of Man Is Woman* by Zhang Xianliang

In 1985, when *Nanren De Yiban Shi Nüren (Half of Man Is Woman)* by Zhang Xianliang was published, it became simultaneously popular and controversial.[1] Its rather sensational title suggested to the Chinese reader of the time an unusual sense of eroticism, both because of the words *nanren* (man) and *nüren* (woman), which had long been abandoned by the "clean" dominant discourses,[2] and because of the way the two words were combined: *nanren de yiban shi nüren* (half a man is woman).[3] This story, about a political prisoner, was seen by critics as a tale "about lust and impotence."[4] The combination of eroticism and political implications in the story attracted much critical attention.

Some critics in China were greatly troubled by the popularity of the story. Wei Junyi, for example, was disturbed by sexual implications which, according to her, triggered the "vulgar reception" of the text.[5] These critics frowned on the story and dismissed it for its lack of "aesthetic" values and its expression of sexual desire. For them the explicitly sexual representation of a political prisoner weakened the tragic beauty of his suffering and thus the beauty of the text. Other critics, however, welcomed the story for both its political overtones and its boldness in addressing a topic that had been taboo in contemporary Chinese culture up to that point. Zhang Xinxin, for instance, argued for the legitimacy of sexuality as a subject in what she termed "serious literature." Echoing this second group of Chinese critics were the enthusiastic critics in the West who celebrated the publication of the story and claimed it to be "moving, tragic, and aesthetically beautiful."[6] The brief comment on the cover of the English translation states: "Written in an ironical prose, which combines a spare, humorous toughness, surrealism, and a lyrical feeling for the Chinese landscape, this brilliant, moving account of lives at the mercy of politics introduces a literary voice of world importance." Martha Avery, the English translator, notes in her introduction that Zhang "writes about human resilience and the costs of survival."[7] These comments represent a more sympathetic reading, usually based on assumptions about "human nature," in this case acknowledging the existence of sexual desire as part of "natural" aspects of human life. The desire, or the representation of the desire, is celebrated as a call for respecting human nature. Within the Chinese context, an appeal to the notion of human nature has strong political implications. Given the historical conjuncture of events at the time when the novel was first published, it spoke to the desires of a people who had lived under a political structure that strongly discouraged expressions and representations of complex human desires.

In short, the discussion of and the controversy over the novel were focused on the subject of sexuality. For the most part, critics who support its representation in the story often link it to its political implications. As long as it is politically subversive, the representation of the protagonist Zhang Yonglin's sexual desire remains unquestioned. One of the problems with this kind of reading, however, is that it understands the notion of desire only as a primordial force which belongs to the "natural" side of a human being. While it welcomes the representation of desire, it fails to examine how the desire is constructed and represented. As a result, this reading does not bother, or may be simply unable, to question the nature of the desire, to ask whose desire it is, and to examine how, in the representation of the desire, women are turned into objects, the "site" or the "space" within which the desires are structured.[8] Critics such as Wei Junyi and Zhang Xinxin have expressed strong reservations about the representation of Zhang Yonglin and his relationship with the woman character Huang Xiangjiu. As a female reader, Wei was offended by the explicit sexual implications, while Zhang Xinxin questioned the protagonist's action after regaining his potency. These two critics, however, did not expand their arguments. Few other critics have pointed out that the desires evoked in the story are male desires with women as their "legitimate" objects. Hardly anyone, for that matter, has questioned this "legitimacy." Such a reading is, of course, gender blind.

More recently, gendered readings of *Half of Man Is Woman* began to appear, generating further questions pertaining to the politics of reading male suffering represented in the novel. A gendered reading of the story has been questioned, however, by those who believe that there is a separation between the political and the gendered. They insist on reading the "political dimension" of the body, namely, the political aspects of the story's representation of sexual desire.[9] But what is meant by the "political dimension" of the body? Whose body is it? Is there such a thing as "the body"? What does it mean when such arguments privilege the political over the gendered aspects of these issues? Is this privileging of the political based on an invocation of "cultural specificity"? Can Chinese men and women, because of China's recent political history, be exempted from the challenges of gendered subjectivities and their construction? If China continues to remain within its existing political power structure, does that mean gender issues should never be considered as important as political issues? And finally, what does this separation between the political and the gendered itself mean?

In this essay I argue—and it is far from repeating a cliché—that gender is political and politics is always already gendered. When Zhang Xianliang constructs "human nature" around issues of sexual desire to show how political repression twists human nature, the way he represents that desire is gendered and linked to patriarchal relations of power. I first take issue with the complacency embedded in the representation of male sexual desire in relation to its object— woman—by associating the notion of desire with the politics of the unconscious. I then take up the argument that opposes a gendered analysis of Zhang's book to a "political" analysis. This opposition is problematic because it fails to recognize that power *is* gendered, that the male desire represented in *Half of Man Is Woman* is closely related to the construction of gendered subjectivity, and that, among other things, Zhang simultaneously occupies the positions of both object of oppression and subject of patriarchal relations. Indeed, what I examine in this essay goes beyond Zhang's book and has important political implications in the broader realm of cultural production.

Woman, "Half of Man," and Male Desire

Half of Man Is Woman tells the story of a political prisoner, Zhang Yonglin, a writer who is imprisoned first during the antirightist campaign and then again at the beginning of the Cultural Revolution. Although the story formally consists of five parts, for all practical purposes it is divided in two by Zhang's second release from labor camp. The first half focuses on the degree to which Zhang Yonglin is sexually repressed in the labor camp and the manner in which that repression is manifested in his dreams and fantasies. It ends with an unlikely encounter between him and a woman prisoner who is bathing nude by a pond. At the sight of the nude woman, his fear wins out and he runs away. In the second half, Zhang is released from the camp and sent to work on a labor farm, where he meets the same woman he saw by the pond. The woman, Huang Xiangjiu, was imprisoned for alleged sex crimes and has since been released to the labor farm. Not long after they meet, Zhang decides to propose, and soon they get married. On their wedding night, however, he discovers that he is impotent. A painful battle follows between him and Huang, and within himself. But after performing heroically in a fight to stop a flood, Zhang regains his potency. Soon after, he decides to participate in political struggles. Fearing that his participation may cause Huang Xiangjiu trouble, he divorces her.

Throughout the novel, Zhang Yonglin's sexual desire is represented with explicit eroticism in his dreams and fantasies, in his first encounter with Huang Xiangjiu, and in his battle against and triumph over his impotence. These images are meant to reflect the twisting of "human nature" under an abnormal political situation and to contrast the "naturalness" of human desires with the "unnaturalness" of political repression. The intensity of the "anomaly"—the simultaneous presence of desire and absence of the ability to possess the object of desire—establishes the pretext for telling the story. It also constructs the "legitimacy" of the storytelling, which further establishes a subject-object relationship between he-who-desires and she-who-is-desired. Within the framework of my argument, however, that "legitimacy" constitutes a problem: women here are employed merely as the bearer of meanings imposed by men. It is precisely this relationship, constructed too comfortably in the narrative, that necessitates another story. That story would allow us to see that in a politically oppressive situation, power relations between the two sexes can still function within the existing patriarchal order under the guise of "natural sexual differences"—regardless of the specific political situation. That is to say, the story's representation of Zhang Yonglin's sexual hunger, the humiliation of his impotence, and his recuperation of potency reinforce the notion of "natural sexual differences" between men and women. Women are objectified, scrutinized, and patronized in the service of a male desire whose real object is to restore "male dignity." Ultimately, it is this dignity that haunts the text.

The story begins with Zhang Yonglin imprisoned in a labor camp. The focus is on sex. The purpose, as I have mentioned, is to reveal how political oppression represses "human nature." One of the ways the male prisoners resist such repression is to talk constantly about women, dwelling on crude descriptions of sexual relationships and cracking jokes about female sexuality. Like his fellow prisoners, the protagonist feels a strong desire for women, the intensity of which is manifested, in his case, through his "twisted" sensual feelings. In his fantasies woman is sometimes "something fuzzy and ungraspable." Other times, says the protagonist, "she took a more familiar form. She melted into other things that gave me pleasure. She was the gentleness and gracefulness, the beautiful curves of my cigarette-smoke. She was the rustling, skin-white paper of my book. She was the well-used smoothness of my shovel handle. With all these things in mind as she came to me, I entered the abyss. In the darkness I, too, found a physical pleasure."[10]

The representation of this unidentified "she" whose image can provide such pleasure to the male imagination is what is at stake here. Semantically, words such as "gentleness," "gracefulness," and "beautiful," which are understood as "natural" feminine qualities, and "curves," "skin-whiteness," and "smoothness," whose erotic implications provide an immediate source of pleasure for a male imagination (a constructed male imagination), all suggest the "bodiness" of woman (as supposed to the "brainness" of man). Other words such as "abyss" and "darkness," and the fact that they are so "naturally" joined with erotically suggestive words, figure the female body as an object and associate it with the irrational and with danger. At the symbolic level, when the image of "she" can only be realized through Zhang Yonglin's scrutiny of things, and when the emphasis on the prolonged withholding of the object of desire is employed to stress the extent of his suffering, the representation of an ideal image of the object of desire somehow serves to transform the representation of the suffering into a pleasurable act. If the act is part of the prisoner's survival mechanism, it is the image of woman represented here that is problematic. That which constitutes "womanness" for him, as I have argued, is none other than a beauty whose manner and body meet the traditional norms of femininity. In the moments of his most twisted sexual hunger, woman remains objectified as the focus of sexual desire.

By the same token, in spite of all his fantasies and his desire for women, Zhang Yonglin can be "turned off" by those who fail to meet his standard. On a very rare chance encounter with a group of women prisoners, he describes his experience:

Sexless, these women had descended to a state even lower than ours. The term "woman" was used only by habit. They had no waists, no chests, no buttocks, as one after another their dark red faces passed by. Although they lacked the "snake wrinkles" of the men, they had the boorishness of female animals . . . My stomach suddenly turned and a stream of acid came up my throat. I looked away, I couldn't go on looking. They would destroy my hope for life itself. To think that the femininity I had enjoyed before, women I had loved before, had come to this. To imagine that they had been arrested and brought to this end—what was there left outside that was still worth longing for? . . . It suddenly came to me that the first primitive animal to use a leaf or the skin of an animal to cover itself must have been a female. (p. 36)

Whether or not there is any proof of his last speculation, it is clear that he is making a connection between his lament and what he believes to be the "natural law" of femininity, as a gesture of protest against sexual repression. Nonetheless, the protesting "I" of these reflections feels sorry not for these women but rather for himself. His psychological pain at watching these "unfeminine" women passing by does not differ from an owner's pain over the loss of a treasured object. All he laments is the loss of the "feminine" appearance and manner of these women. The desire-object relationship between him and women, both in his dreams and fantasies and in his observation of the women prisoners, is sustained. More interesting, perhaps, is what Zhang's own subject position may indicate in this desire-object relationship. The subject is frightened by what he might find in this "twisted" other because he cannot find his "normal" image reflected in it.

This loss of a "normal" self, or to be more exact the loss of "manhood," manifested in the bathing scene and later in Zhang's impotence, constitutes his most deeply rooted fear, the fear of his inability to act as a "normal" man. In the first part of the story, when Zhang Yonglin accidentally sees Huang bathing nude by a pond in the depths of the reed marshes, the image of her upper body dumbfounds him. He trembles at the sight and is seized both by flames of desire and by fear mixed with shame and a sense of inferiority. He runs away. If the subtext of the scene is meant to suggest the negative impact of repression on the protagonist, it also suggests the absence of a "normal" self that could reconcile the tension between desire and fear—the desire to be a "normal" man (in this case, to be able to possess a woman) and the fear of his inability to do so. The dichotomy between desire and fear is employed not only to indicate the tension between him, the man, and her, the woman, but also to indicate the tension within himself. Repression has made it difficult for him to be a "real" man both in relation to a woman—that is, to satisfy his sexual desires—and in relation to himself, to satisfy his belief in what a man should be like. This conflict, of course, demands that the story go on. Zhang needs to find the "man" in the other, "to regain possession of the self, and to reclaim the endeavor that has defined it."[11] In Zhang's story, however, this process of regaining the self is in fact a process of affirming a relation between man and woman whereby the man desires to reclaim his designated position within the "normal" social structure of patriarchy.

In the second half of the story, as the protagonist is released from labor camp and sent to work on a farm, he is now freed from a world without women. Direct contact with women becomes possible. His urgency to become a "normal" man leads him, despite much hesitance and uncertainty, to court Huang Xiangjiu and to propose not long afterwards. Along with the tension between the lack of self and the desire to recover it there exists another source of tension: Zhang's discomfort with Huang Xiangjiu, who obviously belongs to the category of women he painfully depicted earlier in the story. A woman imprisoned for alleged sex crimes, she in no way matches the images of the women in Zhang Yonglin's dreams. Realizing, however, that he is in no position to court a woman who would fit his ideal or be his equal in social status, and that Huang is the only woman available whose social status is "low" enough to match his political status, he embarks on a courtship. This courtship in no way excites him, but he keeps at it. On a deeper level, direct contact with Huang Xiangjiu increases his desire to become a "real" man. But his recovery is full of tensions between himself and his desire, and between the woman and his desire both to possess and to transcend her in order to regain his sense of self. These unresolved moments within the text indicate the constructed nature of the male subject position in relation to woman. On the one hand, he tries to show that, in spite of the fear he has acquired as a result of political oppression, his desire for the woman is a feeling any "normal" man "naturally" has: "To this day, I was moved by that image, the beautiful lines of a naked body. It had excited me countless times, aroused a lust in me, made me realize that despite my outer husk of prison black, or blue, or now, labouring green, I was still a man inside" (p. 77). He continues: "I was caught in an irreconcilable dilemma. On the one side was the voice of reason, held down and controlled by the force of culture; on the other side a primal, non-rational urge, aching to screw another living, breathing body. It didn't matter who she was, as long as she excited the male sex in me" (p. 78). So the decision to surrender himself to his own desire is an affirmation of a male desire: "What the hell—when I'd eaten, I'd go and look for her!" (p. 78).

On the other hand, the object of his desire, Huang Xiangjiu, is also a source of doubt and sorrow about his own position. When he proposes to her, her response seems to him too matter-of-fact; her concern is chiefly financial. As a result, after his awkward proposal and their agreement to marry, he laments: "Was this really love? Had that really been a marriage proposal? I tossed and turned under the covers that night, unable to sleep. It had all happened much too fast, as though it were missing most of the links in the middle. Even though the end result was firmly in hand, I felt cheated, as though it were not heavy enough" (p. 117). He feels cheated because his marriage proposal turns out to be not romantic at all and, perhaps more important, because his betrothed is not the kind of woman he wants. He continues: "Fate was a worldly magician, making jokes that people could not handle: he had created imagination and ideas, and in the end made none of it come true; he created disappointment, chimera and falsehood, and then put idealism and hope into the minds of men" (pp. 117–118). Thus, he is unhappy with the woman he is about to marry but is helpless because, as a former political prisoner, he is left with no other choice. His desire to be a "normal" man is checked by the social and political status in which he is positioned and which, in turn, limits his choice of women; he can choose only women with an "unclean" history (if a "good woman" chooses him, that is another story). Therefore, his choice is a former woman prisoner. One difference between his "unclean" history and hers is worth noting, however: his is of a "political" and hers of a "sexual" nature. Regardless of the political situation, he is still a "virgin." She, by contrast, has not only long since lost her virginity but has gone to prison for her sexual behavior. Culturally, therefore, she is "unclean." That is to say, women who transgress certain political and cultural boundaries are stigmatized as "unclean," while male intellectuals are heralded as heroes or sympathetic victims. This taint on the part of the woman is one element that forebodes their divorce. This peculiar way of using political oppression to justify Zhang's sense of superiority over the woman is problematic and reveals the tensions inherent in his quest to recover his manhood.

By marrying Huang Xiangjiu, the protagonist, instead of ending his troubles, enters another battlefield. The night of their marriage he discovers, to his greatest dismay, that he is impotent, a "castrated" man rather than a "real" man, and his failure to possess the woman frightens him: "Her condescension toward me cut into my peace of mind. A sort of pity hid under her solicitude, and her smile was unnatural. I felt inferior to her. This ruined my sense of well-being" (p. 134). Later he remarks:

> She had slowly expanded, in our so-called "home," until she filled all the empty space. She had taken over the store-rooms until there was no room for me. Before, when I lived in the bachelor dormitory, I had still felt that my space was my own. It was small, but mentally I had felt there were no bounds. Now, our space was larger, but my mental space had shrunk. I knew now what people meant when they said that their minds were being suffocated. (p. 153)

He discovers that she is not the woman who will help him find his manhood. She is rather a threat, one he has to struggle to turn into his possession in order to recover his "true" self.

Subsequently the narrative attempts, on the one hand, to describe the pain of Zhang's impotence, attributing it to the husband's inability to possess the wife and the wife's infidelities with the village's party boss. On the other hand, the narrative restores the dignity of phallic power through Zhang's "conversations" with his horse and with some well-known historical and fictional figures, Chinese as well as foreign, ancient as well as modern. Prior to his dialogues with those male figures, and immediately after his discovery of his wife's affair, he holds an imaginary dialogue with his workhorse, a gelding who laughs at his mental castration and urges him to remember Si Maqian, whose corporeal "'castration punishment' was a crippling measure . . . to spur him on to greater mental resentment, to forge a powerful motivation for completing what are now known as the *Annals of History*" (p. 144). When he "converses" with the male figures (a scene to which I return in the next part of this essay), he receives various bits of advice. As I read these conversations, they exist not for the content of the advice he receives (because the advice is contradictory), but for helping Zhang recuperate his masculinity by aligning himself with these well-known men. These imaginary relationships reveal rather obvious marks of narcissism. Ideologically, however, they may provide the only resort for a wounded sense of male superiority, the only means to maintain the masculine position as the subject of desire.

Meanwhile, the woman as threat is represented only at the level of her role as a sex object. The pain Zhang suffers and the struggles he wages within himself have nothing to do with Huang's own desire as a woman, but only with what he finds reflected in her: his impotence. His triumph over the threat of castration restores his power as a man, and empowers him to convert the woman from threat to possessed sex object. His relationship with his wife changes when he becomes a "normal" man: the "perverse" order in the family is reversed, and the woman is shifted back to the "normal" secondary position. At this point, the story is near its end, where it will reinforce phallic power by endowing the "reborn" man with more access to desire. The performance of the sexual act—not fulfilled until a prolonged period of suffering is completed—is pleasurable beyond mere physiological satisfaction. It is part of Zhang's reclamation of masculine power, a triumph of "male dignity." It is the "triumph" of a male dignity which is realized in the male subject's transformation from the "half man" who fled the bathing scene in awe of a woman he was incapable of possessing to the "whole man" who finally succeeds in possessing and eventually dispossessing her. In relation to this victory, woman serves only as the space in which the enunciation of male desire is realized.

While the woman has fulfilled the function of restoring Zhang Yonglin's male dignity, she has simultaneously been transcended at the symbolic level with the additional implication that she is, after all, not a desirable woman according to the patriarchal norms because she appears to possess too much desire of her own. The divorce, initiated by Zhang at the end of the story, becomes inevitable. Huang Xiangjiu has become a "used tool" for the restoration of his male dignity, but she is also too much of a threat to it. There is little possibility for Huang, as a woman with her own desire, to be recognized as "normal." For a man whose name could be rehabilitated when the political situation changes, she is not a woman who, as the social and cultural norms require, could help him maintain a sense of integrity.

The Politics of Reading Male Suffering

I have so far problematized the representation of the image of women and questioned the nature of male desire represented in *Half of Man Is Woman*. The story I have tried to tell indicates that male desire has been reconstructed according to its own logic. "Half of man is woman," but which half? Why is a man not a "real" man without woman? What is it in woman that contributes to making a "real" man out of a man? These seemingly legitimate questions are unfortunately of little significance to the story; woman is important only insofar as man can find himself in her. This is especially true in the second half, where the tension between Zhang's desire to possess the woman and his fear of failure is generated from the anxiety that he is not a "real" man.

While the novel focuses on repression and its effects (Zhang Yonglin's sexual desires, his dreams of and fantasies about women, his impotence and related humiliations), in order to demonstrate how "human nature" is "twisted" under political oppression, male desire is represented as "normal." The story, in other words, is constructed on the basis of a repressed but not crippled male desire, which is represented by means of unquestioned assumptions. This brings us to the issue of ideology, in which we find that desire itself is characterized as male—for the "maleness" manifested in the desire slides conveniently into traditional patriarchal values when it fastens upon women. The need for the man to win if he is to survive prolonged suffering is combined with a narcissistic complacency supported unconsciously by prevailing patriarchal values. Not only does the image of woman exist in the text chiefly as an aspect of representing male desire, but in the process woman becomes the "bearer of the bleeding wound."[12] That the manifestation of male desire is achieved by representing women by means of unquestioned assumptions is precisely where I find fault with the construction of the narrative.

Let us turn to the political dimension argument. This argument assumes the "political dimension" to be ungendered, and suggests that there exists a conflict between a "political" reading and a gendered reading of male suffering. The question, then, is what it means to insist on arguing for the political dimension of the body in response to a gendered reading of a story that represents male suffering. There are several issues at stake here. First, such an argument continues to work within the existing power and gender relations. It is within these existing patriarchal power relations that such an argument privileges the political over the gendered, and insists on perceiving male suffering as the suffering of the whole nation and therefore as a more important issue than that of how woman's body is employed as the "site" of such suffering. (Once again we find ourselves confronted with the same old assumption that men occupy a gender-neutral position when it comes, among other things, to the political domain.)

Second, and relatedly, given the context of recent Chinese history in which we read the novel, this line of argument is geared toward emphasizing the political dimension of the body and the protagonist's position as the object of oppression at the expense of questioning both the gendered dimension of the body and his position as the speaking subject. The political dimension argument, in other words, emphasizes the protagonist's position as the object of oppression and the relationship between him as the object of oppression and the existing power structure as the subject of oppression. How do we then reconcile seeing *his* body as the site of oppression and accepting *woman's* body as the site of his representation of that oppression? Or can we reconcile the two? I would argue that there can be no reconciliation as long as his body is perceived as or assumed to be gender free, and as long as his subject position is perceived only as the object of oppression.

Third, and perhaps most important, within the framework of the political dimension argument, because it identifies male suffering with the political, any challenge from a gendered perspective becomes questionable. The point, in other words, has to do with how such an argument understands "male suffering." Male suffering is equated with the suffering of the nation, and therefore is conveniently viewed as representing the cultural and historical specificity of Chinese politics. It is this underlying assumption that brushes gendered aspects of the issue aside as marginal. According to this logic, the political dimension is culturally and historically specific, and therefore more important, while a gendered reading is merely an application of western feminist theories and is therefore discredited. By equating male suffering with national suffering, such arguments thus uphold the political dimension as culturally specific, while dismissing the gendered as a foreign concept whose application must therefore remain problematic.

My reading of the novel has demonstrated that "the body" actually means "his body." Having engendered "the body," I further contend that the argument for the political dimension of the body is made within the existing gendered power relations. To expand my argument, I turn to the story again, this time bringing the notion of gendered subjectivity deeper into the picture in order to examine the relationship between the political dimension of the (his) body and his (gendered) subjectivity.

In the story, writing as a victim or object of political oppression, Zhang Yonglin at the same time occupies the position of the speaking subject. This subject-object position which he simultaneously occupies is precisely what I targeted in my earlier reading. I have argued that by exploring a taboo topic, namely, sexual desire, in so-called socialist literature, Zhang Xianliang stages a protest against political oppression. But the representation of desire is realized by employing women as the site in which such desires are structured. Such representations indicate the workings of patriarchal power relations and the discursive construction underpinning the representation of the subject position of the speaking subject.

In the narrative's most politically charged moments, in which the protagonist confronts the meaning of his oppression, or the political dimension of the body, the speaker's position itself is subject to constant shifting, and therefore is never so innocent or so purely political. It is his representation of his struggle that is at stake here. Zhang Yonglin is represented as the object of oppression, and the women in the story seem to occupy a similar position—the position of the oppressed. Do women, then, naturally occupy an equal position with him in his mind? In my earlier reading I argued that they do not: women continue to exist for him only as objects. What is more, even in relation to his oppressor, the protagonist does not occupy the same position as women. He wants to compete with the "father," a desire embodied in his struggle to identify with an alternative father figure. His desire is not just to denounce the "father" but eventually to replace him with himself. As I have noted, soon after Zhang discovers that Cao Xueyi, a party member and his superior, is having an affair with his wife, he engages in a series of imaginary dialogues with various male figures: Song Jiang, a famous character in *Shui Hu Zhuan* (Water Margin); Shakespeare's Othello; Zhuangzi, an ancient Daoist philosopher; and Karl Marx. The first two characters each kill a woman because of her alleged adultery. Their ghostly appearance before Zhang is meant to remind him how a "real" man should act in such a situation. Whether or not he carries out their advice, of course, is not the issue here. Such dialogues are employed to provide him an opportunity to express his doubts about the existing power structure and his desire to find an alternative father figure. In these exchanges one point becomes clear: there is something fundamentally wrong with the current power structure, and it is not Zhang's fault that he is being persecuted.

Among the four dialogues, his conversation with Marx is the longest. By calling Marx "master," the protagonist indicates his wish to discover the "Truth" from him. And within the context of the narrative, he does find the "Truth." Marx disapproves of the existing power structure which claims to carry out his ideas of revolution. Toward the end of their conversation, the protagonist asks Marx: "Looking at the future of our society, is there any guidance you can give me? This question concerns not only how I deal with life, but also with my very life and death" (p. 176). Marx replies, "Economics! You must look at every problem from the standpoint of economics"

(p. 176). The author goes on putting what he believes to be the Marxist theory of economics into the mouth of his imaginary Marx. Then Marx says: "Right now, your productive power has essentially been neutralized. You're trying to scrape by with words and hot air rather than real action. It's ridiculous that at this time the mouth is developing rather than the hands or the body. Do you really think it can continue much longer?" (p. 176). Just at that moment Cao Xueyi comes out of his house. This prompts the protagonist to reflect: "To think that this man, who was one of those offending the great soul of the deceased, was a Communist Party Member!" (p. 177). Through Marx, the "master," the protagonist is thus able both to criticize the current political situation and to identify with "true" authority, an alternative symbol of power in another father figure. His concern over his wife's adultery, then, is turned into a political issue. The real struggle, as it is suggested here, is between him and another man, who symbolizes a corrupt power system; his relationship with the woman is only a manifestation of his weak position in relation to that power. It is not the woman who dominates him but the man who has the power to possess "his" woman. His desire is to fight against that power. To be able to possess the woman, then, also becomes a political act. He gains an equal position not with the woman but with the man; woman's body is merely the site of this power struggle.

Immediately following these dialogues, the protagonist gains back his potency after participating in fighting a flood. In the battle against the floodwaters, he is praised by the villagers for behaving heroically. When he finally gets into bed with his wife that night, he realizes that he has become potent. What is the connection between the two events? Having performed a "manly" deed, he is rewarded by finally becoming a "real" man. Battling the flood is an action reminiscent of Da Yu, a legendary figure who succeeded in fighting a flood and was rewarded by heaven by becoming an emperor. Once again we find the shift of identification with an alternative father figure. The return of potency through fighting the flood, and thus the dominance over women, becomes a trope for the protagonist's struggle against the father in power. Both the representation of the woman character in this narrative and Zhang Yonglin's desire to identify with an alternative father figure in order to regain his sense of power are intertwined in such a way that together they manifest the protagonist's desire for "normal" power in relation to both women and his oppressed condition.

In conclusion, the choice whether to make visible or to ignore the existence of *gendered* subjectivity in the domain of the political is where the difference lies between the political dimension argument and my own argument. To insist that gender is political is not only to argue for including women in the political sphere of the social structure. It is also to argue that to exclude gender from politics is to define the political as gender neutral. By making visible gendered subjectivities in the political, I am arguing that both men and women are always already gendered subjects. Equating the gendered only with women is to continue to marginalize and therefore trivialize them.

I have questioned two highly problematic assumptions: (1) as the result of "his" suffering, the political becomes "his" domain; and (2) what is political is therefore gender free. I have argued that in *Half of Man Is Woman*, it is precisely in relation to these implications that women are employed as the site within which a man's struggle is staged. I have also argued that looming behind the objection to the gender analysis of this story is an insistence on specifying the Chinese political landscape as a gender-neutral zone. But to do so is to continue to assume a separation between the political and the gendered and to believe that men are somehow ungendered. In the name of the political, such an argument continues to single out women's issues or gender issues as special issues and thus to further marginalize them as less important than and inferior to "political" issues. One of the political implications of a gendered reading of stories such as *Half of Man Is Woman* is to raise questions about the assumptions of a gender-free male voice, to engender that always already gendered position, and to bring the issue of constructed male subjectivity into focus in relation to the issue of gender in China.

III | Where Liberation Lies

CHRISTINA K. GILMARTIN

9 | Gender, Political Culture, and Women's Mobilization in the Chinese Nationalist Revolution, 1924–1927

The issue of women's emancipation was closely inter-twined with the entire course of the National Revolution which unfolded in China between 1924 and 1927. It was a prominent component of the revolutionary rhetoric of both the Chinese Nationalist and Communist political parties, which had allied for the purpose of creating a unified nation-state, and it motivated untold numbers of women from all social classes to participate actively in the revolutionary cause. This massive mobilization of women challenged patriarchal social power and endeavored to reconstitute society and gender relations in a more equitable form.

The disastrous unraveling of the alliance between the Communists and the Nationalists in mid-1927 brought the women's mobilization campaigns to a dead halt. With the onset of backlash, repression, civil war, and a Japanese invasion and occupation in subsequent years, the cause of full-blown gender transformation lost its political backing and no longer commanded much public attention. It is not surprising, therefore, that scholars have attributed very little historical import to the effort during the National Revolution to promote essentially feminist goals,[1] in large part no doubt because the outcome seemed so paltry. By the same token, the National Revolution generally has been treated in the scholarly literature as a rather insignificant historical event, except perhaps for its having given birth to the Chinese communist model of peasant revolution.[2]

From the vantage point of the late twentieth century, the very notion that Chinese revolutionaries many decades ago imagined that they could effect such fundamental and far-ranging social changes to the gender order in such a short time seems chimerical. Accounts in recent years of the resurgence of infanticide, the kidnapping and sale of women, rampant violence against women, high rates of female suicide, parental control and interference in marriage choices, and the persistence of pervasive social attitudes maintaining the inferiority of women offer sobering evidence of the durability of patriarchal values.[3] Consequently, we have little sense now of the strength of the ideal of women's emancipation in the mid-1920s for these revolutionaries, of the specific ways in which they translated this ideal into action during the National Revolution, or of the role of women as historical actors in the women's mobilization campaign.

Although gender issues came to the fore in every revolutionary movement in China during the twentieth century,[4] the National Revolution constituted the most radical political effort to overcome women's subordination and transform gender relations in the family, society, the economy, and the polity. A comprehensive discussion of the full gender dimensions of the National Revolution is beyond the scope of this essay. But an examination of the role of the three major political parties involved in the endeavor—Nationalist, Chinese Communist, and Soviet Communist (through the Comintern)—to mobilize women in the one province of Guangdong reveals much about the extent to which a feminist agenda could be pursued in the context of a militant nationalist movement and a strongly patriarchal society.

Although the geographic terrain of the National Revolution was quite extensive and ever expanding, this essay focuses on the gender dynamics of the revolutionary experience in Guangdong between 1924 and 1927 because this province was the first center of the revolutionary effort, and it had a functioning government in place longer than in any other locale that was brought under the control of the National Revolutionary Armies. As such, it allowed for the earliest and most concerted attempt to alter existing gender arrangements. The manner in which women's emancipatory issues were infused into the political culture and the patterns of female participation that emerged in Guangdong served as a model for revolutionaries as they extended their operations into other southern and central provinces of China.

The social terrain of Guangdong, especially the Pearl River delta, was characterized by its large, powerful, and affluent patrilineages, which perpetuated a strong patriarchal ideology that placed little value on females and generally regarded them as expendable.[5] Yet certain aspects of women's culture, labor participation, and political activism in this province diluted the potency of traditional norms governing female conduct and thereby contributed to the creation of a receptive cultural context for initiating the women's mobilization campaign of the mid-1920s. Ono Kazuko's and Rubie Watson's discussions, for instance, of women's ballads, girls' houses, festivals, and sisterhoods reveal the existence of women's rich expressive culture that facilitated the fostering of ties between women and their articulation of a countervailing social vision of gender relations.[6] If the prevalence of footbinding among the Cantonese-speaking population (the Hakka had never practiced this custom) is taken as a measure of the tenacity of traditional norms regulating female propriety, then it is significant that this custom was definitely on the decline by the early 1920s.[7] According to one foreign sojourner, footbinding was "almost unknown" in the entire province, a claim that is supported by the fact that revolutionaries did not make it an issue in the women's mobilization campaigns in Guangdong during the National Revolution, whereas in Hubei it became a main focus of revolutionary activity.[8]

By the same token, it is difficult to characterize Guangdong women as "insiders" *(neiren)*, entrapped within family compounds without much knowledge of the outside world, for many were involved in agricultural production.[9] Surveys conducted by Chen Hanseng in the 1930s revealed the surprising reality that more than half of the day laborers in the fields throughout the province were women.[10] Indeed, the scene of large numbers of women working in the fields in the East River area seemed quite remarkable to Zhu De, a communist general, when he passed through with his Nanchang armies in 1927.[11] Of course, it was difficult for many patrilineages to keep women as *neiren* inside the family compound when their men had gone abroad to find work. Indeed, the practice of male outmigration, particularly among the Hakka, to various parts of Southeast Asia, the Pacific Islands, and the West Coast of the United States was quite extensive by the 1920s.[12] If the Hakka stood out in everyday life for their lack of conformity to many prevailing gender practices, they also were well known for their direct onslaught on gender customs during the momentous Taiping Rebellion in the mid-nineteenth century.[13] This revolutionary tradition was subsequently augmented by the strong participation of Guangdong women in the 1911 revolution, and through the bustling activities of a host of women's groups—more than in any other province in China—that sprang up in the May Fourth era.[14] The legacy of a century of agitation for gender transformation in this province perpetuated an image of Guangdong women as the leaders of the Chinese women's movement and thus laid a strong foundation for the women's mobilization campaigns of the National Revolution.

The mass mobilization of women in Guangdong during the mid-1920s was pursued through the strikingly innovative and extensive use of cultural symbols, propaganda, and organization based on practices developed in the Soviet Union after the Bolshevik Revolution.[15] The explicit aim of this intense effort of mass mobilization was to bring women into the political process, usually for the first time, and make them feel like an integral part of the new political order that was being created. Secondarily, this mode of mobilization aimed to challenge traditional norms regulating gender conduct by promoting the formation of new values and beliefs about the role of women in the political, economic, and social arenas of a modern nation-state. The Chinese adoption of Soviet mobilization practices reflected the tremendous prestige and special role accorded the Soviet Union and representatives of the Moscow-based Third International (Comintern) in the National Revolution. Ever since the issuing of the joint declaration between Sun Yatsen and the Soviet diplomat Adolph Joffe in January 1923, the Soviet Union had provided money, political and military advisers, and arms to the Nationalists in Guangzhou in order to facilitate a revolutionary effort to establish a unified nation-state in China.

While the specific mode of the women's mobilization campaigns that unfolded in Guangdong bore a distinct resemblance to the programs of the Zhenotdel (the Women's Section of the Soviet Communist party), it would be erroneous to suppose that what transpired in the Guangdong women's mobilization campaigns of the 1920s was a direct transplant of the Russian revolutionary experience. To begin with, the National Revolution occurred soon after the upsurge of feminism in China of the 1910s in the context of tremendous cultural, social, and political ferment, which later came to be called the May Fourth movement (1915–1921). The cause of women's emancipation influenced many political activists of both the Nationalist and Communist parties and predisposed them to support the development of a large-scale women's mobilization campaign around May Fourth issues such as marriage reform; the abolition of polygamy, concubinage, and prostitution; female employment in the public sector; and far-reaching legal reforms that would guarantee women's suffrage and property rights.[16] A close examination of the mobilization programs reveals much about the ways in which these May Fourth issues were translated into action during the National Revolution as well as about the emergence of political constraints on this effort of gender transformation.

The Revolutionary Context for the Women's Mobilization Campaign

The transformation of Guangdong into a revolutionary center in the mid-1920s was brought about by the consolidation of Nationalist power in the province with the critical support of funding from the Third Communist International.[17] The Nationalist party was reorganized along lines specified by Mikhail Borodin, the Russian Comintern special adviser to Sun Yatsen. The successful Nationalist military campaigns in eastern and western Guangdong in 1924 and the first part of 1925 created a relatively safe haven for revolutionary discussions and undertakings, areas decidedly preferable to other sections of the country where political control was in the hands of menacing warlords or Westerners. However innovative and promising these social movements initially were in places such as Shanghai and Beijing, their expansion was always checked by the warlords or western authorities. Public discussions and gatherings were subjected to stiff police regulation, and political organizers had to plan actions in a piecemeal fashion from "underground" nooks. Organizers worked under constant threat of police persecution, as was so dramatically demonstrated during the May 30 incident (1925), when the International Settlement police disputed protesters' access to the streets and closed down institutions involved in the protest, including Shanghai University.[18]

Ultimately these Shanghai police actions precipitated a spectacular outpouring of mass nationalist sentiment and gave rise to the emergence of a profound revolutionary consciousness throughout much of urban China. Throngs of students and intellectuals, now confident that a revolution was actually achievable, streamed southward to Guangzhou, which they viewed as the revolutionary capital of the country. This reputation had swelled with the calling of a massive Hong Kong seamen's strike involving tens of thousands of workers, which proved to be one of the longest general strikes (lasting sixteen months) and boycotts of foreign goods in Chinese history.[19] Moreover, a reenactment of the May 30 tragedy occurred right in Guangzhou when foreign police opened fire on a large group of Chinese demonstrators, causing many casualties and deaths in what came to be called the Shaji (Shakee) incident. The combined impact of these events activated a large number of people in Guangdong to participate in the revolution alongside those coming in from outside the province. These new political actors, both mobilizers and mobilized, became involved in the complex process of creating a new nation-state through revolution.

From the early formation of a revolutionary center in Guangzhou, Nationalist and Communist leaders consciously worked to construct a cultural system that would solidify public support for the new order. A new set of political rituals, revolutionary symbols, festivals, and press publications was devised, which had an immediate impact on popular life, particularly in Guangzhou. For many people, participation in political life—rallies, parades, public meetings, holidays—became routine, indeed almost a daily occurrence, prompting western journalists to refer to the city as "Red Canton" in their dispatches.[20]

Women's emancipatory issues were integrated into this revolutionary political culture and were strongly promoted by the new government as an indication of its commitment to gender reform. Women's issues were inserted into newspapers and journals, the theater, and celebrations of most revolutionary public holidays. The cause of women's emancipation as an abstraction seems to have been widely embraced by all the parties involved in the revolutionary coalition, but the initiative to invent an appropriate revolutionary tradition that would give greater credence to the anticipated women's mass mobilization campaign was left mainly to the Chinese Communist party and Comintern advisers. Much of the specific content of the political culture that was created was appropriated directly from European socialist-feminist traditions, and then explicitly linked to the goal of achieving a National Revolution.[21] Intertwined with this internationalist political culture were practices and symbols derived from the May Fourth era. In such a charged environment, for instance, fashion became a political statement. Many of the urban women who assumed visible roles in the political arena expressed their revolutionary modernity through their hairstyles. As in the 1911 revolution, when men cut their long queues as a sign of defiance to the Manchu rulers, women in the National Revolution appropriated the May Fourth practice of bobbing their hair to symbolize their emancipation from the traditional codes for women. In Guangzhou it became the most important way for a young woman to signify that she was an active participant in the grand effort to construct a new order.

Many festivals that promoted women's emancipation had a decidedly internationalist tone. Thousands of people streamed into the parks in Guangzhou every May 1 to celebrate the socialist Labor Day. They called for a variety of changes in working conditions for women, including the granting of paid maternity leave and equal pay for men and women performing the same job. Although Chinese radicals, particularly communists in Shanghai, had held small gatherings to celebrate this socialist holiday previously, this was the first time that it was widely observed as a public occasion in a Chinese city. Similarly, for the celebrations in recognition of the Bolshevik Revolution, official addresses and speeches expounded on the great changes that Russian women had experienced under Soviet rule. Most important, the Nationalist government, following the practice of western socialist parties, incorporated International Women's Day into its calendar of rituals, a holiday that was originally created at the suggestion of Clara Zetkin at the International Conference of Socialist Women in Copenhagen in 1910.[22]

The first Women's Day celebration was held in Guangzhou on March 8, 1924. More than three thousand people participated in this inaugural celebration, which called for gender equality in wages, educational opportunities, and the law, as well as the elimination of concubines, prostitution, child brides, and girl bondservants. During the next few years the slogans became more radical and included calls to end the arranged marriage system, permit divorce, and oppose capitalist exploitation of women.[23] The size of the gatherings grew substantially over time as well: by 1926 the numbers of people attending the March 8 festivities in Guangzhou expanded to more than ten thousand; by 1927 they were estimated around twenty-five thousand. For those city dwellers unable to attend the rallies, the significance of this occasion was impressed upon them through articles in the press and the circulation of pamphlets on buses and in the streets.[24]

One indication of the role that male political leaders initially played in defining the rituals and symbols for promoting the ideals of women's emancipation in the National Revolution is that Liao Zhongkai was the featured speaker at the first March 8 rally in 1924. Significantly, although he was invited to proclaim the importance of this holiday, the soon-to-be-appointed female head of the Nationalist Central Women's Department, Zeng Xing, stood by his side on the podium.[25] No doubt Liao's tremendous political stature as Sun Yat-sen's plenipotentiary and as governor of Guangdong, coupled with his reputation as an eloquent speechmaker, lent great legitimacy to this women's festival. But over the next few years, as the power and prestige of the Nationalist Central Women's Department grew, women leaders came to dominate the proceedings.

No changes appear to have occurred in subsequent years in the internationalist tone of these celebrations, however. The recollections of Vera Vladimirovna Vishnyakova-Akimova, who as a twenty-one-year-old Russian woman had participated in the 1926 Women's Day celebration in Guangzhou, provide a graphic portrayal of the event. In response to a request by the Nationalist Central Women's Department, she and some other Russian women staged an amateur performance for the occasion, which began with their singing the "Internationale." Then they put on a skit which portrayed women of the world looking to the Soviet Union as a beacon of inspiration. Vishnyakova-Akimova recalled how they all dressed up in international costumes to symbolize the many different countries of the world.

[We] surrounded Soviet Russia—the wife of the adviser Rogachev in a *sarafan* and a *kokoshnik* [a type of old Russian woman's headdress] holding a red banner. I was made up as a Chinese woman— dressed in pajamas embroidered with dragons and shod in ancient satin men's slippers on high wooden soles. My head swam in a jet-black wig, parted in the middle, with a bang and long braids, fastened from both sides near the ears; the hairdo was not in the least Chinese. I portrayed awakened China and stretched out my hands towards Soviet Russia. No matter how surprising it may seem, the Chinese recognized themselves in me and applauded deafeningly.[26]

The internationalism of the symbolic framework that was constructed in Guangdong was also reflected in the tribute to the memory of Rosa Luxemburg, the famous Polish-born woman leader of the German Socialist party who was brutally murdered during the ill-fated communist uprising in Berlin in 1919. Not only Communist but also Nationalist journals and newspapers carried articles every January on the anniversary of Rosa Luxemburg's death. Official ceremonies were held to honor her memory as well. She came to represent revolutionary virtue, commitment, and self-sacrifice. Biographers portrayed her as a woman who had dedicated her entire life's work to the cause of revolution, who was willing to go through with a fictitious marriage in order to obtain German citizenship and thereby continue her revolutionary activities in Germany, and who ultimately died for her convictions.

By 1927 Rosa Luxemburg's visual image alone was used to represent the ideal of women's emancipation. Her photograph was featured in many Chinese publications, particularly around March 8.[27] In the rural areas her picture was hung in public spaces, such as the office of the Huaxian Peasant Association at its opening ceremony, as a model of a woman revolutionary, alongside pictures of Sun Yatsen, Lenin, Marx, Engels, and Liebknecht.[28] Over time, new meaning was given to the image of Rosa Luxemburg: she came to epitomize militancy as well. When local conflicts intensified and became violent, hundreds, perhaps thousands of women took up arms for the peasant associations and fought in Rosa Luxemburg battalions.[29]

With the advantage of hindsight it seems curious that the revolutionary government made no significant effort to invent a more Chinese female revolutionary tradition, perhaps featuring Qiu Jin, who later came to be venerated by both Nationalists and Communists as the second most important revolutionary of the 1911 revolution after Sun Yatsen.[30] Like Rosa Luxemburg, she too had been a dedicated woman revolutionary who had defied the old regime and died for her ideals. In some ways she would have been an even more appropriate symbol of female militancy than Rosa Luxemburg because she had consciously identified with the image of a woman warrior. Known for her fondness for donning male attire, riding a horse, brandishing a sword, making bombs, excelling in marksmanship, and downing large quantities of wine, Qiu Jin viewed her decision to become a revolutionary as following in the footsteps of illustrious male heroes in Chinese history and historical fiction, such as Jing Ke (celebrated for making an attempt on the life of the first emperor of China, for which he was summarily executed), Liu Bei and Cao Cao (famous rival heroes in the romanticized Three Kingdoms period, ca. 220–280), and Li Shimin (a founder and great sovereign of the Tang dynasty in the first half of the seventh century).[31]

But the revolutionary leaders in Guangzhou did not show much interest in retrieving the memory of Qiu Jin from history and infusing her image with political symbolism. Although the Nationalist party's Central Women's Department did make a feeble attempt to gather some information about Qiu Jin, and her name was mentioned in passing in the local Nationalist newspaper, *Guangzhou min-guo ribao*, nothing more came of these efforts.[32] This inertia may well have stemmed from a lingering animosity on the part of Nationalist party members for the Restoration Society, a loose-knit revolutionary organization which had collaborated with Sun Yatsen's Revolutionary Alliance party before the 1911 revolution, but later became involved in a contentious factional struggle with Sun's group. Although Qiu Jin had joined the Revolutionary Alliance in Tokyo in 1905, on her return to Zhejiang she became a member of the Restoration Society and conducted her revolutionary activities on its behalf. Once animosities between the Restoration Society and the Revolutionary Alliance came to a head in 1912, Qiu Jin's reputation among Sun Yatsen's clique was tainted.[33]

Qiu Jin's close women friends believed that Sun Yatsen was acting on this animosity when he refused to support the construction of a grand mausoleum to honor Qiu Jin's contributions to the overthrow of the Qing imperial government. Not long after the 1911 revolution, Qiu Jin's friends arranged to have her remains brought back from Hunan, where they had been interred at the site of her husband's family's graveyard, a fate they knew would have been objectionable to Qiu Jin because of her unhappy marriage. They planned to construct a magnificent mausoleum complete with an elaborate epitaph on her revolutionary activities written in the elegant calligraphy of one of her best friends. Just when construction was to begin, however, Yuan Shikai objected to this project on the grounds that it would eclipse the nearby shrine for Yue Fei, the eminent general of the Song dynasty. Qiu Jin's friends believed that they would have mustered enough local elite support to override Yuan's objection had it not been for Sun Yatsen's personal intercession in the dispute.[34]

If Sun Yatsen decided in favor of maintaining male dominance in the realm of symbolism in the 1910s, his own image was increasingly being used in the mid-1920s to imbue the National Revolution and the state-making endeavor with a distinctly male identity. In fact, Sun Yatsen became a more powerful figure in the public eye and for the party after his death than during his lifetime. The tremendous force of his memory as a national symbol was first demonstrated at his funeral in March 1925, when thousands upon thousands of people poured out along the procession route from Beijing to the Western Hills to commemorate his memory, despite the strong opposition of the warlord government to any sort of public demonstration. At that moment Nationalist leaders recognized the tremendous political potential of a purposeful and well-designed effort to enshrine the memory of Sun Yatsen as widely as possible in the public consciousness.[35]

Although the glorification of Sun Yatsen through these means occurred throughout China, Guangdong became the center of this endeavor. His picture was hung everywhere in the city, and even appeared on the currency. Streets, buildings, and parks increasingly bore his name, and the name of Guangdong University in Guangzhou was changed to Sun Yatsen University in 1926. In March of that year the revolutionary government in Guangdong held province-wide commemorations to mark the first anniversary of his death in order to foster the notion that Sun Yatsen was the incarnation of Chinese nationalism. Thus, within a short time this somewhat problematic and not terribly successful politician was converted into the overarching symbol of the nation, the embodiment of nationalism, the father of the revolution. The nationalist revolutionary ideology of the mid-1920s in Guangdong was so strongly imbued with a male identity that it militated against the creation of a full-fledged comparable mother of the revolution from either the international socialist tradition, such as Rosa Luxemburg, or from the annals of Chinese revolutionary history, such as Qiu Jin.

The Organizational Infrastructure of the Women's Campaigns

A Central Women's Department was established by the Nationalist party early in 1924 to oversee the women's mobilization drive for the National Revolution. Although no specific tasks were initially assigned to this department, its general purpose was articulated in the proclamation of the First Party Congress, which pledged to advance the principle of gender equality in the law, economy, education, and society, as well as to promote the development of women's rights.[36] While the basic sentiment of this statement was acceptable to party members, the actual impetus for incorporating a gender plank in the party's proclamation and for creating a women's department came from Mikhail Borodin, the chief Comintern adviser assigned to the Nationalist party. After his arrival in Guangzhou in the autumn of 1923, he had devoted his efforts to drafting a new Nationalist constitution and a reorganization plan for the party along the lines of the Russian Communist party.[37]

The person most responsible for giving explicit meaning to this women's emancipation declaration and organization was He Xiangning, a veteran woman party member who assumed the post of director of the Central Women's Department in August 1924. She held tremendous stature in the Nationalist party in her own right as the first woman to join the Revolutionary Alliance in 1905 and as a member of Sun Yatsen's inner circle in the 1920s. Her legitimacy among Nationalist leaders was further enhanced by her marriage to Liao Zhongkai, one of the most powerful political figures in the Nationalist party and the Guangdong revolutionary government at that time. Moreover, this appointment seemed entirely appropriate because of her long-standing interest in women's rights issues.[38] Indeed, she demonstrated her potential as a future pioneer of the Chinese women's movement even as a child. Inspired by the model of Hakka women warriors in the Taiping Rebellion, she took the extremely unusual action for the daughter of a prosperous businessman in the 1880s of refusing to have her feet bound.[39] This strength of character was again manifested when she was living in Japan as a young married woman and decided to join the Revolutionary Alliance without consulting her husband. When Liao Zhongkai returned from Hong Kong, she persuaded him to become a member as well. For many years thereafter, however, she maintained a fairly low profile in politics, coming back to China from Japan only with the revival of the Nationalist party in the 1920s. By accepting this appointment as director of the Central Women's Department in 1924, He Xiangning for the first time in her political career stepped from the sidelines of her party onto center stage.

During the three years that He Xiangning headed this department, it succeeded in overseeing the social mobilization of large numbers of women for the National Revolution. To this end it not only expanded its organizational networks and developed a core of its own organizers but also coordinated the work of several mass organizations, particularly the communist-run Women's Emancipation Associations and the Peasant Associations, which were also involved in arousing specific constituencies of women for the cause. In Guangdong alone, Comintern advisers estimated in their reports that approximately 113,000 women were mobilized (25,000 workers, 80,000 peasants, 8,000 in the Women's Emancipation Associations).[40] According to Nationalist party records at that time, 1.6 million women joined the ranks of the Nationalist Revolution, which included 350,000 women workers, 150,000 peasant women, and 600,000 women students and "ordinary women" *(putong funü)* nationwide.[41]

These spectacular figures mask the immense difficulties that He Xiangning faced as she tried to breathe life into the Nationalist Central Women's Department in August 1924. Her two predecessors in this position, Zeng Xing and Liao Bingjun, had failed to make the department operational.[42] Although they were highly respected members of the Nationalist party, they were plagued by inadequate financial support from their party. Even though the party had agreed to establish the Central Women's Department at the First Party Congress (January 1924), it failed to commit any funds to its operations. At least some influential members of the Nationalist party, it seems, regarded with disdain the prospect of a full-scale women's mobilization under the auspices of the Women's Department, and preferred to have it remain a nominal organization that primarily held receptions for various women's groups and issued a few press releases.

This lack of financial support ultimately proved so frustrating that He Xiangning took the highly unusual step of mentioning it in her official report to the Second Party Congress in January 1926.[43] But she did not want to wait for this convention before beginning the programmatic development of the women's mobilization campaign. Instead, she prevailed on Mikhail Borodin (through his wife, Tanya) to provide the Nationalist Central Women's Department with an operating budget from certain discretionary funds under his control.[44]

Another serious problem that He Xiangning faced was unifying her staff, which was divided along generational, political, linguistic, and geographic lines. These differences became more pronounced over time as newcomers were added to what originally had been a rather close-knit group. The earliest members were Guangdong women who had been active in provincial women's groups, such as Wu Zhimei of the Guangdong Women's Alliance, or in one of Sun Yatsen's previous political parties, such as He Xiangning and Zeng Xing, who had joined the Revolutionary Alliance soon after it was founded in Japan in the early 1900s. Some members of He Xiangning's staff were in their late thirties or forties by the time of the National Revolution; she herself was forty-six years of age in 1924, when she was appointed director of the Nationalist Central Women's Department. The original core of activists spoke the Cantonese dialect and could not communicate in standard Mandarin, relying instead on a Mandarinized version of Cantonese to communicate with those who came from the north.[45]

The main influx of newcomers came after the May Thirtieth movement of 1925, when the belief that a revolutionary effort might actually succeed became more pervasive and credible. It was at this time that the Chinese Communist party sent a group of its women leaders down to Guangzhou, including two high-ranking women, Deng Yingchao and Cai Chang, who were assigned to work at the Nationalist Women's Department. Politicized during the May Fourth period, both were considerably younger than many of the Guangdong women who were part of He Xiangning's original staff. Deng Yingchao was well known in women's circles for her articles in the *Women's Daily,* and as a founding member of the May Fourth Awakening Society in Tianjin, the Tianjin Women's Rights Association, and the Tianjin Committee to Promote Women's Participation in the National Conference. Cai Chang had become politicized through her involvement in the Xinmin Xuehui (New Citizen's Society) in Changsha during the May Fourth era, but she had very little stature in Chinese women's circles in 1925 because she had only recently returned from five years abroad, where she had studied in France and then in Moscow at the University of the Toilers of the East.

Although Cai Chang technically held the higher-ranking position, as she was a secretary in the Central Women's Department while Deng Yingchao was the secretary of the Guangdong Provincial Women's Department,[46] Deng Yingchao immediately assumed a more visible role in the Nationalist cosmos. Believing that the Guangdong masses could build the revolution in their province under proper political guidance and then serve as the "revolutionary vanguard" for the entire nation, she traveled up and down the province tirelessly organizing municipal and county party women's departments, and eliciting women's support for the National Revolution.[47] She was particularly vigorous in promoting women's activities in Shantou, where she was the keynote speaker for the March 8 rally in 1926, reportedly attended by more than one thousand people.[48] She also published extensively in *Funü zhisheng* (The Voice of Women), the main organ of the Central Women's Department, perhaps because she was assigned to edit it along with Li Peihua, He Xiangning's secretary. She was selected as a delegate to the Second Party Congress in 1926, delivered a detailed speech on the state of the women's movement, and was elected by the Congress to serve as alternate member of the Nationalist party's Central Executive Committee.[49]

When Deng Yingchao spoke of "our party" in her speeches and articles, there was no doubt that she was referring to the Nationalist party. In every article she urged women to support the party because it was leading the revolution, and because through its Women's Department it represented the interests of women.[50] Although she usually refrained from invoking the memory of Sun Yatsen, she did bolster her nationalist message with a strong explanation of the importance of rallying against western imperialism, which she portrayed as posing a constant threat to Chinese sovereign rights, as had been so blatantly evidenced in the Shaji incident.[51]

At the same time, Deng Yingchao did not conceal her communist convictions. She frequently denounced capitalism and called for its overthrow in her articles for Central Women's Department publications. Moreover, she often promoted the communist-sponsored Guangdong Women's Liberation Association as the ideal mass organization, with two-thirds of its members of worker or peasant background, and as the "core organization of the Guangdong Women's Movement."[52] Like most communists of her day, Deng Yingchao placed great stock in the importance of organization, especially the construction of national or provincial organizations. Thus, her identification of the Guangdong Women's Liberation Association as the "core" group signified her aspiration that it would serve as the main force working with the Central Women's Department to unify the many disparate independent women's groups of the province.

The effect of extremely energetic young communist women such as Deng Yingchao on the development of the Central Women's Department and the simultaneous mushrooming of these mass women's organizations throughout the province in the second half of 1925 tilted the entire political climate in Guangdong women's circles toward the left. The increasing numbers of younger, more radical women who had became active in the revolutionary movement often found themselves discontented with the moderate pace and policies of the more senior, established women leaders of Guangdong, including He Xiangning. These young women wanted to politicize gender issues and activate women for the National Revolution on this basis.[53] To them this meant stressing the potentially divisive issues of free-choice marriage, the right to divorce, and the abolition of concubinage and polygamy.

He Xiangning's principal concern in this situation was to prevent the growth of deep divisions in her staff. To this end, she stressed the importance of promoting women's issues in the context of the wider struggle to win the Nationalist Revolution. She did not oppose the more feminist actions of radical women, and she even adopted their boyish bobbed hairstyle.[54] But she chose to place her main emphasis on developing programs that were designed to promote women's practical interests in the new order, such as drafting legal codes to protect women, developing a cadre school, urging the government to hire women, opening up literacy schools, hosting teas for various women's groups that supported the National Revolution, setting up a People's Drama Society, and organizing women's Red Cross units, which would be needed to care for the wounded and work in hospitals once the Nationalist Revolutionary Armies launched the Northern Expedition in the summer of 1926.[55] Thus, even though she was willing to sponsor a resolution at the Second Party Congress in January 1926 explicitly stating that the party had to deal with gender oppression if it wanted large numbers of women to support the revolution,[56] most of her speeches and publications stressed the great importance of women's becoming involved in the revolutionary effort for nationalist reasons.[57]

These views were consistent with He Xiangning's early views on women's emancipation. Moreover, by constructing a moderate role for herself, He Xiangning was able to retain sufficient support of Nationalist leaders for her program. In so doing, she succeeded in building a strong organization with a staff that was able to develop its own agenda, one that embodied two different approaches to mobilizing women but nevertheless was under the control of women.

Although the differences between He Xiangning's and Deng Ying-chao's mobilization strategies were quite striking—one aimed to activate women primarily on the basis of programs designed to overcome women's subordination, the other through programs that essentially stressed nationalist issues—they managed to coexist with relatively few tensions and often proved mutually supportive. No doubt He Xiangning's style of leadership facilitated this compatibility.

The Guangdong Women's Emancipation Association

The nationalist mission of the revolution was reflected in the programs and propaganda of the Guangdong Women's Emancipation Association (Guangdong Funü Jiefang Xiehui), the principal nongovernmental women's group involved in the mobilization campaigns. Founded in early May 1925, it benefited from the strong outpouring of nationalist sentiments generated by the May 30 and Shaji incidents, and within a short time it had attracted several thousand members throughout the province. Its first director, Xia Songyun, from the outset stressed nationalist priorities as a basis for female participation in the association. At times she seemed to conflate issues of women's emancipation with nationalism by arguing that female emancipation could occur only through the consummation of a nationalist revolution.[58]

The intense nationalism that was exhibited in the mobilization activities of this organization in Guangzhou and its environs was matched by a vehement articulation of gender issues. Although this type of mass women's organization was promoted by the Chinese Communist party in many provinces during the National Revolution, only in Guangdong and the neighboring province of Guangxi was the word *jiefang* (emancipation) inserted in its title, signaling its strong May Fourth orientation on women's matters.[59] The founding declaration of the Guangdong Women's Emancipation Association placed much emphasis on May Fourth issues such as marriage reform, improving women's access to education, and granting women legal rights of inheritance and suffrage.[60] During the next two years, branch organizations of the Guangdong association were established in approximately twenty-seven counties in the province and spilled over into neighboring Guangxi. They stirred up a great deal of contention through their zealous promotion of marriage reform issues and their willingness to give strong support to women contesting arranged marriages, for which they earned the derisive epithet of "divorce and remarriage bureaus" or even "high-class brothels."[61]

This organization attracted five thousand women from a wide cross-section of the population during its two years of existence.[62] The founders were primarily young women students from secondary schools such as the Kunwei Girls' Middle School in Guangzhou. A distinguishing characteristic from the outset, however, was the participation of women workers from the "red" telephone operators' union, such as Ma Xiaofen, who was selected to be on the first executive committee.[63] When the Hong Kong seamen's strike was called a few weeks after the May 30 incident, it provided a working-class focus for the mobilization program of the Women's Emancipation Association. Seizing on the fact that over ten thousand women workers and their family members were involved directly or indirectly in the strike, these women activists took to the street to present plays dramatizing the plight of the Hong Kong workers who had dared to resist imperialist pressures. They also organized bands of women students from the various girls' schools to go around to all the shops asking for contributions to the strike support fund.[64] Later, He Yizhi, a member of the executive committee of the association, set up a part-time school for women workers. Over forty students enrolled in the program, which incorporated revolutionary ideas in its academic curriculum.[65]

These successful experiences of raising money or offering classes to women workers were ancillary to the main tasks of working-class organizing. Activists of the Women's Emancipation Association, aided by communist labor organizers and Women's Department personnel, were pleased to see that more than four thousand women weavers, two thousand garment workers, and three thousand women working in match factories were willing to form unions.[66] But according to Communist party reports, women workers in Guangzhou, particularly in the textile mills, were suspicious of party organizers pushing them into unions dominated by men, and which ultimately represented only male interests in most conflicts or negotiations with management. In one instance union leaders succeeded in getting much larger wage hikes for male workers than for women, and throughout paid little attention to the issues that women workers were raising. Moreover, in any conflict between male and female workers the union leadership always decided in favor of the men, with the result that women workers often felt that they would have been better off without a union.[67]

These problems were compounded by the disdain of many male communist labor organizers in Guangzhou for the very idea of organizing women or working with the women's movement. In situations where the work force was predominantly female, such as match production and certain garment trades, efforts to build unions were more successful. But labor organizers for the Chinese Communist party and the Emancipation Women's Association seemed unable to make inroads in organizing the female silk workers in Shunde.[68] No doubt these organizers found it disappointing that the radical marriage practices pursued by some of these women silk workers—delayed transfer marriage, compensation marriage, and sworn spinsterhood—did not predispose them to supporting the revolution.[69] According to Robert Eng, this seeming paradox is explained by the fact that the silk workers of Shunde were under the tight control of the patrilineages of the surrounding villages. While outside labor agitators were thwarted because they posed a distinct threat to the economic power of the patrilineages, unconventional marriage practices were not considered particularly threatening to patriarchal power because the women were still economically tied to their natal families.[70]

Also difficult but more rewarding was the effort of the Women's Emancipation Association to mobilize rural women for the National Revolution. Motivated by a shared commitment to create a new type of society for women in both urban and rural areas, the young urban women activists in Guangzhou recognized quite early that they needed to address the plight of rural women. To what extent their gaze may have been steered in that direction by Communist party officials is unclear, but certainly the successes of Peng Pai in organizing peasant associations in Haifeng and Lufeng counties were well known throughout Guangdong by this time.

Shortly after the founding of the Guangzhou Women's Emancipation Association, its women leaders launched their rural strategy by sending letters to potential organizers in rural areas encouraging them to consider starting up branch associations. Then traveling performers were dispatched to counties such as Meixian, Chaoan, Jieyang, and Denghai in order to attract the interest of illiterate peasant women. The following March, Women's Emancipation Association activists designed an International Women's Day program, which they sent out to various counties.[71] Such activities contributed to the establishment of more than twenty-two branches of the Guangdong Women's Emancipation Association outside Guangzhou between June 1925 and 1926. The first was founded in June 1925 in Haifeng by six women students, for which they earned a reputation as the "six famous stars."[72] By the end of the year, branches had been established in Chaoguan, Meixian, Qiongya, Renhua, Shantou, Shaoguan, Xinhui, and Shunde, and in the next six months another thirteen became operational.[73]

One of the most perplexing problems facing women activists involved in rural communities was identifying an organizational base. They found it difficult to situate a Women's Emancipation Association physically in a rural community because of the shortage of public space available to women. Unlike in the cities, where the women's mobilization campaigns of the National Revolution could readily utilize the resources developed by previous women's groups, there was no recent history of public action by women in most of these rural communities. Deciding that local girls' schools were the preferred site if at all possible, teams of Women's Emancipation Association activists set out to investigate local conditions. Tan Zhushan made a study of Huizhou and found that school authorities of the only girls' normal school in that county were quite hostile to May Fourth notions of female emancipation and ardently held to their belief in the need to develop women into good wives and mothers.[74] Tan found this bias particularly unfortunate because the school contained the largest number of women students in the area; few female students could be found in the county-run elementary school. Without access to a progressive girls' school, Tan clearly despaired about the possibility that the Huizhou Women's Emancipation Association could extend its influence into surrounding towns such as Huishu. To her this rural terrain seemed a bastion of "backwardness," in which communities "stubbornly resisted" ideas about social change, and women's educational level was too low for them to understand what the revolution was offering them.[75]

Women organizers sometimes found that a change in administration at a local school could radically alter their ability to reach young women in a community. In Meixian, for instance, Deng Yingchao was able to use her stature as an official in the Guomindang Women's Department to have Huang Yusheng, a Shanghai woman who had graduated from Xinan University, appointed principal of the Meixian county-run women's normal school. This action, coupled with the simultaneous removal of a problematic official in the local Nationalist Women's Department, allowed for the rapid development of the Meixian Women's Emancipation Association. Within a short time it became one of the most active branches in the province, and even published its own journal, *Meixian funü*.[76] Once women activists were able to gain a foothold, they could be quite effective in implementing their programs of action.

The most active women's associations outside the Guangzhou environs were located in Hakka communities and in areas with high levels of outmigration or with large minority populations, such as Hainan Island. At a grass-roots level there seems to have been little mention of nationalist issues made by these women's associations; rather, feminist programs were emphasized. These associations were often inundated with pleas from women who wished to escape arranged or abusive marriages. These women's petitions were clearly extremely contentious in their communities because they struck at the heart of social life, the marriage contract. If women had the right to decide their own marriages, they were ultimately challenging the basic assumption that they were a form of property. Indeed, from a patrilineal perspective the payment of a hefty bride-price did confirm that assumption. By all accounts these marriage cases taken up by the Women's Emancipation Association, often with the help of the Nationalist Women's Department, caused tremendous strife in local communities. Sometimes women who were granted divorces had to be extricated from their communities with the support of the women's associations and the Nationalist Women's Departments. In at least one case a woman had to be sent all the way to Moscow to attend Sun Yatsen University in order to remove her from a vengeful husband. This effort to change the marriage system posed a fundamental challenge to the patriarchal mode of power in the family.

Gender Issues in Peng Pai's Peasant Movement

The Nationalist Revolution's mobilization of women was also conducted through the peasant associations, which ultimately attracted the largest sector by far of women in the revolutionary forces of Guangdong. At the peak of revolutionary fervor, in mid-1926, as many as eighty thousand women reportedly were involved in the provincial peasant associations, more than fifteen times the membership of the women's associations. Admittedly this number was inflated owing to the common practice of automatically extending peasant association membership to the wives of male recruits. Nevertheless, an examination of female activism in the Guangdong peasant associations indicates that more women were willing to involve themselves in the National Revolution around community and class issues than around feminist issues. In this way the gender orientation of the peasant association programs contrasted sharply with those of the women's associations.

Peng Pai, the foremost communist organizer of the Chinese peasantry in Guangdong, placed much emphasis on involving women in the revolutionary movement. Unlike other male communist organizers of the working class, Peng Pai made a concerted effort to activate women in the organizations he oversaw. In this respect he stood out as one of the Guangdong communist male leaders most dedicated to the proposition of encouraging female participation in the peasant associations. After he rose to a leadership position in Guangdong in 1924, he was influential in implementing this policy as a grass-roots organizer of peasant associations, as the commanding figure in the Guomindang Peasant Department, as director of the Chinese Communist Peasants' Committee, as a leading figure in the Guangdong Peasant Association, and as a teacher and director of the Peasant Movement Training Institute.

As a grass-roots peasant organizer in Guangning, Haifeng, and Fengshun counties, Peng Pai encouraged and even personally recruited women into the cause. When necessary, he was willing to take the time to provide peasant women with explanations of the most basic political vocabulary, such as the meaning of "organize" (zuzhi), a term that stumped Li Jianshen when she first heard Peng speak out on the importance of establishing a peasant association in her village of Baixi. His patient coaching and encouragement was instrumental in Li's decision to assume leadership positions in both her village and district peasant associations.[77]

In 1924 Peng Pai was a critical leading figure in the intense and violent conflict to establish a peasant association in Guangning, an out-of-the-way county in the West River region of the province which was infamous among radical organizers for its "feudal" practices, including higher-than-normal tenancy rates and even virtual serfdom.[78] Although Guangning was not the type of place where high levels of female participation would have been expected, Peng Pai worked with the local student leaders to build a peasant association that claimed the largest female membership in the province—thirty thousand.[79] A significant number of these women were quite active in the building of this peasant association, both in behind-the-scenes supportive activities, such as preparing glutinous rice cakes decorated with the ideographs for "revolution" (geming) for a large meeting of more than five thousand members, and at the center of public occasions, such as the presentation of petitions to Cai Huoping, the county magistrate. When fighting broke out in February 1925 against landlord militia, women worked behind the lines of battle and even participated in the fighting.[80]

Peng initially supported the spread of the women's associations in the rural areas. When women students and workers from the Nanfang weaving factory established the first women's association in the province outside Guangzhou in June 1925, Peng Pai honored the occasion by delivering the inaugural address at its founding meeting.[81] The peasant association in Haifeng, where Peng Pai turned his attention again in early 1925, also reported a significant number of women members, perhaps as many as 1,700.[82]

Ultimately Peng created a peasant organization of unique resilience in this county, one that succeeded in establishing its own soviet government after the collapse of the alliance between the Guomindang and Communist parties in 1927. Significantly, in this time of great crisis, more opportunities opened up for women in leadership and the militia. A few women were elected to important positions in the soviet government, and thousands of women took up arms to fight for the existence of the peasant soviet. Gender issues also came to the fore, with the women's association advocating the abolition of enslaving girl bondservants and the elimination of brothels. At the same time, the peasant association found that 30 percent of the cases being brought to the arbitration department concerned marriage issues, including the sale of wives by their husbands.[83]

Peng Pai's support of women's issues and activism in the peasant movement was often qualified, however, by the practical realities of rural society. As early as 1922, when the glow of May Fourth feminism was still quite bright in the Communist party, Peng Pai encountered a potentially thorny problem for his fledgling peasant association when a six-year-old child bride drowned in a latrine in Chishan, a village in his native Haifeng county. The family she was living with was accused of having contributed to her death by beating her so severely that she lost her balance and fell into the privy. As the girl had been living in the home of a peasant association member, Peng was concerned that any proof of wrongdoing might have a negative impact on his organization. When thirty or so of the girl's relatives arrived in Chishan to press the issue, Peng Pai refused to open the casket and prove that the girl had not been beaten. Rather, he assembled the entire peasant association and finally intimidated the accusers into dropping the charges through his officious manner and the militancy of his group. Afterwards Peng commented revealingly that this incident showed that "powerless men will be tricked" and thus served as living proof of the value of a united peasant association.[84]

Thereafter, Peng Pai exercised caution when dealing with gender issues in the peasant movement. He showed little interest, for instance, in encouraging female enrollment in the Peasant Movement Training Institute, which was established in July 1924 as the main means for extending the reach of the revolution into many rural communities in Guangdong.[85] Although many communists were involved in this school, including Mao Zedong, it was Peng who served as director of the first class and thereafter exerted the most profound and consistent influence over the shaping of the school and the orientation of the curriculum. During its three years of operation, only 30 or so of the 996 graduates of the Peasant Institute were women.[86] The only female teacher on the staff was Li Yichun, a Hunanese communist who was in charge of the singing classes. It was probably difficult to encourage household heads to send female members of their families to attend what was essentially a male-dominated school. Nonetheless, Peng Pai's influence over the peasant associations was sufficiently powerful to elicit a higher number of female applicants if he had been so inclined.

From the little that is known about these thirty female students, most were selected by their peasant associations, and upon graduation went back to their localities. With a few exceptions, they were not inclined to promote feminist issues. The women with a clear interest in overcoming women's social subordination were not assigned to work in peasant associations, but rather were sent directly into the women's associations or into the Guomindang Women's Department, particularly if they manifested any strong interest in gender transformation issues. Gao Tianbo, a member of the first class, found herself assigned to the Guangzhou Women's Emancipation Association, and Zhong Zhujun (1903–1929) primarily worked as a women's association activist after graduation, setting up a branch in Suiqi county.[87] Such practices suggest the intention to restrict feminist influences in the peasant associations.

Even more telling than the small numbers of women students and their assignments was the lack of emphasis on women's issues in the curriculum. In fact, Peng Pai specifically instructed all his male students to desist from spreading May Fourth notions about freedom and equality, and never to fall in love with a peasant woman.[88] Peng's main concern was to avoid any criticism of the arranged marriage system as it was practiced in rural localities. Moreover, his position was shared by other communists involved in peasant work, such as Ruan Xiaoxian, who encouraged young male peasant association members to go along with parentally arranged marriages unless the woman was physically defective. Nor should the men divorce their wives. The widest latitude a May Fourth–oriented organizer could have on this issue was to encourage peasant men to put off agreeing to a parentally arranged marriage until they had met a woman of their own choosing.[89]

Yet, as Peng Pai was only too well aware from his travels through rural Guangdong, for most male peasants the issue was not finding a wife of one's liking but being able to afford a wife. In many localities where Peng Pai organized peasant associations, 50 percent of the male members were not married. And many of those who did marry were able to do so only by arranging for a young girl from a poverty-stricken family to be raised in their home, with the result that the marriage partner was often ten to twenty years younger than the man. From Peng's perspective, these child bride marriages stood as yet another sign of peasant oppression.[90]

Peng Pai could easily empathize with the misfortune of peasant men going through life without a wife, and he even was saddened to learn that they would ask to have wooden plaques placed on their graves with the names of fictitious wives in a last bid for conventionality. Yet he rarely seemed to consider peasant adversity from the point of view of poor women or child brides.[91] Peng Pai's perspective on these issues was consistent with the identity of the peasant associations that was being constructed. Peasant association publications, for instance, were directed at a male audience. The infrequent images of women that were published in these journals tended to portray them as possessions of men. One cartoon featured a landlord using his beautiful wife to bribe leaders of the peasant association.[92] Indeed, it appears that these associations were intentionally imbued with a male identity in order to solidify their legitimacy in the community and increase their acceptability among skeptical local conservative notables. To this end, communist peasant organizers decided in 1925 to coin the slogan "The Nationalist Party is the father, and the peasant association is the son."[93]

In his leadership of the peasant movement, Peng Pai also seems to have steered clear of organizing peasant associations in localities where women dominated agricultural work. Such was the case in Meixian, for instance, which had experienced heavy outmigration of its male population for many years.[94] Although Peng Pai was in charge of the Chaomei regional board which oversaw the Meixian region, no peasant organizer was sent out to that county, despite the protests of women activists in the area who complained that the peasant association leaders were not interested in helping them form an organization because of the preponderance of women peasants.[95] Perhaps Peng Pai was concerned that an existing women's association in the county that was as dedicated to the proposition of gender transformation as the one in Meixian would be a constant thorn in the side of a peasant association, or that the peasant association would develop programs that were not in harmony with those of other associations in the province.

These expedient measures eventually altered the ideas and work styles of the radical leaders themselves, many of whom fancied themselves quite progressive. Peng Pai is a case in point. Whereas in his early days as a peasant organizer he had sought out the opinions of association members about his policies, as his reputation grew, he increasingly adopted a patriarchal leadership style and assumed that his reports and orders would be accepted without question or objection. As he toured the countryside, throngs of peasants would hail him as "the emperor."[96] Even in Guangzhou he was known as "the king of the Hailufeng peasants."[97]

Peng Pai's relationship with his wife over time became increasingly patriarchal as well. The scion of a wealthy landlord Hakka family, he agreed to an arranged marriage but then made a serious attempt to convert the relationship into a more modern marriage. In 1912, for instance, he persuaded Cai Suping, his new wife, to unbind her feet, and he often was seen strolling through the town of Haifeng holding her hand. Later, when he went to Japan to pursue his education, he continually encouraged her in his letters to study, with the result that she acquired a certain degree of literacy. Later, he also encouraged her involvement in the peasant associations as a women organizer, and she seems to have shared many of his activities.

This modern marriage was transformed in December 1926, when Peng Pai invited Xu Bing, a woman student he had met in the Communist party office in Shantou, to move into his home, where Cai Suping was also residing. When Xu Bing accompanied Peng Pai on his trips to Guangzhou and Wuhan, they appeared as a couple in public; but in the rural community where he lived, he cohabited with the two women. Peng Pai may well have reasoned that it was more humane to allow Cai Suping to remain in his household than to subject her to the painful humiliation of a divorce. Moreover, he most likely would have objected to the allegation that he had essentially turned Xu Bing into a concubine. Nonetheless, that is how the arrangement must have been seen by his peasant following, particularly after both women gave birth to children over the course of the next year or two.[98] In any event, this behavior was exceedingly unusual for a high-ranking Chinese communist leader, and it directly contradicted strongly articulated principles in the communist movement opposing polygamy and concubinage.

From the vantage point of the late twentieth century, we can see that the feminist orientation of the women's mobilization campaigns during the National Revolution did not prove durable. The Nationalists' and Communists' subsequent retreat from many of these feminist programs had multiple causes, some manifested during the course of the revolution, others related to fallout from the acrimonious and bloody breakdown of the collaboration between the Communist and Nationalist parties.

From the beginning to the end of the women's mobilization campaign, the feminist agenda was hampered by difficulties arising from within the revolutionary coalition. Although both parties were willing to signal a radical break with tradition in the cultural sphere by extolling the ideal of women's emancipation as an abstraction in many of the new festivals, publications, and theatrical productions, they were reluctant to use their fiscal resources to support the actual mass mobilization of women into active political involvement. Without the initial financial backing of the Comintern through Mikhail Borodin, it is unlikely that the Nationalist Central Women's Department could have sustained the level of vitality necessary for a campaign of that magnitude.

Moreover, just as the effort to create a broad symbolic framework for women's emancipation was hemmed in by a nationalism imbued with a personalistic male identity, so the feminist-oriented women's mobilization campaign was curtailed by the dual operations of nationalism and patriarchy. He Xiangning's need to wrap her Women's Department programs in a nationalistic cloak was clearly echoed by the Women's Emancipation Association in Guangzhou and was paralleled by Peng Pai's conformity with rural patriarchal practices. In spite of these constraints, the implementation of a feminist agenda proved contentious within the revolutionary coalition, particularly in the rural areas, where it was discredited as morally debased.

After the mass mobilization of women came to an end because of the breakup of the alliance between the Nationalists and Communists in April 1927, neither party was willing to repeat the full-scale assault on gender oppression which had occurred in the National Revolution. Both the Nationalist government based in Nanjing (1928–1937) and the Chinese Communist government established in 1949 sought to institute gender policies that preserved a measure of legitimacy, which fundamentally meant maintaining male authority.[99] To some extent, this occurred because the tragic struggle that ensued between the two parties over the next few decades included a propaganda war over the politicization of gender issues. The Nationalists found that the charge of sexual immorality was an extremely effective weapon for discrediting Communist party organizers, particularly women, who were portrayed as sexually promiscuous and a danger to the moral order. The identification of morality as a significant social issue had profound implications for both parties. The Nationalists embraced traditional values and promoted domesticity through its New Life Movement of 1934.[100] The Chinese Communist party also became more conservative socially, even somewhat puritanical, in the 1930s. Much of the original women's program was modified or abandoned, and feminists such as Ding Ling were chastised for their inappropriate emphasis on gender transformation.

The massive demonstration of support for changing gender relations that was manifested in the National Revolution did not go totally unheeded, however. It prompted both the Nationalist and Communist authorities to promulgate new legal codes that granted unprecedented rights to women under the law. Indeed, the Nationalist government's Civil Code, which contained the heart of its provisions on female rights in the new state, and the first Communist marriage regulations, which were enacted in the Chinese Soviet Republic of Jiangxi, were drafted almost simultaneously in 1931. Meanwhile, the outlawed Chinese Communist party kept alive much of the language and rituals of women's emancipation as it continued its efforts at revolution, a factor that was to have an enduring impact on the cultural and social order in China after 1949.

10 | Liberation Nostalgia and a Yearning for Modernity

We were enjoying the midday break for cadres. Yu Shifu, Tang Shan, and I had gathered in our customary spot, the cramped reception office of the Zhenfu Silk Weaving Factory in Hangzhou, historically the silk capital of China. It was the winter of 1985, and, with economic reform in full swing, Zhenfu's reception office often appeared more like the waiting room of a train station, with various people from around the factory running in to use one of the few available phones, or visiting engineers and cadres at Zhenfu for collaborative meetings coming in to grab teacups and thermoses of boiled water. But at this moment, when most cadres were resting after lunch, the office was unusually still.

Tang Shan, an earnest twenty-seven-year-old former prep worker,[1] had recently risen to become the factory's Party Youth League secretary. She had been assigned to take care of my needs. Despite our political differences, and somewhat to my surprise, we were becoming friends. Yu Shifu, then in her late forties, was also a former prep worker. She had managed, some ten years previously, to secure the much less onerous position of factory receptionist. She had succeeded in such an enviable accomplishment through a combination of good fortune, good politics, and good *guanxi,* or connections. As Zhenfu's receptionist, Yu Shifu received visitors, answered the factory's main telephone, and, for a time, looked after me.

Many at Zhenfu gave Yu Shifu the unofficial title of "backbone cadre" in recognition of her long years of devotion to the party. Some said it with admiration and others with a barely perceptible sardonic tone. In the midst of post–Cultural Revolution cynicism, Yu Shifu was perhaps one of the few who stood by the party out of earnest conviction, a belief in the need to serve rather than a will to command power. She still invoked the socialist guiding phrase "Serve the people," and continued to dress in the simple, unadorned blue jacket and pants that signified an earlier era of class politics. No one could have accused her of the increasingly common complaint about party cadres: corruption for personal gain. My own respect for strong political commitments meant that, despite misgivings, I found myself somewhat drawn to her. On her own initiative, Yu Shifu had assumed toward me the position of surrogate mother and ideological guide. When I arrived at the factory in the morning, she offered me tea to ward off the winter chill; she kept a check on my movements and contacts within the factory, and occasionally sang the praises of the party to me.

Over the weeks I realized that Yu Shifu was exerting a great effort to do "thought work" *(sixiang gongzuo)* on me, to educate and convince me, the outsider, about all the positive transformations in China since Liberation. One point on which she held especially strong convictions was the liberation of women in China. "Women and men are equal now in China," she would press on me over lunch, during walks, while we sipped our tea. "Women can go out and work, just like men." "Women have been liberated," she would continue in a slightly anxious and overly eager tone.

I silently disagreed with her, but I always politely nodded my head. I took her comments with an equal measure of respectful intellectual interest and political frustration. Anthropologists have laid to rest the myth of the classic participant-observer who only listens and records.[2] Through numerous self-reflexive descriptions, we have acknowledged that the anthropologist's presence is inevitably a complicated affair of involvement.[3] Yet most recent calls for representing the anthropological encounter portray a dialogue that ultimately culminates in a relation of equitable exchange. Challenging Yu Shifu, I knew, could potentially be a more acrimonious affair.

But that day in the office the strain of anthropological disinterest had grown too great. I decided to engage her. I was moved to do so, in part, through having met a variety of women in the factory who felt themselves capable of far more challenging work than the low-skilled, marginalized positions into which they had been shunted. Also, just the previous day I had been a bemused bystander to a playful argument between Yu Shifu and one of the inspection shop's rakish young men over which sex could claim a more burdensome life, women or men. Yu Shifu, rightfully I thought, claimed that women carried more of the burden, what with shopping, cooking, laundry, and then holding a job as well. Her interlocutor, in the midst of cleaning his bicycle, argued that men had to take care of all the dirty work women would not, or could not, handle. (Cleaning bicycles, not unlike fixing cars in the United States, is considered "men's work.")

Yu Shifu's convictions about women seemed intriguingly contradictory. I decided to be direct. "If women and men are equal," I challenged, "how is it that there are so many competent women in this factory who don't get promoted to be managers?" Yu Shifu replied that women and men are equal but that they are different, and men have qualities more suited to managerial work. I pressed the point, asking bluntly what those different qualities were. She responded that men are stronger than women. Assuming she meant physical strength, I countered that strength does not lead to intelligence. Didn't people in China have a popular saying, anyway, to the effect that those who have brawn do not have brains? Yu Shifu appeared to be without a response. Or perhaps she thought the situation was skidding dangerously close to a breach of the relatively unencumbered social relationship we had built. Whatever the reason, she broke off the discussion. Tang Shan, who had stood watching silently from the sidelines during this interchange, appeared both amused at my comments and slightly appalled at my brazen challenge, which might easily have caused Yu Shifu to lose face.

In the Hangzhou silk factories, where I spent a great deal of time in the mid-1980s, a particular cohort of women workers repeated to me, with much insistence, that the revolution had liberated them. These women were of the generation that had come of age in the factories during the late 1940s and early 1950s. What does one make of these statements? One can easily trace the lines of Maoist feminism through which these women give "voice" to their lives. Certainly that version of socialist feminism legitimized only one way in which women could frame their life stories. As with other forms of discourse, it would be impossible to distinguish the way Maoist feminism "spoke" through these women from the way they spoke about themselves.[4]

Perhaps, then, one should just mark these powerful effects and move on. One might also view these statements from the position of the younger generation of women workers, whose search for a meaningful sense of womanhood has been caught up in the post-Mao rejection of state-induced feminism. Then one might argue that the "truth" of socialist China is that women were never "really" liberated at all.

But can we not find a way to recognize the historicity and particularity of these older women's statements? In what follows I begin to search for possible answers to that question by arguing for an approach that links positionality with knowledge. I begin by situating myself in relation to a genealogy of the question of women's liberation in China as it has been analyzed in Euro-American feminism. A politics of location, insisting that all knowledge is situated, problematizes the objectivist conceit that a transparent reality—Chinese woman, Chinese socialism, Chinese culture—awaits description.[5] It maintains that all descriptions are context bound and historically contingent. Most important, a politics of location clarifies the responsibility of ethnographers—and their readers—to account for the shifting terrain of power and meaning on which the anthropologist and her various interlocutors—often known as "informants" on the one side and "theorists" on the other—strain to communicate with one another.

A genealogy of Euro-American feminist deliberations on women's liberation in China leads one to recognize the need to break up the monolithic category of "Chinese woman." One can then attend more closely to differences among Chinese women as they have been politically and historically constituted. Identities as "women," "workers," or "women workers," far from having an essential sameness for different cohorts of workers, as if resting on a single ontological foundation, have been constituted through divergent systems of meaning.

In the silk factories of Hangzhou, four generations of women workers labored side by side: those who came of age in the 1950s; the Cultural Revolution generation; the post-Mao generation of urban women; and the most recent cohort of young, unmarried women from the countryside. I address only two of these cohorts in this essay: the oldest and the post-Mao urban workers. The vivid contrast between these two groups of women highlights the issues of feminism and representation I wish to explore. In discussing the narratives of the oldest cohort, I situate them not only in the past but in the present, where their stories of liberation take on the hue of nostalgic memories for a period of innocence and heroism. Their "personal" narratives differ markedly from those of the younger generation, who yearn for nothing more than to pursue post-Mao versions of modernity.[6] Acknowledging that the meanings of womanhood and work in China differ by generation allows one to recognize that a history of feminisms exists in China as well as in the United States. This recognition of the contingency of feminisms in both places is inextricably linked to positioning one's own political and intellectual commitments.[7]

Decentering the Interlocutor

My heated engagement with Yu Shifu was not the act of a neutral observer with a disinterested curiosity in the effects of China's process of economic reform on women workers. Rather, my explosive challenge must be positioned within a history of Euro-American feminism and its representations of Chinese women as our political others. That history can be divided into three periods.[8]

From the late 1960s to the mid-1970s, Chinese women held a special place in feminist and socialist writings. During that time western feminists, like male socialists, looked to China as the utopian answer to political dilemmas. Chinese women in this context became heroes. Within a broader feminist framework that criticized the promotion of modernization theories through an emphasis on women's oppression, European and American feminists argued that Chinese women had fought against the oppression of traditional Chinese patriarchy. In the vanguard of revolutionary battles, they had rallied to abolish footbinding and insisted on "free" marriage, "free" divorce, and the right to something called "work."[9] This romanticization of Chinese women may have orientalized them through abstractions about the essence of patriarchy in Chinese tradition against which they were said to be fighting. It nonetheless recognized real agency on the part of Chinese women that, at the time, inspired both white feminists and many Asian American feminists. Euro-American feminist participation in socialist politics may also have partaken of socialism's colonizing gestures, but there was a history of differences that did not reproduce exactly the same rhetorical strategies or textual effects as socialist writings on imperialism and world history.[10]

This earlier romantic period gave way, under the weight of western feminist disillusionment with the left, to a critique of women as caught in the structures of a patriarchal socialist state. Gone were the larger-than-life portraits of Iron Women who held up half the sky. As stories filtered out about the chaos of the Cultural Revolution, feminists situated in the West began another revision of Chinese women's story: women were objects of a communist state that had used women's liberation rhetoric to further its own ends.[11] In this version, Chinese women were still victims, but of a new form of socialistic patriarchal family; they were not liberated by "work" but were instead now doubly burdened by a socialist state's demands. Those women who proclaimed themselves liberated by the Chinese Communist party were perhaps exemplars of ideology's power. As we in the West learned more about the Cultural Revolution and how ideology was seemingly force-fed to "the masses," this explanation seemed reasonable. The idea that women in China had been liberated was then treated by some feminists in the United States as misogynist instrumentality on the part of the state, while others argued that this claim was the state's ideological recuperation of woman as sign of socialist modernity.[12] Given that the role and position of women had seemed to be of central concern to the architects of the Maoist polity, Euro-American feminists felt cruelly betrayed. Perhaps these issues had, after all, merely figured as part of the "rhetoric" of the Chinese state.

My response to Yu Shifu's argument about women's liberation in

China, then, had a long genealogy. My culturally inappropriate behavior clued me in to something I was doing wrong, but what was it exactly? Recent postcolonial critiques of Eurocentric scholarship have led to a third period in which to contextualize a possible answer. Postcolonial scholars have argued that the production of western knowledge about China and other "nonwestern" countries is far from a matter of neutral or objective description. This knowledge is infused with and implicated in the long history of European and American colonialism. The effects of power in this Eurocentric scholarship are evident not just in the content of what is said but also in its relational quality, whereby the assumption of a universalizing narrative of progress (be it Marxism or modernization theory) leads to authoritative statements that represent peoples outside the United States and Europe as unalterably "other" to the West in a dichotomous and fixed relation of difference. This alterity creates a self-referential world in which the West-as-self is the authority of and measure for progress.[13]

Feminists have traced the marks of colonial discourse in feminist recuperations of the "nonwestern" woman (even through claims to sisterhood). In one early definitive piece, Chandra Mohanty argued that, under western eyes, the heterogeneity of female subjects in third world nations is suppressed through the discursive production of the "third world woman" as a singular subject. Women in third world countries, then, never rise above their generality to become subjects of a counterhistory.[14] Aihwa Ong has argued that women in China and elsewhere are often used as "case studies" whose analysis takes as its referent feminist interests as they have been articulated in the United States and Europe.[15] Yet I would also contend that the recognition of Chinese women as subjects, however caught in the web of dominating representations, has been in striking contrast to the nonfeminist literature on China, in which women barely figure.

In light of these critiques, we as western feminists are compelled to reflect on how we have written and spoken about Chinese women. For our writings have arrived at what Lata Mani has called the "age of multinational reception," in which feminist dialogues occur with diverse interlocutors.[16] In what ways, in the earlier periods, did we assume a universal standard for feminism, plopping it down, rather like an ill-fitting hat, onto our diverse objects of study? Through what sorts of representations did we create the truth about the oppressed Chinese woman? In what sense did we make Chinese women our political others? What were the effects of these representations? To what extent did they elide any sense of agency or ineluctably lead to a view of "Chinese women" as a singular noun?

This genealogy of past representations is crucial, not because mea culpas are in order, but because the subject of women's liberation in China continues to cast a long shadow on current research about Chinese women's lives conducted by feminists in the West as well as women's studies scholars in China. Reflecting on the power inherent in the knowledge western feminist scholars have created (and continue to create) is essential for moving toward dialogues between women in China and western feminists in which the latter are not the only legitimate analysts in the conversation.

Most concretely, we feminists must reconsider our encounters with those women in China who continue to insist that they were liberated by Liberation. This question is not of historical interest only, for the issue of women's liberation also reverberates across the post-Mao social landscape in China. Women's studies scholars, women workers, soap opera fans, sexologists, and numerous others have engaged in a reinvigorated debate about the meanings of gender. In what follows, I attempt a reconsideration of the meaning of liberation for the oldest generation of women workers. My approach is but one possible way to bring about an intersection of these debates in China with postcolonial critiques in the United States.

Liberation Feminism and Liberation Nostalgia

As with feminist interventions into socialist politics in the United States during the 1970s, Yu Shifu's analysis of women's liberation in China was similarly a political critique by a certain generation of women, who must be situated historically. These were women who came of age at the moment of Liberation. Yu Shifu began silk work at the age of ten, just prior to Liberation. Her family had moved to Hangzhou, where her father worked in the silk factories. But then her father died, and her mother and three children lived tenuously in the countryside, where her mother worked as a maid for various wealthier families. Yu Shifu returned to Hangzhou with her mother when she remarried but felt uneasy about being dependent on her stepfather, who in any case also earned a meager wage. Through personal introductions, Yu Shifu entered the Zhenfu Silk Weaving Factory to engage in the most difficult and laborious of tasks: spinning the silk thread out of the cocoons.

Yu Shifu entered the factory at a time when women who worked in the few Hangzhou factories in existence were considered "broken shoes," a term for prostitutes and other shameless women who appeared openly on the streets. One male engineer from Hangzhou's Silk Engineering Institute explained: "Women fell into the factory like a horse falls on the battlefield." That is, "if a woman fell into a factory, it was the same as an injured horse—nobody wanted her. They would say she was sexually loose." This, after all, people would tell me of that time, was not the sinful, "modern" city of Shanghai.

This cultural construction of the meaning of work reveals the politics of location through which different feminist conversations begin to intersect and diverge. Western feminists have argued that the Chinese revolution merely reconstituted gender inequality in a different form. But to understand why Yu Shifu might feel liberated by that Marxist revolution, we must turn to the meanings of womanhood and the gendered spatial geographies of the late 1940s and early 1950s, prior to the nationalization of industries in 1956.

At that time silk production in Hangzhou took place almost exclusively in the household. The production of silk was intertwined with the production of family relations. The weaving of silk was "men's work." It was the custom in Hangzhou, I was told, to think that only men could do the weaving. "Custom" thus carried shades of a normalizing practice through which the institutionalization of specific knowledge about gender and labor allowed arbitrary arrangements to appear natural. Silk weaving was the medium through which the ideological possibility of "autonomy" was created—for men. Or, rather, for a man as head of a household cum small business whose labor he represented as if congealed in his own by being the one who had the "skill" of weaving and who went "outside" the family to sell the finished cloth. Men in this way achieved not only a skill but, through it, the project of manhood.

A significant part of the labor in Hangzhou's family workshops was women's preparation of the silk thread for weaving. Location also shaped the meaning of these activities for women, but in the opposite sense than for men. Women's home-based activities were not a statement of autonomy, for women and men construed women's location "inside" to be eminently natural. Women and men understood female gender identity through a dichotomy of "inside" *(li)* and "outside" *(wai)*. Although women were obviously engaged in "labor," this was not the category through which people conceived of womanhood.

This inside/outside dichotomy was not unique to silk producing households nor to Hangzhou. Margery Wolf has succinctly summarized this dominant ideology of appropriate womanhood in pre-Liberation days: "Only women who had gone out of the family and were therefore outside the rules of respectability appeared openly in the streets. These were the beggar women, the slave girls, the prostitutes, the vendors, the servants. Few women, no matter how close to starvation, made the decision to go out easily, for there was no going back."[17] The ability to remain "inside" was thus intimately tied to one's class standing and its attendant resources.[18]

Women sought to remain "inside" as a spatial statement of virtuous femininity. But the contrast of "inside" and "outside" that marked appropriate activities for women did not necessarily refer to the literal physical structure of the home. More stress was placed on the importance of remaining within an "inside" social sphere in which women interacted only with other family members and not with strangers. Inside/outside divided tasks within the household workshop into those done within the social sphere of the home and those that entailed external social contacts. Inside/outside also meant working in a family workshop, which was "inside," versus doing prep work in a factory, where women could be seen by strangers.[19]

The interpretation of inside/outside was thus not homologous with a dichotomy that opposes "family" to "work," for women's "inside" activities were not construed primarily in relation to motherhood or caring for a family or doing housework. Older women in the silk factories freely admitted, without any sense of shame or regret, to not having taken care of their children in that period. Yu

Shifu spoke of those days when they were child laborers in the factory not as a time of lost mothering—or alternatively of a lost childhood—but as a time when their relationship to their mothers was structured through location in the factory.

If women's activities "inside" the household workshops were not construed through an elaboration of "home" and motherhood, neither were they opposed to the category of "work." Those women who prepared the thread "worked," they just did not engage in labor outside the home. But if labor inside the home maintained both female and family honor, or social face, labor outside the home degraded a woman and her family. This sense of shamed womanhood was the cultural context from which Yu Shifu and other women of her generation were interpellated, or caught up, in the new Marxist discourse on work.

Chinese Marxism, of course, cannot be separated from ideas about the nation and nationalism. In the colonialism of the early twentieth century, western imperialists in China cast "her" as a feminine, weak counterpart to the masculine strengths of heroic western nationhood.[20] The language of gender became central to the way people in China have defined their modernity. In the writings of early republican reformers, raising the status of women and strengthening the nation were presented as inseparable projects. In the language of the reformist discourse, the subjugation of Chinese women came to symbolize the subjugation of China in the world of nations. The Chinese Communist party developed its politics within this context. It fought to strengthen the nation in part by emphasizing the need to strengthen women's position within it. In a Marxist framework, this meant constructing a new sense of womanhood in relation to a category called "work."

With the 1949 revolution, the socialist party-state began to institutionalize a different set of oppositions through which to evaluate Chinese womanhood. In place of an understanding of woman as tied to a sociospatial relation of inside/outside, the party-state put a new measure of importance on women's relationship to "work." In a discourse that soon became the official and dominant one, "work" was itself constructed as a new category: activity that produced surplus value for the state, acknowledged with a wage. Of course, certain activities became valued as "work" and not others. Activity in household workshops became petit bourgeois labor, privatized and opposed to the state.

Women were said to have been enslaved by domestic chores and could be emancipated from that bondage only through participation in "work." This party-state representation was not a straightforward description of women's realities but an interpretation of them. It recast womanhood in several important ways. By introducing "work" into the category "woman," it redefined proper women as those who worked. They were not simply their husbands' dependents. Moreover, women performed labor in the workplace, along with men. This interpretation of women and labor has its contradictions, as American feminists have pointed out. Yet Yu Shifu and other women of her generation embraced these new subject positions presented to them. Yu Shifu quickly joined the party and became part of the production of this discourse, for she could then switch the terms of pride and shame, invert the social bottom and top, and shift the grounds for interpreting the meaning of her place in a silk factory—from a "broken shoe" who had transgressed the gendered inside/outside spatial dichotomy to a revolutionary "liberated" woman. Now, Yu Shifu was no longer a fallen woman but a worker, and workers were rhetorically praised as the most progressive urban class.

Many of these women workers called on their newfound subjectivities as workers to challenge local gender relations and the conservatism—only recently discovered as such—of Hangzhou. Not all women of Yu Shifu's generation agreed with this analysis or took up this new subject position. Those who had been shaped by laboring "inside" family workshops, later labeled as petit bourgeois, and those of intellectual and capitalist family backgrounds were positioned differently in relation to the power of what quickly became hegemonic cultural representations. Women assigned the latter class labels, for example, became the targets of repeated political campaigns to divest them of their privileges and purportedly unrevolutionary consciousness. Thus, I am delineating the cultural work history of a relatively small group of women within a specific cohort.

One can never overlook the fact that these interpretations of work and gender were produced through the state. Yu Shifu's feminism and her sense of self were the products of a discourse on what Tani Barlow has called the "national woman" (funü).[21] Barlow has argued that the revolution resituated Chinese women inside the state under a Maoist inscription. Women could be represented *as women* only through the state's Women's Federation. That is, the socialist state in China, in marked contradistinction to the state in the United States, colonized and produced feminism. The "national woman" became the only viable feminist under Maoist politics. She was a revolutionary who had reached an elevated status through commitment to class politics and wholehearted support for state policies.[22]

In the post-Mao era, younger generations of women have heaped disdain and loathing on the Women's Federation version of the political woman, distancing themselves as far from it as possible. Nonetheless, one would do well to remember that any reduction of Yu Shifu's embrace of this feminist politics to something like "patriarchal manipulation" only reproduces the very problem of ahistorical feminisms I have delineated in this essay. It would be more fruitful to trace the complex interplay between this official discursive production and Yu Shifu's own history, a task beyond the bounds of this essay.

One must also bear in mind that the interpretation by Yu Shifu and others of her generation who came of age inside the factories of the 1950s were stories related to me in the mid-1980s. They constituted a set of memories, a reconstruction of the past framed, as memories always are, in relation to the present. They were told to me when economic reform in urban areas had just begun to erupt in full force. With economic reform, workers have become decentered and displaced as heroes of the nation. No longer the bearers of a revolutionary consciousness, they have been newly mythologized as a quite different sort of cultural artifact. Workers have become, in the political imaginary, a category of person marked by what they lack. They lack productivity, efficiency, incentive, knowledge, and all the markers of the "modern" worker. They are portrayed as the drag on the Chinese nation's will to modernity. The discourse of economic reform has led to a coherent and commonsensical mode of understanding that workers can be grasped only as subjects whose consciousness, whose very being, is motivated by economics divorced from political goals, indeed from any view of social relations they might hold. Any sentiment expressed by workers is construed in these terms by managers, state bureaucrats, and the media. Workers are captured metonymically, but also in their literal physicality, through measurement and calculation, as displayed in gigantic productivity charts hanging over their heads.

It is widely held, both in the United States and in China, that this is the essence of what a Chinese worker is "really" all about. This essence is said to derive partly from history: the chaos of the Cultural Revolution is said to have taught workers those unconscionably bad habits of foot dragging. But at the same time, this description is offered as the ahistorical truth about workers, one obscured by Maoist politics. Workers in China no longer have any ideological ground on which to claim a special place in the tale of national progress.

This is the context in which Yu Shifu and others told me their life stories. They drew portraits of themselves as heroes who had eaten much (gendered) bitterness. "Eating bitterness" had been a narrative trope much used by the state to signify the exploitative days before Liberation. Their picture of themselves as those who fought against prior assumptions about the natures and proper places of women and men, who stood at the forefront of the nation's hopes and dreams for the future, took on the distinct hue of nostalgia. The nostalgia resonated in the way they framed the present as an experience of loss—a loss of anachronistic frames of reference that had featured them in the center.

Their nostalgia was a complicated affair. Several dominant strains of nostalgia for the 1950s could be detected amidst the fanfare of economic reform. There was the nostalgia for the 1950s as a moment of innocent idealism. One could believe in the possibilities of the new state before the various political upheavals turned the idealism into sour cynicism. One could feel unified, whole, at one with the nation. One could engage in self-sacrifice in good faith. This form of liberation nostalgia is evident in a number of intellectuals' memoirs and courses through Yu Shifu's story as well. Then there is the hegemonic nostalgia of the state, put forth as a desire to return to the high rates of productivity the economic experts found in the 1950s. No human subjects figure in this picture.

Yu Shifu and others weave these strands into a marginalized but potentially resistant strain of nostalgia. With nowhere to turn in the current moment, no location from which to speak with any pride, these workers of the oldest generation turn to their memories as the only thread that leaves a trace of more complex selves, of selves who belong in the nation as socialist subjects because they have spoken bitterness and therefore deserve recognition. Let there be no misunderstanding. Yu Shifu, as a loyal member of the party, wholeheartedly supports economic reform. It is precisely the contradictions in her position that give rise to nostalgia. One can no longer speak the bitterness of workers which she has spoken and have it lead anywhere but to the past.

Yet rather than treat Yu Shifu as a product of state ideology whose fractured consciousness is apparent to the western observer—that is, rather than conclude that her remarks are not the "real" feminism and that she is the "informant" to my western feminist analysis—I argue for an alternative, postcolonial gesture: the recognition of the existence of and possibilities for various feminisms, both Chinese and U.S. Different generations of thought exist, in China as well as in the United States, about what counts as feminism. If we western feminists are to grant historicity to our own feminisms, we should recognize the historicity in Chinese women's voices as well. Moreover, we need to recognize the heterogeneity of Chinese women's subjectivities so as to decenter the Chinese woman as she has been created by white western feminists and by the Chinese state. Yu Shifu, then, is not my informant, but an analyst and producer of feminist discourse in her own right, someone with whom I might, in fact, disagree. My argument with her, in one sense, then, is predicated on respect for her position, even as my aggression was misplaced and my sense of Pyrrhic victory overdetermined.

Yearnings for Modernity

Yu Shifu's is one generational voice among several in China speaking about gender, difference, and inequality. Tang Shan, who was listening to our argument that day, is two generations younger than Yu Shifu. She vehemently disagrees with the feminist position Yu Shifu takes, as she confided to me some time after my outburst. Her discomfort was not at the content of my words but at the manner of my performance. For Tang Shan is of a generation now marginalized in a women's industry and further marginalized as a worker in a period that celebrates intellectual labor.

Tang Shan and others of her generation, who reached adulthood at the end of the Maoist era, have come of age as the Chinese state has ushered in a new imaginary, or symbolic vision, of political economy better known as economic reform. This vision is impelled by two goals of the party-state: to erase the Cultural Revolution and the Maoist politics and ideology of which that revolution was, retrospectively, the culmination; and to attain new levels of wealth and power that will speed China along the road to that ever elusive goal of something called "modernity," whose shifting ground of meaning is caught up in the global stakes of national and multinational political and economic power.

I arrived in China in 1984, just as the state was beginning to institutionalize this vision in urban areas. Much of my time was spent on the shop floor of the Zhenfu Silk Weaving Factory, in Hangzhou, where I learned about the changing discursive constructions of women's bodies and women's subjectivities in the silk industry, which over the previous decades had gradually shifted from men's work to women's work. In the winter of 1991 I returned to China and Zhenfu to renew old ties and to discover what had changed in the lives of the women workers I had known.

One day, while I was in the factory, Xiao Bo burst into the reception room and threw her arms around me. We hadn't seen each other since the end of 1986. Four years had passed. She was wrapped in a glorious fur coat, full of the high energy and laughter I remembered. We spent the afternoon catching up. When I knew her last, Xiao Bo had been the leader of the A shift in the Number Two Prep Shop at Zhenfu. Twenty-three at the time, Xiao Bo had been quite young to supervise a group of about fifty women. But the shop supervisor had promoted her not only because she was a diligent prep worker, skilled at knotting silk threads. She also represented the youthful body so admired by the current economic reform state for its potentially high production capabilities. The older bodies of Yu Shifu's generation, their skill notwithstanding, would no longer do for the state's new regime of high productivity. Nor would the Cultural Revolution generation of workers suffice, for they still talked back to any managerial authority, having learned their political lessons well in the Cultural Revolution. Borrowing from Maxine Hong Kingston, one could describe them as "outlaw knotmakers."[23] But Xiao Bo, having come of age after the Cultural Revolution, was not. During the time I spent at Zhenfu, I would sometimes follow her around as she took on the shift leader's double load of fixing production problems and disciplining workers. Xiao Bo was always quick with her tongue, and her temper regularly flared as invariably the Cultural Revolution group of workers hanging around off the shop floor ignored her calls to return to their positions. Workers of the oldest generation also sloughed off her attempts to appear as an authority figure. They demanded the respect due their long experience and seniority—and thus demanded a lack of supervision. Xiao Bo, even as she diligently went around knotting broken silk threads and changing overfilled spindles, would voice her frustrations to me about her lack of success on the job. Always she blamed herself and her lack of ability. Doing silk work, she also lamented, meant eating bitterness. Xiao Bo and other workers who invoked the sense of eating bitterness did not refer to a pre-Liberation past. They had turned its meaning around to imply a criticism of the present.

Xiao Bo and others of her generation had come of age in a 1980s social landscape whose topography only dimly resembled that of earlier eras. Now the dominant vision of economic reform is to recast workers' bodies so that they will become more "productive" and "efficient." Intellectual labor has become much more highly valued than the "mere" execution of ideas, and the division between mental and physical labor has grown even greater than in the past. This mental/physical hierarchy is refracted through a long history of social mobility in China through intellectual status. Juxtaposed with this image of workers as in need of raising their productivity is another state-produced image—that of the individual. The abandonment of the Cultural Revolution's class politics and the creation of the individual subject are part of the same state project. Differences in people's social positions are therefore held to be the result not of structural inequalities among social groups but of the ability and willingness of individuals to apply their talents.

The meaning of doing silk work has consequently changed. Prior to economic reform, silk production work was still one of the most highly skilled jobs in Hangzhou. But it no longer has the flash of the electronics industry or nuclear power plants, which stand as icons to modernity. Since the early 1980s, no urban working-class youths have come to work in Hangzhou's silk factories. Factory cadres now recruit poor peasant women in remote mountain areas of the province. Silk production work is now construed as unskilled physical labor.

The gendered signification of job tasks has also shifted, as those tasks considered manual labor—weaving, preparation of the thread, and inspection work—are increasingly considered to be women's work. One party cadre at Zhenfu defined these tasks as boring, of low skill, but requiring energy. Women are said to have the requisite patience to accomplish these tasks, to complain less than men about boring work, and to have nimble fingers, which, according to this biopowerful technique for reconstructing women's bodies, uniquely suits them to silk work.

This is the context in which I met Xiao Bo as a fiercely hardworking woman who labored at tasks she thought of as bitter. When I first knew her, Xiao Bo, though of marriageable age, was in no hurry to tie *that* knot. The union representative for the prep shop and the woman in charge of birth planning both teased her, but Xiao Bo was biding her time. On my last visit Xiao Bo caught me up on both her marriage and her transition to motherhood. She described the kind of husband she had sought—one who was more even-tempered than she and who would let her have the last word whether she was right or wrong. She spoke of the birth of her child and the fact that she was on an extended maternity leave. I wondered if there had been complications with the birth, for she had already taken more than three months over the six months allotted for maternity leave.

But Xiao Bo was visibly pleased with herself for having stayed out of the factory for so long. Rather than comment on possible health problems, she spoke about the bitterness of silk work. She confided that her leave had run out but she had no plans to return. "What if someone from the factory pressures you to go back?" I asked. She rolled her eyes to the ceiling in mock innocence. "Well, I guess I won't show up and then they will have to remove my name. I won't count as a person in this work unit anymore."

"But what will you do?" I persisted, knowing that abandoning the lifetime security of a state-run factory job also meant giving up one's food rations and child supplements.

"Stay home as long as possible," was her answer.

Perhaps the economic reform state's most effective denunciations of the Cultural Revolution—and most pressing calls for greater efficiency to produce modernity—have been through discussions of the nature of women and men, for it is on this terrain that the party-state can convincingly claim that Maoist politics—in all of its aspects—overturned the "natural" order and that state leaders and managers now in power are simply turning the world right side up. Their naturalization of their specific vision of the body politic has revolved critically around gendered natures. The Maoist state proclaimed women's liberation as the sign of China's qualifications for entrance into advanced nationhood in a western-dominated neocolonial world order. Thus, reform significations of gender have been posed in opposition to Cultural Revolution heroics about women holding up half the sky.[24]

Ideas about biology have become central. Biology is inescapable and determines capabilities. This has replaced the emphasis on social explanations for women's oppression prevalent in the Maoist era. Much fun has been made of the "Iron Women" image of the Cultural Revolution, an icon now used to reduce Maoism to the claim that women should be like men in every respect.[25] This production of knowledge that biology is inescapable is tied to the notion that individuals should engage in those activities for which they have the most biological talent. This has meant that women are becoming more strongly tied to domesticity and motherhood. Women's activities in the home are no longer condemned as feudal social arrangements. Rather they are said to be a natural expression of the female self.

Women workers' self-perceptions have emerged in relation to hegemonic images of laziness, productivity, the individual, silk work as physical and demeaning labor, motherhood, and marriage. This is not one coherent discourse but a field of intersecting and competing discourses, in which these images serve as signifiers whose referents, or cultural meanings, are continuously contested.

Xiao Bo was not alone in her movement into the subject position of mother. Others who took leave and then returned were congratulated by their sister workers for their ability to stay out of the factory so long. These women have placed themselves in opposition to the state's ever encroaching reach on their bodies to make them more efficient at production. By certain western feminist standards, this generation's embrace of motherhood is not in "women's interests." But before one judges their actions, it is critical to appreciate that this generation has come of age with a legacy of forty years in which the state has claimed and defined feminism, mainly through the Women's Federation. Most workers in the silk factories of Hangzhou, schooled in political thought work through various campaigns, have become cynical about the state and thus reject the grounds of feminism as those of official discourse. To search for the seeds of feminism in China by recognizing only demands for careers, intellectual achievement, and individual equality—demands that most resemble the needs of white, middle-class women in the United States—is the kind of colonialist gesture I believe we must move beyond.

These women who embrace motherhood and reject productivity are voicing their resistance to the state and attempting to wrest from it some measure of control over the definition of their bodies.[26] They do so, as do various women in the United States and elsewhere, by embracing and rejecting available subject positions. If the state is increasingly ordering work and work life, women workers have thrown up motherhood and family life as barricades. The state, of course, is involved in the disciplinary regimes of femininity. But motherhood is a floating signifier that women workers—as well as state cadres—struggle to pin down in various ways. If the official language of feminism has been discredited as a means for social change, these women workers are nonetheless stitching together a patchwork of creative alternatives from the experiences of their daily lives.

But there is one more wrinkle to my story. For if class positioning fundamentally depends on gender, and if their discursive interrelationship varies historically, then it is also important to realize that women's positioning in relation to them varies within any one time period. To return to the contemporary period of economic reform, women's construction of their subjectivities in relation to work and family depends on what kind of work they do. Women who are managers in the silk industry are positioned in a somewhat different relation to these official discourses than are women workers. If women workers were trying to prove they could not be good workers by insisting on their womanhood, women cadres were attempting to demonstrate their capabilities as good managers by showing that biology and family did not hold them back. With economic reform, managerial positions were once again highly desired, even more so now that they more clearly represented intellectual status.

One such female manager was a woman I call Huang Lin. Huang Lin was in her mid-thirties when I knew her and had become Zhenfu's only female technician. The child of a middle school teacher and thus an "intellectual youth," Huang Lin had been assigned to work in a silk factory during the Cultural Revolution. She became a weaver, assuming she would be a worker for the rest of her life. But just after the Cultural Revolution she managed to test into Shanghai's Textile Engineering Institute.

With her recent college degree, Huang Lin had a certain standing in the factory. She was chosen to take one of the coveted places on a trip planned to Como, Italy, to buy ten new shuttleless looms for Zhenfu. As one of the few young "intellectuals" on the trip, she had been asked to serve simultaneously as technician and translator, using English. I thus became her English tutor for several months in the winter of 1986.

We met each day, but only after the first month did I learn that Huang Lin had recently given birth. When I first met her, in fact, she had just returned to work after a maternity leave she had cut short after learning of her trip to Italy. Among our efforts to practice the English words for everyday problems about food, lodging, and travel, we spoke of how she juggled child care and household responsibilities with her job. Huang Lin insisted, matter-of-factly, that child care did not interfere with her work. She had hired a full-time, live-in maid *(baomu)*, who cared for her baby all day. This, despite the fact that Huang Lin's salary, at the bottom rung of the cadre scale, did not yet exceed that of most workers and her maid's wages took up most of it. But what of household chores, I wanted to know. Surely they must take time away from work. "No," she replied easily, "I have a washing machine."

Huang Lin was in a situation not much different from that of Xiao Bo, who had prolonged her maternity leave. Unlike her, however, Huang Lin had raced back to work as soon as was culturally forgivable (that is, after the thirty days in which women are supposed to stay at home so as not to catch ill winds). And unlike Xiao Bo, Huang Lin sometimes skipped the breast-feeding hour, studying English with me instead. The difference in their approaches was obviously due to the different burdens and rewards associated with the kinds of work they did in the factory. Class differences thus make gender a complicated affair, as women like Huang Lin attempt to ignore or maneuver around popular conceptions of motherhood even as they submit to the discipline of work.

I began this essay with a quandary of representation for western feminists writing on women in China and in other countries ideologically constituted as "nonwestern": how do we begin to move beyond the categories and modes of analysis that can make this writing slip into orientalism? Is there a way to engage with the so-called other while simultaneously trying to break down the western self/nonwestern other dichotomy?

The answer is not for Euro-American feminists to cease writing and speaking. As Chandra Mohanty has insisted, western feminist work on women in third world countries is essential for combating western solipsism.[27] Rather, I have argued for a double, and linked, practice: to pull apart this entity, "the Chinese woman," as a unified subject, and then to hold that in tension with a refusal to establish a unitary standard for feminism and, by extension, liberation.

Attention to the historicity of knowledge led me to begin by positioning my own voice within the various paths American and European feminisms have taken as they have constructed Chinese women, first through a socialist agenda and then through a post–Cultural Revolution politics of nostalgia. The beginning, then, of a path toward postcolonial discourses about women's lives in China is to decenter the voices of western feminism through situating their/our knowledge. Recognition that there is no privileged "we," no position of authoritative observer in this world, must infuse all current work. There is no one recognizable subject position called feminism, especially not in a world of transnational, criss-crossed flows of commodities and values. Western feminist voices need to be marked as but one voice among others.

In breaking up this "we" of the West, those of us who write from a western feminist position must recognize the politics of location that involve shifting positions and subjectivities both on the part of women who live in the United States and on the part of women who live in China. Toppling the figure of "the Chinese woman," as I have tried to do, is critical for moving toward a postcolonial feminist analysis. I have argued that there is no one fixed space from which all Chinese women speak in a sovereign voice. Rather, I have tried to disrupt that category by arguing that Chinese women stand in a variety of generational and class positions which have been discursively articulated in history. Those who, like Yu Shifu, were located in urban factories at Liberation embraced a Marxist ideology of women's liberation that indeed changed their place in a new social order. If their voices later came to represent a state whose feminism has been caricatured by a younger generation, western feminists would nonetheless do well to remember parallels in the history of American feminism, in which current notions of labor and race have led many to reject earlier feminist truths about women and work.

To move in the direction of postcolonial feminist ethnographies, those of us who write from the position of western feminism must open up a new textual geography of situated feminisms by engaging in dialogues that move in diverse, and sometimes conflicting, directions. The choice is not between one stance of authoritative feminism and complete silence. The point is rather to have multiple conversations in which western feminists are not the only analysts in the room.[28]

My emphasis on the agency of women in China is far from a denial that relations of gendered domination continue to exist there. It is within a context in which that point has been hammered home over the past decade and a half that I advocate choosing a different angle of vision. I stand even further from a relativist claim that disallows cross-cultural feminist agendas. Recognition of the inextricable links between knowledge and power is not relativism. This is, however, a call to abandon the dangerous fantasy that North American feminists can establish a unified analysis for the global situation of women. Alliances must be created—requiring continuous negotiation and dialogue—with those in China evolving new forms of feminism in the post-Mao era who may strongly reject what constitutes feminism in the United States.[29]

Yet precisely because these multiple conversations are situated, the power of representations in these dialogues must be continually recognized. Feminist dialogues are exchanges that occur in a global political and cultural economy, one dominated by the United States. Moreover, feminist debates are engagements with interlocutors who have diverse histories as active readers and activist producers of knowledge. The production of feminist knowledge thus moves both in and out of texts through a committed political agenda about power and inequality that must speak itself both through and about these issues.

Dual and conflicting risks exist in a position that lacks engagement with other voices, on the one hand, and in one that assumes an overly familiar appropriation of those voices, on the other. The commitment to navigate these dilemmas means a commitment to struggle with western feminists' projections onto Chinese and other nonwestern women. It means reflecting on the effects that fieldwork can have on one's perspective. And it calls for striving to write feminist ethnographies that can take into account the diverse conversations by and about the sexes in different fields of power; the local, national, and transnational contexts of various interlocutors; the disciplinary assumptions of anthropology; the institutionalization of area studies in the West; and the location of various feminist political practices. No position anyone takes up will be pure. I think, however, that the stakes of politically engaged feminist dialogues are worth fighting for.

11 | The Origins of China's Birth Planning Policy

Since 1980 China's strict birth limitation policy has become one of the most notorious ever enacted in the People's Republic. The attempt to limit most couples to only one child provoked comment and controversy worldwide, and contributed to a broad-ranging debate about the politics, economics, and ethics of state-enforced birth limitation directives. As part of that debate, commentators have attempted to situate the policy in a historic context, usually by summarizing a widely accepted view of how the family planning program evolved. That history relies heavily on political and economic factors that led to several changes and reversals in China's policy prior to the 1970s. It also focuses on how a few key leaders in Beijing had complete power over the family planning agenda. Mao Zedong is blamed for opposing family planning and birth limitation until the population problem grew very severe, and Zhou Enlai is given credit for pushing for a strict birth limitation campaign beginning in the early 1970s.

When this standard narrative of China's family planning policy is viewed comparatively alongside the histories of reproductive rights movements elsewhere, three elements are especially striking. The first is the powerful role of the state in fashioning a birth control policy and the conscious link between collective economic goals and birth control programs. The second is the apparent marginalization of women within that process. Whereas individual women and women's movements figure prominently in the evolution of such policies elsewhere, they do not appear to exist at all in the Chinese case, except as objects of state regulation and control. Third, like birth control initiatives elsewhere, the Chinese initiative was, and remains, extremely controversial and hotly contested. Unlike the struggles elsewhere, however, the struggle in China is not interpreted as one in which women position themselves against the state. Instead, the terms of debate are understood to be ideological and policy issues among revolutionary state actors. Women's sovereignty over their own bodies is muted, while elite struggle over the direction of socialist transformation and development looms large.

This absence of women from any meaningful role appears compelling in the context of the 1980s and 1990s, when the state-mandated program of contraceptive use and strict childbearing limits placed enormous burdens on women of childbearing age and took reproductive decisions out of their hands. The Chinese program, viewed from a distance, seemed to be a chilling reminder of what can happen when women forfeit personal sovereignty to an oppressive state. By focusing relentlessly on this relatively recent turn in China's policy, however, we make two serious mistakes. First, we infer from current policies that women have had no historic role in shaping China's birth control policies, and second, we interpret the absence of an overt women's struggle against state policy as confirmation of women's marginal role in the policy process.

The purpose of this essay is to consider the role women have played in the construction of China's family planning program. I argue that the standard history obscures the role played by women in early struggles to gain access to birth control. On the policy level, women fought for a reversal of the early pronatalist policy that severely limited access to any form of birth control. Given the revolutionary character of Chinese politics in the 1950s and 1960s, however, that was not enough. The policy of allowing access to birth control and promoting fewer births had to be secured from assault by those who opposed it on ethical or political grounds. The construction of such a theory, the second level of struggle, was crucial to policy formation and implementation. Yet this very act of theory construction eventually became the mechanism by which women were subjected to tight regulation by the state. Chinese women were not simply the objects of a changing state attitude toward the need for birth control; their need to link up policy preferences to a defensible political argument produced unintended consequences—new and stricter forms of state control.

Origins of China's Birth Control Policy

When the People's Republic was established in 1949, the Chinese Communist party faced the immediate tasks of completing political consolidation, restoring social order, and reconstructing the economy. Unlike previous rulers, however, the CCP was committed in victory to a second revolution—the transformation of China's backward, agrarian society into an advanced socialist society. In Marxist-Leninist terms, the first steps toward that goal were the destruction of class relationships that had prevailed in traditional China, the expropriation of private property on behalf of the proletariat, the transformation of the agricultural sector along socialist lines, and the extraction of the rural "surplus" to fuel urban industrialization and development. In practical terms, however, the first step was to provide a basic level of subsistence for more than 500 million people.

Outside China, many observers were skeptical about the ability of the CCP to accomplish the basic goal of feeding its people.[1] Mao's response was to condemn this "pessimistic view" as reactionary, Malthusian, and "utterly groundless," and to insist instead that China's large population was a great asset.[2] Although this aggressive public stance no doubt hid some private anxieties, in 1949 Mao Zedong was basically confident that, absent the class exploitation, foreign imperialism, and bureaucratic corruption that had burdened previous regimes, the new people's dictatorship could feed, clothe, educate, and gainfully employ China's growing population while simultaneously maintaining a high rate of investment in social and economic development. Between 1952 and 1957, however, three factors converged to bring about a fundamental policy reversal. The first was pressure from women to expand access to contraceptive methods and loosen restrictions on abortion and sterilization. The second was the movement toward a comprehensive economic planning process, which required some means of measuring the size and the rate of growth of the population. The third was increasing anxiety about economic expansion and performance, particularly in the agricultural sector. Of these three factors only the third has been examined closely for its influence on policy-making and policy evolution during this period. The role of women and the impact of the development of the central planning system have been neglected.

Women and Contraception

For Mao Zedong and the other senior leaders of the CCP, the only real population issue in 1949 was the macro one: whether population growth would outpace food production and retard economic growth. For women within the CCP, however, there was another population issue: whether or not they would have control over childbearing decisions, including access to contraceptives, sterilization, and abortion.

For women within the party, particularly those from elite ranks who had been in Yanan, access to contraceptives was one part of a larger issue they had confronted in the 1930s and 1940s. As a party, the CCP had committed itself to the liberation of women and the provision of equal rights to men and women. During the war years, therefore, women were used in the work force and encouraged to participate in labor. By engaging in the work of the revolution, it was argued, women would bring about their own liberation from the feudal society in which they had lived.

In practice, the women of Yanan found themselves struggling to cope with the short-term reality of "liberation." They were freed to labor equally with men, but they remained responsible for the household—caring for husband and children. They were given a new burden as the price of liberation, but the old burden of domestic obligations and expectations was not lifted. As Ding Ling put it in her essay "Thoughts on March 8" (International Women's Day): "If women did not marry, they were ridiculed; if they did and had children, they were chastised for holding political posts rather than being at home with their families; if they remained at home for a number of years, they were slandered as backward. Whereas in the old society they were pitied, in the new one they were condemned for a predicament not of their own making."[3] The frustration captured by Ding Ling went far beyond the party's stance on population and birth control, but the central dilemma of how to raise children while simultaneously serving the revolution made access to contraceptives a crucial piece of the agenda for women.

During the 1930s and 1940s, party policy on population growth was pronatalist; high birth rates among the peasantry were seen as the only means of compensating for losses due to war, disease, and high infant mortality. At the same time, the demand for access to birth control by urban intellectual women led to an official policy advocating delaying marriage until the end of the war with Japan; for married couples, birth control was sanctioned as a way to delay childbirth.[4] This policy did not go unopposed, however. Opponents writing in the newspaper Liberation Daily (Jiefang ribao) stressed that birth control surgery was dangerous and bad for women's health. Others opposed birth control on moral grounds, arguing that giving birth was a natural human phenomenon that should not be artificially regulated.[5] In the face of this opposition restrictions were placed on access to abortion and sterilization, but birth control after marriage was officially sanctioned.

At liberation, this birth control policy remained in force despite the adoption of a pronatalist line. With the party leadership dealing with more pressing issues than regulations governing access to birth control, however, control over this issue devolved to the newly created ministry of Public Health. Dominated by medical professionals whose social conservatism, western training, and missionary background led them to reject birth control as immoral, the Ministry was quick to draw up regulations that imposed severe restrictions on access to contraceptives as well as abortion and sterilization. Those restrictions were in keeping with the pronatalist policies and slogans of the 1949–1952 period, but it is unlikely that they were developed in direct response to party instructions. During this period of organizational consolidation, the party relied heavily on nonparty cadres and experts to help stabilize basic government services. In some cases policy decisions made by these individuals did not conform entirely to party preferences. But because regulations developed by government ministries were not channeled to the party for approval, regulations were sometimes in force before party leaders turned their attention to them. It was precisely this gap in party supervision that led Mao to criticize the Ministry of Health on a number of issues in the early 1950s.

In April 1950 the Ministry of Health and the Health Department of the Central Military Commission implemented regulations governing access to abortion by female cadres in party, government, and military posts in the Beijing district. The regulations apparently specified six conditions under which abortion was permissible, but precisely what those conditions were remains unclear. What is clear is that the regulations were designed to limit access severely. Access to abortion, even for those who met the conditions, was predicated on obtaining a series of approvals. First, the woman's husband had to authorize the abortion in writing. Second, the head of the department or organ where the woman worked had to authorize the procedure. And third, the attending physician had to approve the decision. Failure to obtain all the necessary approvals would result in administrative punishment.[6]

By May 1952 the Ministry of Health had drafted regulations that would apply nationwide. On December 31, 1952, the regulations were approved by the Culture and Education Commission of the central government and disseminated on a trial basis.[7] The regulations outlawed sterilization or abortion except in cases of severe illness or threat to the woman. In addition, no woman was eligible for sterilization unless she was thirty-five years old, had six or more children, and had one child aged ten or above.[8] Reinforcing this strict line, the Ministry of Health also moved to limit access to contraceptives. In January 1953, only days after the regulations were approved, the ministry notified customs officials that they should stop the import of contraceptives.[9] This ban, combined with the restrictive policy that discouraged the production of contraceptives domestically, meant that contraceptive supplies would continue to be extremely scarce.

By early 1953, then, the combined forces of social conservatism and ideological radicalism had produced a set of official state regulations that virtually eliminated access to birth control. Just as they were coming on line, however, the logic of the women's movement in China was moving in the opposite direction, leading at least some women (particularly cadres) to press for increased access. For female cadres the new regulations on contraception represented a policy setback and posed a threat to their pursuit of active political careers. During the 1940s the party had quietly maintained a two-track policy—allowing urban, educated women to practice birth control while encouraging childbearing among peasant women. The Ministry of Health was now moving to establish uniform regulations that would abolish the two-track policy, and it was doing so just as the female cadre force and female labor force were beginning to expand. As a result, women within the senior ranks of the party began to press for a change in policy, linking access to birth control to the larger movement for women's liberation that was already under way.

During the recovery years of 1949–1952, the focus of the women's movement had been on the liberation of women from the oppressive effects of a feudal society. The primary weapons in that movement had been the Marriage Law of 1950, which guaranteed women the right to make their own marriage decisions and equal rights and status within the household, and the mobilization of women into the labor force, with a guarantee of equal pay for equal work.[10] Certainly these weapons were not strong enough to eliminate the deeply entrenched attitudes and behaviors of traditional Chinese society in only three years. Nevertheless, by 1953 the women's movement was looking ahead to a new phase of development, one that would parallel the new period of economic construction outlined in the First Five-Year Plan (1953–1957).

Moving toward this new phase of development was the central theme of the Second All-China Women's Congress in April 1953. Speakers at the congress noted the gains that had been made since liberation, and stressed in particular how economic liberation—that is, employment in the labor force—was crucial to achieving women's equality.[11] After describing how CCP policies on day care centers, maternity leave, and women's health clinics were benefiting women laborers, however, they also pointed to the difficulties women faced in juggling work and the household. With those problems in mind, Deng Yingchao's report on future work stressed a series of problems that had to be reconciled during the five-year plan period. They included "striving for equal pay for equal work, . . . solving women's special problems, the popularizing of the new methods of maternity and child care, the training of midwives for villages and child-care workers for the factories."[12] This list reveals the extent to which maternity and child care issues had emerged as priorities for the women's movement. And although there is no public reference to birth control at this time (a predictable omission in a climate where public discussion of sex-related topics was taboo), the vague reference to "women's special problems" may well have been designed to encompass the popularization of birth control methods.

The question was how to effect a change in the restrictive regulations on access to contraception. Fortuitously, advocates of birth control were aided in the spring of 1953 by the "three-anti" campaign. The campaign was directed against corruption and bureaucratism in government, but more generally, it was designed to prevent a widening of elite-mass cleavages by keeping the bureaucracy open to mass input. As a result, people were encouraged to write letters to government officials or visit government offices in order to voice their opinions or complaints.[13] Taking advantage of this climate, women in the labor force and female cadres began to send letters to the Women's Federation, the official trade union, and party and government headquarters, complaining of the tight restrictions and requesting access to contraceptives.[14] It is unclear just how many complaints were registered in 1953, but in response, Zhou Enlai undertook an investigation of living conditions in worker households, comparing the situation of working couples with many children to that of families with fewer children.[15] The results, which favored households with fewer children and thus access to contraceptives, were passed on to health cadres.[16]

By August 1953 proponents of relaxed access to contraceptives were rewarded by a shift in central policy. The changes were set forth by Vice Premier Deng Xiaoping, whom Zhou Enlai would later claim had the "inventor's patent" *(famingquan)* on the birth control issue.[17] In a report to the Women's Federation, Deng instructed the members to begin to promote birth control; he also instructed the Ministry of Health to revise their regulation banning the import of contraceptives and to publicize the new policy of promoting birth control to all medical personnel.[18] Shortly thereafter the ban was reversed, and new, more liberal regulations were issued by the ministry in July 1954.[19] The new regulations promoted the voluntary use of birth control methods, but they continued to express reservations about abortion and sterilization, maintaining strict limits on access and tight regulation. Hospitals and health units were instructed to give full and correct guidance on contraception, the Ministry of Light Industry was ordered to speed up production of contraceptives, and the Pharmaceutical Company was made responsible for their distribution. Contraceptives were to be sent directly to supply outlets for marketing; access would no longer be controlled by medical personnel. Following up on the question of supply and sale, the Ministry of Commerce and the Health Ministry issued a separate circular in late November stating that, in general, contraceptives should not be sold in minority nationality districts, nor would supplies be sent to rural areas.[20]

By 1954, then, central policy on access to contraception had been relaxed dramatically. As a result, most women could go to women's health units at local hospitals or clinics and expect to receive guidance on birth control issues. Alternatively, they could go directly to pharmaceutical retail outlets to purchase contraceptives; a doctor's prescription was no longer necessary. In practice, of course, birth control remained extremely controversial, medical personnel were hostile to disseminating birth control information (or incompetent to do so), cadres delayed giving the necessary approvals for sterilization and abortion, and contraceptives were extremely scarce and of poor quality. Nevertheless, an official policy supporting access to birth control had been established in principle.

In short, women played an important but neglected role in influencing state policy on contraception. That is not to say that their campaign alone was responsible for policy change. Two other crucial developments converged with their mobilization during this period: the emergence of a comprehensive process of economic planning, and growing anxiety about China's economic performance.

The First Five-Year Plan and State Advocacy of Birth Control

By the end of 1952, the CCP had basically completed the task of consolidating its power nationwide. In addition, the first stage of the rural revolution—implementing land reform and waging class struggle against the landlord class—was nearing completion. With those accomplishments to their credit, the Chinese leadership began to concentrate more intensively on the problem of how to bring about rapid industrialization and development, an issue that required two sets of decisions. The first was substantive: what mix of policies would yield the most rapid pace of development at the lowest political, economic, or social cost. The second was administrative: how was the new communist government to oversee and administer a socialist economy. The substantive question proved so controversial that it devoured the remainder of the decade; I will return to this issue later. The administrative question was more straightforward, at least at the outset. The Soviet experience with centralized economic planning and administration had allowed Stalin to industrialize rapidly, and it was the model of choice for the Chinese leadership. Beginning in 1952, therefore, the Chinese began to create the central organs necessary for developing a nationwide planning process and apparatus. The State Statistical Bureau was established in October, and by the end of 1953 each province had set up a statistical department.[21] Similarly, the State Planning Commission (SPC) was established in November, and subordinate organs were set up in the provinces. The SPC was given responsibility for both short-term (annual) and long-term (five-year) economic planning. Its job was to coordinate the production and distribution needs of individual economic organs, and to set priorities for investment and growth.

The creation of these and similar economic organs gave China the semblance of a central planning apparatus, but in practice the system was loose and incomplete, lacking both the hard data and the coordinating mechanisms that were necessary for a tight, efficient planning process. Nevertheless, these steps paved the way for the development of the First Five-Year Plan (FYP), which was to commence in 1953. The plan set basic targets for industrial and agricultural production, as well as targets for related work in areas such as health, education, and scientific development. To set those targets, the leadership needed reliable figures on indicators such as the size of the urban and rural work force, the likely growth in employment needs over the coming five years, and the number of students who would be enrolling in schools and graduating, to cite only a few examples. Most fundamentally, they needed a reliable figure on the overall size of the Chinese population, as well as data on its composition and age structure.

Since 1949 the Chinese communists had used a population figure of 475 million in all public statements. By the end of 1952, however, the leadership knew that the actual number was much higher. In 1951 the State Statistical Bureau estimated that the Chinese population (including Taiwan) exceeded 564 million at the end of 1950; in 1952 the Internal Affairs Ministry reinforced that figure, estimating a population of over 575 million at the end of 1951.[22] Though far closer to the actual number than the official figure of 475 million, these estimates were inadequate for long-term economic planning. As a result, in late 1952 the Central Committee ordered a census for June 30, 1953. The State Statistical Bureau was put in charge of carrying it out, and Vice President Deng Xiaoping oversaw the process for the central leadership.

The completed census results were not published until more than a year after the census, in November 1954.[23] In preparation for elections to local people's congresses, however, the preliminary total was announced in June of that year. As head of the General Election Commission, Deng Xiaoping announced a total of 583 million living in the People's Republic; the total Chinese population, including Taiwan and overseas Chinese, numbered 601 million. This population total was close to the estimates made in 1952 and 1953, and therefore less startling to the leadership than earlier accounts have assumed. Nevertheless, this figure, and the high population growth rate of 2 percent per year, raised serious questions about how to meet the performance goals of the First Five-Year Plan.

The centerpiece of the plan was the development of heavy industry. With Soviet assistance, 156 new plants were to be built, and industrial growth was to expand at a rate of more than 14 percent per year. Investment in agriculture, by comparison, was extremely modest, and expectations for agricultural growth were set at 4.3

percent annually. Although meeting these targets would mean impressive gains over the five-year period, it was not at all clear in 1953 that doing so would resolve basic problems left over from the period of reconstruction (1949–1952). One of those problems was unemployment and underemployment. In mid-1952, 2.8 million laborers remained unemployed, despite the creation of 3 million new jobs after 1949. In the countryside, land reform had left many households without sufficient land to employ all members of the household. As a result, many peasants began to migrate to urban areas in 1952 and 1953, in anticipation of the high-paying jobs in new industries to be created during the First Five-Year Plan.[24] Despite a government directive to prevent this migration, the influx contributed to a jump in urban population of nearly 28 percent between 1952 and 1953, increasing substantially the pressures on cities to expand their employment base.[25] More important, the influx also contributed to the second major problem that confronted the planners at this time: continuing food shortages.

Between 1949 and 1952, the CCP's rural policy concentrated on the implementation of land reform, the overthrow of the landlord class, and the restoration of stable agricultural production. By 1953, however, the party began to look toward the process of collectivization as the long-term solution for China's agricultural sector. In 1953 the party proposed a fifteen-year process of transition from private farming to socialist collectives, a timetable that would be accelerated dramatically in 1955. But in the short run, rural private markets continued to flourish, and peasants were able to sell to rural traders or state purchasing agents if they so desired. By early 1953, however, this system of rural marketing was under serious threat. Despite the successful economic recovery efforts after 1949, the cities continued to suffer food shortages, which were increasingly blamed on the low peasant grain marketings. As a result, some within the leadership argued for the implementation of a system of mandatory purchases and sales of food grains, allowing the state to guarantee the stability of grain supplies and food prices in the cities. The system would also add stability and predictability to the overall planning process, since food grains were a primary export item and a key input into the industrial sector.

Others argued against such a move. In March 1953 Deng Zihui, head of the CCP Rural Work Department, criticized the imposition of a system of unified procurement, advocating instead a readjustment of food prices in order to give the peasants higher incentives to sell to the state. By October, though, he had been overruled. With state grain sales exceeding purchases by 38 percent, the food supply and the economy as a whole were in peril. Accordingly, the system of unified procurements was implemented in the winter of 1953–54, with each locality assigned a procurement quota by the next higher administrative level. All private trading in grain was made illegal, and designated grain shops or supply and marketing co-ops were allowed to sell grain. Urban residents would be supplied grain through their workplace, with purchases made at low, state-subsidized prices; enterprises that needed grain for business purposes (such as restaurants) were given a set quota for purchase at state-run grain shops.[26]

The system of unified procurements resulted in a dramatic increase in grain purchases in late 1953 and 1954, solving the immediate problem of food grain shortages. By its very success, however, it created a new problem. By late 1954 and early 1955, so much grain had been sold to the state for supply and reserves that the narrow margin of excess left in the villages was a source of growing anxiety for the peasantry. Under the system in force, peasants were due to receive grain for consumption in the spring of 1955. Before the designated time of distribution arrived, however, many began to complain of hunger on account of inadequate supplies of grain. In many cases the claims of hunger were bogus, but the general anxiety over supplies was very real. Moreover, the peasants expected to see an increase in their quota for sale in 1955, a step that would increase production pressures and potentially draw off more of the surplus grain. Responding to those fears, some peasants began to cut back on their grain production or simply neglected it, concentrating instead on other crops. Recognizing this threat, the state took steps to allay their fears, including fixing the grain quotas and prices for three years. Nonetheless, despite their efforts a "grain supply crisis" emerged in the spring of 1955, forcing the leadership to mobilize party leaders at all levels to go into the villages to rectify and stabilize the situation.[27]

It was in this context—with census results that showed a rapid rate of population growth and a growing conflict between the ambitious plans for development and the short-term dilemmas of rapid urban growth, tight food supplies, and an uncertain rural political climate—that the CCP leadership formally shifted to an antinatalist policy. In July 1954, just as the more liberal regulations on contraception were being drafted, the Ministry of Health submitted to the State Planning Commission an outline plan for controlling birth rates.[28] And in December a special government group was convened to discuss population and birth control questions. Demonstrating how rapidly the thinking of central leaders had evolved, Liu Shaoqi made a remarkable speech before the group.[29] He acknowledged the ongoing debate within the party over the advocacy of birth control, noting that articles opposing birth control continued to be published. He argued that it was time to bring that debate to an end, announcing officially that "the party endorses birth control." He went on to use Soviet history and the CCP's Yanan policies to construct a rationale for permitting open access to contraception. Arguing that the Soviet Union's policy toward birth control had changed to fit changing circumstances, Liu made a similar case for change in China. He claimed that the pronatalist Yanan slogan "People and livestock are flourishing" *(renshu liangwang)* had been adopted as a response to the high infant mortality rate (over 50 percent) during the Yanan period, but only after the party had made an unsuccessful effort to introduce new childbirth methods that would reduce this figure. When the peasantry resisted, the party resorted instead to encouraging more births.[30] Now that the CCP was out of the hinterlands and in power, he argued, circumstances had changed dramatically:

The difficulties of giving birth to many children are very great, the parents, household, and the child itself all [have] difficulties, the society and the country also [have] difficulties. Clothing, food, medicine, schools, and so on are all insufficient, and they cannot be solved all at once. Because of this, we should endorse [*zancheng*] birth control, not oppose it. None of the opposing arguments hold water. It is incorrect to say that birth control is immoral. To say that birth control has a bad influence, this is not a real problem.[31]

Liu then gave instructions that reveal both the true depth of the controversy surrounding the propagation of birth control and his determination to prevail. He called on the health department to publish guidance manuals on birth control and to educate health workers on the subject. He also called for using every means available to increase the production and supply of contraceptives, including more research, private factory production, purchase in Hong Kong, and imports from capitalist countries.[32] He also called for propaganda and study within the party in order to unify thinking among cadres, but only oral propaganda for public consumption. He explicitly ruled out a print campaign in newspapers as premature. Most telling, he advocated extending this propaganda campaign into the countryside, noting that "it is not the case that there is no demand for birth control in the countryside." He called on cadres involved in "women's work" to find ways to discuss birth control with rural women, but he made clear that a mobilization campaign would be inappropriate and premature.[33]

Liu's instruction to concentrate first on educating party members and cadres was a sensible and measured approach to the revolutionary idea of encouraging contraception and providing birth control guidance on a massive scale. The 1950s were a time when issues of contraception and reproductive control remained extremely controversial, even in the industrialized world. It is hardly surprising that many members of the peasant-based Chinese Communist party found the idea of mass contraceptive education and distribution unpalatable, or that the initiative would encounter extreme resistance throughout Chinese society, including among medical professionals. Before going forward with a public campaign, therefore, it was essential first to propagate the new line within the party, since it was by no means assured that the rank-and-file members would carry it out willingly. Mobilizing within the party first was the standard approach to policy dissemination and implementation within the CCP, and it was particularly important for a sensitive and controversial topic such as birth control.

After Liu's speech, the Second Office of the State Council responded by organizing a special small group for research on birth control issues, with members drawn from the ministries of health, light industry, commerce, and foreign trade, and from mass organizations such as the Women's Federation. The group met four times in early 1955, and submitted a report to the Central Committee on January 31, detailing the steps to be taken to promote birth control.[34] The report was approved by the Central Committee on March 1, and released as a document titled "Directive on Population Control." The directive argued for the promotion of birth control on explicitly economic grounds, stressing that birth control was directly related to the people's livelihood, and to the welfare of the country, individual households, and the next generation. Unlike policy statements that began to appear in the 1970s, this one made no effort to link the policy specifically to women's health. Instead, the general welfare of parents (*fumu*) and children was stressed. Moreover, the use of the term "population control," or *renkou kongzhi*, left no question about the state's decision to adopt an antinatalist policy, moving a step beyond women's demand for contraceptive access.[35] The only remaining questions were how this policy would be put into operation and implemented; but before those questions could be addressed, a political backlash against the policy began.

Comprehensive Birth Planning

By the time this birth control policy was in place, the debate over the pace and shape of socialist transformation in China had begun to overtake and reshape it. Over the next few years, China's leaders would confront the consequences of excessive centralization of decision-making, rapid growth in the state bureaucracy and the state payroll, excessive growth in the urban population (with a consequent drain on food supplies and consumer goods), and, most troubling, very sluggish growth in the agricultural sector. By 1955 two distinct viewpoints were emerging on how to resolve the problems of agricultural performance—one favoring a slow-to-moderate pace of transformation that would take place over many years, the other favoring a more aggressive approach and an accelerated pace of collectivization.

By the spring of 1955, the Chinese countryside had been thoroughly penetrated by the CCP and a foundation for collectivization had been put in place. Land reform had been followed with the organization of mutual aid teams; the private grain market had been abolished, and a system of unified purchase had been instituted; and a small number of cooperatives and collectives had been formed. Although the leadership agreed that these were only preliminary stages toward the goal of collectivized agriculture, the question was how, and at what pace, to proceed toward that goal. Those responsible for agricultural work argued for a slow pace of transition, adhering to the fifteen-year timetable set out in the first FYP. Faced with widespread difficulties in the countryside resulting from the excessive extraction of grain in 1954, these officials feared that speeding up the pace of collectivization would further dampen the peasants' enthusiasm and undercut their incentives to produce. To avoid that possibility and ensure an adequate food supply, they advocated price increases for grain and a relaxation of quotas for extraction. Those responsible for overall economic planning, in contrast, argued for a moderate increase in the pace of cooperativization and an expansion of the number of collectives. From their perspective, price increases and relaxed grain quotas would be far too costly, in both political and economic terms, and concessions to agriculture would detract from the rapid development of heavy industry. Only steady movement toward collectivization could remove this threat by securing state access to the agricultural surplus, for a minimal cost.[36]

By midsummer Mao Zedong had rejected both positions in favor of an accelerated plan for cooperativization. In July 1955 he summoned provincial leaders to a work conference and called for the completion of cooperativization by the end of the decade and for an accelerated pace of collectivization. He asked the leadership to formulate new plans on this basis and report on their progress within two months. By the time the Central Committee met in October to hear the leadership report, collectivization was moving ahead with a speed that vastly exceeded even Mao's goals, and within a year the process was complete. When he convened a symposium on the nationalization of industry in late October 1955, he determined that the pace of development in the industrial sector could also be accelerated; rather than wait twelve years to complete the nationalization process, he proposed that it be done in two.

Behind Mao's press for more rapid transformation was a growing belief that the main barriers to progress were political. He concluded that the "conservative work style" and "right deviationist mistakes" of the party and state bureaucracy were responsible for the slow pace of rural transformation, a belief that was apparently confirmed by the swift completion of the process under his direction. To solve this leadership problem, Mao called for the cultivation of a "progressive work style," a leadership style that emphasized three basic elements: (1) more investigations of local conditions; (2) better, more rapid communication in the bureaucracy; and (3) comprehensive planning.[37] It was this last element, comprehensive planning, that irrevocably refocused China's approach to population policy.

In pushing for a progressive work style, Mao aimed to foment the momentum for mobilization which had been developing since July. Impatient with Soviet-style bureaucratic methods that seemed to breed a climate of pessimism and caution within the party and government apparatus, Mao saw the campaign approach as an effective and superior alternative. Adopting mobilization methods did not imply a deemphasis on planning, however; planning per se was no obstacle to progress, only pessimistic planning. Rather than using the lowest common denominator or the poorest-performing units as the basis for setting goals and targets, progressive planning would be based on the most advanced achievements and ambitious targets. And rather than a rigid top-down process of centralized planning and dissemination of targets, progressive planning would involve the mobilization of each sector and each government level in a comprehensive bottom-up process of plan development and implementation. In short, Mao saw comprehensive planning as a synthesis of the best elements of systematic planning and mass mobilization—disciplining mobilization to the needs of the plan and infusing the planning process with the potential for mobilizational breakthroughs.

In response to Mao's call, each ministry and each province began to lay out short- and long-term plans ranging from three to twelve years. In an effort to avoid the errors of "right-deviationism" or conservatism, each organ proposed ambitious targets, and lower-level governments pushed their targets even higher as a statement of their political resolve. Calls went out to complete the First Five-Year Plan by the end of 1956, a year ahead of schedule, and under

Mao's guidance work began on a twelve-year comprehensive plan for agricultural development.

It was in the context of this "planning campaign" that the focus of population policy began to shift from *birth control* to *birth planning*. In late 1954 and early 1955, birth control advocates such as Shao Lize began to write and speak about the subject, encouraged by the steps already taken to relax birth control restrictions. They stressed that individual couples should *plan* for their children and use birth control to prevent early or unwanted pregnancies.[38] In other words, while linking the need for family planning to the larger issue of China's long-term development, they basically called for family planning in the liberal sense of individual couples taking advantage of new contraceptive techniques to make voluntary and conscious decisions about the timing and spacing of children. Within a year, however, this relatively liberal concept of "planned childbirth" had become fused to the very different concept of comprehensive socialist planning. The result was a profound change in the meaning and implications of China's birth control policy.

The first step was the insertion of a provision on birth planning into a draft twelve-year plan for agricultural development.[39] The draft, which Mao Zedong submitted to a meeting of the Supreme State Conference in January 1956, comprised forty articles. Article 29 emphasized the need to "propagandize and popularize" birth control *(jiezhi shengyu)* in all densely populated areas, and "to promote childbirth according to plan" *(tichang you jihuade shengyu zinü)*.[40] To those familiar with the language being used to encourage individual couples to adopt birth control, the phrase "to promote childbirth according to plan" could be understood to refer to household-level decision-making about the number and spacing of children. To rank-and-file party cadres, however, the nuances of meaning were completely lost. For them, planning was a collective activity, and in early 1956 they were in the midst of a campaign to achieve more comprehensive planning. If births needed to be planned, they would set birth targets and mobilize to achieve them on a mass scale, shifting the planning process from the individual to the state. Accordingly, over the next two years various localities began to draw up plans relevant to the birth control effort. Guangdong and Hebei provinces drew up formal twelve-year plans for birth control work, while Hunan and Sichuan provinces issued directives on strengthening birth control work.[41] Shanghai announced that it planned to reduce its birth rate by half during the Second Five-Year Plan (1958–1962), from 40 per thousand to 20 per thousand; Changsha committed itself to a birth rate of 30 per thousand by 1962, but announced a further goal for the third FYP, a birth rate of 21 per thousand. Women workers in some localities were required to sign "birth plans" of their own; women with two children agreed to have no more during the second FYP, and women with one child or none agreed to have only one. Even a few rural cooperatives pledged to cut their birth rate drastically by the end of the second FYP.[42]

As a result of this activity, by 1957 the *concept* of "births according to plan" *(you jihuade shengyu zinü)* was rapidly becoming the *doctrine* of planned births *(jihua shengyu),* even though most senior leaders continued to advocate birth control rather than birth planning. In September 1956, for example, Zhou Enlai's report on China's second five-year economic plan endorsed birth control measures and propaganda but made no reference to "birth planning," and in November he expanded on the issue in a Politburo talk on the 1957 annual plan:[43] "At yesterday's Politburo meeting I said we should promote birth control . . . It is now clear that we will not be able to employ everyone within a short period of time, and wage increases will not enable workers to support the population of many households. I believe that going so far as to promote late marriage even has some advantages."[44]

Similarly, in August 1957 China's leading economic planner, Chen Yun, spoke pointedly about pressing economic problems, including the large migration of peasants to urban areas in search of alternative employment. The migration threatened to put additional pressure on the central budget, since urban residency would entitle the migrants to a variety of state subsidies, and it also put pressure on the urban food supply. Noting that the current problems were directly related to the rapid pace of population growth, and that the effects of birth control measures would be seen only after ten to twenty years, Chen called on each province and municipality to create a specialized committee to handle this work. Acknowledging the difficulty of promoting birth control in Chinese society, he called for widespread propaganda to overcome the "shyness" *(paxiu)* of both men and women when it came to buying contraceptives. In a more practical vein, he indicated that the price of contraceptives would be lowered *again,* even to the point of free distribution *(baisong),* and that the party was prepared to spend "several tens of millions" a year on subsidies. Most striking, he made what was perhaps the first reference to a general limit on childbearing, suggesting a "call on Communist party members not to give birth to a third child."[45] Yet he did not make any reference to the formula of "birth planning."

In contrast, Mao Zedong stressed the dual themes of birth control and birth planning throughout 1957, laying the foundation for an official doctrine of comprehensive birth planning. A new text of Mao's February speech, "On the Correct Handling of Contradictions among the People" (most likely the transcript of a tape recording made at the time) reveals that Mao understood quite well the dimensions of the population problem in 1957, and the economic and planning issues that made birth control a priority.[46] After noting several of these problems, he went beyond the advocacy of birth control to call for comprehensive population planning.

Our plans, work, [and] thinking all should start from the [awareness] that we have a population of 600 million. Here [we] need birth control; it would be great [if we] could lower the birth [rate] a bit. [We] need planned births. I think humanity is most inept at managing itself. It has plans for industrial production, the production of textiles, the production of household goods, the production of steel; [but] it does not have plans for the production of humans. This is anarchism, no government, no organization, no rules. [*Loud laughter.*] If [we] go on this way, I think humanity will prematurely fall into strife and hasten toward destruction. If China's population of 600 million increases tenfold, what will that be? Six billion: at that time [we] will be near destruction. There'll be nothing to eat; and with advances in hygiene, sanitation, inoculations, the babies will be so many that it will be disastrous, with everyone being of venerable age and eminent virtue. [*Loud laughter.*] . . . Perhaps this government should establish a department, establish a planned birth department—would that be a good idea? [*Loud laughter.*] Or how about establishing a committee, a birth control committee, to serve as a government organ, [or we could] organize a people's group? Organize people's groups to advocate [birth control]. Since [we] need to solve a few technical problems, [we will have to] provide funds, think up methods, propagandize.[47]

In October 1957 Mao reiterated these views at the Third Plenum of the Eighth Central Committee, with provincial, municipal, and county cadres in attendance. By this juncture, however, the antirightist campaign was well under way. Intellectuals who had advocated birth control were under attack, and leftist political momentum was building rapidly. Yet Mao's growing ambition for exceptionally rapid economic gains had not altered his views on birth planning. In summary comments at the plenum, Mao said: "[As for] population control, [if we] have three years of experimental propaganda, three years of popularization, and four years of universal implementation, this is also a ten-year plan. Otherwise, if we wait until the population reaches 800 million to carry it out, it will be too late. [We must] achieve planned births step by step." In a second set of comments for the plenum, he continued:

In the future, China will become the country with the highest production level in the world. Currently, some counties have already reached 1,000 *jin* per *mu* [equivalent to about 500 kilograms of grain per .067 hectares of land]: are we capable or not of raising it to 2,000 *jin* per *mu* in half a century? In the future will it be 800 *jin* per *mu* north of the Yellow River, 1,000 *jin* per *mu* north of the Wei River, and 2,000 *jin* per *mu* south of the Wei River? To reach that target by the beginning of the twenty-first century, we still have several decades; perhaps we don't need that much time. We rely on intensive cultivation in order to eat; if there are a few more people, there will still be food to eat. I think a per capita average of three *mu* of land is too much, if in the future there is less than one *mu* [per capita] there will be enough to eat. Of course, there still must be birth control, I don't mean to encourage births.

. . . There is also a ten-year plan for planned births. There is no need to go propagate it in minority regions and sparsely populated localities. Even in places with a large population, [we] must carry out experiments, gradually popularize [it], gradually achieve universal planned births. [We] must carry out public education on planned birth, nothing other than a free airing of views, a great debate. With respect to births, mankind is in a state of anarchy, the self is unable to control the self. In the future we want to achieve the complete planning of births, but without a societal strength, unless everyone agrees, unless everyone does it together, then it won't work.[48]

Mao's insistence on the need for birth planning, not simply birth control, and his description of human reproduction as an anarchic and uncontrolled process set his words apart from those of other leaders and mark him as the author of the birth planning doctrine. By framing the issue in this way, he separated birth planning as a goal entirely from the question of whether China's large population was or was not an asset, and from the increasingly rancorous debate over China's economic development strategy. If population planning was desirable for the same reasons that economic planning was desirable, if anarchic and unregulated human reproduction was as "antisocialist" as was the anarchy of the market in the material and economic realm, then the issue was no longer overpopulation. The question was how to bring birth planning and material planning into balance.

The passage also demonstrates that Mao's commitment to birth control and planning coexisted with his growing optimism about rapid agricultural advances. It is true that Mao was far more sanguine about China's large population than other leaders, and optimistic about the future of a more populous country. Rather than showing Mao as torn between his faith in the masses as a productive asset and his advocacy of birth planning, however, the passage reveals his singular confidence in the combined processes of unified planning, propaganda, and grass-roots party mobilization as the key to the overall mission of socialist development. Birth planning was not to be equated with a pessimistic view of China's productive capacity, or with the need for a fertility reduction campaign, or even with the special needs and burdens of women in the revolution. Birth planning was one part of a desired pattern of unified social organization that Mao increasingly believed to be within reach.

Mao's vision began to crystallize in 1958, when the combined momentum of progressive planning and the antirightist campaign culminated in the Great Leap Forward, a massive political and economic campaign that emphasized campaign methods of implementation, the substitution of mass mobilization for material and technical inputs, and further decentralization of planning to the provinces and localities, with national plans built from the bottom up.[49] As the momentum for a Great Leap started to build, it became increasingly difficult to express any reservations about China's capacity for a rapid breakthrough to advanced socialism and communism. As a result, those who had warned of the negative consequences of population growth became vulnerable politically, and high-level opponents of the birth control policy within the CCP went on the attack, denigrating supporters of the antinatalist policy as reactionary enemies. Most birth control advocates retreated from their positions in an effort to blunt the force of the attack, but Ma Yinchu, a nonparty intellectual, a delegate to the National People's Congress, and the author of a 1957 tract, "New Population Theory," refused to back down. As a result, he became the focus of the attack and in 1959 was branded a rightist.

In similar fashion the political momentum created by the Great Leap Forward led to exaggerated estimates of increased agricultural production, leading Mao to feel more optimistic about China's population and the capacity to maintain an adequate food grain supply. In contrast to his statements in 1957, therefore, by August 1958 Mao's view on the population burden had shifted. Rather than emphasize the need for state intervention to promote birth control and planning, at the Beidaihe conference he advocated a more relaxed approach: "[Our] views on population should change. In the past I said that [we] could manage with 800 million. Now I think that 1 billion plus would be no cause for alarm. This shouldn't be recommended for people with many children. When [people's] level of education increases, [they] will really practice birth control."[50]

This newfound optimism, and the overall tenor of the Great Leap Forward, account for the collapse of the birth control campaign in 1958. What is important, however, is that Mao did not go so far as to repudiate either birth control or birth planning. When his twelve-year agricultural development plan was revived in 1958, for example, it continued to advocate birth control and birth planning. Only the antinatalist focus of the program was rejected.

The Post-Leap Revival of Birth Planning

The leftist environment surrounding the antirightist campaign and the Great Leap Forward undermined the fledgling program to make contraceptive information, supplies, and procedures available to couples of childbearing age. Support for contraception became temporarily dangerous, and the Women's Federation, like other organizations, retreated from the issue without explicitly endorsing the diatribes of the leftists. In the aftermath of the Great Leap, however, the economic problems that had spurred the birth control policy remained pressing. By 1962, therefore, the architects of the post-Leap economic recovery, Liu Shaoqi, Zhou Enlai, and Deng Xiaoping, helped push through a new directive on population control.

The new document reiterated the logic for birth control which had been articulated in the 1950s, but it was striking in one crucial respect. Whereas the leadership—apart from Mao—had steered clear of the doctrine of "planned birth" in 1956–57, Mao's language and logic was now embraced as the centerpiece of the program. The December 1962 directive was titled "On Enthusiastically Promoting Planned Births," and it began by declaring: "It is the set policy during our country's socialist construction that birth control be promoted in the cities and in densely populated rural areas, and that there be appropriate control of the rate of population growth, in order to gradually move the birth problem from a state of anarchy to one of planning."[51] The directive went on to establish the link between birth planning and the process of planned socialist development, and to refute any allegation that the policy was Malthusian. It also called on party committees and governments at all levels to place birth planning at the top of their work agenda, and gave a mandate to party committees to organize all relevant departments and organizations in the development of a comprehensive birth planning program.[52]

This directive marked a turning point in the evolution of China's birth planning strategy. It unequivocally legitimized birth control and birth planning by stating that it was the established policy for the period of China's socialist development. This blanket endorsement, coming so closely on the heels of the anti-Malthusian diatribes that permeated the Great Leap Forward, left little room to doubt the seriousness of the Center's intentions. Any doubt that did remain was quashed by the demand that all party and government leaders make birth planning a part of their most urgent business and organize accordingly. In addition, the directive advocated birth control as a means to "appropriately control the rate of population growth."[53] Using Mao's own words to reject the anarchy of unplanned human reproduction in a planned economy and society, the leaders of the economic recovery were able to preempt neatly any opposition or criticism from leftist critics.

The new state strategy of planning rates of population growth had immediate and far-reaching consequences for women of childbearing age. Party and government leaders, as well as all relevant sectoral departments and mass organizations, had been ordered to place this work at the top of the agenda; they had also been directed to pursue birth control with the goal of controlling population growth. But how were these directions to be put into operation? How was progress to be measured? And how were basic-level cadres to be mobilized to carry out this work? Answers to these questions were provided nine months later, at the second urban work conference, held in September 1963. Convened by the Central Committee and State Council, the month-long meeting produced the first set of short-term and long-term planning targets for urban population growth, setting the stage for all subsequent planning. Propelled by sample surveys that indicated population growth rates over 27 per thousand in 1962 and over 33 per thousand in 1963, the participants agreed that during the remaining three years of economic readjustment (1963–1965) the rate of urban population growth should be brought under 20 per thousand.[54] During the Third and Fourth Five-Year

Plans (1966–1970, and 1971–1975, respectively), urban growth rates were scheduled to continue their descent, with an average annual drop of 1 per thousand. By the end of the third FYP the target was set for under 15 per thousand; the fourth FYP target was under 10 per thousand.[55] The plan, in short, would unfold in two stages: first, a three-year campaign to induce a rapid drop in urban population growth, which had exceeded 30 per thousand; and second, a steady decrease over the following ten years.

These steps toward comprehensive planning were reinforced in 1965, when Zhou Enlai articulated China's first long-range population goal: reducing the rate of population growth to 1 percent or less by the end of the twentieth century.[56] And after the disruption of the Cultural Revolution (1966–1969), Zhou Enlai included birth planning work in the draft outline program of the Fourth Five-Year Plan in 1970, arguing that "birth planning isn't a health question, it is a planning question. If you can't even plan the rate of population increase, how can you have any national plan?"[57] With these comments, Zhou cemented the conceptual and policy shift that had begun with Mao in the 1950s, redefining population goals as part of the centralized state plan and the crucial prerequisite to successful economic planning. This shift completely secured the birth control program from ideological attack, and compelled local leaders to take population targets seriously as part of the national economic plan. To that extent it served also to secure women's access to contraceptives on a mass scale, even in the countryside. But it also meant that the regime would apply to birth control goals the same target-oriented approach that was the standard tool of policy implementation in the material sector, where numerical targets were routinely used to set production levels and determine standards of performance in production units. With population planning thus linked to the primary obligation of the socialist state—the production, allocation, and distribution of material goods—childbearing became subject to those same mechanisms of depersonalized centralized planning. Under this rationale, women were production instruments subject to the structure of state monopoly and supply, and children became a planned product of the socialist state.

There is little direct evidence about the reaction of women to this reinterpretation of the population control policy at either the elite or the mass level. Several factors suggest the likelihood of official support for the policy, at least at the outset. In the early 1960s, when Mao's birth planning concept was used to justify the revival of birth planning programs and attention to reproductive health, it is very likely that it genuinely received elite-level support from the Women's Federation as the necessary means for securing the program from ideological attack. Without that security a state birth control program could not be launched, and access to quality contraceptives would be delayed indefinitely. With Mao Zedong's imprimatur, the program could survive, a condition that proved all too necessary during the Cultural Revolution years. Despite these initial calculations, however, the Cultural Revolution marginalized the issue of birth control in the late 1960s, and the adoption of contraception remained entirely a voluntary affair. Only in the early 1970s were administrative and planning directives brought to weigh on childbearing; ironically, the circumstances of the 1950s now played themselves out in reverse. Whereas the leftist mobilization of the late 1950s had aided social conservatives and reluctant male party cadres who opposed the birth control program, the leftist climate of the early 1970s was used to mobilize the party and society for state-enforced contraceptive use and birth limits. What women had begun as a struggle to undo an official pronatalist policy in the early years of the People's Republic thus became an obligatory and intrusive program of state-enforced contraception and birth limits.

By the end of 1975 the conceptual and policy shift that had begun with Mao in the 1950s had been cemented. As a result, population goals were redefined as part of the centralized state plan and the crucial prerequisite to successful economic planning. In theory, the health and welfare of women and children continued to be the primary justification for family planning and birth control programs until after Mao's death. In practical terms, however, from 1970 onward the logic of centralized economic planning provided the rationale for population control plans. This shift meant that the regime would apply to birth control goals the same target-oriented approach that was the standard tool of policy implementation in the material sector, where numerical targets were routinely used to set production levels and determine standards of performance in production units. With population planning thus linked to the primary obligation of the socialist state—the production, allocation, and distribution of material goods—childbearing became subject to those same mechanisms of centralized planning.

It was this underlying conception of birth planning as the reproductive corollary to planned material production that immunized it from radical assault at the beginning of the Cultural Revolution and provided a safe political haven for the development of a far-reaching birth control program. To that extent, it was essential in securing the access to birth control that elite women had demanded in the name of women's liberation. The theory created the potential for a new form of tyranny, however, and one in which the official state representatives of women were complicitous. When put fully into operation in the 1970s and 1980s, the theory translated into a state-enforced program of birth limitation that claimed full sovereignty over women's reproductive lives. In the 1980s those consequences began to be increasingly contested, and as the necessity for a strict ideological grounding for population control receded in favor of a pragmatic economic rationale, the birth planning doctrine itself was subjected to growing criticism and debate. The policy stood, nonetheless, as the distorted legacy of the doctrine. Thus we see that struggles waged from within the state, like struggles explicitly waged against it, can produce unintended and ambiguous consequences.

MARGARET Y. K. WOO

12 | Chinese Women Workers: The Delicate Balance between Protection and Equality

In its forty-two-year history, the People's Republic has undergone numerous changes, and the role of women in China's work force has fluctuated with each change. Most recently, beginning in the late 1970s, China turned from the chaos of the Cultural Revolution to embark on a period of pragmatic legal and economic reforms. In the legal realm this has resulted in the reestablishment of institutions that were previously abolished. In the economic sphere reform has led to the decentralization and autonomy of industries, the appearance of private enterprise, and the elimination of the "iron rice bowl" employment system. With these changes, issues of women and work have surfaced with a new prominence in China. How has the Chinese state and society with its newly reinstituted legal system dealt with these issues?

For urban women workers,[1] China has turned to "protective" legislation which focuses on the biological differences between women and men. While these laws make an effort to accommodate women's reproductive needs in the workplace, they also reveal the latest reality that "women's problems" are increasingly discussed as a matter of biology, and less as social problems. These laws constitute a marked departure from the prior policies of the Cultural Revolution, which emphasized the belief that "women are the same as men."

It is important to note that these laws and regulations embody an inherent tension between multiple goals reflecting the ambivalent and complex relationship between the Chinese state and women in China. In tone and focus, these laws have their origins in Confucian tradition and ever changing socialist goals. Any strategy for addressing women and work issues in China must take account of these roots and the realities of socialist politics.

Laws and Regulations since 1982

The Constitution adopted in 1982 offers a strong promise of equality for women. It guarantees that women enjoy "equal rights with men in all spheres of life," and that the state "protects the rights and interests of women, applies the principle of equal pay for equal work to men and women alike, and trains and selects cadres from among women."[2] This promise of equality was reaffirmed by the adoption in 1992 of a Women's Rights Protection Law, which pledged to protect "women's special rights and interests granted by law."[3]

Although the Chinese regime does provide some limited antidiscrimination legislation to ensure similar treatment of men and women in the workplace, recent legislation by and large takes the approach of emphasizing the differences between men and women and "protecting" women. Thus, while prohibiting discriminatory hiring, pay, and termination, the Women's Rights Protection Law states that there are "certain work categories or positions that are unfit for women" and also affirms women's differences from men by requiring all "units to protect women's safety and health at work in accordance with law."[4]

This strong strand of protective legislation can also be seen in the "contract labor" regulations,[5] which require that enterprises hire women, but only where "suitable," a term very much left to the discretionary interpretation of employers.[6] Similarly, the Labor Insurance Regulations, first instituted in the 1950s and reinstituted in 1979, differentiate between men and women by requiring women workers to retire at age fifty, as compared to age sixty for men.[7]

Perhaps the clearest examples of the focus on the "protection" of women's biology are two regulations promulgated in the late

1980s—the Provisional Regulations for Health Care for Women Employees (Trial Implementing Draft), known as the 1986 Health Care Regulations, and the Regulations Governing Labor Protection for Female Staff Members and Workers, known as the 1988 Labor Protection Regulations.[8] Both were the joint product of the Ministry of Public Health, the Ministry of Labor and Personnel, the All-China Federation of Trade Unions, and the All-China Women's Federation.[9] The stated purposes of both regulations were to protect women's health—meaning their reproductive capabilities—and to "enhance the quality of the nation."[10]

These two sets of regulations, under the headings of health care and labor protection, imposed limits and rules explicitly structured around women's reproductive cycles. The regulations identify the five periods in the life of a woman worker in which she must be accorded special treatment *(wuji baohu):* menstruation, pregnancy, delivery and nursing, and, in the case of the 1986 Health Care Regulations, menopause.[11] For each of these periods, the regulations impose limits on the types and conditions of work women can perform.

Thus, for example, during menstruation women workers must not be assigned "to work at high altitudes, in places with low temperatures, or in cold water."[12] During periods of pregnancy and nursing,[13] women cannot be assigned to work overtime or on night shifts,[14] or to jobs that will expose them to industrial poisons.[15] Women workers, during menstruation,[16] pregnancy,[17] and postpartum,[18] cannot perform work requiring labor of third-grade intensity and are barred from fourth-grade labor at all times, whether or not they are in a critical period.[19] Significantly, higher-grade work is paid more than work of lower grades.[20]

Both the 1986 Health Care Regulations and the 1988 Labor Protection Regulations provide for specific leave and rest time during each of the critical periods. For example, the 1988 Labor Protection Regulations provide for a paid maternity leave of ninety days, fifteen of which may be taken prior to delivery.[21] For the pregnancy period, both regulations mandate rest breaks,[22] and for the nursing period, they specify two thirty-minute nursing breaks per day.[23] A pregnant female worker may exercise her right to reduce her workload or voluntarily be assigned to other work with a certificate from a medical department.[24]

Both regulations emphasize the importance of health education[25] and prenatal[26] and postnatal care. The 1988 Labor Protection Regulations also call for the provision of specified health care facilities during the designated periods, such as health clinics in units that employ over one hundred women,[27] rest areas for pregnant women, nursing rooms, child care centers, and kindergartens.[28] Finally, the 1986 Health Care Regulations require that employers maintain records of the menstruation cycles of their women employees.[29] Married women employees are encouraged to ask to be examined if they have missed a period.[30]

In sum, while there are stated guarantees for women workers of equality and nondiscrimination, the strong tendency of recent regulations is to carve out special protections for women structured around their reproductive functions, thus defining the treatment of women along biological lines.

There is certainly much to be praised about these regulations. For one thing, they represent advances in addressing the health needs of women. For another, the recognition of positive guarantees is consistent with international standards, which encourage the provision of support services and benefits to women workers.[31] The "protective" regulations provide benefits for women workers that other countries, such as the United States, are still grappling with. In the United States, although women have formal equality, the lack of support structures for child care, parental leave, and benefits continues to disadvantage women workers.

Yet these "protective" regulations can themselves contribute to the problems of discriminatory hiring and occupational segregation. Because they are primarily directed at and structured around a woman's reproductive functions, the regulations run the risk of reinforcing the stereotype that the primary role of a woman is reproduction. Additionally, the regulations can have the practical effect of keeping women out of certain categories of work, ostensibly because of the need to protect them. For example, the protective restrictions on hours and times women can work and restrictions on lifting and on working in cold water and at certain heights are extremely broad and may apply to a wide variety of jobs. While, theoretically, women are prohibited from these categories only in their critical periods (menstruation, pregnancy, delivery, nursing, and menopause), the reality is that these restrictions may deter employers from hiring women at all. More problematically, the regulations also deter employers from hiring women because of the cost of benefits that must be provided to women workers.

It is perhaps unsurprising that these regulations focus on protecting women's biology. This approach can be understood in the context of both socialist ideology and Chinese tradition. As a preliminary matter, the protective approach is part and parcel of the socialist ideology of protecting against "exploitations of the working class,"[32] an ideology that can be traced to legislation promulgated in the early years of the People's Republic.[33] The specific focus on protecting women's *biology*, meanwhile, reflects traditional images and medical beliefs about women as well as fluctuating Chinese state policy toward women.

Traditional Confucian thought defined a woman in terms of her obligations to her husband as a wife and to her son as a mother. Women were perceived as the weaker sex, meriting special protection. This vision of women is reflected in present-day Chinese law, in which women are classified, along with "the elderly and the young," as a group in need of special protection.[34] According to modern Chinese legal treatises, women occupy a special status in the labor force in light of their special reproductive responsibilities.[35] This idea of special protection for women is reinforced by traditional medical beliefs that women are weakened by their reproductive responsibilities. According to a study by Charlotte Furth and Ch'en Shu-yueh, menstruation in traditional Chinese medicine was viewed as analogous to childbirth, creating an imbalance of the body and rendering a woman weakened.[36] In traditional medical texts devoted to women, "menstrual regulation" received the lengthiest discussion. During menstruation and pregnancy, and after childbirth, women were subject to certain restrictions such as avoidance of baths, cold water, and heavy exercise, and were advised to eat particular foods as "support" to renew their energy.[37]

The 1986 and 1988 regulations track these traditional beliefs, which are today reinforced with the authority of modern biomedicine. The Chinese regulations do not simply limit the "special protection" to pregnancy and postpartum but rather extend protection to periods of menstruation and even menopause. Meanwhile, the ninety-day maternity leave (two weeks of which is to be taken prior to delivery) is based in part on the belief that a woman needs fifty days to recuperate from delivery, a period traditionally called *zuo yuezi*.[38] Similarly, labor law textbooks in China defend limitations on the kinds of work women can do on the grounds that lifting more than twenty-five kilograms may cause dislocation of the uterus for women workers, and exposing menstruating women to cold water may cause irregular cycles.[39]

More important, perhaps, the focus of these regulations on protecting women's "biology" is the latest in a series of fluctuations in the Chinese policy toward women, which has consistently placed gender equality second to the exigencies of economic development.[40] During the initial period of collectivization in the 1950s, when there was surplus labor, the Chinese government instituted the Five Goods Campaign, which encouraged women to stay home as "socialist housewives."[41] During the Cultural Revolution, when state policy heavily favored a leveling of class differences, women were called back into the work force under the slogan "Anything a man can do, a woman can do also." Women and men during this time were viewed as unisex, and women's issues were seen as societal, not biological.

In the more recent period of economic reforms, gender equality has again been asked to take a back seat to the socialist goal of economic development, with a renewed focus on woman's domestic role and her reproductive biology. With the shift in emphasis toward privatization and economic efficiency and away from the prior policy of full employment, unemployment has again become a major problem for China.[42] In a situation of high unemployment and privatization, women workers have been the last to be hired and the first to be laid off, and even when hired, women have been segregated in specific, mostly lower-paid light industries.[43]

In a development reminiscent of the 1950s, some enterprises have actually implemented formal "return home" policies,[44] whereby women workers, especially older women and nursing mothers, have been paid a percentage of the wages they formerly received from their work units for staying at home.[45] Additionally, women workers have been offered maternity leave, ranging up to two years, while receiving 60 to 70 percent of their former salary.[46] For some women workers, the reduction of income has caused a marked drop in family and social status.[47] Both policies have proved to be controversial.[48]

Viewed positively, then, the focus in recent legislation on the "protection" of women benefits them by restructuring the workplace to accommodate their reproductive role. Viewed more cynically, protective legislation, in its unusually detailed restrictions, is a form of "biologization" of women, which can be seen as part of an effort to push women out of the work force during an era of surplus labor. The focus on women's biology reinforces the rhetoric encouraging the return of women to the home as "socialist mothers."

This is certainly not the first time the Chinese state has defined the "natural role" of women. For example, women's fertility has been shaped by China's population policy.[49] In an attempt to hold its population at 1.2 billion by the turn of the century, China implemented in 1979 the fourth birth planning campaign, more commonly known as the One-Child Campaign, a strict regime of state-imposed family planning with elaborate rewards and sanctions. In China the ideal socialist family is the single-child family.

Interestingly, then, there is a tension between China's protective regulations and the state's goal of population control. While the state supports the "return home" policy and, at least superficially, the protection of a woman worker's reproductive health, the state must, at the same time, emphasize the contrary duty of women workers to bear only one child. It is perhaps not surprising that the 1986 Health Care Regulations contain provisions that protect a woman's reproductive health as well as provisions that establish a menstruation card system for women employees, presumably to keep track of workers' pregnancies.

Maintaining both these policies demonstrates the complexity of the Chinese state's attitude toward gender equality. It is evident that the goal of gender equality is once again subordinated to a higher national goal: the one-child family. Hence, a woman worker who has a second child outside the mandates of state population policy is not accorded the benefits provided by the labor and health regulations. Rather, she is subject to different regulations relating to family planning.[50] In sum, the 1988 Labor Protection Regulations and the 1986 Health Care Regulations reflect the delicate balance the Chinese state is trying to maintain between women as workers and mothers, but only as mothers of one-child families.

The extent to which the regulations serve more to bolster the rhetoric regarding women as mothers than to give women the benefits they need is further revealed by the manner in which these regulations have been implemented and the impact they have had on women workers. By and large, the regulations have not been uniformly implemented, for implementation depends largely on the discretion of factory managers and on the economic conditions of the factory or enterprise. When forced to implement these regulations, some factory managers simply respond by not hiring women workers, or by laying them off.

Indeed, despite the massive propaganda effort that accompanied the implementation of these regulations, it is unclear how many women workers know about the regulations or to what extent they are actually being implemented. One fact is clear, however: employers have not been overwhelmingly receptive to these regulations. Enterprises that employ many women have complained that they must bear a greater financial burden to provide benefits to their workers than enterprises that mostly employ male workers.[51] New smaller enterprises and private businesses, meanwhile, have complained that they may not even be financially strong enough to set up a benefits system. Many factory owners have argued against these requirements on the grounds that they reduce efficiency, decrease profits, and create incentives for not hiring women.[52] Thus, many reports indicate that these regulations have not been widely implemented.[53]

This conclusion was validated in a 1990 trip I made to Wuhan, where visits to factories revealed that the implementation of these regulations varied, depending on the leadership and the economic condition of the individual factories.[54] If the leadership is, as the workers term it, "democratic" or "reform-minded," then implementation of the labor regulations can be extensive. Similarly, if the factory can afford to implement the various regulations, it is more likely to do so. Hence, one well-run and lucrative factory was able to offer longer rest breaks and maternity leaves, earlier retirement, and better facilities, including a library and a small garden for its workers.

When faced with providing protective benefits, some factory managers simply chose not to hire women workers, or to dismiss them. Thus, in the city of Nantong, women constituted 70 percent of the total number of workers fired from their jobs in 1988.[55] Factory managers blame this outcome on the requirement to provide protective benefits. They embrace the old saying, "Ningyao shige Wu Dalang, buyao yige Mu Guiying," loosely translated as "Better to have ten weak men than one strong woman."[56] It would appear, then, that the protective regulations have added fuel to the fire of discriminatory treatment of women workers. In recent years the number of complaints to government bureaus, trade unions, and the Women's Federation has increased despite, or perhaps because of, these protective regulations.

Ultimately, the conclusion that women's interests have been subordinated to the state's goal of economic development is best supported by the conditions in the "special economic zones," which the government has set up to promote economic development. In these SEZs, where female labor is needed, the "return home" policy is not promoted, and protective regulations are nonexistent. While some SEZs have a broadly stated provision which requires enterprises to "implement special health protection for women workers in accordance with the provisions of the PRC,"[57] the SEZs have not been vigorous in implementing the national requirements and, to date, have not promulgated parallel regulations themselves. In the SEZs, where the need for protection is the greatest, the conditions are the worst.

Specifically, women workers constitute the majority of the labor force in the special economic zones, as much as 90 percent of the work force in some factories.[58] As temporary or contract workers, these women are not accorded many of the benefits normally guaranteed by state enterprises, and their employers often ignore central guidelines on sex discrimination and labor protection of women workers. Thus, women in special economic zones face sexual harassment, low pay, poor working conditions, long hours (including mandatory overtime of four to eight hours), and heavy workloads.[59] Factories in special economic zones provide few of the benefits normally provided by state enterprises, such as housing and meals. Housing in the SEZs can be ten to a room, and dining facilities are nonexistent. In one Shenzhen factory, workers stopped work twenty-one times between 1986 and 1988 to protest violations of their labor rights.

Chinese Women's Strategies

What strategies, then, might Chinese women pursue to better ensure gender equality in the workplace? The possible strategies are numerous, and, although they are not limited to the legal domain, legal strategies are a good place to begin. China now professes to be a state ruled by law, and the Chinese population is turning more and more to the legal arena for resolution of its problems. Chinese women have begun to work through the legal process to achieve their equality, and will likely continue to do so.

The official women's organizations have by and large pursued a strategy that takes into account socialist reality and reflects the "collectivist" tradition of China. There are, however, a growing number of voices representing the changing views of Chinese women. In 1988 the official women's magazine *Zhongguo funü* sponsored a year-long debate among scholars and readers titled "Women's Way Out" *(Nüren de chulu)*, focusing primarily on the "return home" policy.[60] Over thirty-eight articles and letters were published.

Some of the authors expressed the view that society must give greater recognition to women's contributions but also that women should be self-reliant. Others supported the continued recognition of differences between men and women, in part in order to help strike a balance between work and family. A third view was that women must have some choices in the system. The multiplicity of outlooks expressed in these articles and letters reflects Chinese women's changing lives and their perception of their role in the reformed economy, their definition of gender equality, and thus their varying strategies to achieve this equality.

A Collectivist, Not Individualist, Strategy

Chinese women have continued to push for further action on the part of the state to address discriminatory hiring and treatment. Some Chinese women recognize that regulations which provide benefits for women but do not prohibit discrimination against women can cut against women's competitiveness.[61] As I noted earlier, some factories and enterprise owners have refused to hire women on the grounds that women workers are more costly than men. Thus, for example, the Women's Federation pushed for the passage of the new national Women's Rights Protection Law in 1992 to clarify, coordinate, and reaffirm the legal protections accorded by existing regulations. During the debate on the law, the Women's Federation also lobbied, although unsuccessfully, for the elimination of the disparity in retirement age between men and women and for establishing a quota for women delegates to the National People's Congress.

It is unlikely, however, that a strategy that calls for doctrinal neutrality and similar treatment of the sexes would be adopted by Chinese women. This is primarily due to the collectivist emphasis of Chinese society and thus of Chinese law. In China there is no "individualist" or "natural rights" tradition, which views women as individuals "endowed with inalienable rights" against the competing claims of state and society. The natural rights tradition has, in countries such as the United States, led to a development of antidiscrimination legislation requiring that women be treated similarly to men.[62]

By contrast, women in China are viewed primarily as members of a family and of a community, not as autonomous, isolated individuals. As Andrew Nathan has explained, in traditional Confucian thought, social order and harmony require each person to understand and to abide by his or her rights and obligations in relation to others.[63] This collectivist tradition is bolstered by Chinese Marxism, which subordinates individual interests to the higher interests of party, class, and nation.[64] Hence, Mao wrote, "the individual is an element of the collective. When collective interests are increased, personal interests will subsequently be improved."[65] Members of a socialist society are expected to behave selflessly and sacrifice themselves for the greater good.

With the focus on the collective, the Chinese concept of rights and laws also emphasizes the imposition of duties on the individual citizen.[66] In this view, law is designed not simply to protect individual interests, but rather to enable individuals to meet their obligations to the state. Reciprocally, the state has a duty to provide and guarantee certain social and economic benefits to the individual.

Gender equality in China must be viewed in the context of the Chinese preference for collective rights. Under this analysis, the state owes women a duty to protect and guarantee certain social and economic benefits. Yet in return, rather than viewing gender equality as an inalienable natural right, the Chinese socialist state sees gender equality as an instrument of political movement toward the greater collective good of socialist construction. The appropriate concept of equality for women is dependent on what the state perceives as the needs of the collective.

Consistent with this focus on the collective, Chinese women have, and are likely to continue to pursue, a "collectivist" strategy—a strategy to define the rights and interests of the collective in a way that ensures greater equality for women.[67] In 1990, the Department of Women Workers of the All-China Federation of Trade Unions, the *Workers' Daily,* and the local workers' newspapers in China held a six-month-long debate on the "correct" understanding of women workers and childbearing values in the development of a "commodity economy."[68] The stated purpose of this discussion was to "educate" people on the public and social values of childbearing and maternity, not as subordinate to the economy but rather as a collective good in themselves.

There have also been discussions in China about the need to adjust workdays and hours to accommodate family needs as an important collective goal. At present, work hours in China are very long. Some studies report the yearly minimum to be 2,448 hours,

600 to 800 hours a year more than in some developed nations.[69] In some small towns, work periods often extend to 4,000 hours a year, two to three times the national average elsewhere in the world. A study by the China Science and Technology Development and Research Center, however, found the work efficiency among industrial and commercial laborers in the country at only 40 to 60 percent of optimal standards.[70] Experiments to improve efficiency have obtained favorable results. Recent attempts to shorten the work week have resulted in both improved efficiency and increased family time.

Improved Implementation

Coming from a collectivist society based on relational concepts, most Chinese women continue to recognize differences between men and women and prefer a strategy that recognizes those differences. Thus, some Chinese women scholars have argued that the idea that women are the same as men is a "male-centered" way of thinking.[71] At the same time, many women appear to accept the importance of "special protection" for women. Hence, there has been little open discussion in China challenging the protective nature of the 1986 and 1988 regulations. In a 1990 conference on women in China, the protections offered by the labor regulations were justified as important and necessary in safeguarding the legal rights of women because "women have their own physiological features and have the task of bearing children so as to carry on the race."[72] The women at the conference expressed the view that labor regulations should protect the health of women workers as well as their labor rights because health care for working women is an index of the liberation of women, and because protection of women's health is not simply for their own benefit but also for the benefit of a future generation.

According to this viewpoint, one strategy for women workers is to improve the implementation of existing regulations. Guo Tong, director of the Women Workers Department of the All-China Federation of Trade Unions, reports that negative effects from the 1986 and 1988 regulations are the result of insufficient measures to implement the regulations. The issue of enforcement of laws in China is not limited to these labor regulations, but there are obstacles unique to the 1986 and 1988 regulations that could be addressed to ensure better implementation. Enterprise owners have complained that the social and economic benefits guaranteed for women workers by the labor regulations are too costly. Better implementation of these regulations may mean supplementing these measures with companion programs to distribute the cost of the benefits guaranteed by the regulations. For example, the city of Nantong in Jiangsu is experimenting with a municipal women worker's maternity fund to relieve enterprises of this burden.[73] In Nantong every working employee must pay twenty yuan annually into a special fund, which is used to compensate enterprises for the subsidies they give women workers on leave.[74]

Another suggestion that has been raised, though not tried, is that tax rates for enterprises be adjusted according to the proportion of women employed (resulting in reduced taxes if more women workers are hired).[75] A final suggestion, helpful only for married women, is to divide the cost of child care and maternity benefits evenly between the husband's and wife's employer.[76]

Yet, better implementation alone may be insufficient to achieve equality for women. An acceptance of differences between men and women would require a greater awareness of what constitutes true biological differences between men and women and an approach that accepts those differences in a "nonhierarchical way and nonpejorative way."[77] This is important in China, where 30 percent of women, in a nationwide survey conducted by the Women's Studies Institution under the All-China Women's Federation and the State's Statistics Bureau, expressed the view that men are naturally more capable than women.[78] Thus, some Chinese women have also begun to emphasize the need to raise the "self-respect, self-reliance, self-confidence, and self-love" (zizun, zijiang, zicong, zi'ai) of women as an important step in achieving equality.[79]

Changing Voices of Women's Equality

Finally, while many women may want the protections accorded by the labor regulations, there may be others who choose not to take advantage of the protections. The changing voices of Chinese women show that some see a woman's choice as the route to equality.[80] In a society with an intrusive state, the issue of choice requires China to protect existing notions of rights as "zones of noninterference."[81]

On an individual level this would mean a greater sense of individual rights as well as duties to state and society. On a legal plane it would mean that the restrictions and benefits contained in any protective regulations ought to be enforced at the election of the individual woman worker. To the extent that these laws "protect" women, women must be able to choose whether and how they want to be protected. As in the area of human rights, a minority member should be able to opt out of mainstream culture or, in effect, choose the terms under which she will participate in it.[82] In this instance, Chinese women should be able to opt out of the protections and restrictions contained in these labor regulations. While the protectionism of the regulations may be explained in the context of Chinese socialist culture, the explanation does not justify imposing the standards on those members who do not want them.[83]

Ultimately, the strategy of choice would require that the goal of women's equality in China stand apart from the state's goals, and apart from economic development. Women's equality must be important because women are important apart from their roles as mothers or wives. This is particularly true when the political and civil rights of women run up against the social and economic development priorities of the state. Taking the definition of gender equality away from the state would further require the development of an independent women's movement, separate from state and party control, which encourages the multiplicity of changing women's voices.

Chinese women have worked toward equality through the collective effort of women's groups, and will continue to do so. The All-China Women's Federation theoretically represents the interests of women in China, with offices and representatives at nearly every level of society. It is an organization that has actively worked for the interests of women. Yet, even as this organization advances the cause of women, it is also an arm of the government and a wing of the party. This is true of the trade unions as well, including the Women Workers Department of the All-China Trade Unions.[84] As arms of the state, then, these organizations accept the position of the state which places economics over women's equality and which focuses on the traditional role of women.

Absent an independent women's movement, there has been no critical examination of this historical strategy to remedy the inequality of women, and only limited debate about alternative strategies. An independent women's movement is also important if Chinese women are to be the ones to define their roles in society. Since the late 1980s, the field of women's studies has been further developed in China, and international conferences have been held there to discuss the issue of women's equality.[85] These developments will assist in promoting gender equality as a separate goal, apart from its role as an instrument of social change and political campaigns, and should help individual women define for themselves what their role in society will be.

In sum, recent Chinese regulations on women and work reflect a strong trend toward the biologization of women's issues as the latest in a series of fluctuating state policies toward women. While gender equality requires the delicate balance between protection of women's reproduction and equality of opportunity for women, these regulations can be subordinated to the state's goal because of the malleability of the focus on women's biology and the concept of the "natural role" of women. Furthermore, the manner in which these regulations are implemented can further reinforce discriminatory practices against women in the work force.

In response, Chinese women's consciousness of gender equality is growing and changing. This can be seen in the continuing debates and the multiplicity of strategies for achieving equality. Some Chinese women are continuing to fight the negative implications of protective regulations, while others work for better implementation and enforcement. Gender equality can include protection of women, but the costs must be spread more equitably. There is also room for more antidiscrimination legislation to ensure that protective legislation does not become the pretext for not hiring or promoting women workers.

Finally, because of the strong emphasis on the importance of the collective in China, Chinese women will continue to develop collectivist strategies to achieve gender equality. These strategies must further define gender equality as important apart from other national goals. Ultimately, the achievement of gender equality will depend on the development of an independent voice for women in China, one that expresses the full variety of choices and views of Chinese women.

IV | Becoming Women in the Post-Mao Era

LI ZIYUN
Translated by Zhu Hong

13 | Women's Consciousness and Women's Writing

It was during the May Fourth movement in 1919 that Chinese women writers first appeared as a group on the cultural scene. But it has been only since 1976 that women's awakening consciousness has been significantly reflected in the writing of mainland women writers.

The history of Chinese literature is certainly sprinkled with women's names: Cai Wenji, Li Qingzhao, Zhu Shuzhen, and Xue Tao are some of the better-known ones. But they are rare exceptions. These early women writers were either from among the handful of educated women of elitist families or were trained courtesans. They mostly wrote poetry bemoaning the pains of parting and the emotions of loneliness and longing. Hemmed in by moral restrictions and female proprieties, these women produced works that were tame in comparison to the daring intensity of the erotic poetry of male writers. History and tradition have stifled women's voices. At most these women of the past have murmured in their loneliness and expressed a vague longing for love.

During the May Fourth movement, with its slogans of democracy, sexual equality, and liberation of the self, a new culture was born, and women writers appeared on the scene. The decade from the inception of the movement in 1919 to the end of the 1920s produced a remarkable group of women writers, pioneers in the drive against feudalism. Reading them now, however, one cannot help but feel that the demands they raised—freedom in love and marriage, self-liberation—were identical to those of male writers. At the time they did not realize that there were other issues special to women, such as economic independence, which were essential to ensuring their equality with men. In these works of the twenties, women were in league with men in their common struggle against the dark forces of feudalism. Actually, some women writers proved even more courageous than men. This is not surprising for, as in real life, once a woman makes the break with family and society, there is no turning back for her. What the women writers of this generation did not realize was that no matter how courageous their pose, what they were fighting for was merely the right to choose a man to attach themselves to. This, of course, was understandable, since for thousands of years Chinese women had been confined to the family, at the mercy of their husbands. Thus, the moment they discovered for themselves the stirrings of democracy, the first right they wanted to acquire was the right to a man of their own choosing. The consciousness of sexual inequality and the realization of the importance of economic independence came later. On this issue it was a male writer who offered deeper insights. Lu Xun, the greatest figure in modern Chinese literature, in his short story "Remorse" *(Shang shi)* first made the point that without the right to work, without economic independence, the Chinese Noras of the age were only exchanging one form of patriarchy for another. The heroine of "Remorse" succeeds in marrying the man of her choice, but ends in tragedy nonetheless.

Ding Ling, the leading female figure in modern Chinese literature, might be said to be the first woman to express an awareness of the sexual inequality underlying patriarchal oppression. Her stories from the 1920s, such as "Miss Sophie's Diary" *(Sha Fei nüshide riji)* and "Wei Hu," were concerned with the situation of women and their future in the society. The characters in both stories are liberated young women from well-to-do families with the freedom to leave home for a higher education and to mingle freely with young men. The naive young girl in "Wei Hu" falls in love with a socialist. Miss Sophie's emotional makeup is more complex. She is pursued by a very proper young man who is devoted to her, but she loves someone else, a worthless scoundrel, married, and a frequenter of brothels. Both young women, though free, are confused and do not know what they want. The love of a libertine is not dependable, of course, but even being loved by a revolutionary figure has its risks, as there are always the conflicting demands of love and revolution. The male lovers who figure in "Wei Hu" and another story, "Shanghai 1930," both desert their lovers for the sake of revolution. The stories do not pursue the fate of the young women after they are deserted, but since they have no means of support, it seems likely that they must drift into the arms of other men, or even sink into something worse.

Ding Ling was the first woman to sense that freedom in love and marriage would get women nowhere if they were not politically and economically independent. Her works also gave the first intimations of what was to become the normative theme in the literature of the decades that followed—that revolution and love are mutually incompatible. Sexual love was considered corrosive to the revolutionary spirit. In the leftist literature of the thirties, love was invariably identified as an expression of bourgeois ideology and repudiated. Thus, in revolutionary literature natural human impulses were just as repressed as they had been previously, only in another form. And this also raises the question of the place of woman in this literature. If we go over the writings of the leftist thirties and later, it becomes apparent that the description of an all-devouring love as the expression of self-definition has practically disappeared. The images of women in this mainstream literature have lost all claims to femininity. Except for women from well-to-do families who are described as negative images, women who espouse the revolution are described as sexually neutral as far as personal character and the emotions are concerned. When it was officially established that workers, peasants, and soldiers should be the central figures of literature, all descriptions of the more subtle feelings of educated women disappeared from the scene. Descriptions of love were limited to resistance to arranged marriages, mostly in rural areas, or at the other end of the scale relationships based on the common revolutionary cause. What was missing was the representation of love itself. After the thirties, except for the works of Xiao Hong and Zhang Ailing (Eileen

Chang), images of women with complex personal thoughts and emotions vanished from mainstream writing.

Xiao Hong and Zhang Ailing were two heretics on the literary scene from the 1930s throughout the 1940s. Over a span of twenty years, they were the only ones who broke through the repression of female consciousness. Not only were they set apart from their contemporaries, but the two women's writings were also very different from each other. Xiao Hong could be compared to a little cactus flower struggling to survive in a desert, whereas Zhang Ailing would be a red poppy flowering on the ruins of war and devastation. Each stood alone, struggling against great odds.

Xiao Hong's writing career was intimately associated with the literary left. *The Field of Life and Death (Shengsi chang)*, her groundbreaking work, was published under the auspices of the leftist camp, and on the whole her writings stayed within the conventions of the leftist mainstream. She wrote about rural conditions in northeast China before and during the Japanese occupation. What made her unique, however, was the fact that she not only described the abysmal conditions under which the peasants subsisted but also was particularly concerned about the fate of women, who bore an extra burden of suffering over and above what they shared with the men. For instance, in the story of a little child bride, the girl's curiosity about life and her stubborn struggle to stay alive are delineated in all their excruciating painfulness. The expectations of her mother-in-law leave no way out for the girl; she must end in madness or death. And then there are all those young women who die in childbirth. Occasionally a spark of love is kindled among the young, only to be snuffed out immediately. And women always have to pay a heavy price for one fleeting moment of tenderness. The gentle swain evolves into a brute of a husband, or the heroine has to bear the stigma of being a "fallen woman" for the rest of her life. Xiao Hong was the first woman writer ever to expose intimately the conditions of existence for women in the vast backward areas of China.

Zhang Ailing, unlike Xiao, was totally detached from the revolution and the literary mainstream. She excelled in stories of the well-to-do wives and daughters of degenerate merchant and bureaucrat families, stories that communicate an all-pervasive stench of decay. These women commit adultery out of boredom, or use all their wiles to land a good catch. One of Zhang's most outstanding stories—"The Golden Cangue" *(Jinsuo ji)*—describes the ordeals of a resourceful young woman who marries above her station. Zhang Ailing classified her stories under the general title of "romances," and at first glance they do read like popular romances. But on closer inspection what emerges is an exposé of the conditions of life for women and the way these evolving conditions affected their inner lives.

Xiao Hong conveys the deadly monotony of the lives of rural women who suffer silently and die unnoticed; their unending cycle of mute suffering leaves the reader stunned. Zhang Ailing, by contrast, puts each of her individual characters under the microscope so that we see not only every single strand of their hair but into the very core of their being. Xiao Hong's women are innocent victims who cannot even grasp the idea of defending themselves, whereas Zhang Ailing's women are very much aware of their true situation. They realize that they are the playthings of men, or the tool for producing an heir. They muster all their wits and wiles to play on men's need for them in order to secure something for themselves—official status in the family, or economic security. In the long struggle they become full of hate and resentment, even against their own offspring. They end up mentally exhausted and emotionally drained, every spark of humanity stifled.

Xiao Hong and Zhang Ailing come from different backgrounds; the characters they describe and their narrative methods are totally different. But they have one thing in common: they both broke free from the inhibitions of mainstream literature, which did not acknowledge sexual differences. They both started out from a woman's point of view to describe women's sensitivities. Although neither they themselves nor the characters they describe can be said to have attained an "awakening," they did manage to leave a feminine touch on the writing of the 1930s and 1940s.

The nonrecognition of gender issues lasted into the post-1949 era. Before 1949 this neglect may perhaps be explained by the war, a time when the issue of national survival overshadowed all others. But after the war was over, there must have been other reasons for the persisting neglect. The communist bases established before 1949 had laid down the policy of equality between the sexes throughout a period of wartime communism tempered with vestiges of peasant ideology. Under conditions of extreme scarcity, women were encouraged to work outside the home and join literacy programs. Although sexist discrimination still existed, the official policy upheld equality between the sexes and provided equal political, economic, and cultural rights for women. Thus, a number of women joined the labor force, took part in politics, even joined the army. It must be pointed out, however, that the so-called equality between the sexes was flawed from the outset by the fact that women were required to meet male standards of performance. For instance, women had to undertake hard manual labor, or even take up the gun. Under those circumstances women themselves took pride in being masculine. All manifestations of femininity were denigrated as "housewifeliness." Women themselves tried to hide their own femininity. This mentality lasted into the 1970s. Throughout those years gender differences were wiped out; not only the cut and color of their clothes but even the wristwatches worn by men and women were of the same design.

As far as writing under communist rule was concerned, the tradition of the 1930s took over and became the official line: national war and class struggle became the dominant themes. This emphasis on belligerence stifled women's voices. Under the circumstances, it is understandable that few women writers emerged. The handful of women who did write fiction wrote according to the male standards.

Xiao Hong and Zhang Ailing had done their writing in the Nationalist-controlled area. The first was considered to have betrayed the leftist tradition in which she had started her career. The other was outside the leftist tradition altogether, at one time probably even considered a target of the revolution. It was only in occupied Shanghai, where literary writing was cut off from all traditions whatsoever, that a writer such as Zhang Ailing could find fertile soil. Neither before nor after could she have thrived as a writer.

In a word, women's issues were consistently ignored from the earliest leftist writings right up to the postliberation years. If anything, the situation was aggravated after 1949. New China made provisions for women's political, economic, and legal rights. With one flourish of the pen, Chinese women acquired the right to vote, something their sisters in the West had spent decades, even centuries, fighting for. The government also provided employment for women, with equal pay for equal work, ensuring their economic independence and their dignity as individuals. But the economy, based on a still backward agricultural sector, relied heavily on manual labor, thus further "remolding" women according to male standards and accentuating the masculinization of women. Any expression of female impulses or feminine sensitivity was invariably stamped out, in literature as in life. In the early days of the newly founded state, art and literature had for a brief period abounded in images of women expressing their gratitude to the party for freeing them from unwanted marriages, or reveling in the joys of their newfound independence as members of the labor force. This of course was mostly limited to worker or peasant women. But as time went on, even these disappeared, and the depiction of women in literature was further distorted. This state of affairs was pushed to an extreme during the Cultural Revolution, in the so-called eight model operas, where women were mere vessels of class ideology, sexually neutralized revolutionary militants.

But the emotional yearnings of women could not be totally stifled. After all, even under the feudal system the "rose" had managed to peep out from behind the high walls of tradition. There were Liang Shanbo and Zhu Yingtai in "The Butterfly Lovers"; there was Cui Yingying in "The Romance of the Western Chamber" *(Xixiang ji)*, and there was Zhuo Wenjun, the courageous young widow of the Han dynasty two thousand years ago, who eloped with the man of her choice. And if it had been thus with these women, so much more so with a generation of women with the May Fourth movement behind them. It is worth noting that as early as the fifties, two women writers appeared who wrote from a woman's point of view and groped after women's consciousness—Zong Pu and Liu Zhen. Interestingly, these two writers, although about the same age, were widely divergent in personal backgrounds. Zong Pu, brought up in an academic family, was one of the most cultivated writers of her generation. Liu Zhen, by contrast, was a product of the communist base areas, having joined the army in her early teens. But each in her own way felt that the storm of revolution had wounded women emotionally. The heroines created by these two writers in stories such as "The Red Beans" (*Hongdou* by Zong Pu) or "Long Flows the Stream" (*Changchangde liushui* by Liu Zhen) had put the demands of the revolution and the needs of the collective before everything else; they did not allow themselves to be crushed by shattered love. All that their heroines did was to give way to some of their internal conflicts or express some of the pain they felt. But that was enough to incur accusations and attacks. After the writings of Liu and Zong, all expressions of womanly feelings, tastes, and sensitivity disappeared from the scene. In the first thirty years after liberation, these were the only two low moans of the female voice; after that, complete silence. In the folk songs of remote border regions, themes of female erotic longings continued to be heard. For instance, folk songs of the northwest spoke straight from a woman's heart. But these voices, too, were soon silenced.

The year 1976 marked a shift in political, economic, and cultural policy, a shift that erupted out of the self-imposed isolation of three decades and opened China up to the outside world. Art and literature, repressed for so many years, enjoyed a revival, and writers one after another began to take up their pens. Women writers, though not numerous, were outstanding from the outset. For the moment they occupied themselves with social or political themes, not with women's special issues. This was understandable, as the country was just emerging from social turmoil, and public attention was fixed on larger issues which affected people's very survival. Women, like their male counterparts, wrote about the atrocities of the Gang of Four, making their own contributions to the so-called literature of the Wounded Generation. Or they engaged in rethinking the rights and wrongs of the immediate past. In the latter mode women writers actually pioneered.

Once the repression was lifted, if only marginally, the rebel voice began to make itself heard. The first two writers to rip off the facade of sexual equality in contemporary Chinese society were Zhang Jie and Zhang Xinxin. Zhang Jie's "Love Should Not Be Forgotten" (*Ai shi buneng wangjide*) and "Gathering Wheat" (*Shi mai sui*), and Zhang Xinxin's "How Did I Miss You?" (*Wo zai nar cuoguole ni?*), all published in 1978, could be considered trial balloons before the attack proper.

Moving cautiously, Zhang Jie attempted to break the silence by challenging the taboo on the subject of love. She raised the issue on two fronts: sexual love, and human relationships in general. She did not preach a moral but allowed the message to seep in naturally through narration and dialogue. "Love Should Not Be Forgotten" describes two elderly veteran cadres who have been silently in love with each other for most of their lives, but owing to the fact that the man was tied down in a loveless marriage, they never spoke of their love to the day of their deaths. This self-denial, although exaggerated, brings out the inhumanity of the so-called moral restrictions on people's natural feelings. "Gathering Wheat" seems like a supplement to "Love Should Not Be Forgotten." It is a sketch of a little girl, an ugly duckling, and her warm relationship with a poor old man, a candy peddler. Such a tender description of a human relationship was absent in the literature of the revolutionary period. What the author is saying is that men and women, old and young, all need to love and to be loved, and that it is inhuman to repress that need.

Zhang Jie was the first woman to stand out and make an appeal for love in a loveless desert. Zhang Xinxin protested on behalf of women in another way—by asking questions. Indignantly she asked, how has woman come to lose her feminine characteristics? How has she become so coarse, so awkward? In her stories, all the sights and scenes to which we have become accustomed through daily contact suddenly take on the aspect of the unfamiliar and the unnatural once they are put in the spotlight. In her short story "How Did I Miss You?" Zhang Xinxin chose for her protagonist a ticket seller on a public bus. The young woman is good at her job, but is also a talented writer whose play has been accepted for performance by an amateur dramatic group. Her job requires her to fight and shout her way through the crowd on the bus. Wrapped in a shapeless padded jacket, stamping about in her big clumsy boots, she has lost all trace of femininity. At the rehearsal of her play she meets and falls for the director. He admires her talent but is repelled by her aggressiveness and her rough, masculine manner. Zhang Xinxin describes her heroine's feelings of frustration and hurt. She asks, now who made her what she is in the first place? Is it not men themselves, who make all the rules? Why did they "remold" her into such a shape and then reject her for being what they have made of her? The young woman realizes that what she has lost is not only one missed chance for love but her very nature as a woman.

In appealing for "the right to love," in attempting to take back the femininity of which women have been robbed, Zhang Xinxin and Zhang Jie challenged the firmly entrenched conventions of communist writing, and thus they came under attack. But by the 1980s the Cultural Revolution was over, times had changed, and the fate of Zong Pu and Liu Zhen in the 1950s could not be repeated. In the new cultural environment Zhang Xinxin and Zhang Jie were defiant and stood their ground. In the aftermath of the affair, Zhang Xinxin described Zhang Jie admiringly as a "witch." Actually both of them were regarded as wicked witches by the conservative old guard, who still held on to the communist prescriptions for writing.

Once the defenses were breached, the situation got out of control; women's pent-up resentments over the years burst out and swelled into a flood. Now the lid was off, and the subjects were not limited to "love should not be forgotten" or "how did I miss you?" Other women writers introduced other problems such as sexual discrimination, sexual harassment, sexual abuse, and the persecution of women under the old ethical code: in short, all the obstructions and frustrations that women face in the search for self-realization.

In this general attack it was still Zhang Jie and Zhang Xinxin who stood at the forefront. They followed up the earlier stories with a string of notable works even more outspoken about women's causes. Zhang Xinxin's "On the Same Horizon" (*Zai tongyige dipingxian*), "The Dream of Our Generation" (*Women zhege nianjide meng*), and "The Last Haven" (*Zuihoude tingbo di*), as well as Zhang Jie's *The Ark (Fang zhou)* and "Emerald" (*Zumu lu*), were among the most outstanding. Zhang Xinxin bluntly pointed out that men and women do not take off from the same starting line in today's competition. She particularly emphasized the conflicts of family, love, and career that beset women. Zhang Jie exposed the sexual discrimination and sexual harassment with which women are regularly confronted.

A demand for equal and fair competition runs through these

three stories by Zhang Xinxin. All deal with the fate of ambitious young women who try to compete on an equal basis with their husbands, and the price they have to pay. The couple in "On the Same Horizon" have been through the rural reeducation ordeal and are now back in the city, both looking for a chance to make something of themselves. The story focuses on their conflicts in this process, describing everyday occurences that forcefully bring out the existing inequality in society, despite the letter of the law. In addition to the demands of a social role, women have to carry the extra burdens of a family role, bearing and rearing children, looking after the house, even supporting their husbands in their careers. Under the circumstances, how can women compete with men as equals? Besides, women are required by convention to be "womanly" and support their husbands in adversity, to give in to their fits of temper and to nourish them when tired. In a word, they are expected to sacrifice themselves to their husbands. Men reciprocate by letting their wives bask in their glory once they achieve it. The young woman in "On the Same Horizon" complains: "He expects me to love him, but what about me? Has he ever thought of loving me?" "He wants to enjoy family happiness and he expects me to give up everything else to supply it for him." She points out rightly that "when I have given up everything for him, I will not be his intellectual equal anymore, and he will lose interest in me." She keeps asking: "What about me? Where do I come in?"

The questions she raises are still valid today. For instance, in popular culture there are dozens of examples of a wife's being praised for supportiveness when the husband is honored for his achievements. The words of a popular song in honor of military heroes goes something like this: "This medal of honor, one half is yours, one half is mine." Actually, we all know that the real honor goes to the husband, who did the fighting. And anyway, how can a husband's achievements replace one's own achievements? The assumption behind the words of the song is that women are just an appendage of their husbands.

After painful deliberation and hesitation, the heroine of "On the Same Horizon" chooses career over family. She has an abortion, gets a divorce, and enrolls in a drama institute. "The Last Haven" reads like a sequel. Here the heroine is a divorced actress who has achieved a measure of success. She feels a void in her life, however, for she misses the love of a man. But by now she has lost the aggressiveness of the heroine of "On the Same Horizon." She is overcome by weakness and self-doubt. So once again our heroine is back where she started out, torn between career and family. This seems to be the perennial state of most of Zhang Xinxin's heroines.

Zhang Jie's heroines, by contrast, have given up all illusions of love. They have given up on men as hopeless, and have decided to prove their own worth in society at large. *The Ark* exposes the presence of sexual discrimination, sexual harassment, and sexual abuse, and describes women's rebellion. All three women in the story have marital problems. Liu Quan and Cao Jinghua are both divorced. Liu could not bear the nightly rape that her husband subjected her to, while Jinghua's husband divorced her because she had an abortion. Liang Qian remains married in name only; her husband will not give her a divorce because he still wants to use her father's powerful connections. Their collective message to these husbands is: "We are human beings, not sexual tools."

These three women also encounter problems in pursuit of careers. Liu is not only sexually abused by her husband but also subjected to harassment by her boss. Liang Qian has used her father's influence to secure an apartment for her two friends and to help Liu Quan transfer to a better job. But in her own work as a film director, she is hedged in on every side by male colleagues who do not want to work under a woman, as well as male censors who find fault with her film.

Zhang Jie's women are more aggressive than Zhang Xinxin's. Although they have given up on men, they still long for someone to love, and want to be loved in return. But they have learned through hard experience that all men, whether husbands or lovers, only want women to be playthings in their lap, that no man wants an independent-minded woman. These women have realized that equality on paper is not enough, that "one must fight tooth and nail to assert one's own value." Zhang Jie sometimes sounds hysterical and tends to go to extremes. But her grasp of women's predicament is firm and clear-sighted.

Many women followed in the wake of Zhang Jie and Zhang Xinxin and explored further the problems confronting women, approaching them from different angles. Some were plaintive, listing the injustices that women were subject to. Others portrayed a new type of woman, one who decides to ignore what the world may say and goes her own way.

The first group wrote on a wide variety of subjects but concentrated on one basic issue: the destructive effect of traditional ethics on the lives of women. Wen Bin's "Silent Commemoration" *(Xin ji)*, a story set in the sixties, and Zong Pu's "Tragedy of the Walnut Tree" *(Hetao shude beiju)*, set against the background of the Cultural Revolution, describe women as victims in the grip of the feudal ideal of chastity. The protagonist of "Silent Commemoration" was widowed when young and went through unspeakable hardships to raise her five daughters. With the children all grown, she wants to marry a cousin from her home village, a childhood friend who has remained faithful through the years. But she is fiercely opposed by her daughters. They are the new generation, educated, with government jobs, yet they feel that their mother's remarrying would be a disgrace. The mother submits to her daughters' verdict, ashamed that she has ever harbored the thought of remarrying. The woman in "The Tragedy of the Walnut Tree" lives in a prison of her own making. Her husband left to go abroad and never returned. The woman waits year after year until, thirty years later, she receives a letter telling her that he is not coming back but will be responsible for their daughter's education abroad. In response she decides to cut down the walnut tree in the courtyard. Not only was the tree a witness to their vows of undying love, but it has also been her companion throughout her solitary years. In cutting down the tree, she cuts off her emotional links to her husband and frees herself from the outdated ethical codes which have tied her down. The two stories are quiet in tone, but their condemnation of traditional ethics is nonetheless truthful and poignant.

Feudal concepts of virginity were overthrown during the May Fourth movement, yet they linger on, casting a chill into women's hearts. Even to this day women have been ruined for breaking the taboos of virginity and chastity. Chen Jie's story "The Big River"

(Dahe) presents this issue in an extreme form. The story revolves around an incident in which a woman middle school teacher and a casual male friend, a poet, lose their way while walking in the woods and do not come out until they get help from a local peasant the next morning. This is enough to create a storm in the little world of the school. The poet's wife seeks out the teacher and slaps her face in public. The party cell at the school makes a case out of the incident and sets up a team to investigate. The poet is interested only in protecting his own skin. Two other characters are described in remarkable depth. One is the party secretary of the school who herself has had an extramarital affair and now goes to extraordinary lengths to present herself as virtue outraged. Her questioning of the poor teacher is an outright inquisition. The other character is the betrothed of the young woman. He himself once seduced a young girl, and was slapped in the face by the man she subsequently married. Like the party secretary, the more guilty he feels, the more intolerant he becomes. He keeps saying magnanimously, "Never mind, never mind," but repeatedly asks the poet, "What exactly did you do to her?" The teacher finally throws herself into the river, not to prove her innocence but rather in despair at the shameless hypocrisy engulfing her, and as a protest against the insults to which she has been subjected.

Lu Xing'er is an author who writes exclusively on women. Her works include two volumes of short stories—*Born Women (Tiansheng shige nüren)* and *A World in Herself (Yige nüren de yitai xi)*. A recurring theme in her writings is that in the relations between the sexes, woman is always the loser. According to Lu Xing'er, women are too obsessed with love, too ready to give up everything for love, while men consider women only one part of their life. "The Sun Is Not Out Today" *(Jintian meiyou taiyang)* and "The One and the Other" *(Yige he yige)* are representative of her approach. The first story takes place in a clinic, where a group of women are lined up waiting for abortions. The schoolteacher's husband had neglected to take precautions. The actress has finally gotten a chance to play a lead role and does not want to jeopardize her career. One young woman is unmarried. Another is carrying the child of a married man. None of these unwanted pregnancies was the result of violence or seduction. All the women had engaged in sexual relations willingly, and now bear sole responbility for the results. We are naturally led to ask: "Is this fair?" The second story describes two women who are totally different in every way. One woman has ordered her whole life around her husband: he has been the center of her existence. Now that he is dead, she finds herself lost. Her neighbor is a successful career woman, an artist, the typical liberated woman, independent, enjoying life. The widow admires and envies her. She later finds out, however, that her artist friend has been carrying on a lifelong affair with a married man, and through it all the man has kept playing the model husband to his wife. So the widow is confronted with the question, if this is being liberated, is it worthwhile? Which of the women is leading a fuller life after all?

Among the writers registering the sufferings of women, Zu Lin occupies a significant place. In her novel *Female—Human (Nüxing ren)*, she traces the universal fate of women in the lives of three generations. A grandmother, a mother, and a daughter live under different social systems, and the circumstances of their life stories differ, but there is a striking similarity in their sufferings and final fates. The grandmother left home for the sake of love but ended up being deserted. In the second generation, the husband was a weakling and committed suicide during the antirightist campaign. To bring up her daughter, the mother supplemented her income by prostitution. When the daughter discovered her mother's secret, she left home, outraged, and went to settle in a remote rural area. After undergoing countless sufferings and seeing something of life in the country, she returned home, sick and destitute, and married a man she did not love. As she is about to give herself to him, she realizes in a flash that she is following in her mother's footsteps.

Sooner or later someone was bound to make a stand and end the general tone of plaintiveness in writing about women. The first to strike this positive note was Dai Qing. In "The Unexpected Tide" *(Buqide chaoxun)* she tells the story of a young widow with a child, who decides to marry a man several years younger than herself. This act is in itself a challenge to tradition and displays a new attitude. Here a new type of woman has emerged, one who will not submit to fate and is not afraid to attempt the impossible.

Dai Qing is still a member of the middle-aged generation who has had to overcome her scruples to carve out a new path in the portrayal of women and their problems, as in "The Unexpected Tide." But a younger generation has gone even further. They have grown up in the environment of the new period; their values and their codes of behavior are different from those of the previous generation; they totally ignore so-called public opinion and just go their own way. With one group of young writers, a new type of individualistic heroine takes center stage. The pop singer in Liu Suola's story "The Pop Star" *(Gewang)*, the artist's model and the manager in Liu Xihong's "You Cannot Change Me" *(Ni buke gaibian wo)* and "The Black Forest" *(Hei senlin)*, all belong to this type. They make their own decisions about jobs, career, and marriage, and never allow themselves to be moved by what the world will say. They do not dream of love everlasting, do not place men at the center of their lives; they may not even need a man in their lives at all. "Blue Sky and Azure Sea" *(Lantian lühai)*, for instance, describes the friendship of two young women. Critics on the mainland consider these unburdened young women models of the new style of liberated, independent woman. In this fictional world it seems that these young women are not restricted by the manmade rules of male-centered society. But we must take into account the fact that these women are a tiny fraction of the female population. When the overwhelming majority are not liberated, the liberation of a few does not have a firm basis. The part is subject to the whole, after all. And what is more, within the limits of the stories sexual inequality is not abolished; it just has not come into the confines of these young women's lives. The road to women's liberation is long and arduous, but these young women could be the first swallows of spring.

Other writers leave women's conflict with the establishment aside for the moment to study some innate women's problems, for instance, the problem of sexual repression. Sex has been a taboo subject for Chinese women from time immemorial. According to this view, sex equals lasciviousness, the epitome of evil as far as women are concerned. Thus, although sex is a fact of life, it is nonexistent in literature. In the literature of the May Fourth movement, only "Miss Sophie's Diary" expressed women's sexual urges, and it shocked the public. Other works of the era stopped at the edge of emotion. More recently, "Love Should Not Be Forgotten" avoided all hints of sexuality, keeping love strictly platonic. But a new group of writers is doing the opposite, portraying sex as instinctive. Wang Anyi's trilogy "Love in the Barren Mountains" *(Huangshan zhi lian)*, "Love in a Small Town" *(Xiaocheng zhi lian)*, and "Love in a Beautiful Valley" *(Jinxiugu zhi lian)* is typical, as are Tie Ning's story "The Haystack" *(Maijie duo)* and her novel *The Rose Gate (Meigui men)*. Interestingly, these two writers started their careers by describing the growing pains of innocent young girls, then shifted to portraying love nakedly, as an instinctive urge. In her distinctive, intimate narrative style, Wang Anyi describes the sexual awakening of young women and their ultimate satisfaction. Tie Ning, by contrast, depicts the sexual frustration and pain of women, and their psychological and emotional scars.

"Love in a Beautiful Valley" describes the casual affair of a well-seasoned woman; the other two stories in Wang Anyi's trilogy portray the growth of women from naive youth to full sexual maturity. Cutting across the differences in circumstances and setting, one common theme runs through the descriptions of all these young women: once aroused, they are insatiable. They are shameless, out of control, and care nothing for consequences; in their search for sexual satisfaction, everything is swept away. Only pleasure prevails.

Wang Anyi's trilogy attracted a lot of attention on the mainland. It was the first time the bedroom was brought into view. According to tradition, sex was unmentionable. Previous descriptions of sex in writing, from the 1930s right through to the 1980s, had always been linked to specific social problems, not excepting the writings of the male author Zhang Xianliang. It was Wang Anyi who first described sex as an instinctive drive, uncontrollable because it represents the ultimate happiness. All the characters concerned, men and women, cultivated or ignorant, derive unutterable ecstasy from sexual experience, whether carried out under the veil of romantic love, or thrust forward in crude and naked, even perverted form. It makes no difference. On most occasions it is the woman who takes the initiative. In their mutual contest, physical and spiritual, it is always the female who is stronger. Sometimes she might play the submissive little woman, but only to arouse, and eventually to dominate. Contrary to the conventional way of presenting woman as a passive tool for male satisfaction, Wang presents women as the active party. The literary world was stunned.

Tie Ning perceived sex as an unchanging part of human nature, modified by social conditions. She studied the forms of these modifications, especially as they affected women. The haystack in "The Haystack," a hideout for lovemaking, is a witness to sexual games through historical changes. *The Rose Gate* portrays the varying responses to sex across three generations of women under changing historical conditions. The rose gate, of course, is the writer's symbol for the female genitals. Describing a young girl's puberty, she writes: "This year, the spring is so rosy." And later, as the young woman painfully gives birth to a girl: "Another woman has forced open the radiant gate." Taking Tie Ning's symbol of the rose for the female genitals one step further, one could say that the war between the sexes is "the War of the Rose." The grandmother's involvement with sex is a long story. Born to a good family, she first gives herself to a revolutionary, and then marries a rake against the wishes of her family. He soon deserts her for another woman, but she is not one to accept defeat. She carries on a long-standing battle to take back her husband: if not his heart, at least his body. Broken in spirit by several failures and sexually starved, she repeatedly tries to revenge herself on her husband and his family and develops a perverted interest in other people's sexual secrets. She spies on her daughter-in-law and follows her granddaughter, but all her wiles harm only herself. She ends up a physical and mental wreck. Hers is the tragedy of an intensely clever woman defeated by circumstances.

The second generation, the aunt, is a different type altogether. Without making scenes, she quietly goes about getting what she wants—marriage, divorce, affairs, everything is handled smoothly. She looks her mother-in-law straight in the eye when caught in adultery. Even so, she also ends up losing the man she has set her heart on.

The third generation seems more clear-headed than the elders as far as relations between the sexes are concerned. For a fleeting moment the granddaughter is attracted by two of her aunt's lovers, but she resists temptation. But her marriage does not turn out a success either. One thing Wang Anyi and Tie Ning have in common is the absence of any kind of perfect sexual relationships in their works. Also, women are always stronger than men, usually taking the initiative in relationships. This kind of description may seem somewhat exaggerated and far-fetched at first sight, but perhaps it is logical that the first stirring of sexual revolt should take on a hint of the hysterical, just as the earlier reactions against sexual inequality exemplified by the works of Zhang Jie and Zhang Xinxin were also exaggerated.

This quick overview of recent women's writing highlights only the most significant details. Actually there were many more women writing on women. Their works include Shen Rong's "Divorce? Why Bother?" *(Lande lihun)*, Xu Naijian's "Just Because I'm Thirty and Unmarried" *(Yinwei wo shi sanshi sui de guniang)*, Hu Xin's "Four Women of Forty" *(Sige sishi sui de nüren)*, and many others. Another interesting aspect of the new writing on women is the description of women living in remote, backward areas of the country, as in Chi Zijian's "Northern Wilderness under Snow" *(Beiguo yipian cangmang)*. In these areas women are still being publicly bought and sold; their lives are still men's to dispose of. These women are just as enslaved as they were during the thirties and forties, the difference being only one of form. One can easily imagine the force of their revolt if they were roused from their current state of semistupor.

As is quite apparent, all the women writers mentioned herein are writing within the limits of a state control which does not officially recognize sexual inequality. Some are writing, consciously or not, under the general assumption of a "femininity" which they wish to reclaim as part of a woman's right. Others are more concerned with social issues. All tend to identify with their heroines in getting their message across. But whatever the differences in their theoretical assumptions, they are all actively engaged in raising the long-overdue Woman Question.

And yet there has always been a tradition of women writers who do not necessarily concern themselves with gender issues, but primarily write about social and universal human issues, and this tradition is still alive today. Any larger study of women's literature in China should not ignore this other aspect of women's writing, which is outside the scope of this essay.

14 | Women, Illness, and Hospitalization: Images of Women in Contemporary Chinese Fiction

What is most noteworthy about Chinese women's fiction of the "new era" is not just the proliferation of women writers. Nor is it the articulation of women's themes, although that has reached remarkable proportions. Most noteworthy in recent women's fiction is the changing language of the imagery, the new way that women image themselves.

At the very outset of the post-Mao era, Zong Pu enlisted a series of mixed metaphors of illness and hospitalization in her novella *The Everlasting Stone* (1980) to describe the vicissitudes of a literary woman caught up in the toils of the Cultural Revolution. With the launching of the reform of the early eighties, Shen Rong stunned the literary world and the reading public with *At Middle Age* (1980), which opens with a woman dying in hospital. Midway into the decade, the younger writer Lu Xing'er summed up woman's position in the age of reform, her gains and her losses, in a story set in an abortion clinic, "The Sun Is Not Out Today" (1987). If we put aside Ding Ling's tubercular Miss Sophie as belonging to an earlier tradition where descriptions of disease have more romantic associations, we could say that these women writers have effected a quiet revolution: a revolution in the sense of exploring new ways of representing women, breaking away from old stereotypes and prescriptions.

The representation of women has always been a problematic issue in contemporary Chinese fiction. In a society in which the local version of Marxism does not recognize sexual inequality, writing overtly about women's issues is at best risky. As late as 1987 the visiting feminist scholar Ruth Perry was told by a representative of the official All-China Federation of Women that Chinese women are "liberated and equal." Thus, any thinking and writing about women's problems must necessarily be framed within this larger context and inevitably marginalized and trivialized. What is worse, women can be blamed for their own problems. The federation's official slogans of "Self-Respect," "Self-Reliance," and "Self-Strengthening," with their emphasis on individual effort, do not leave much room for looking at women's problems in relation to anything outside their own willpower. This can be motivating, and yet it can also be guilt-provoking.

From 1949 right up to the end of the Maoist era, tied down by official prescriptions and taboos, writing by women about women has not flourished, and women writers have been largely cut off from their literary foremothers of the twenties and thirties. The situation in Maoist China was comparable to that in the former Soviet Union, where invariably "the images women create of their gender are made with a male tradition in mind."[1]

Apart from the lack of justification—political, ideological, and theoretical—for taking up gender as a separate issue, women's writing is constrained by a hierarchy of theme and subject matter. Such a hierarchy is part and parcel of the literary orthodoxy and implicit in much current literary criticism. In the afterword to *Essays on Contemporary Women Writers,* even Li Ziyun, a critic who has worked for many years to promote women's writing, finds herself ranking the achievements of women's writing by theme and subject matter. She begins with "those works concerning major social conflicts, on which hang the destiny of millions." Descending in the scale of values, she comes to writings "on various conflicts in the society . . . touching on problems of personal dignity, private fates," this second category being justified by the way it "reflects the world in a nutshell." She ends with the topics of "love and marriage," which are not exclusively the province of women, she concedes, although "women writing on the subject attract more attention."[2] By an unspoken code it is assumed, first, that the subject closest to women's interests is that of love and marriage, and second, that this particular subject ranks lowest in the literary scale of values. This, of course, gives rise to the very difficult question of the difference between the man's and the woman's point of view on what constitutes the importance of any subject. Could it be taken for granted that "a scene in a battlefield is more important than a scene in a shop"[3]—assuming, of course, that the man is on the battlefield and the woman in the shop?

In addition to the hierarchy of theme and subject matter which tends to demean women's issues, women writing about women are also inhibited by the tyranny of models. Just as women are put on a pedestal in the western tradition—the madonna, the angel in the house, in a word the unattainable—so are they "privileged" in socialist writing. Woman in much of the writing of the Maoist era is put on a revolutionary pedestal, where she plays out her exemplary role, more often than not ending in sacrificial death on the altar of the revolution.

In the post-Mao era this model has been transformed, yet the situation is not essentially changed. Instead of the revolutionary heroine, the new fiction has developed a breed of "superwomen," the female counterpart of the "tough guy" phenomenon. As one critic writes, "Hemingway could not have foreseen that, owing to the specific historical and social factors in the China of the eighties, the tough guy of the East has reared his rugged head."[4] Muscular frame, cold exterior, invincible will, steadfastness of purpose, and strong leadership are some of the distinguishing marks of the "tough guy," setting up a new aesthetic model. Basic to all this is strength—the strength with which the hero sweeps all before him in the struggle against great odds, be it the forces of nature or of human institutions. The heroes of Jiang Zilong, Zhang Chengzhi, and Liang Xiaosheng are the best illustration of this larger-than-life idealized male.

The "superwoman" image shares some of the characteristics of her male counterpart, though considerably diminished in glory. Jiang Zilong, who has set a number of his recent works in the reform era, published a novella, *At Sixes and Sevens,* with a woman at the center. Bu Tianxie is a brilliant scientist and chief engineer of an electronics engineering institute. "She works like a whirlwind," sweeping from her path all petty scheming and underhandedness. But with an uncontrollable temper and naïveté in handling personal relationships, Bu is surrounded on all sides by traps and obstacles, and ends up—significantly for the purpose of this essay—a wreck in the hospital. The actress-writer Huang Zongying's work of literary reportage, "The Flight of the Wild Geese," eulogizes an obscure botanist working tenaciously on herbal medicine high up in the mountains of northwest China. Qin Guanshu had been discriminated against and repressed for most of her working life because of her family background. Yet she herself played into the hands of her enemies with her own general moroseness and harsh temper. It seems that where the male is tough and authoritative, his female counterpart manages only to be quarrelsome and offensive, an aberration from true womanliness, so to speak.

Another dimension of the "superwoman" model lies in the portrayal of moral superiority, as if what women lack in strength and authority they make up in moral virtue, suffering "moral and ethical pressures beyond female endurance,"[5] as one critic points out approvingly. Contemporary fiction abounds in illustrations of this double standard of "toughness," by male and female writers alike. The poor peasant woman up in the mountain cabin, deserted by the man whose life she had saved and whose child she has borne (Zhang Xuan, "The Woman Up Eight Temple Mountain") or the woman who forgives her philandering husband and brings up his illegitimate child as her own (Hang Ying, "An Oriental Female") are but some of the examples held up for emulation. Thus, through the evolution of types, the basic expectation of the selfless female remains the same. The post-Tiananmen soap opera hit on national television, *Aspirations,* projects the saintly figure of a female "do-gooder"—"selfless," "obedient," "caring," "never angry." A report in the *New York Times* expressed surprise that the hard-line government seems to have discovered this figure and seized on her as a tool to propagate communist morality.[6] Actually, what could be more logical, seeing that this tearjerker fulfills all the requirements of the selfless female role model? A gushing article in *People's Daily* for Woman's Day, March 8, 1991, eulogizes this "Virgin Mary of the East" and holds up her virtues for emulation, first and foremost among them "giving in and giving way."[7] If we take it that "self-denial plays a significant role in the ideology of the modern age as reflected in contemporary Chinese literature,"[8] then the representation of women has certainly been co-opted to fit into this scheme. If the revolutionary heroine of an earlier age was the revolutionaries' male fantasy, likewise the superwoman of the new fiction is but an alternate form of this same fantasy, a new intrusion of "those patriarchal definitions that intervene between herself and herself."[9] Hampered by value judgments regarding theme, subject matter, and role models, one may well echo the words of Patricia Spacks as she contemplates women writers of eighteenth- and nineteenth-century England as they set pen to paper: "So what is a woman to do, setting out to write about women?"[10]

Repossessing Her Own Body

One significant way women writers slip through the hierarchy of theme and subject matter and outwit prescriptive role models is by putting their heroines "out of work," divesting them of social and domestic duties for the time being and putting them in bed—not in a marital bed, which is not "duty-free," but in a sickbed. Once in a sickbed, the female is no more the selfless, indefatigable superwoman, ceaselessly performing, endlessly giving, silently enduring. Paradoxically, "to be selfless is not only to be noble, it is to be dead,"[11] whereas to be ill, weak, even dying is to be alive again, not "giving in and giving way," but struggling for self-assertion in the act of fighting for one's life and health, both physical and spiritual. Thus the irony of an alternate image of woman: no longer standing on a pedestal but lying in a sickbed.

A formidable array of sick and dying women people the new literature. They range from the dying doctor Lu Wenting in *At Middle Age* to the dying communist cadre Tian Jing in "Sons and Daughters" by Ru Zhijuan; from the talented doctor Yen Xiaoyan in "The Old Maid" by Li Huixin to the dedicated village schoolteacher

Liu Qing in "Four Women of Forty" by Hu Xin, and finally to Peiti in *The Everlasting Stone* by Zong Pu, all diagnosed with cancer. And then there is the beautiful young woman paralyzed in bed in "The Serenity of Whiteness" by Gu Ying, the deranged doctor Jin Naiwen perennially confined to the hospital in "What's Wrong with Him?" by Zhang Jie, and the many other ill and dying women in Zong Pu's stories. There they lie, waiting for treatment, giving birth, undergoing abortions, struggling with death.

Since male appropriation of the female body is deeply inscribed in the literary canon, women writing themselves cannot be really free until they repossess and redefine their own bodies. Through the imaginative act of putting women in the hospital, new dimensions are opened up for more intimate ways of experiencing women's lives, alternate ways of representing women.

While not going so far as to "place the female body at the center of a search for female identity,"[12] as cautioned against by Elaine Showalter, the Chinese woman writer does show a new awareness of woman's body as soon as she shakes off the pressures of constricting role models. The situation is comparable to that of Virginia Woolf, when she "murders the angel in the house" and is confronted with her own body. For the first time, women's bodies and physical appearances are described in these works in a truthful and significant manner, free of the cluster of values and taboos that cling to the conventional revolutionary female stereotype. What Virginia Woolf had in mind when she confronted the experience of her own body was obviously sexuality. A number of women writers in China, Wang Anyi for one, are exploring the same path. The writers under consideration here, however, discover woman's body while rejecting sexuality. In traditional Chinese literature rarely was a woman's body and physical appearance of interest except as an object of male desire. There are changes, certainly, in the new tradition of socialist literature, but only in order to make women's bodies vessels of unlimited capacity to take on suffering, for instance, as in the much-admired description of Elder Sister Jiang in *The Red Crag*, calmly combing her hair before she goes to meet her executioners, in a veritable sacrifice-made-easy formula.

Zhang Jie, Zong Pu, Lu Xing'er, and others, however, discover woman's body not in relation to male desire, nor as a tool for worthy ends, but from a woman's own point of view, in relation to herself and her own situation. They begin by rejecting the sexual role. Sick, in the hospital, women have ceased to function, not only in a social, political, or domestic capacity, but even as sexual beings. In "The Serenity of Whiteness" it is apparent that Shao Xueqing is of no use to her husband as they lie side by side in her hospital ward, she tied to her bed, he on a board wedged between her bed and the radiator, among three other sick women and the husband of one of them stretched across four chairs placed together. Here it is precisely Shao Xueqing's sexlessness that is at the bottom of the war between the couple. Yet she is described as beautiful as she reclines in bed against a background of pure white, which emphasizes her sexlessness. Her legs are two withered sticks, which her husband "shoves into a basin of warm water" as he performs his nursing duty, for which he receives a stipend. Her bloodless hands, also still beautiful, are engaged in a feminine activity—knitting. Ostensibly she is knitting for her neighbors, the nurses, anybody who asks her for the favor. In reality, like a latter-day Madame Defarge, she is remembering and plotting her own future. Whiteness, her distinguishing mark, combines sexlessness and a determination to wipe out the past in a powerful symbol of a dying woman launched on a search for her own identity now that what she had held onto—marriage and family—are lost.

The sick woman is not even a pleasure to behold, contrary to the conventional ways of portraying women as objects of beauty in men's eyes. Zhang Jie's *The Ark*, the first avowedly feminist novel of the new era, portrays three professional women sharing a flat and struggling against a hostile male-dominated environment. Here, physical descriptions function as clues to the inner being of these women. Cao Jinghua lies on the floor completely exhausted after she finishes unloading coal briquettes for winter storage. Unable to move, her thin frame racked with the pain of arthritis, her eye sockets deeply hollowed, her feet filthy with coal dust, she is a pitiful sight. Liang Qian, the filmmaker, is worn out and often hysterical. In a pane of glass at the studio she sees her own face, "pale, worn, dishevelled, but eyes still looking out defiantly under angry brows . . . certainly not a face to attract." Liang Qian feels like the little tree that clings to the horizon in her own film: "helpless, forlorn, crooked, knobby." Helpless, yes, but knobby, that is, not smooth or soothing to the touch. In the description of these women there is no effort to soften or adorn. Earlier on, the philandering Bai Fushan arrives to spy on his estranged wife, Liang Qian, and startles her two housemates out of bed on a Sunday morning—huddled in nightgowns, dragging their slippers, with unwashed faces and messy hair. Ugliness, pain, and dirt here form a literal description of the condition of these women, and something else besides: they are a symbol of the injustice and frustration that bear down on them and threaten to ruin them.

The Ark has many striking descriptions of women as they appear in men's eyes. Ill, dirty, worn-out, aged, they attract contempt. "Knobby" and defiant, they attract hostility and fear. Bai Fushan, the estranged husband, looks Liang Qian up and down and notices her "thin, sticklike legs and wasted hips." Moving his eyes upward, he sees her "sunken chest and thin yellow face." He can no longer find anything lovable or even interesting about her. "How on earth could she have sunk to this?" he asks himself, as he proceeds to negotiate with her to obtain a favor from her powerful father. This is, incidentally, the reason he still hangs on to the marriage despite Liang Qian's wasted looks—the useful connection. Mr. Xie, the bribe-taking head of the department where the third housemate, Liu Quan, works, has his own unpleasant perception of Liang Qian. After a painful conversation on the phone when she accuses him of breaking a promise, Mr. Xie visualizes her as "a piece of stale pastry, hard and dry, with a smell of grease." "If all women were like that," he thinks to himself, "what will the world come to? And what would be the point of having men at all?" Fortunately for him, not all women are like that, and he turns with pleasure to his favorite assistant, Qian Xiuying, characterized as "the woman who always remembers that she is a woman." "Her belt was drawn tightly across her waist; the excess fat in her middle was pushed down, making her belly protrude under her colorful dress, like a butterfly about to break out of its cocoon." The comparison is a perfect symbol for Qian Xiuying, fluttering around her boss like a butterfly.

Of the three women, only the English interpreter Liu Quan has a youthful figure and good looks, but her eyes are always red and swollen from crying, and her looks only draw the harassment of her boss, who opens his fly as he makes her "report" her work to him. These are women whose "looks" are literally ranged against them in the battle of the sexes.

Incidentally, the deathblow to Liang Qian's artistic ambitions is dealt by nothing other than an image of female anatomy—a woman's breasts. Liang Qian's film is finally finished and is being reviewed by the censors. "Why does the lead actress have such high breasts? Are they real or padded?" growls one of the censors. "If padded, then we have a problem on our hands." Liang shoots back, "Why don't you give them a squeeze to find out?" And that, of course, draws the death sentence for her film.

The Ark is an angry book—angry at men's selfish cruelty, cynical greed, and shamelessness, and at women's powerlessness. This anger saturates the plot, which consists of a string of frustrations for the three women, all trained professionals who have given up on love and ask only for satisfaction through practicing their professions. The anger vibrates through the narrative voice, indignant, bitter, ironic, cynical, contemptuous. And last but not least, the sheer physical description of the three women as they appear to themselves, to one another, and in men's eyes is invested with an anger that strikes out savagely.

Best known for the sexless ethereality of her female characters, Zong Pu constructs a paradigm from extreme physicality to extreme spirituality in *The Everlasting Stone*. The story begins with a double death sentence for the heroine, the thirty-eight-year-old Peiti, writer and teacher of Chinese literature at a major university—physical death by cancer and political death by the assignment of an "enemy" label.

In a clinically precise representation of operations, exposed organs, squirting blood, and mutilation, Zong Pu completely demystifies the female body. She starts with the basics: cells. The reader is introduced to the heroine through her cells. Peiti goes to the hospital for a biopsy and gets a chance to look through the microscope at her own cells. The "bad" cells, a deadly green-black, seem to glare at her maliciously. She shivers. After all, they are right inside her own body. The "good" cells are pink and soft and kindly looking. But this is only the beginning of a complex metaphor. Peiti is also invaded by "cancer of the soul." Just as the individual physical body is invaded by cancer, so is the collective political body. The descriptions of violence, sadistic cruelty, pervasive dirt, and the accompanying smells all testify to a deeply sick society, torn by the contest between "good" and "bad" cells. The good cells are people like Doctor Fan (who eventually marries the heroine), old Doctor Han, Peiti's friend Tao Huijun, and the decent, hardworking people whom Peiti meets in the hospital and who weave in and out of the story. They are the good cells of the political body; they help maintain sanity and humanity. Cancerous cells are followers of the Gang of Four, who take part in the organized frenzy of the Cultural Revolution for personal ends. Then there are the naive young people who are caught up in the storm. Last are the worldly wise who wrap themselves up in a protective coating of noncommitment. They are infected with "hardening of the heart," a spiritual and moral cancer.

Peiti, herself an upright and idealistic woman, is also infected with this "hardening." She begins to lose faith in human relationships under the monstrous persecution that she herself, her father, and her friends undergo, while many look the other way. Peiti's own moral as well as physical survival depends on the outcome of the contest between the two kinds of cells, in the body politic and in her own physical organism. Zong Pu's moral philosophy may be naive, but it is the only source of optimism in the story. In the end, because of a botched operation Peiti is still threatened by the "bad" cells, which she visualizes scuttling through her body. But she has overcome the "hardening of the heart" through unalloyed love. From the cell to the soul, Zong Pu represents a woman who is extremely vulnerable and yet manages to recapture a deep moral integrity and inner strength. Her political death by means of a mere externally imposed label Peiti can afford to treat with pure contempt.

If Zong Pu works through a complex metaphor that operates at multiple levels and is sustained throughout the story, Zhang Jie goes to the other extreme. In "What's Wrong with Him?" she focuses on one part of a woman's body—the hymen. "What's Wrong with Him?"

is a collage of disjointed, absurdist images, sinister on the one hand, wildly hilarious on the other. The setting is mainly the mad world of a hospital, a replica of the world at large. Here patients die because elevators do not work, are maimed during minor operations because the lighting is bad. One doctor borrows the title of professor for a trip abroad, while another doctor applies for the temporary loan of an apartment to entertain a visiting foreigner. This is a hospital where the annual report is copied from the previous year's and that from the one before, where "half the staff are children of the other half."

Most outrageous of all, however, is the image of a young woman, Ding Xiaoli, being examined by a troop of doctors concerned with the state of her hymen. Her husband, a medical student, had missed the significant red spot on the bedsheets on their wedding night and immediately filed for divorce. When her hymen is discovered to be intact, her husband promptly falls back in love and withdraws his divorce suit. But Ding Xiaoli, having been stretched out and prodded by these men, feels "like a pig fresh out of a slaughterhouse after examination with a blue chop stamped on its big white rump." "No matter where she was, she felt she was still lying, legs wide apart, on the gynecologist's table." So it is Ding's turn to file for divorce.

As the divorce suit drags on, Ding Xiaoli is haunted in her dreams by the image of a huge hymen. "She dreamed that she had grown larger, thinner. Turned into a huge hymen so thin it rustled in the wind." Ding fantasizes that she ought to "take a scalpel and cut the hymen into bits two centimeters square to sell to women whose husbands were of no use, to guarantee that at one puff they would break. She could make a fortune that way, and the divorce rate would drop."[13]

This monstrous image of a woman turned into a hymen rustling in the wind dominates all the absurdities of the hospital world, an emblem of exactly what one half of the population means to the other. It acquires a life of its own, like the pessary in *The Group* (Mary McCarthy), with its own history from the Greeks, the Jews, and the Egyptians, all the way to Holland and finally the United States. This image of a monstrous hymen is metaphorically flung at the heads of sexist creatures who appear in the shape of medical students, doctors, heads of departments, directors. It hangs over them like a screaming accusation, a banner of protest, or of triumphant celebration. Never before in contemporary Chinese writing had a single piece of description of the female anatomy been so eloquent.

These stories cover a wide range of issues from outright feminist protest to concern for the moral being of the individual and the society. What unites them, however, is a unique approach to female physicality, devoid of shame and guilt, candid, direct, defiant, even accusatory, repulsing male appropriation. It is a repossession and reexperiencing of her own body, a crucial step in woman's consciousness.

Metaphor for Victimization

It is not by accident that one of the central works of the reform period, critical of the establishment, should open with a scene, like a tableau, of a woman dying in a hospital. In *At Middle Age* Lu Wenting is the suffering female, emblem of victimization. The hospital, with its associations of infection, disease, decay, and death, provides an appropriate setting in which to invoke the problems of the society and women's place in it. To all the volumes of words written on Lu Wenting, perhaps it could still be added that in the context of the story she is a passive figure having things done to her—more and more straws piled on her back until it breaks. This angle of presentation detracts nothing from the power of the work. It is actually the whole point, showing the demands that the society makes on the individual, and the added burdens a woman has to bear if she wants to be a good citizen, a good professional, a good wife, and a good mother. It is, consciously or otherwise, a variation on the "one day in the life" theme, the description of a woman's permanent condition through a glimpse at one day in her life. As in Solzhenitsyn's *One Day in the Life of Ivan Denisovich*, this particular day in Lu Wenting's life is just one out of hundreds and thousands of such days following one upon another. What we see at the beginning of the story is the result of the accumulation of too many such days. Lu Wenting is the Everywoman of contemporary Chinese fiction. As

Lu Wenting totters home on the arm of her husband, we can foresee her going back to the old routine. Nothing is changed.

At Middle Age, among other things, started a vogue of representing women at the end of a "process." The reader's attention is drawn to the process of victimization and its agents in various forms. *They* are the center of interest rather than the victims themselves. Thus, Mrs. Qin Bo, the minister's wife who contributes to Lu's collapse, draws the reader's attention to herself and manages to put Lu Wenting in the shade, so to speak. Lu Wenting's trials merely illustrate the workings of this victimization process. In the poetics of protest literature, she is the sum of what has been done to her, the object of victimization in unadulterated form.

Stories of victimization within this model follow a pattern, beginning at the end, as required by the accusatory nature of the theme itself. In "The Old Maid," for instance, Yan Xiaoyan, the young woman of "bad" family background, is systematically deprived of everything—love, career, friendship—and at the age of thirty-eight is diagnosed with breast cancer. The hard life she has led as a village doctor and the constant humiliations she has suffered as the offspring of a "bad element" have not only ravaged her health but also destroyed her self-esteem in the process. She refuses the love of a young man in the same degraded position as herself, not wishing, as she tells him bluntly, to "propagate this inferior species." The story begins in the hopeful post-Mao era, but for the "old maid" diagnosed with breast cancer, it is the beginning of the end and a silent comment on the age.

"Four Women of Forty," a parade of defeated women, is another example of illness as a metaphor for victimization. The most pathetic case is that of the talented Liu Qing. The author goes back in time to give us a glimpse of Liu the young graduate as she flings back her plaits imperiously and declares that she is going to be a writer. This is juxtaposed with the present scene, twenty years later, as she wipes her worn face with the back of her hand like any peasant women, a little detail that reveals so pathetically the corrosive effects of half a lifetime of deprivation. Hers is a life laid waste. After years in the country, she ends up with no family, no love, no career, no achievements, and diagnosed with breast cancer. In the cases of Liu Qing, of Yan Xiaoyan in "The Old Maid," and of Peiti in *The Everlasting Stone*, the affliction of cancer—unromantic, repulsive, carrying in its wake the inexorable verdict of a painful death—is a perfect metaphor for victimization of the innocent.[14] Breast cancer carries an additional suggestion of sexual repression, though this is only hinted at: "Breast cancer patients should marry. The reasons are complex," says the doctor to Peiti in *The Everlasting Stone*.

In a short story, "The Sun Is Not Out Today" (Lu Xing'er), the effects of victimization are brought out in the contrasting images of women lined up waiting for an abortion. At one end of the line we see the young and fresh; at the other end, like a warning, or a portent, is an older woman whose sagging body is like an empty sack. In between are tired and worn-out women. Like a tableau, they seem to represent the progressive stages in the life of a woman.

The hospital in itself could be an agent of victimization. One Chinese official has been quoted as saying that "corruption in China is like AIDS,"[15] and hospitals, with "a more complex hierarchy than other organizations" *(At Middle Age)*, are steeped in it. With varying levels of medication, depending on one's status in the power structure, the hospital is a perfect emblem of the social system itself. Thus, in the hierarchy of medication women's exclusion takes on a symbolic significance.

As a repository of care, the hospital stands for the unattainable, like Kafka's castle. This is what is said to a young woman experiencing labor pains: "This clinic is taken over for emergency service [infighting during the Cultural Revolution]. All the women have been sent away—those that have had their babies, and those that haven't got round to having them" (Gu Ying, "Jingjing Is Born"). In fact, the whole story of "Jingjing Is Born" is the "pilgrimage" of a woman trying to get into a hospital—the unattainable. Even Lu Wenting's husband has to stop a truck to get his dying wife to the hospital, though she herself is a doctor who has collapsed from overwork.

Hospitals are symbols of the bureaucracy. This is what is said to women waiting for abortions: "Without a certificate, the doctor will not do the operation—even if you break in and lie down on the table." What certificates? "The card from your medical file, your employment card, your marriage certificate, your residence registration booklet, the letter of recommendation from your work unit . . ."

The hospital, instead of taking in, exemplifies exclusiveness. In terms of hierarchic exclusion, Liu Qing ("Four Women of Forty") must start off at daybreak from her own poor village and walk to the county center to catch the bus for her train connection to the provincial center. But this is as far as she can make it up the medical hierarchic ladder—a symbol of her low status. To go further, to a major Shanghai hospital, for instance, one has to rely on "connections."

As for political exclusiveness, Peiti *(The Everlasting Stone),* diagnosed with cancer, has to ask for a special dispensation to go to the hospital, and to get this dispensation must submit to a ritual of abuse from the big boss. Even after going through this, she is considered "not worth a thorough operation" when she does get to the operating table. In these stories only one woman gets prompt treatment— Yin Mei, the wife of the chief of the public health bureau; she is literally wedded to power (Zhang Jie, "The Pieces of the Puzzle").

Descriptions of hospitalization open a window on women's special pain. The representation of pain is also ruled by hierarchy. "Female suffering is . . . less pertinent, less significant, less threatening than the pain which befalls men."[16] Describing women's pain, especially in stories of abortion, puts pain in a new perspective. As the sign on the landing in the gynecological clinic says, "Male Comrades: No Admittance" ("The Sun Is Not Out Today"). This is the only area where women enjoy privacy—the area of pain.

To women waiting for abortions, hospitals are hostile and intimidating: the unbending rules, the tyranny of authorization papers, the long wait, the impersonal handling, the stifling "Silence!" signs everywhere, the probing—"Grilled to see if she was married or not" (Tang Min, "Bearing the Unbearable").[17] The doors of the operating room like gaping jaws about to chew up the women, the operating table with women laid out like victims under the knife, and from which the women depart doubled up with pain: this is where women are thoroughly degraded. The young writer Tang Min describes her own experience: "The clinic was packed with pale, wan creatures, all of whom seemingly had given up any attempt to look presentable for the occasion. With the lower parts of our body naked for examination, the self-image changes, seeming loathsome" ("Bearing the Unbearable").

In stories of abortion in the West, women think more in terms of personal choice and thus more in terms of guilt: the child willed out of existence, "the day it should have been born" (Joan Didion, *Play It As It Lays*); whether the woman should have done it (Margaret Drabble, *The Middle Ground*); the child "scraped into a bucket—thrown into the sewers" (Margaret Atwood, *Surfacing*). For Chinese women, by contrast, the choice is made for them: lack of married status, official birth control policy. What remains is not self-questioning or deliberation but rather pain and humiliation. With no alternative, women are still made to feel guilty: "If everybody behaved like you," says the head nurse to a woman who has been forced to have three abortions in six months—and we would expect her to warn the woman of health hazards, but she finishes the sentence with, "we would not be able to cope even if our feet were turned into extra hands!" ("The Sun Is Not Out Today"). In the end, pain is the only thing left in common for women East and West. Anna the drifter in Jean Rhys's novel *Voyage in the Dark* loses blood after an illegal abortion. As she lies in bed, there is only a long yellow ray coming in under the door from the light in the passage—"Yellow, always the color of fear." The women queuing for abortions in "The Sun Is Not Out Today" are also haunted by yellow—the pale yellow globe of the street lamp shimmering blankly on a cold morning, like a half-ripe grapefruit, reminder of the unripe fruit inside themselves that has to be "scraped off."

Hospitalization as Liberation

As we look through women's writing of this period, it is remarkable how many women have acquired a new consciousness through hospital experience. *At Middle Age* tells us that "for years, [Lu Wenting] simply had no time to pause, to reflect on the hardship she had experienced or the difficulties lying ahead. Now that all physical and mental burdens had been lifted, she had plenty of time to examine her past and to explore the future." Here a woman is seeing herself for the first time. The scenes in the story—the emergencies, the fatigue, the humiliations and injustices—are all presented through Lu Wenting's flickering consciousness. Though life has not changed, though there is no clue to the future, still the experience provides a woman's first awareness of herself.

Putting women in the hospital is also a narrative strategy to get women to talk, to give them a chance to review their lives and make new decisions. In the first place, it provides an opportunity to get them together. Chinese women do not spend hours on the phone chatting with their friends. To judge by the evidence in the Soviet-era collection of stories *The Women's Decameron* by Julia Voznesenskaya and the stories under consideration here, women living under socialism can stop to talk only when they are in the hospital, away from husbands and children, free from the daily routine of household chores and tensions of the workplace. We see them talking to one another, exchanging confidences, saying things they would never tell their nearest and dearest or of which they were not aware themselves.

Hospitals provide healing through women's mutual opening-up. For instance, in "Four Women of Forty" there is no place the four former classmates could conceivably have met except in the hospital at that particular moment. Ye Yun, the actress, cured of infection of the pelvis, is on the point of leaving; Liu Qing, diagnosed as having cancer, has just arrived; Cai Shuhua, the "women's work" officer, is on the hospital grounds on business with the birth control office; Wei Linling, the only one living a soft and pampered life, is there on behalf of her husband's network of useful connections. Meeting after twenty years' separation, they take turns telling one another about their lives since they last parted. By recounting, comparing, and reflecting, they see their own lives as they have never done before. It is a revelation for each of them. Wei Linling realizes that she is just an appendage of her successful husband and a servant to her son, that she is raising another man just like her husband. A professional career thrown away is the price she had to pay for the "good" life. Cai Shuhua's values are challenged as she realizes for the first time that her husband has contempt for "women's work," Cai's own job. But he is just echoing the prevailing attitude: party, government, army, workers, youth, women—this is the official order of priorities. Ye Yun, considered a "fallen woman" after two divorces—note the suggestiveness of the pelvic infection—is now married for the third time to an older man and cynically taking advantage of her newly acquired status. Only the poor rural schoolteacher Liu Qing, worst off of them all, still clings to her illusions, partly because she is shut off from a wider mental horizon, and partly because she has nothing else. The story, actually a long conversation, ends with questions: "Career, ideals, struggle, love, marriage, family. It is so hard for women. Questions at every turn. But where are the answers?" The questions are unanswered, but what the women acquire is an awakened consciousness. Illness and hospitalization for women is a test of survival in more senses than one. Apart from the physical struggle for survival, there is a test of the will and the spirit. In the stories of women such as Liu Qingyi ("The Tragedy of the Walnut Tree"), Peiti *(The Everlasting Stone)*, and Shao Xueqin ("The Serenity of Whiteness"), the struggles to survive on the physical level and on the emotional and mental level go hand in hand and are mutually illuminating.

Liu Qingyi, in "The Tragedy of the Walnut Tree," is the archetypal deserted wife, familiar in traditional Chinese literature, which abounds in stories of women whose husbands leave to take the imperial examinations and never return. Qingyi, their modern counterpart, has been deserted by a husband who left for the United States, and she bears the stigma of the deadly "overseas" connection. The story begins on the day when things come to a head. Helpless in bed, racked by asthma, Qingyi is taunted by a group of adults who sadistically trample on her roof and jeer at her helplessness. And on top of that, she gets a letter from her husband, after thirty years of silence, telling her that he is not coming back. The two calamities seem to work together, the rampage over her head and the chilling letter in her hand. At this crisis Qingyi decides to cut down the walnut tree in her yard. It was the tree *he* had loved. It was the tree under which she had stood as she greeted the "liberation." It was the tree which had given her consolation during those thirty desolate years. Now Qingyi, weak, ill, but shed of illusions, decides to cut down that tree. This act deliberately cuts her emotional ties to a past that has betrayed her. More important, it is also a gesture of defiance against the tyrannous present. In a scene merging fantasy and reality, suggestive of Nathaniel Hawthorne (whose works the author has translated into Chinese), Qingyi picks up an axe, panting and trembling with weakness, and cuts down the tree as if by a miracle. The miracle, of course, is in herself, in the fact that she has overcome her own emotional paralysis. Qingyi returns to reality as she prepares to pay the fine for cutting down the tree without a permit, and is ready to start life on her own.

Shao Xueqing in "The Serenity of Whiteness" would have lived out her humdrum life with a worthless husband if she had not been stricken with chronic rheumatic heart disease and near-paralysis, owing to delayed diagnosis and lack of care. Illness becomes a moral test that brings out the worst in her husband and unrealized strength in herself. At first Shao clings to the marriage out of spite. All her dormant energies and resourcefulness are brought out to trick and catch her husband in an affair, but it is a Pyrrhic victory. The party's intervention on her behalf gets her nowhere. Lying in the hospital, thinking while she knits, observing the different kinds of marital relationships among her ward mates, Shao decides to give her husband his coveted divorce and bring up her child properly. Faced with death, she comes to terms with the meaning of life.

In this context it is interesting to note these women's struggle against the determinant of age, which is perhaps special to Chinese culture. Nearly all the women in the stories concerned are about forty: the four women in "Four Women of Forty," the three women in *The Ark*, the old maid in "The Old Maid," Peiti in *The Everlasting Stone*, Shao Xueqing in "The Serenity of Whiteness." They have reached, or are nearing, "that relentless number," when "youth takes leave, never to return, and age takes over, never to be shaken off" ("Four Women of Forty"). This gives an added poignancy to these women's efforts to "liberate" themselves. Instead of giving up, they make forty "the middle ground" (Margaret Drabble, *The Middle Ground*) from which to review the past and plan the future.

"The Sun Is Not Out Today" is one of the outstanding works of the eighties which extensively explores images of hospitalization for what they say not only about women's pain but also about women's choice. Using a gynecological clinic for the setting foregrounds the problem of choice.

Before the women waiting for abortions are swallowed up into the operating room, they sit on a bench in the waiting room and achieve a moment of solidarity and collective consciousness. All are equally victims of unwanted pregnancies. There is a sense of collective indignation at husbands and lovers. The older women, always tired, bear sex like an inevitable affliction. The pretty young woman, being "modern," has experimented with premarital sex but is now trapped. Her wedding has been called off, and she is led by the union officer to this abortion, reduced to just another figure in the birth control work report. So much for her modernity. After the women undergo their operations, they are collected by their husbands or lovers in a scene reminiscent of Jean Rhys's cynical ending in the doctor's words in *Voyage in the Dark:* "Ready to start all over again in no time, I've no doubt."

But two women in the story make their own decisions. For the sake of her career, the young actress is determined to get her abortion. She is without the requisite papers, true, but she has another kind of paper—two tickets to the theater to bribe the doctor. She is set to appear onstage that same night, on the road to success. The teacher Dan Ye, on the verge of an abortion, changes her mind and decides to keep her baby, despite the social ostracism that will surely fall on a child born with no father. She decides to "give it a try," just as Rosamond Stacey decides to have her baby in *The Millstone* (Margaret Drabble). She decides to enter a world from which men are protected: after the planting of the seed, all the rest is up to the woman—the pain, the decisions, and the long years ahead. Just as Rosamond in *The Millstone* does not tell George, her baby's father, of his paternity, Dan Ye decides to break off with her married lover and bring up her child alone.

From flickering consciousness to new awareness and on to decision-making, we see how illness and hospitalization can be a liberating experience.

Few Chinese women writers, if any, claim to be feminists. Rather, many disclaim the dubious distinction. Traditional attitudes toward women, combined with the weight of official intolerance of any possible suggestion of sexual inequality in a socialist state, gives feminism a bad name. If women writers are concerned with women's issues, they certainly do not advertise it, and even when writing overtly about women's problems have to weigh their words. In the afterword to her own collection, Zhang Jie, author of the first avowedly feminist novella in contemporary China, says enigmatically: "Did I say all that I had wanted to say? Can I say all that I want to say?"[18]

And yet, since the conditions of existence for men and women are so different, it is inevitable that a special female awareness should emerge from the writings of women, and this is even more true when women write about women. Thus, in spite of a reigning ideology which categorizes human beings under the headings of "class," and where gender issues are submerged in "class" issues, women writers still manage to give voice to the reiterated basic protest, "How hard it is to be a woman!" (Zhang Jie, The Ark).

So far, avant-garde women's writing has been mostly identified with fiction on the subject of sexuality. Certainly the writings of Wang Anyi (Love Trilogy), Tie Ning (The Rose Gate), and Yu Luojin (A Winter's Fairy Tale) have broken new ground in representing female sexuality and exposing sexual oppression. But the perception of women against a background of illness and hospitalization is another breakthrough, and one that is just as significant. Without identifying themselves as feminists, women writing about sick and dying women have given shape to new forms of self-definition and effectively brought about a total reversal in the way women are perceived. They have laid open the problematics of gender in contemporary Chinese society without resorting to themes of love, marriage, or sexuality. The house of women's fiction has many windows. It is up to women writers to open them one by one.

15 | Politics and Protocols of *Funü:* (Un)Making National Woman

This essay is a genealogy of the discursive construction of woman in post-Mao China.[1] Specifically it concerns the theoretical debates over gender politics among Chinese women scholars during the 1980s. My object is to show how Chinese theory was a localized recoding of women's liberation politics worldwide, but the debates also possess certain irreducible specificities because they address discursive subjects *(funü, nüxing, nüren)* with long, complex histories in China.[2]

Each of the words of key importance in this essay— *funü, nüren, nüxing*—signifies women differently. *Funü,* in commonsense Chinese just the word for "women," can also be understood to mean "female subject in Maoist state discourse." During the 1980s *funü's* protocols and powers were both an effect and a constituent part of Maoism's once powerful state rhetoric. *Nüxing,* which possesses a genealogy as old as European colonialism in China, is most accurately glossed as "woman the sexed subject, the other of humanist Man." (The best equivalent of *nüxing* in contemporary North American feminist usage is probably "essential woman.") *Nüren* corresponds to "women" with a small "w," analogous to what Denise Riley has called woman as a category in anglophone European social history.[3] The words have ordinary roles to play in contemporary everyday standard Chinese; collectively they structure elements of quotidian reality and collude in its maintenance. But each also has efficacy (some would say potential agency) as a position that invites or allows subjects to engage in purposeful action.

It is perhaps best to begin by clarifying my general assumptions, as they may not seem commonplace in a history of women. First, this essay is a history of female subject positions in discourse—since *funü, nüren,* and *nüxing* all mean "female subject"—rather than a study of individual, "concrete" women. I do not believe that written documents provide unmediated access to the lives of Chinese women. Sources do not just reflect social subjects, since evidence is never self-evident. Given the very nature of representation, documents are precluded from presenting woman and women in their entirety since they are, after all, activated and realized by means of writing and speech.

Asking questions about how woman is represented in discourse— the kinds of female subjects constituted by the terms *funü, nüren,* and *nüxing*—allows us to move away from the mythology of the indivisible, bounded, essential subject. It shifts our attention to the ways that female, like male, subjectivities are provisional and strategic constructions. The term *subject position* calls attention to the power of discourse to situate the meanings of woman multiply and always in relation to one another. This view holds that because subject positioning is discursive, it is also always social.

Second, the use of the word *discourse* indicates that power is generated by means of language. What is written and spoken about people situates them in ordinary and powerful commonsense realities. Historical research, for me, therefore consists of reading critically to discover where precisely these referents position woman, and then asking what conditions suggested that particular formation of woman over and above some other.[4]

Third, I do not assume that words can be translated in and out of representational economies without violence. Unlike the translator who shifts words from one language to what she judges is a roughly equivalent place in another, I consider how key terms operate in synchronic contexts, particularly where social subjects themselves actively attempt to bring a context to crisis. By glossing prosaic terms as subject positions, I mean to emphasize the specificity of language and politics. This is as true of positions in state discourses (*funü*, for instance) as it is of oppositional discourses, such as those based on the alleged essential nature of *nüxing*.

My argument is divided into three parts. The first, titled "Reassembly," examines terms and their contexts. I focus on the decision of the Women's Federation (Fulian) in the late 1970s to document women's gains under communism, thereby reviving *funü*. The second part, "Contesting *Funü*," examines how the historians of women's history whom Fulian had empowered actually set into circulation a counteridentity which they referred to as *nüxing*, who should, they implied, supersede the older Maoist collectively defined *funü*. The third part, "*Nüren* and the Economy of Women's Studies," speculates that *nüren*, an intermediate subjectivity within nonstatist Marxian discourse, might well emerge from these debates as the favored theoretical subject. *Nüren* scholars make the insurrectionary claim that the writing of universal women's history holds out great promise for creating a transnational theory and practice of women's liberation.

Reassembly: Protocols of *Funü*

In the late 1970s and early 1980s the Chinese Communist party attempted to restore its pre–Cultural Revolution control structure. Institutionally this meant reviving mass organizations such as Fulian, the Women's Federation. Authorities assigned Fulian the task of "steadfastly protecting the interests of the masses whom [it] represents," while in fact tacitly restricting the scope of its concern to the Central Committee's understanding of what constitutes a "woman."[5] Fulian's job, in other words, was to represent *funü*. Older federation leaders, such as Kang Keqing, Deng Yingchao, and Cai Chang, resumed control of the women's bureaucracy in the years immediately following the fall of the Gang of Four. The National Women's Congress met in 1978 for the first time in twenty years; gradually Fulian began recovering resources it had lost during the Cultural Revolution.

As an arm of the government, Fulian heeded the Central Committee's call to reinstate *funü,* an older ideological subject, as the agent of post-Mao modernization. Fulian's senior leaders, however, were critical of some aspects of Deng Xiaoping's reforms. They argued that one undesirable effect was the resurgence of feudal misogyny and its expression in outright official bias. According to Tan Xiang-bei, for instance, although socialist China's legal codes had long promised protections for women exceeding those offered in bourgeois capitalist nations such as France, Chinese women now suddenly found themselves encountering rollbacks of even their earlier legal guarantees—all justified in the name of economic privatization.[6] Articles in the Maoist theoretical organ *Hongqi* (Red Flag) illustrated the escalating prejudice facing women in the "reformed" Chinese Communist party itself.[7] Critics also noted a vicious new intolerance of female college graduates in male-dominated work units and a monstrously swelling inequality between the conditions of urban and rural women.[8]

Critics less sanguine about a reinstated Fulian's prospects read the same harbingers similarly, but insinuated that the federation was not competent to handle such an enormous problem. Privatization of domestic relations, retreat from social justice, tacit approval of retrograde beliefs about women's intellectual inferiority, and collusion with those who would shut women out of politics (a crudely masculinist bid to force women into unremunerated domestic servitude, the so-called "back to the kitchen" argument), all were effects of reform that could potentially demoralize women since they foreclosed women's access to the state for even minimal redress. Under such circumstances, internal critics insinuated, Fulian's task would certainly short-circuit. The ideological work that brought women to consciousness of their own mass subjectivity would falter without legal safeguards. Ultimately women would feel the effects of "reform" not simply in terms of outright privation but also as invidious, colonizing self-doubt.[9]

In the face of Deng Xiaoping's move toward economic privatization, Fulian's restored central leadership chose to combat tangible loss with venerable pre–Cultural Revolution political weaponry. First, the organization sought once again to reform its "work style." The drive to recruit "good" women's work cadres and to staff offices with educated urban female workers was consistent with Fulian precedent and most certainly an offshoot of pangovernment efforts under way to combat "bureaucratism" and local corruption.[10] Second, to rectify its mass mission Fulian turned once again to sloganeering. Its motto "Protect women's and children's legal interests" did initiate efforts to raise consciousness and combat illegal bias. Yet this offensive, like the effort to discipline "good" cadres, seemed a hackneyed and tired tactic in light of roundly condemned Cultural Revolutionary ideological excesses.[11] When it came time to specify which legal protections required the organization's special attention, Fulian opted for a campaign propagandizing yet another version of the Marriage Law rather than addressing, say, labor or education.[12]

Was Fulian's strategy anachronistic in being firmly wedded to a rapidly disintegrating Maoist imaginary, or was the organization capable of responding to fresh oppressions? Some Fulian initiatives implied the former and suggested that, at least for veteran Fulian bureaucrats, the road home was going to be the road back. Intransigence apparently lay behind the revival of earlier styles of propaganda work and the decision to recycle rhetoric that was in some cases already forty years old.[13] A good example of the old-fashioned style was the resurgence in the press and media of mini-propaganda campaigns touting model women who, though undoubtedly heroines of the CCP women's movement, were, by the fall of the Gang of Four, either on the edge of retirement or quite simply dead.[14]

Just restoring Fulian's previous powers would probably not have proved sufficient in any case. The effects of reform were stimulating new problems. Moreover, no amount of Fulian posturing could obscure the fact that the agency had from the beginning of its existence been a branch of the ideological state apparatus. The declining fortunes of government propaganda machinery in general tended to problematize Fulian's foundational claim that it had been *funü*'s sole avenue of social and political representation between 1949 and the outbreak of the Cultural Revolution in the late 1960s. To undermine Fulian's claim to have represented Chinese women, it was necessary only that a nonstatist women's movement step forward and lay claim to an alternate past.

Fulian made the momentous decision in 1980 to establish archives and research centers at county and urban units, and to encourage amateurs to write true local histories of the Chinese women's movement. According to Deng Weizhi, women's history projects sprang up all over the country as a consequence of the decree. As I suggest later in this essay, they made possible the production of the very "woman /*nüxing* theories" and global *nüren* historical genealogies that eventually relocated categorical "woman" beyond Fulian's compass altogether.[15]

Deng Yingchao seems to have recognized the dangers inherent in a popular history movement. She constantly reminded audiences that documenting the women's movement meant reestablishing the inextricable relation between proletarian national revolution and communist women's liberation.[16] To no avail. The truism that without the Communist party there would be no women's movement could not be sustained in 1981. Post-Maoists were rediscovering the May Fourth movement and beginning to speculate about a Chinese women's history before communism. As women historians would eventually argue, the Communist party (and therefore Fulian) had in fact colonized the May Fourth period, obscuring its historical importance with an elaborate formulaic policy of veneration. What this lavish praise had long masked was evidence that the independent women's movement had not so much supported the communists as loyally sacrificed its own autonomy to further a national revolutionary Bolshevik agenda. In doing so, it had lost its historical efficacy.

Fulian's task from its earliest genesis had always been, as it turned out under the new historian's scrutiny, to promote *funü* in a forthrightly statist regulative propaganda discourse. When the CCP Central Committee resurrected Fulian, it stood to reason, the long-term goal was nothing more than inserting *funü* back into civic discourse. As in the past, a rejuvenated federation's mission should reinforce the subject *funü* and construct "woman" on these terms. As one element of the federation's renewed mission, the women's history movement was initially just another means of situating *funü* back where she belonged, at the vanguard of the vanguard of revolution.

But the state subject position that Fulian struggled so valiantly to recuperate in the early 1980s just would not stabilize. *Funü* meant national female subject. It had originally taken shape during the years of the party's guerrilla war, within powerful propaganda discourses that set *funü* up against "imperialism," "the West," "bourgeois feminism," and "landlord oppression." *Funü* repeatedly participated in the state's primary concern, which was to link the CCP's own mix of cultural nationalism to a mandate that would allow it to govern on behalf of the dictatorship of the proletariat. The CCP offered itself as the nation's salvation and justified its own authority in part on the grounds that it had liberated China's women: as the Central Committee was to the people, so Fulian was to the *funü*. That is why *funü* meant national woman, or, more precisely, national woman under a Maoist-communist state inscription.

Kang Keqing, Deng Yingchao, and Cai Chang, who presented themselves as a single, exemplary, unified *funü* subject in a volume of their jointly selected works, demonstrate what was at stake for the imbricated national Chinese woman subject. To summarize the protocols or constituting behaviors of *funü* as they appear in the official script of Kang-Deng-Chang[17]: *funü* oppose feudalism, imperialism, individualism, and bureaucratism, while supporting the thought of Chairman Mao; share many interests with the oppressed proletariat; contribute to the nation's overall well-being precisely because they are neither bourgeois feminists nor ultraleftists unmindful of women's special characteristics;[18] and enthusiastically accept that "in our country the interests of the individual and the interests of the state are one."[19] *Funü* are particularly noticeable when mass mobilizations socialize domestic labor and bring women from the shadow of family and kin, to the liberating light of state positionalities. Thus, Kang Keqing names the May Fourth movement, land reform, and the Great Leap Forward as periods of particular gain. Any period in which (1) *funü* are a revolutionary force, (2) their liberation is a condition of proletarian revolution, and (3) productive labor is the basic condition of women's liberation can count as a progressive era.[20]

The Fulian high command offered such rhetoric of state as a vernacular political imaginary. Like all bits of state rhetoric, it empowered because it justified state sovereignty. Indeed, in earlier days this very language had exercised real hegemony by constituting and convincing masses of citizens that it possessed a general truthful reliability. But as the rest of this essay elaborates, by the time Deng-Cai-Kang launched their offensive, many women simply did not identify as *funü* at all. As Li Xiaojiang so succinctly put it, "I knew I was female [*nüren*]. But I didn't recognize that this implied special characteristics, that a difference existed between me and other people, or rather me and men."[21] So completely had the state colonized *funü* that no one considered herself one. No sooner had this contradictory interpellation opened up than theorists such as Li undertook to reposition themselves as *nüren* and *nüxing*—that is, as other than "men" and far outside the state's purview.

Contesting *Funü*: Uncoupling Mao and Women's Liberation

Funü never really recovered. While the state reassembled Fulian, the post-Mao subject positionalities *nüxing* and *nüren* surfaced, which were not overtly linked to the state's discourses. The multiple crises stimulated by the reforms simply exceeded Fulian's capacity to monopolize representation, or even to regulate female subject positions adequately. Challenges to the specially privileged and bureaucratized subject position *funü* multiplied until, in the late eighties, Fulian could no longer contain them all within the terms of its own unitary discourse.

By then, critics had shifted to a consideration of Fulian's own culpability, and particularly to its often-stated claim that only it had properly represented Chinese women. In the end, after subjecting this claim to thorough scrutiny, commentators agreed that Fulian needed to shoulder some responsibility: not only was *funü* not a hegemonic subject, or even the only subject position available in Chinese women's movement discourse, but Fulian itself had not fulfilled even its own restricted mission of representing *funü*'s limited interests. Either Fulian would have to rework its mandate or it was going to have to admit that it was ineffectual. Pan Suiming adroitly summarized such criticism, arguing in exasperation that Fulian's basic problem was that it saw itself as "an institution of social administration when it ought to be representing [*daibiao*] women." The federation's self-effacing posture in relation to the state meant that it "lacks an independent will" and thus the very wherewithal to represent anything![22]

The most damaging question of all was, "If it doesn't represent women, what is it Fulian 'represents'?" One answer (consistent with Pan's critique) was that Fulian represented *funü*. From there it was but a step to the repudiation of *funü* itself. Liberation, Pan opines (again, this view is widely echoed elsewhere), did not define ordinary Chinese women. On the contrary, such women saw so-called liberation as a "gift" from on high, a kind of ambiguous endowment. The widespread belief that the CCP had liberated women by fiat was proof that, in a strange twist of logic, women themselves must never have asked for liberation, never wanted it, and therefore, more likely than not, had had the state force it upon them! "Real women," as opposed to the liberated Fulian subject, had needs that far exceeded the federation's tepid wish list. Official feminism would have to accept the special needs of real women, or real women would continue to dismiss it, since, according to this critique, most women felt that "representing *funü* is Fulian's business and has no connection to me."[23] The alleged disjuncture between "women's" interests and Fulian's representations was a telling offensive in the campaign to undo Maoist *funü* and break its hold on Chinese women's liberation theory.

This line of criticism opened up what in the early 1990s remained a key issue: the question of sex difference. During the late Maoist period (1966–1976), went this argument, high-tide mobilizations had masculinized women and obliterated natural sex difference.[24] In the words of one essay, "If feudal 'women's way' turned women into men's inferiors, then the high tide of leftist thought obliterated sex difference, making it impossible for women to be women [*nüxing*]."[25] Stripping women of their female nature and by default masculinizing the feminine, this argument continued, placed women in an impossible historical double bind. According to those who charged Maoists with masculinizing women, in order to return to natural sex difference patriarchy would simply have to be reinstated. No doubt male dominance was unjust. Nonetheless, it did distinguish between male and female, and therefore guaranteed harmony with nature and maintenance of the natural sex difference. Equality should, indeed would, eventually occur, of course. But it would emerge only as the effect of historical overcoming, in which the patriarchal stage, predicated on slowly evolving "natural" logic (i.e., logic inscribed in historicized nature), and thus superior to arbitrary, "unnatural" CCP political lines, was finally just transcended.

This formulation, which I call the *xingbie* problem, clarifies what was at stake theoretically when these insurgent liberationist arguments grounded themselves on a foundational sex difference. The term *xingbie* may be translated literally as "sex difference"; it is also, in fact, the preferred Chinese translation of the English theoretical term *gender.* A significant incongruity exists in the fact that as some Chinese theorists are interpreting gender in sexed, othering, binarial terms, some anglophone theory is seeking to do exactly the opposite. The effort to dethrone biological physiology from its conventional authoritative position in Anglo-American and French feminisms has sought to overcome precisely the ground of physiological difference that much *xingbie* theory opens up so richly inside China when it translates *gender* in this way.

Gender as sex difference proved a tremendously powerful critical weapon in Chinese academic debate. It provided a way of theorizing essential difference at the very heart of nature and therefore—allegedly—at a profounder, deeper level than claims laid by the CCP's regulative ideology. Essential *xingbie* raises an immediate categorical problem, however. Human sexual difference and women's humanity tend not to coexist in the same frame: not in European Enlightenment discourse, not in bourgeois feminisms, and not in *xingbie* theory. Either women are "people" *(ren),* meaning "human," a category therefore by definition ambivalently gendered, split, and doubled, exceeding the impoverishing biological reduction man/woman, or women are essentially different from men; man is a euphemism and woman is definitionally "other." The struggle of women to be different from men and to be human beings and therefore essentially like men is logically and practically very difficult.[26] Many partisans of women's difference could not adhere strictly to *xingbie*'s implications, and ended up actually siding with Wang Jinling, who introduced Margaret Mead's critical notion that although sex difference may *feel* natural, it is always historically contingent and thus amenable to directed change.[27]

A second key strategy for undermining the old construction of womanhood comes from theorists of "woman culture" *(xin nüxing wenhua)*. Like Huang Hongyun, they seem eager to construct a female culture that would nurture a sense of womanhood against prevailing misogynist, masculinist cultural domination. Strategically, Huang expanded on Ernst Cassirer's idea that culture supplies access to the category of the person in order to argue that half of Chinese humanity has historically found personhood inaccessible since tradition made women "vulgar, passive, dependent virtuous wives and good mothers." Sex difference, she argued, should imply separate but equal cultures, one male and one female. The problem facing advocates of a woman's culture, in Huang's view, is that Chinese traditional culture had failed women even in this.[28]

Nüxing, the word culturalists such as Huang chose to replace *funü* in their writing, literally means "female sex." Culturalists particularly have made *nüxing* the naturalized starting point for all discussion of women's past or future. Indeed, they have made *nüxing* into the "other" of *funü*. Whether the target was party weakness vis-à-vis women's liberation, the insufficiencies of party-inspired women's history, or backwardness in the party world of Fulian cadres, the antidote always turned out to be a *nüxing* operating under her own free will in a terrain beyond the Women's Federation. The simple rhetorical association of *nüxing* with alternatives and *funü* with apparatchik-style political categories is strikingly consistent. To phrase the point crudely, *nüxing* took *funü* as its oppressor.[29] Li Xiaojiang's essay *Zouxiang nüren* helps explain why making oneself a *nüxing*-subject offers so much critical maneuverability. In an autobiographical piece Li represented herself as a girl who had excelled in a meritocratic world because she possessed a wholly androgynous will *(yizhi)* and could expend heroic effort in pursuing her goals. She grew up, she said, in the peculiar world of Fulian-style "equality," and never suffered really egregious sexual discrimination. Schooled under the ultraleftist political line, she later became a professor—and all this without ever having to consider herself a woman. Motherhood finally opened her eyes. Suddenly she confronted the "typical eastern woman's fate" of selfless domestic sacrifice on top of the burden of her salaried work. Li realized that "the double roles brought dual standards, like a double-edged sword . . . making it impossible . . .

to find a relaxed, real sense of self [*ziwo*] whether . . . in the home
or outside in society. I failed to understand why this happened only
to women, why only those who had female bodies should be forced
to endure this . . . What I knew least, even after all my disciplined
nights of reading, was precisely 'woman' [*nüren*]."[30]

Li's formulation suggested two more issues that theorists took up
very profitably. First, when *nüxing* made *funü* "other," made it "nonwoman" in relation to itself, it positioned itself as a sexed and foundational subject in relation to yet another term, "family role." As Li's
description makes clear, she identified herself (albeit provisionally)
as a *nüxing* when she found herself suddenly forced into the role of
mother. Second, because *nüxing*-subject was always a self in relation
to an original statist subject, *funü*, it could not easily stand alone. If
nüxing was the "real" subject position (as opposed to the nonwoman
funü), then, *nüxing* had to show that it, and not *funü*, truthfully
represented women as they *really* are. Theoretically speaking, any
such claim to prior being, to what I have been calling foundational
status, must reveal the ground (e.g., nature or history or reproductive physiology) upon which her claim rests.

A strong critical effort on the part of theorists such as Wei Bingjie,
Ruo Shui, and Feng Yuan, therefore, has attended Li's insight, extending and placing into discursive tension not two but three linked
tropes—"personality" *(renge)*, "roles" *(jiaose)*, and "female" *(nüxing)*.[31]
All female roles, the argument goes, but especially "virtuous wife,
good mother," have historically repressed the emergence of personality in Chinese women.[32] When some Chinese women did develop
a sufficiently stable self to begin winning high social position and
emerged into society with "independent personal character," men
panicked. They reacted by seeking to force *nüxing* back into the
demeaning, emotionally laborious, traditional female role categories
such as wife, housekeeper, and child care nurse.

Theorists of *nüxing* argued that some sexually defined roles
should be retained. As Ruo Shui put it: "Roles are the positions
people make out of the net of relations [*guanxi zhi wang*] in nature
and society . . . Roles make people into people. The more roles a
person has, the more completely a person can develop qualities and
the more richly life can be enjoyed and realized." Roles in this

construction both oppressed and liberated females, since "that is the double nature of roles."[33]

The role theorist Li Ying actually offered readers a history of the relation of self and role. An Edenic matriarchy had once existed, she theorized, where female personality flourished. But historical necessity empowered patriarchy and imposed on society a sexual division of labor that effectively quarantined women inside the family. There the emotional expectations linked to "virtuous wives/good mothers" sapped woman of her self-consciousness and destroyed her personality. She survived, enslaved to "traditional psychic consciousness," for thousands of years until the rise of capitalism and socialism. According to Li Ying, then, Chinese women needed to recover their ability, lost since the matriarchy fell, to "recognize the personality of the self." Wei Bingjie and Li Ying felt that the condition wherein roles undermined women's personality would be resolved only when women themselves developed a stronger sense of their "essential consciousness." Women consistently failed to achieve equality with men because they did not have sufficient gender consciousness and thus had difficulty maintaining their sense of self.[34]

The *nüxing* critique of role and character had an inflammatory effect. Its highly confrontational, accusatory sense of grievance has pried "woman" out of a statist context and set it into an economy of Marxian nature. *Nüxing* criticism opened a new terrain for "women's studies" beyond the self-congratulatory political annals of the Communist party because it exploited the biological and historical possibilities inhering in the flexible category "woman." Whether it went by *nüxing,* as in role theory, or *nüren* in the textual economy of women's studies, the critique of Fulian's national female subject has ended the ability of *funü,* the state's woman, to act as a hegemonic signifier. That, in turn, appears to have altered the terms by which female subjects can be formed in most discourses.

Nüren and the Economy of Women's Studies

Women's studies *(funü xue)* and woman theory *(funü lilun)* are academic fields that have since the late 1980s attracted scholars, teachers, bureaucrats, Fulian workers, urban readers, literary figures, college students, and for-profit publishers.[35] Advocates of women's studies endorse the government's reform politics but express, at the same time, their preference for a historical interpretation of woman as a social category in a mode-of-production narrative. Together they represent a fusion of the community of women (*funüjie*) and the theoretical world, and suggest further that Marxism has a stake in resolving the woman problem and that woman theorists should colonize the party theoretical establishment. Women's studies is also a discipline in the Foucauldian sense, an academic field of action. Women's studies scholars argue that activists, readers, and writers should recolonize Fulian's institutional structure in the name of global women's history.

In the late 1980s Deng Weizhi, Li Min and Wang Fukang, and Li Xiaojiang all argued that there existed an obvious need for "woman theory."[36] Li Min and Wang Fukang contended that since Marxism was a good deal more than Mao's Red Book,[37] Marxists should recognize the insufficiency of existing theory as it pertained to women, and should take steps to resolve the problem. The resulting woman theory aimed at stopping several gaps. It was conceived as a way for scholars to systematize nearly a decade of critique. It made an inclusive gesture that sought to embrace progressive Fulian cadres still more comfortable in the world of Chinese Marxist categorical certainties. It also linked current goals and the genealogical past, for it insisted that the Chinese woman problem constituted a historical offshoot of the European Marxist tradition. Most of all, perhaps, woman theory opened what in other academic contexts would be considered feminist questions.

Li Xiaojiang brought feminist questions into women's studies through Marxist history. She argued as a Marxist that history has produced three stages of theorizing about women: (1) "bourgeois feminist theory" (the Paris Commune and the middle-class female rights movement against androcentric traditional society), (2) the proletarian women's movement (the Commune to the Second World War), and (3) revival of the global women's movement (the rise of woman theory in socialist and capitalist countries as women ready themselves for the final battle).[38] The reference to history as the ground of truth neutralized the old charge that "bourgeois feminist theory" is a poisonous weed, since it is easy to demonstrate multiple connections between European and Chinese women's rights movements. The family resemblance of crude bourgeois feminism to Chinese woman theory has, Li argued, long since faded. Unlike current western feminists, Chinese women sought not so much rights for individuals as the larger collective guarantee that Chinese women would be allowed into the world of human beings. Women's social liberation in China was just one specific departure point in the global struggle for human liberation.[39]

The second thrust of Li Xiaojiang's woman theory was to re-problematize the subject woman *(nüxing)*. Chinese woman theory, in this argument, should not consider *nüxing* (essential woman) its subject because gendered subjects are by definition historical constructs. Obviously, Li argued, physiology and sexual science play their parts, but that does not justify taking biological woman as the subject of a women's theory that must serve activists and scholars. At this point woman theory split decisively from the powerful *nüxing* critique. For Marxian woman theorists, the subject of theorizing, "woman" *(nüren)*, is not a historical essence so much as a marker or empty place. The subject "woman" occurs only historically as a category *(fanchou)*. "The responsibility of the women's movement has always been to face women's reality and concretely measure and strategize ways of pushing women's liberation forward onto a practical course. But woman theory makes woman in the abstract into its foundation and grasps the intrinsic qualities of the women's movement by connecting 'woman as a category' on a conceptual level to other social categories."[40] Unlike social classes, however, women-as-a-category is not "for itself," as, for instance, the revolutionary bourgeoisie or a slave class might be.[41] Women, unlike men, "evolved" within hegemonic social stages that men had determined. For that reason, women's "evolution" is always played out, as Simone de Beauvoir would say (according to Li Xiaojiang's citation), in a secondary relation to male history and thus a secondary "historical" evolution.[42]

A compelling apocalyptic tone pervades woman theory and Chinese women's studies generally. It suggests that Chinese women must seize the category "woman" and produce their own subjectivities within its framework. By its own lights, the conceptual breakthrough arrived when the reforms finally exacerbated long-standing historical contradictions, breaking the bureaucratic stalemate that had trivialized Fulian's mission. Now theory's historical task is to conjure into existence a Marxian female subjectivity, beyond Fulian's *funü*.[43]

Yet, unless Chinese women appropriated a local practice for women's studies, Wan Shanping argued, simple theory itself would never mediate the "difference" separating women's and men's history (to say nothing, she implied, of the multiform differences between Japanese and Chinese women, European and Chinese women, or North American and Chinese women). Part of the reason why localization of women's studies was so pressing was the fact that the discipline and its theoretical justifications were all imported. According to Wan Shanping, the term "women's studies" first entered Chinese discourse through a book review in *Studies of Social Sciences Abroad* of Shirai Atsushi's *Women's Studies and the History of Women's Movements*. Serious collective discussion of how the notion might be appropriated into local contexts came at the First National Conference on Theoretical Studies of Women, which Fulian sponsored in late 1984.[44]

The way to guarantee local practices for Chinese women's studies, Deng Weizhi argued a year later, was to seek a popular audience for its scholarly and theoretical projects.[45] But Deng also wanted to legitimate women's studies as a field of knowledge. Women's studies as a discipline entered academic circulation under the sponsorship of social science methodology. "'Women's studies' does not just take 'woman' and attach a 'studies' to it," Deng wrote. It is no simple, untutored advocacy of women. It is instead "a highly articulated interdisciplinary" field encompassing "sociology of women, female pedagogy, philosophy of women, female psychology, female physiology, study of female health," to say nothing of ethics, aesthetics, history, women's legal studies, "and even a brand-new discipline of women's literary criticism," and other academic possibilities as yet unformulated.[46]

The ground of Chinese women's studies as a social scientific discipline is, then, neither nature nor culture. As a field it need not, its founders argued, justify the local practice of women's studies or its theoretical mission by reference to an allegedly natural human instinct such as "sexuality," or discrete cultural practice, as the so-called "women's culture" advocates had. Rather, it should undertake scholarship that seeks to provide a rationale or ground for political strategies aimed at alleviating women's oppression. Women's studies, in this view, must "ground" itself in accurate social scientific representations of women, and deploy female subject positions in a field of knowledge as a means of instigating and justifying liberatory political direct action.[47]

Without actually saying so, Chinese women's studies, therefore, offers a way to legitimate an extrastatist, nonsanctioned subject positionality other than *funü,* namely, the subject *nüren,* or woman. The subject *nüren* commonly occurs in texts that address the popular-scholarly reading audience of academic readers and literate or "good" Fulian cadres. These essays provide critical reviews for scholars located in remote areas of the country who might not have access to materials or the time to read more widely. One such essay listed major founding figures and described their current work (e.g., Li Xiaojiang's program at Zhengzhou University, Henan; Zhu Qi's work at Tianjin University deconstructing the notion of matriarchy; Li Zhongming's work on patriarchy in Hubei; Nan Xi's scholarly work at Sichuan Foreign Languages Academy) and attached a critique that connected these research projects to one another.[48]

Nüren also appears consistently in historical monographs. Li Min's book *Chinese Women's Studies* provided what amounts to a historical genealogy for *nüren.* Li traced what she called Chinese "women's speech" through various stages.[49] She reexamined Chinese women's representational practices and their relation to western feminism, arguing that the historical connection between western scholarly and theoretical practices and empirically verifiable Chinese women's experience began very early. The May Fourth movement produced the first genuine "women's speech," because it systematically linked Chinese texts to western analysis, that is, to the sort of women's studies Chinese scholars should invent for themselves.[50]

Deng Yingchao's concern became reality in the writing of historians such as Li Min, Ren Qing, and Li Xiaojiang. The invitation Fulian had extended to archivists in 1980 that they document the linkage of Chairman Mao and the *funü* of China had given rise instead to innumerable historical rereadings of that very premise. In each case, because women's studies frames itself within the social sciences, its claims to represent history correctly can be contested only on historical grounds. To put it another way, as *funü* is to ideology, so *nüren* is to history. To take one example of how difficult it is to refute women's studies analysis: Xiao Li and Xiao Yu periodized the three major discussions of women's liberation as the reforms of the 1890s, the 1911 bourgeois revolution, and the May Fourth movement.[51] To denounce such a historical periodization, critics cannot just point out so-called ideological errors but must provide alternative proofs or evidence that the historian's argument is incomplete or inaccurate on documentary grounds.

Chinese scholars have recently shown tremendous interest in reperiodizing the chronology of the Chinese women's movement, suggesting a turn to more "accurate" representations than have been available in the past. Cai Yu, a typical revisionist, looked across the ocean to overseas Chinese scholars and backward to May Fourth figures such as Chen Dongyuan for accurate, inspiring representations, implying that what fell between—thirty-five years of Communist party history—was simply useless.[52] Chang Ying not only credited the revolutionary bourgeoisie with inventing and sustaining the women's rights movement but pointed out that historically the women's independence movement had not flowered because the proletarian movement had run roughshod over it. Even the most patriotic women would not, she seemed to hint, so willingly sacrifice their own struggle to forward a nationalist agenda again. And that was because, Chang Ying concluded, not only had the proletarian movement not freed Chinese women (reversing Deng Yingchao's first premise), but it had in the end aborted the autonomous women's rights movement altogether.[53]

The women's studies movement has changed the academy in an institutional sense, establishing women's studies departments in universities. It has also reflexively created a "community" that scans its own products, positioning and repositioning itself in relation to other social sciences and in relation to groups of women outside China. In this constant self-surveillance, scholars are producing a subject, "woman" *(nüren),* which forms an irreducible "identity" for anchoring advocacy politics.[54] As Qing Ren self-consciously wrote: "If one could say that the period of the early 1980s was concerned with researching the women's question as it affected women's employment, safeguards, and other concrete matters, the mid- and late years of the decade saw increasing focus on research into women themselves, as a consequence of the elevation of research and the lavish attention paid it."[55]

Another mark of the discursivity of the "women's studies community" is Li Xiaojiang's Enlightenment project, the Henan People's Press women's series, which she projected would consist of twenty to thirty volumes of research on women. Li took a formless feeling that there should be more concerted knowledge about women and turned it into a battleground for women's studies. "Its charge: to use scientific research as its methodological base, human systematic sciences as its background, employ leading specialists to do research on women, and to push for theoretical progress so that we can establish a respectable base for national women's studies."[56] The flood of articles, periodicals, forums, and newspapers targeting female readers inspired her.[57] She fought to bring scholarly order to enthusiasm through a long-term, academically respectable project that would emphasize the Chineseness of Chinese women's studies. Li's interest in qualifying Chinese women's studies as culturally Chinese can be read as her effort to localize *nüren* and make certain that Chinese women's studies inoculates itself against colonization by the larger, often either insensitive or indifferent North American women's studies establishment.[58]

At its broadest, then, Chinese women's studies is a direction within the social sciences to represent Chinese women in history. It seeks to relocate that history on an empirical, documentary, quasi-scientific ground that will ensure without question that women's experience is represented in scholarship. As an academic discipline, however, it is part of a larger debate over representation and scientific truth claims in post-Maoist China. It participates in dismantling state ideological categories and in the ongoing efforts of the intellectual community to establish a scientific discourse that takes "nature" (in the case of natural science) and "society" (in the case of social science) as its referents.

* * *

Much has changed since the beginning of the 1980s. Before 1985 the dominant subject position open to Chinese women was still *funü*, situated in the powerful discourses of the socialist imaginary. By 1990 Maoism had collapsed, and *funü* with it. As late as 1985 the focus was still Fulian. In the 1990s it became women's studies. The framework within which textual politics played itself out in 1985 was, as before, the state *(guojia)*. Subsequently, despite the events of 1989, it became nationality *(minzu)*. Before the women's studies movement, liberation for women proceeded against "feudalism." Now women struggle against traditional society *(chuantong shehui)*. The dominant category then was politics, which Fulian controlled as the bureaucratic arm of the politicized state. Today women's studies sustains itself as an academic field or *xueke*, far removed from crudely "ideological" political activities. The rhetoric of women's subjectification has been irrepressibly enlarged. *Funü, nüren, nüxing* (and *xin nüxing, xin funü*, and so on) are all circulating simultaneously, a reminder that de-Maoization is as much a matter of language as an institutional project.

All critics apparently concur on the need to serve as advocates for ordinary women enduring the heightened social contradictions reform has visited on everyday life. There appears to be a consensus among women's studies scholars, moreover, that strategically it makes most sense to colonize rather than to abandon Fulian. The desire to extend the institutional reach of women's studies may also explain efforts to deploy the most inclusive, historicized, provisional female subject positions imaginable.[59]

The unmaking of *funü* is both similar to and different from feminist historians' deconstruction of Victorian women in the United States and England.[60] *Funü* and Woman situated themselves analogously, in the sense that for decades each appeared a stable trope, policed the boundaries between itself and others, and thereby dominated much political action.[61] But, as I hope I have demonstrated convincingly, analogy in the end explains nothing. Examined historically, neither "woman" nor "women" survives as a universal, transcendental signifier; no one sign is ever exactly reducible to the forms, terms, and constructions of any other, and thus history writing must remain strategic and contingent.

Even so, women's history practices, like the deconstruction/preservation of *funü* I have traced here, offer scholars and readers outside China other ways of resolving pressing local questions of strategy. Following the theorizing efforts of others is profoundly enabling. It suggests new ways of thinking about one's own local practice, not in spite of but rather in light of tangible historical and circumstantial differences among us. It also forces writing about women into ever more sophisticated efforts at grasping the imbrication of language and politics. In the end, of course, reading someone else's theorizing project clarifies the overall value and potential of liberation struggle, there and here, and thus provides valuable instruction.

LI XIAOJIANG

Translated by S. Katherine Campbell

16 | Economic Reform and the Awakening of Chinese Women's Collective Consciousness

At the end of 1987, through the venue of the Thirteenth Party Congress, we in China acknowledged the basic conditions of our country as standing at the onset of socialism, and we clarified the basic path for pursuing all aspects of intensive economic reform. The trades and professions put forth a variety of political, economic, and social reform programs. China's modernization can already see the first light of dawn: a way out.

The fact that China's path is through economic reform has already made a deep impression on people's consciousness; the road to social progress is also through reform. But why must the issue of "a way out for women" be the first casualty in the course of reform? It is almost as if social and economic reform conflicted with the course of women's development. Is this indeed true? The logical conclusion is that both goals are the same, but real life reflects conflict. Theory and reality, society and women: where did their paths diverge?

The Pressure of Reform

The pressure that reform places on women has actually existed for quite some time. From the post-1978 introduction of the agricultural and industrial contract production systems to the rise of the individual entrepreneurial class and the service industry, new women's issues (in comparison to the thirty-odd years of liberation) are sprouting like herbs in the spring rain of reform. Problems such as women returning to the home, female workers losing benefits or having their benefits reduced, young girls being forced to discontinue their education, and the reappearance of prostitution and concubinage are not just becoming visible today. They have at least a ten-year history.

The Thirteenth Party Congress gave Chinese society a new lease on life. Although the ensuing intensity and fast pace of competition created pressures at all levels of society, people can still acknowledge, with relative optimism, that the reforms have already provided both society and individuals with increased opportunities. Those who most feel the pressure and most sense the uncertainty of those options are women; and the Women's Federation, which represents women as a collective group, simultaneously feels its existence as an organization threatened.

Why is this? Let us look at what has been advocated, attacked, abolished, and publicized in the course of reform.

The "Report on Work" of the Thirteenth Party Congress[1] clearly lays out the theory of the first stages of socialism: so-called reform, including reform of political structures, is intended first and foremost to advance the development of society's productive forces. The congress initiated improvements in economic efficiency in order to realize more quickly the transformation of our country from impoverishment, to relative comfort, to prosperity. It also attacked the bureaucracy of the political world, the dogmatism of the theoretical world, the egalitarianism of the economy, and the apathy of the individual. It proposed a realistic approach to reform and true economic competition. These goals, sought after but unrealized for many years, are all well and good—but they threaten women. In the spirit of realism, we are impelled to face squarely the issue of biology and childbirth for women in social production. In actual economic competition, the fact that the quality of women as workers is inclined to be low and that they have a dual role evidently makes women and the enterprises that employ them less competitive.

Reform has also eliminated life tenure for cadres and the "iron rice bowl" of industry.[2] At precisely the same time that the limited tenure policy and the contract system were being implemented, much of the protection and many of the benefits for women in industry began to disappear one by one. As a result, the problems of "same work–different pay" and unequal promotions for men and women have arisen.

In 1988 a series of women's issues became even more pronounced. Not only women but the many men whose interests are intertwined with women's, and who are with women from morning to night, were affected, as well as all the families concerned about a daughter or a wife. Let us take a glimpse at the issues in the natural course of that one year.

First quarter. In the process of democratic elections for People's Congresses at every level and for the Seventh National People's Congress, few female cadres were elected, highlighting the problem of women's participation in government.

Second quarter. With the simultaneous implementation of enterprise self-management and discretionary hiring and contract systems, women's social benefits, salary, employment, and promotions were all threatened, rendering women workers' problems more acute.

Third quarter. In job assignments for college graduates and those who failed to pass the college entrance examinations, employment problems for women surfaced anew. This directly endangered young women intellectuals' future prospects and development.

Fourth quarter. With the deepening of economic reform and the widespread pursuit in industry of peak work capacity, the increased vigor of enterprises and the increasingly tense double burden for women came into direct conflict. The call for "equal work–equal pay" causes women to face even more severe challenges in light of the adjustment of actual work assignments and the disadvantaged position women encounter returning to work after childbirth. Under the circumstances, some women will inevitably decide to return to the home. But people will interpret this not as the will of society but as the conscious choice of women.

The travesty is that these pressures women endured then and continue to endure are never seen as social problems; they are construed as merely *individual problems.* Criticizing society as unfair is to no avail. The balance of justice has never been the moving force in the progress of history. If one is only willing to face reality, then one must see that the emergence of women's problems is actually a means for society to resolve many other social problems that emerged with reform (such as excess labor, labor productivity, and so on). Women have thus been the cornerstone in the development of society's productive capacity. Historically it has been so; in reality it is so. No wonder authoritative sociological publications are unwilling to print much on women's issues, for to speak excessively of women's liberation at this point would be to say that women's problems are obstructing society's reform and economic development. This means that Chinese women, who have worked hard all along to recognize their unity with society, cannot but acknowledge that women's issues in the midst of economic reform have been abandoned by society. They are truly women's problems, in that they have become sociologically insignificant.

What Exactly Are the Issues?

Discussions of women's issues in the past were always about women enduring oppression, discrimination, and enslavement; these were the pernicious vestiges of feudalism and the product of capitalist exploitation. To put it bluntly, these were mostly the problems of working women, and could be categorized as problems of class.

Today, however, just as issues of class in China and the world have receded, women's issues have gradually become more pronounced. They are reflected not only in the problems of women workers and of all women at work, but also in the lives of women of every class, and in every facet of women's lives. Especially in contemporary China, women's problems come from every direction, creating among those who concern themselves with women's issues a sense of crisis.

It is hard to deny, even for Chinese women accustomed to the catchphrase "Socialism liberates women," that the crisis objectively exists. If we use the obvious "equality of men and women" standard to measure women's actual plight, then Chinese women's liberation seems to be taking the road of regression. In the face of this "reverse tide," the long-parroted, never tested, never deeply researched theory of women's liberation appears exhausted. It is this weakness of conventional theory that compels us to face the reality of Chinese society and the reality of Chinese women, to investigate conscientiously all these earth-shattering women's issues. Are they really problems, and if so, of what kind?

Issue 1: The Women of Daqiu Village Return to the Home

The phenomenon of Daqiu village's women[3] emerged parallel with Daqiu village's economic reform. Now, some years later, Daqiu village has attracted national attention. The key to its fame lies not in its progress toward wealth but in its "women returning home." It seems that Daqiu village has become a new model, attracting economists' attention and women's panic. The phenomenon of women returning to the home emerged in apparent conformity with economic reform: it caters to a male need to participate in a high level of competition, and also lessens the constraints of women's double workday. At the same time, it lightens the burden for industry of tasks not oriented toward production, and supports social stability and enterprise development. In short, the return of women to the home allows men to work to their utmost capacity and alleviates the pressures in women's lives. From the perspective of subsistence and questions about improving the material standard of living and easing burdens in women's lives, one could say that no problems exist—either for society or for women.

From the viewpoint of development, however, and particularly women's individual development, problems become visible. The model of the women returning to the home symbolizes a return to a traditional role for contemporary women faced with a double workday. To put the matter even more bluntly, the suffocation of women's individual self-worth is the price paid for men's realization of their greatest social value. This is nothing new; history has always been this way!

Issue 2: Li Jing: Female Workers Laid Off and Waiting for Work

Layoff of female workers is apparently a local policy. There is no law, document, or regulation, and one never sees the press or scholars publicly promote it, but the phenomenon coincides with enterprise self-renewal and self-adjustment, and has increased in direct proportion to the expansion of enterprise self-management. Li Jing is one such laid-off woman.[4] Filled with the anxiety of seeking self-development, Li Jing tells the story of her own route to adulthood. On the individual level, her luck was bad: industrial reform began just when she was expecting a child and experiencing peak stress from women's double role. If this period had come a little sooner, the problem of layoffs would not have affected her so directly. But the issue of bearing and raising children is one from which no woman (no matter whether she is a worker or a peasant farm woman) can free herself.

Industry faced this problem earlier than women did, and dealt with it resolutely. In order to lessen pressures and expenditures not oriented toward production, industry forced pregnant women into the large contingent of the unemployed. It cannot be denied that this was an expedient measure of economic reform: it ensured the survival and development of industry, yet did not threaten the survival of women. This "laid off and waiting for work" policy is also a prime tactic for resolving excess employment and thus invigorating enterprises. It is not seen as a social dilemma; on the contrary, it effectively resolved certain social dilemmas. So why should it be posed as a women's issue?

Here is a phenomenon worthy of attention. Daqiu village women returned to the home to engage in nothing but household labor, yet they did not vent any grievances. But women like Li Jing find it unbearable to be laid off to care for children, even though they still draw 80 percent of their salary. Why? Because most women who, like Li Jing, have a moderate level of education have experienced self-development. It is impossible for them to return to the condition of illiteracy and be content with an existence in which they eat well, sleep well, and are supported and protected by others. They have already experienced the hope of winning the same opportunities for advancement as men and, through their own hard work, of realizing their desire for individual social worth. It is easy to see that the issue for those who have been laid off, like Li Jing, is not one of women's survival but rather one of women's development as persons in society.

Issue 3: Women College Students Find Placement Difficult

The previous year,[5] difficulties in job placement for female college students occurred at nearly every school in the country. After Hou Baoqin, a Beijing School of Commerce graduate in the class of 1987, was rejected by her work unit, reporters Zhou Lang and Feng Kewei conducted a special investigation of this problem.[6] They found that placement is difficult for female college students not only because of the traditional bias that men are superior to women, but also because there is a standoff between the work units who do the hiring and the women themselves within the context of reform.

On this question women are already accustomed to unfavorable comparisons with men—in terms of grades, competence, ability, and so on—as well as the expected conclusion that men and women are equal and should receive equal treatment. But a society that deals with concrete matters every day must recognize the ineradicable social differences between the two sexes: that is, men's virtual superiority in social production, and contemporary women's heavy burden of a double role.

No matter what a woman achieves in school or what her abilities are, the time for job assignments coincides with the traditional age for marriage. Thus, falling in love and starting a family happen at the same time as taking a job. Given society's low productive capacity and the consequent shortage of social benefits to provide for all human needs, it would be difficult to find any enterprise leader willing to undertake the burden of providing the time, personnel, and material resources necessary to cover for an employee about to undergo childbirth. Without universal social guarantees for pregnant women's needs, to ask a work unit to accept more women graduates (or women workers) is unfair.

It is common knowledge that China has a very small proportion of highly educated people. From a macro perspective, then, the problem of "difficult placement for female college students" simply does not exist. But in the final analysis the question arises, what exactly is the issue? It is not one of job placement itself, nor is it a question of survival. It is rather a question of women's development. Restrictions placed on job assignments lead to inequality of opportunity between men and women, and it is because of this that a whole series of obstructions to the self-development of women intellectuals are created.

Issue 4: The Question of Women in Politics

Women in government, like other political phenomena, is a sensitive topic. In the wake of women's losses in the elections to the Political Bureau of the Thirteenth Party Congress[7] and in the reorganization of government structures at every level,[8] the issue of women in politics has become a very visible symbol for women's liberation. The reaction of the Women's Federation has been fierce, but the common reaction of women in society is still one of indifference—just as in the past.

There are three issues that need to be clarified: (1) the relationship between women and politics; (2) the relationship between women holding office and women's liberation; and (3) the relationship between women holding political power and the interests of women as a whole. This brief essay cannot address the relationships and differences among these issues in detail, but the main points can be outlined.

First, even though the government is run by men, it does not entirely exclude women's interests. Just as the political slogan of "equality" that originated with the bourgeoisie can also include equality between men and women, so it was a socialist revolution, opposed to a feminism of women's rights [bourgeois feminism], that brought women political liberation. This is not just opinion but historical fact.

Second, the fundamental symbol of women's liberation in the political arena is precisely that of women holding office. But we have not yet seen the awakening of women all across society to a consciousness of themselves as social subjects or to a consciousness of democracy. Neither have we seen a large number of women taking an interest in and participating in political life. Perhaps, then, the issue of women in political office is just a sham. To speak in strictly political terms, relying on social policy to specify a particular quota of female cadres is in essence a mockery of political democracy. This represents a government handout to women, not the true political participation of women. This is also not just opinion but historical fact.

Third, women who participate in politics or hold positions of leadership as individuals do not necessarily represent the interests of women as a group. In history, when heads of state such as Wu Zetian,[9] Queen Victoria,[10] and Empress Catherine[11] took up the reins of power, this was not equivalent to exceeding the authority of women's political position. The numbers and offices of women politicians obviously cannot be the only measure of women's political status when these politicians lack collective consciousness.

If we sort out these three issues in terms of female political participation in contemporary China, the nature of the problem becomes obvious: the indifference of most women to participation in government balances with the lack of female collective consciousness among the women holding office. This is not a new problem, either, but has come about since the breaking of the iron rice bowl,[12] and is a reflection in the political arena of a series of problems in women's employment and development. The so-called problem of women's political participation appeared precisely when democratic election was initiated. Thus, it seems not to be a problem in society; on the contrary, it is the result of invisible social pressures on women's self-development.

Issue 5: The Question of Reform in Women's Organizations

The cry for reform in women's organizations has come principally from within the Women's Federation. The disregard shown by every area of society for the Women's Federation as well as the coldness of women themselves toward the federation have existed for a long time. These have acted as dual pressures from both the inside and the outside, threatening the very survival of women's organizations. The Women's Federation could continue to exist with the protection of the government, but it will be difficult for it to find its own space for development in society.

If you do not believe me, try answering this question: Does the Women's Federation as it currently stands have a distinct reason to exist? As a test, we could publish a document announcing that the Women's Federation will be entirely disbanded at every level. Even if it were to be dismantled in a single day, what effect would that have on social production? The machines would run as usual; electric lamps would still light; households would go to sleep calmly; the next day the sun would come up. Even if some Women's Federation cadres claiming to represent women's interests went to Beijing to complain, women themselves would see it as a joke, assuming it was just the act of some "people who eat the rice of women" who are themselves out of work.

In the midst of contemporary reforms, the sensible thing to do is obviously not to review the federation's meritorious record of the past. Opposing arranged marriage, encouraging women to come out of the home, protecting the legitimate rights and interests of women: for now we do not need to enumerate the accomplishments one by one. These are historical facts understood by all. It is exactly these contributions that have brought about the Women's Federation's pervasive presence and have ensured that, through the iron rice bowl of socialism, it would continue to exist to the present. It should be said that the existence of the Women's Federation and the fact that it is widespread is already worthy of esteem among China's women. At the least it has maintained the fruits of liberation that Chinese women have already won. On these grounds alone the federation cannot and should not be dissolved. Even suggesting that it should be disbanded is a latent crime against history: not toward the past, but toward the future.

Why? Because women have not had equal collective privileges in male-centered society, and Chinese women have had their own problems that differ from general social problems. In the course of economic reform, women's problems have been not alleviated but intensified. This in itself implies a definitive need for the existence and development of women's organizations. But from all appearances the situation of the Women's Federation is extremely awkward. It has been rejected both by society and by women. There is no harm in looking back.

Recollection 1. After 1978, when problems for women emerged with the birth planning policy and the implementation of the new marriage law, the Women's Federation worked energetically on behalf of the legitimate rights and interests of women and children. But while "mobilizing to protect families," many Women's Federation cadres sought to appeal to the law on behalf of women who had been abandoned, to ask for the preservation of marriages that were already ruined, the opposite of what the new marriage regulations called for. The federation supported "Qin Xianglian,"[13] and used phrases such as "virtuous, at home, secondary,"[14] and "female superiority"; why was it that not only men frowned at this but women themselves also gave a snort of contempt?

Recollection 2. The Women's Federation made an effort to obstruct the trend in enterprises toward eliminating women and refusing to accept new female workers, yet their efforts were like those of a praying mantis trying to stop a chariot. The campaign was undoubtedly in women's interest, but it was to no avail in solving the real problems facing women. Such an organization is the kind with which even weak women are not willing to throw in their lot.

Recollection 3. After women's losses in the elections to the Political Bureau at the Thirteenth Party Congress (1987), every local government lost women delegates as well, arousing the ire of the Women's Federation. The federation was the first to petition for proportional representation for women cadres. Proportional representation seemingly could continue as it was (there are people who have suggested quotas by social group), but that would contradict the principles of democratic selection. If extension of fair treatment to women in government operated simply according to a quota, there would be at least two kinds of abuses. In the course of reform, incompetent cadres [who would remain in office because of a quota] are harmful to the social collectivity, and that is unfair to society. Also, every woman selected from some group represents mostly that group's interests—but who is working for women's interests?

If we acknowledge that society's reform is also a transformation for women, that economic reform necessarily brings with it an improvement in women's standard of living and quality of education, why do we need to trouble ourselves on behalf of women? And why should the position and status of the Women's Federation be of concern?

Obviously the question of reform in women's organizations is not a social problem that shakes up society at large but is women's own business. The questions are of collective development: first, of women upholding women's collective interests in the face of reform pressures, and second, of ensuring that the structure of organizations reflects the level of social and economic participation of women.

In our country, within a certain number of years the issues that will be defined as "female" will be of every hue and shade and of unprecedented variety, and their boundaries will be difficult to establish. Every class of women has its own pressing issues that are not mutually reinforcing and may even be contradictory. But there is one thing they do have in common: none of these women's problems endangers social existence or creates detrimental effects to society; they do not intensify social contradictions and can even be the result of alleviating other social contradictions. Because of this they cannot be called social problems but are instead the affair of women. They are the problems of self-development of women after their consciousness of themselves as persons has awakened and they demand a realization of their social self-worth.

Logically, women's development and social development are congruent. But why is it that in our country, in the midst of economic reform, the development of society and the development of women have come into sharp conflict? Or that social development and women's development may even be severed at a certain point?

Wherein Lies the Crux of the Issue?

Answering this question touches on at least two basic theoretical points. One is the nature of women's liberation, and the other is the specific characteristics of Chinese women's liberation.

The First Question of Theory: What Is the Nature of Women's Liberation?

Why do we want to liberate women? We have become accustomed to saying, "Women are people, too," as if the principle of fairness played a leading role. Consequently, to liberate humankind *ought* to liberate women; humankind seemingly will use ideal principles to divide up the world equitably. If this were so, women's liberation would simply mean assimilation into an originally male world, and male and female equality would naturally be the symbol of women's liberation. Men see the matter this way, and recognize that women's liberation elevates women but that men must remain dominant and the norm. Women also see it this way; they believe that women's liberation simply means equality between men and women, and they make an effort to use male standards (so-called society's standards) to judge themselves.

Is this the only way? If it is, then women's liberation is just a by-product of the development of society; it is a symbol of self-civilizing in a male-centered society. The liberation of women will then not intrinsically aid the liberation of humankind, but on the contrary will become a burden in the search for the comprehensive development of freedom. It makes the burden of society and of those in charge (men) heavy. As long as society cannot get out from under the threat of mere survival, women's liberation will be considered superfluous. The complaints of contemporary Chinese men and the general atmosphere of grievance toward working households with two heads have definitely not come out of thin air!

The Second Question of Theory: What Are the Specific Characteristics of Chinese Women's Liberation?

Post–May Fourth China[15] found itself in an open world, and had already broken away from the course of isolated cultural development. It could not but recognize elements that had come from every region of the world, as well as the influences and inroads of many cultures. Socialist revolution was one of these.

It is hard to deny that over the course of time, social liberation for women in our country has been extensive; it is embodied in legislation and in daily life. The manifestation in women themselves is the awareness and practice of assimilating into society, becoming part of society. One must acknowledge that, compared with the status of women in the West, the status of Chinese women in social life and the level of recognition by society has been relatively high. This is manifest in that

- society calls on women to join in productive labor;
- the social structure guarantees that men and women receive the same pay for the same work;
- the right to equality between men and women is promulgated in legislation;
- government policy protects the various interests of women;
- a socialist ruling party helped women to the extent of establishing and developing a women's organization.

In the course of eliminating class differences and breaking down great disparities of wealth in order to maintain a standard of living necessary to provide for the basic needs of the entire society, all of these achievements could have been realized, or have been realized.

But if women's social participation comes not from the ideal principles of socialism (principles of equality) but from the internal needs of developing society's productivity, the question takes on a different answer:

- The spontaneous course of the development of productive forces in competition naturally selects the male, who can focus all his efforts on social production, and rejects the female, who must be responsible for human production.
- From the perspective of the situation of China's large population, developing productive capacity is a matter not of insufficient labor but of a glutted labor market. Even if we had no population problems and proceeded from a stable society, the trend would always be to take on young male workers, not female ones.
- As to the limits on the pace of development, the burden of welfare in a period of low productivity obviously impedes rather than advances the development of society.
- If we look at the basic quality and productive potential of men's and women's labor, the formal structure of equal pay for equal work limits the mobilizing of unequal work loads,

imperceptibly letting male competitive consciousness lower the level of benefits for women.[16]

- In terms of women's own situation, participation in double production in a society with a low standard of living and an undeveloped labor force not only will not liberate women but will also make doubly heavy the burden of subsistence. Even if women have the social opportunities for equal development, they will suffer from not having the strength to attend to other work. It is thus difficult to open any real route to individual development.

Therefore, to push for principles of egalitarian distribution and structural liberation for women from an undeveloped economic base restricts not only social development but women's own development as well. That kind of price for the social liberation of women must be paid for by the actual experience of every woman. More than forty years of mental and physical exhaustion caused by the extraordinary stress of a double role is a heavy burden, and one that neither women in history nor contemporary men have experienced!

In terms of our country's low social productivity, the current reforms have realistically restored the relations of production and the system of economic organization previously criticized in theory. The household responsibility system, individual entrepreneurship, and the contract system in industry emerged simultaneously. There is not much to criticize here. But a corollary development was the restoration of women's original social status. It seemed that women were to return to the home, to a social milieu characterized by obvious inequality with men. To Chinese women already accustomed to recognition by society and male-female equality as symbolic of women's liberation, this was certainly an excessive challenge.

At a certain point in time the conflict between economic development and women's development will become more intense as the reforms expand. In this way contemporary Chinese women will find themselves involuntarily pressed between the needs of two different kinds of development. On the one side is the pressure of social development. The conflict between economic efficiency and principles of fairness is concentrated on women's bodies. Women are thus squeezed into the realm of noneconomic labor by the exclusion of women's labor power when enterprises choose to eliminate the constraints that human reproduction places on social production. This coincidentally gives a measure of protection for women and society in the midst of competition.

On the other side are the internal needs of women's own development. History has verified that relations of production can be reworked to align with productive forces during periods of "restoration." Only human consciousness cannot be reversed. Perhaps deep sleep can still be had after awakening, but the new heavy sleep brings with it dream-visions of past awakenings. Consequently, Chinese women who have self-consciously assimilated into society and have simultaneously been recognized by society, who have kept on a par with men in society, are now in a position of unprecedented difficulty, and they cannot but cry for help in search of a "way out."

A Way Out?

Finding "a way out" is an old topic in women's quest for liberation. Women who are self-aware therefore confront this question. But women's liberation has prerequisites; even if social conditions permitted a high level of material and cultural development, there must always be the subjective condition of women's conscious desire to develop, that is, the awakening of women's subjectivity.

If we use these preconditions to judge the course of Chinese women's liberation, the social liberation that Chinese women have won can be seen to have its shortcomings in the two areas of material conditions and ideological conditions. As to the former, the low level of productive capacity means that society has the intention but not the ability to carry out women's liberation fully. As to the latter, Chinese women's collective consciousness is especially weak. A clear example is the way many female writers and cadres expend much effort to distinguish between themselves and women as a group while striving to create signs of equality with men throughout society. If even talented women with status, ability, and education are uninterested in working toward the liberation of Chinese women, how can one ask that of the great mass of Chinese women, who are still unable to extricate themselves from the hard problems of survival and development?

As of now, compelled by the great tide of reform, the first shortcoming has been clearly exposed. The second has been concealed by women's social liberation. For this reason we see that some women have returned to the home (many of them willingly) and some women workers have been laid off (although many pregnant women were willingly laid off). In the midst of reform, society makes no allowances for women's liberation, to the point of refusing to discuss it. One could almost come to the conclusion that the movement for women's liberation in China is at an ebb, or is even going backwards. Is it really this way? This question raises a third theoretical issue.

The Third Question of Theory: What, Finally, Is the Marker of Liberation for Women?

We used to think that the liberation of women meant just the appearance of women in society. Obviously if a woman has not come out into society, her social consciousness of herself as a person is difficult to awaken, and she will not be able to realize her human self-worth in social life. Without a doubt, women's coming out into society is a prerequisite of women's liberation. Nonetheless, qualifications remain.

Point 1: Women's coming out into society, however, is not *the equivalent of women's liberation.* It cannot even be used as a scale to measure women's liberation. Many eighteenth-century Englishwomen came out into society, most to work as cheap laborers or prostitutes. For them, coming out into society was not liberating; indeed, the bondage of society and class was added to bondage to men, and their misery became even more intense. More than forty years after liberation,[17] the women of our country have made a huge leap into social life. But because social productivity is low, they must shoulder the double burdens of work and household chores. Their life's burden thus becomes heavier by a factor of two. The life of a beast of burden is certainly not the liberation which Chinese women have so painstakingly sought.

We used to affirm theoretically that women's liberation is just class liberation, and could collaborate with revolutionary communism. Historically, women's liberation has actually been linked with class liberation: in the United States it was linked to the movement to abolish slavery; in Europe it was linked to workers' movements; in many third world countries it has been linked with nationalist liberation; in the Soviet Union and China it was linked with socialist revolution. Obviously the resistance movements of oppressed classes and nationalities and the path of oppressed women in search of liberation have interrelated interests.

Point 2: Class liberation, however, is not *the same as women's liberation.* It cannot be used as a significant measure of women's liberation. Class is a historical factor, and always belongs to a given historical category. With women it is different. Women's most immediate interests have always coexisted with all of human existence and development; they were a historical constant. But history has already confirmed that the liberation of slaves in the United States and the reform of the Russian serf system did not bring about a corresponding liberation of women. Peasants who gained title to land could still tyrannize their wives at home; men of the bourgeoisie who won their human rights could still discriminate against women in social life to the point of excluding them. China's social practice has also already affirmed that the victory of the socialist revolution did not imply liberation for women but merely provided an advantageous juncture in Chinese women's quest for liberation.

More than forty years after liberation, we are accustomed to acknowledging that women's liberation means the equality of men and women. It cannot be denied that to have the equality of men and women set forth in legislation was definitely a basic goal of the women's liberation movement, and one of the essential conditions for ensuring women's successful fight for their liberation. No matter in terms of a collective of women or an individual, coming into a world that was originally male means that one cannot help but take established male standards as a goal for self-improvement and the measure for testing self-development and individual worth. This is the most convenient measure created by history.

Point 3: Equality between men and women, however, is not *the same as women's liberation.* It can never be the ultimate measure by which to judge women's liberation. Equality between men and women as the standard for women's liberation already includes two mistaken theoretical presuppositions.

The first, in reference to biological differences and historically created social differences, is that in the construction of human existence the two sexes lived and helped each other mutually. Their strengths and weaknesses, as far as human needs were concerned, were a given that could not be defined as positive or negative. Sex difference was not human-made, nor is it a gap that can be bridged by human effort. On this basis any sort of formal equality between men and women can only create inequality on an essential level. Practice has also proven that for women to take on the risks and burdens of competition in a male-centered society and also strive to realize their self-worth is no easy feat; they must still endure their mission of human reproduction mandated by nature. Under such premises the measures of equality place excessive demands on women.

Second, the idea of "equality" is the product of class relations in a class-stratified society, mainly embodied in the bourgeoisie's demand for self-interested political power. Of course, women make the same demand of men; thus, "equality" became the basic measure of women's emergence into society. But the relations between men and women far exceed class, status, and all the other categories of social value. The biological differences between the two sexes are interrelated with the gradual evolution and proliferation of racial groups, and the social differences between the sexes have strengthened in response to the demands of human development. Therefore, human ideals cannot possibly create an equal world on the bedrock of difference, and it was on the foundation of harmonious coexistence of the two sexes that the greatest extent of freedom was won. In this sense, "equality" was intrinsically an impediment to the development of freedom and every kind of individuality.

In the midst of the huge wave of reform, a new idea is coming to the fore, that the liberation of women must improve society's productive capacity, and the expansion of the labor force will necessarily bring with it the liberation of women. Concerning any positive effect productive forces could have on promoting the liberation of women, I have already put forward an argument: that is self-evident.

Point 4: A developed productive capacity, however, is not the same as women's liberation. I have already shown how material civilization undoubtedly created the conditions for women's liberation; but without women's self-consciousness and struggle, we would not have so-called liberation, and we could not have genuine human liberation. Even if "the other half" of humanity enters a world that was once male, is recognized by, and assimilates to that world, what new benefits will that bring to men and to the world?

What exactly, then, *is* the standard for women's liberation? To summarize, it is human freedom and overall development. In order to comprehend this issue, we must first acknowledge that this world of ours (still a male-centered one) is imperfect; it has flaws. Its flaws are not just that one portion of humanity (women) has been lost to social life; this is a question of quantity. Even more important is that, as it has used material measures, social measures, and so-called civilized measures to judge people's worth and thus belittle women, our society also belittles the feminine aspects of human nature, such as coexistence and symbiosis; indeed, it belittles the unconditional acknowledgment of the worth of individual human life. In this sense, so-called women's liberation is not just a demand for power by powerless women, nor is it just a group of people entering another group's world. Even more important, women's liberation means giving a good name to the "incurably" petty qualities of femininity (such as being peaceful, close to nature, emotional) and through women's struggle to promote those valuable human characteristics that have long been undervalued by the standards of civilized society. This noble demand can emerge only after a high level of social development has allowed society to master nature and overcome basic difficulties of existence: it both affirms people's social value and makes possible opportunities to realize fully individual self-worth in society; it affirms the value of human life, and brings about the freedom to possess individual self-worth completely.

Viewed in this manner, women's liberation is both a social issue and an individual one. Without doubt it depends on the progress of men and male-centered society, and even more on all the effort women put into establishing female self-worth. To speak precisely, in the long course of civilized history, men fully developed their skill in the production of material things, for the most part taking up the cross of civilized progress for humankind. Now, in the process of humankind's own self-liberation, the burden of the cross is borne mostly by women. Their task is to establish the independence of female character and self-worth, however that affects the development and perfection of humankind.

Because human liberation and women's liberation are multidimensional, no matter in which direction one exerts effort during development, all paths are viable; any one of them may bring progress. For instance, the development of society and the economy can lessen human dependence on nature, thus alleviating the stress of double roles for women. Alleviating contradictions between classes and encouraging social stability will help advance political democratization and give free rein to individuality, thus establishing the conditions for female self-worth. A choice of professions will measure people's level of initiative; this is the premise for women's economic independence. The ability of men and women to get along with one another equally will also be an important measure for gauging society's degree of civilization; this is the social guarantee for women's development.

Yet if all this is separated from the awakening of female self-consciousness and efforts toward self-improvement, then there is no need to indulge in extravagant discussions of women's liberation or a way out for women.

The problem of a "way out" has been much discussed and fretted over, but as far as that issue is concerned, there is no further need for women to worry. If we look at it only from the angle of subsistence, employment, and the economy, the problem does not exist for most Chinese women. One reason is that the traditionally male-centered society by definition has the natural function of protecting women (the father raises the daughter, the husband provides for the wife, society takes care of the household). A second reason is that the socialist system cannot allow a large contingent of people to stay unemployed for a long period of time. It must always have an appropriate policy to provide for the powerless. Since women are all made powerless, society has also protected women in its protection of the indigent. Under the pressure of reform, some women want to return to the home, and some women want a break from work. But women's return to the home does not necessarily imply the formation of a "housewife class" (peasant women who participate in household economic production are not in the "housewife" category), and women who have already quit working (most are taking part in the labor of human reproduction while pregnant) are not entirely the same as the large contingent of the unemployed.

As enterprises have rid their ranks of excess labor power and cast aside the burden of caring for women involved in giving birth, they have cast many women off the main road of development. But whether women's goal is to subsist or to pursue self-development, they can, as always, come out of the home when the time is right and find many employment opportunities. This is true even if it means taking a side road to development, or pushing a small cart (the sudden rise of women as entrepreneurs or in specialized businesses are examples). They can also make their way into the crevices of society, and there find positions for themselves and space to move. It is only from the perspective of female self-development that we see that these kinds of spontaneously generated routes out are indeed difficult and humble; one can just barely survive, and will have difficulty pursuing self-development. But perhaps it is the very nature of these routes that has stifled the aspirations for self-improvement of a generation of women as well as the possibility that women may develop in step with men.

A positive point is that the history of more than forty years of social liberation for women has enlightened a generation of Chinese women, whetting their appetite for realizing individual development through male-female equality. As society was accepting them and making an effort to assimilate them, Chinese women also put all their thought and will into harmonizing with and blending into that society. Their desire to be persons was intense, but their female self-consciousness was very slight. Society has suddenly pushed women aside, and drawn boundaries with the intention of excluding women. Now women cannot but throw off the swaddling clothes of society's protection, and in the name of the collective of women explore a way out so to develop women's independence and self-improvement.

To demand development, there must be a consciousness of development. Women who have had the desire for development blocked by their gender status are bound to set off an awakening of female subjectivity. This is the ideological basis for women's liberation, and it is also an unavoidable stage on the road to women's liberation. This is just what Chinese women collectively have ignored and avoided.

Until now this issue has not been raised; but it is raised by the pressures of reform. Even though present reforms are in numerous ways not beneficial to women, they offer one benefit that no force of human will could have effected: social pressure has brought about an awakening of Chinese women's collective consciousness of an accustomed dependence on society. With this awakening, it may be possible to realize a thousand or ten thousand ways out.

If the collective consciousness of Chinese women were awakened, then we would definitely see enlightened women actively involved in society, and would see self-improvement and consciousness-raising movements for women. In the painful process of weaning themselves away from society, Chinese women can learn to draw nurturing and strength from women themselves. In the face of traditional theory that has lost its efficacy, they can explore and choose new theories for women. At the same time, they can also choose "organization": new women's groups with various structures or with no structure could come into being one after another. Thus would we find a way toward collective female development even in the difficult organizational predicament of no way out.

Notes

Contributors

Notes

Introduction

1. For helpful discussion of gender as an analytical category, see Joan Scott, "Gender: A Useful Category of Historical Analysis," in *Gender and the Politics of History* (New York: Columbia University Press, 1988), pp. 28–50, 206–211; Faye Ginsburg and Anna Tsing, eds., *Uncertain Terms: Gender in American Culture* (Boston: Beacon Press, 1989), pp. 1–16.

2. Margery Wolf, *Women and the Family in Rural Taiwan* (Stanford: Stanford University Press, 1972); Marilyn Young, ed., *Women in China: Studies in Social Change and Feminism,* Michigan Papers in Chinese Studies no. 15 (Ann Arbor: Center for Chinese Studies, 1973).

3. Kay Ann Johnson, *Women, the Family, and Peasant Revolution in China* (Chicago: University of Chicago Press, 1983); Judith Stacey, *Patriarchy and Socialist Revolution in China* (Berkeley: University of California Press, 1983); Phyllis Andors, *The Unfinished Liberation of Chinese Women: 1949–1980* (Bloomington: Indiana University Press, 1983).

4. See Lata Mani, "Multiple Mediations: Feminist Scholarship in the Age of Multinational Reception," *Feminist Review* 35 (1990): 24–41; Chandra Talpade Mohanty, "Under Western Eyes: Feminist Scholarship and Colonial Discourses," *boundary* 2.12–13 (1984): 333–358; Gayatri Spivak, *In Other Worlds: Essays in Cultural Politics* (New York: Methuen, 1987); and Trinh T. Minh-ha, *Woman, Native, Other: Writing Postcoloniality and Feminism* (Bloomington: Indiana University Press, 1989).

5. On this point, see Rey Chow, *Woman and Chinese Modernity: The Politics of Reading between West and East* (Minneapolis: University of Minnesota Press, 1991); and Aihwa Ong, "Colonialism and Modernity: Feminist Re-Presen-

tations of Women in Non-Western Societies," *Inscriptions* 3–4 (1988): 79–93.

6. Homogenization is not the point here. Rather, we argue that all knowledge is always situated in a particular time and place and is always related to dynamics of power. For an elaboration of this issue, see Donna J. Haraway, "Situated Knowledges: The Science Question in Feminism and the Privilege of Partial Perspective," in *Simians, Cyborgs, and Women: The Reinvention of Nature* (New York: Routledge, 1991), pp. 183–201.

7. See Margery Wolf and Roxane Witke, eds., *Women in Chinese Society* (Stanford: Stanford University Press, 1975), p. 11.

1. Learned Women in the Eighteenth Century

I acknowledge with appreciation astute critical comments on an earlier draft by Lisa Rofel and Gail Hershatter. Yu-yin Cheng corrected errors in my translations. I am also grateful for the advice of my colleague Michelle Yeh.

1. See, for example, Kay Ann Johnson, *Women, the Family, and Peasant Revolution in China* (Chicago: University of Chicago Press, 1984), pp. 8–18; John King Fairbank, *The United States and China*, 4th ed., enl. (Cambridge, Mass.: Harvard University Press, 1983), pp. 22–23.

2. A recent example is T'ien Ju-k'ang, *Male Anxiety and Female Chastity: A Comparative Study of Chinese Ethical Values in Ming-Ch'ing Times* (Leiden: E. J. Brill, 1988).

3. Margery Wolf, *Women and the Family in Rural Taiwan* (Stanford: Stanford University Press, 1972).

4. See, for example, Joanna F. Handlin, "Lü K'un's New Audience: The Influence of Women's Literacy on Sixteenth-Century Thought," in *Women in Chinese Society*, ed. Margery Wolf and Roxane Witke (Stanford: Stanford University Press, 1975), pp. 13–38; Paul Ropp, *Dissent in Early Modern China: Ju-lin Wai-shih and Ch'ing Social Criticism* (Ann Arbor: University of Michigan Press, 1981); K'ang-i Sun Chang, *The Late-Ming Poet Ch'en Tzu-lung: Crises of Love and Loyalism* (New Haven: Yale University Press, 1991).

5. Readers will recognize my special debt to the work of Maureen Robertson, "Voicing the Feminine: Constructions of the Gendered Subject in Lyric Poetry by Women of Medieval and Late Imperial China," *Late Imperial China* (hereafter *LIC*) 13.1 (1992): 63–110. See also Ellen Widmer, "The Epistolary World of Female Talent in Seventeenth-Century China," *LIC* 10.2 (1989): 1–43; and Dorothy Ko, "Pursuing Talent and Virtue: Education and Women's Culture in Seventeenth- and Eighteenth-Century China," *LIC* 13.1 (1992): 9–39.

6. The debate is described in Susan Mann, "'Fuxue' (Women's Learning) by

Zhang Xuecheng (1738–1801): China's First History of Women's Culture," *LIC* 13.1 (1992): 40–62; see also Mann, "Classical Revival and the Gender Question: China's First Querelle des Femmes," in *Family Process and Political Process in Modern Chinese History*, Institute of Modern History, Academia Sinica (Taipei: Institute of Modern History, Academia Sinica, 1992), 1:377–411.

7. Each has an authoritative biography in English. See David S. Nivison, *The Life and Thought of Chang Hsüeh-ch'eng (1738–1801)* (Stanford: Stanford University Press, 1966); and Arthur Waley, *Yuan Mei: Eighteenth-Century Chinese Poet* (New York: Grove Press, 1956).

8. The term *fu xue* was used first by Yuan Mei to refer to the study of poetry by women, invoking as a model the female voices in the *Book of Odes (Shi jing)*. A review of Hu Shi's research on the controversy and a discussion of Zhang's views on gender appears in Zhou Qirong [Chow Kai-wing] and Liu Guangjing [K. C. Liu], "Xueshu jingshi: Zhang Xuecheng zhi wenshi-lun yu jingshi sixiang" (Scholarship and Statecraft: Zhang Xuecheng's Theory of Literature and History and Its Relationship to Statecraft Thought), in *Jinshi Zhongguo jingshi sixiang yantaohui lunwenji* (Collected Essays from the Conference on Statecraft Thought in Modern Chinese History), ed. Zhongyang Yanjiuyuan Jindaishi Yanjiusuo (Taipei: Academia Sinica, 1984), pp. 142–145. Zhang Xuecheng's essay, which is undated, was written to protest the publication of Yuan Mei's *Suiyuan nüdizi shixuan* (Collected Poems of the Women Pupils in Suiyuan Garden), printed in 1796, the year before Yuan Mei's death; hereafter *SNS*. Page references in the quotations from *Fu xue* follow the version in the standard edition of Zhang's collected works, *Zhang shi yishu* (Bequeathed Writings of Master Zhang), ed. Liu Cheng'gan, Jiayetang edition of 1922, *juan* 5:30b–41a; hereafter *FX*.

9. Yuan Mei, *Suiyuan shihua* (Poetry Talks from Sui Garden), ed. Gu Xuexie (1793–1796; rpt. Beijing: Renmin wenxue chubanshe), *juan* 3, no. 50, p. 88; hereafter *SS*.

10. *FX* 5:30b.

11. *FX* 5:31a.

12. These were the three renowned Tang poets Xue Tao (768–831), Yu Xuanji (844–868), and Li Ye (eighth century). An excellent short assessment of their lives and work appears in Sharon Shih-jiuan Hou, "Women's Literature," in *The Indiana Companion to Traditional Chinese Literature*, ed. and comp. William H. Nienhauser, Jr. (Bloomington: Indiana University Press, 1986), pp. 186–187. Biographies of Xue Tao and Yu Xuanji, respectively, appear separately in Nienhauser, *Indiana Companion*, pp. 438–439 and p. 944. A number of Xue Tao's poems have been translated into English.

See Amy Lowell and Florence Ayscough, trans., *Fir-Flower Tablets* (Boston: Houghton Mifflin, 1921); and Jeanne Larsen, trans., *Brocade River Poems: Selected Works of the Tang Dynasty Courtesan Xue Tao* (Princeton: Princeton University Press, 1987). A brief biographical sketch of Xue Tao also appears in Kenneth Rexroth and Ling Chung, *Women Poets of China* (New York: New Directions Books, 1972), p. 125, together with a selection of her poems. Like Li Ye and Yu Xuanji, according to some accounts, Xue Tao donned the habit of a Taoist nun (*nüguan*) and became a recluse in her later years. See Rexroth and Chung, *Women Poets*, pp. 125, 130, 137. A short biographical sketch of Yu Xuanji by Jan W. Walls appears in Wu-chi Liu and Irving Yucheng Lo, eds., *Sunflower Splendor: Three Thousand Years of Chinese Poetry* (Bloomington: Indiana University Press, 1990), pp. 577–578.

13. *FX* 5:34b. Song Ruohua was the consort of Emperor Dezong (r. 779–805); the Lady Zheng is known only as the wife of Chen Miao.

14. See Yuan's comment on poetry and sex later in this essay.

15. *FX* 5:32a.

16. *FX* 5:34b.

17. See *FX* 5:38b. I am indebted to Pauline Yu for her reminder that this is an allusion to the *Shih jing* (Book of Odes). The ode in question is in *Guofeng* (Songs of the States), book 3, the Odes of Bei. The poem describes the distress of a man whose beloved refuses to come out to meet him. See Kong Yingda, ed., *Mao shi zhushu* (The Annotated Book of Odes), Siku quanshu edition (rpt. Taipei: Taiwan shangwu yinshuguan, 1983–1986), 3:72a–76a. The poem is translated in James Legge, *The Chinese Classics*, vol. 4, *The She King*, reprinted from the last editions of the Oxford University Press (Taipei: Wenxing shudian, 1966), pp. 68–69. A Song commentary contrasts the *jing nü* with the *liu nü* (rambling girls) described in another poem, and points out that only "common" women would wander abroad.

18. The poem is *Zhou nan* 1.

19. A line from another section of the Songs of the States, from the state of Bei (Bei 9).

20. The story was preserved for Yuan Mei to record it years later, as a preface to two of Sun Yunfeng's poems included in his *Poetry Talks*. See *SS* 2, no. 31, p. 45. A biography of Sun Yunfeng appears in Shi Shuyi, comp., *Qingdai guige shiren zhenglüe* (Brief Lives of Women Poets of the Qing Dynasty), preface dated 1920 (rpt. Shanghai: Shanghai shudian, 1987), 6:9a–10a; hereafter *QGSZ*.

21. Yuan Mei, *Suiyuan shihua buyi* (Supplement to Poetry Talks from Sui Garden), vol. 2 of *SSH* 2, no. 61, pp. 615–616; hereafter *SSB*.

22. *SSB* 5, no. 5, p. 679.

23. *QGSZ* 6:13b.
24. *SSB* 8, no. 11, p. 767.
25. Xie Daocheng, *jinshi* of 1661/62, was a native of Min county, seat of Fuzhou prefecture. A member of the Hanlin academy, he rose to the position of Grand Secretary under the Kangxi emperor.
26. Zhang Yingchang, comp., *Qingshi duo* (Anthology of Qing Poetry), classified by topic; first printed 1869 under the title *Guochao shi duo* (rpt. Beijing: Zhonghua shuju, 1960, 1983), vol. 2, 22:803–804.
27. *SSB* 6, no. 3, p. 712; *SS* 2, no. 46, pp. 50–51.
28. *SS* 3, no. 42, p. 85. Elsewhere he observes: "Among female poets, most are respectable ladies [*guixiu*]; few are courtesans [*qingyi*]." See *SS* 3, no. 73, p. 97.
29. See Arthur W. Hummel, ed., *Eminent Chinese of the Ch'ing Period* (1944; rpt. Taipei: Ch'eng-wen, 1967), p. 26.
30. *SSB* 8, no. 63, p. 788.
31. S. Wells Williams, *The Middle Kingdom* (New York: Charles Scribners Sons, 1900), 1:573. See also Hummel, *Eminent Chinese*, p. 402.
32. The most commonly cited example of the companionate marriage ideal comes from the widely read memoirs of the erstwhile *yamen* secretary and traveler Shen Fu and his beloved Yun. See Shen Fu, *Six Records of a Floating Life*, trans. Leonard Pratt and Chiang Su-hui (Harmondsworth: Penguin Books, 1983). Shen Fu himself was not a degree holder, and his wife, while literate, was self-taught. But examples of companionate marriage appear among the most eminent scholars and officials. Of the more than sixty-seven noted women writers mentioned in Hummel, *Eminent Chinese*, eleven were concubines; the rest were all wives of noted scholars, including major figures such as Sun Hsing-yen and Ts'ui Shu. See also Ellen Johnston Laing, "Women Painters in Traditional China," in *Flowering in the Shadows: Women in the History of Chinese and Japanese Painting*, ed. Marsha Weidner (Honolulu: University of Hawaii Press, 1990), pp. 87–88. On these and other family networks, see Dorothy Ko, *Teachers of the Inner Chambers: Women and Culture in Seventeenth-Century China* (Stanford: Stanford University Press, 1994). On in-law networks, see comments on learned women of the Zhuang lineage in Benjamin Elman, *Classicism, Politics, and Kinship: The Ch'ang-chou School of New Text Confucianism in Late Imperial China* (Berkeley: University of California Press, 1990), pp. 57–58, 71, 87.
33. *SSB* 10, no. 35, pp. 832–833.
34. *SSB* 10, no. 39, p. 834.
35. *SSB* 8, no. 65, p. 789; *QGSZ* 6:4b.
36. *SS* 3, no. 5, pp. 69–70; *SSB* 4, no. 52, pp. 669–670. The *Elegies of Chu*, long poems revered for centuries, have been translated by David Hawkes, *Ch'u*

Tz'u: The Songs of the South (London: Oxford University Press, 1959). They are tragic because of their association with the life of the poet Qu Yuan, who committed suicide in despair after being banished by the ruler to whom he was devoted. See also Laurence A. Schneider, *A Madman of Ch'u: The Chinese Myth of Loyalty and Dissent* (Berkeley: University of California Press, 1980). To a young woman, the *Chu ci* would have been emblems of separation, loneliness, and longing for an unreachable beloved.

37. *SS* 2, no. 67, p. 60.

38. *SSB* 9, no. 55, p. 813; *SS* 1, no. 53, p. 24. See Waley, *Yuan Mei,* pp. 36–37, for an account of the tragic ruin of Yuan's talented sister Suwen as a result of an arranged marriage.

39. See *SSB* 9, no. 37, p. 807; see also *SSB* 8, no. 20, p. 771; *SSB* 9, no. 9, p. 795.

40. Yeh Shi, "Xie mu," in *Guochao guixiu zhengshi xuji* (Correct Beginnings: Women's Poetry of Our August Dynasty, Second Collection), ed. Yun Zhu, prefaces dated 1836/37, *juan* 3:6a.

41. See, for example, *SS* 2, no. 25, p. 43; 2, no. 52, pp. 53–54; 3, no. 57, pp. 90–91; 4, no. 30, p. 112; and *SSB* 2, no. 24, p. 601; 7, no. 21, p. 743; 8, no. 64, pp. 788–789; 10, no. 23, p. 827.

42. The definitive study of the Double Seven festival is Hong Shuling [Horng Shwu-ling], *Niulang zhinü yanjiu* (A Study of the Folktale of "The Cowherd and the Weaving Girl") (Taipei: Taiwan xueshu shuju, 1988). For standard accounts in English, see Tun Li-ch'en, *Annual Customs and Festivals in Peking,* trans. and ed. Derk Bodde, 2d ed., rev. (Hong Kong: Hong Kong University Press, 1965), p. 59; and Juliet Bredon and Igor Mitrophanow, *The Moon Year: A Record of Chinese Customs and Festivals* (1927; rpt. Taipei: Ch'eng-wen, 1972), pp. 369–374. See in particular Maureen Robertson's translation and comment on a Seventh Night poem by Xu Quan, in Robertson, "Voicing the Feminine," pp. 95–96.

43. Poem by Wu Lingze, in Liu Yunfen, comp., *Cui lou ji* (Collected poems from the Kingfisher Tower [Ming Dynasty Women's Poetry]), preface undated (Qing dynasty), reprinted from the Yexiangtang edition (Shanghai: Shanghai zazhi gongsi, 1936), p. 69; hereafter *CLJ.*

44. Poem by Zhang Yuzhen, dated 1782/83, in *Suiyuan nüdizi shixuan* (Collected Poems from the Entourage of Women Poets at Sui Garden), preface dated 1796, 3:10b; hereafter *SNS.*

45. Poem by Zhang Yuzhen, *SNS* 3:12b.

46. Poem by Shen Yixiu, *CLJ,* p. 72.

47. Poem by Han Pei, *CLJ,* pt. 3, *xin ji* (new collection), p. 25.

48. Wolfram Eberhard, *Chinese Festivals* (London: Abelard-Schuman, 1958), pp. 143–144, describes the cowherd and the weaving maid as husband and

wife, but conjugal love is not a prominent theme in the festival and its mythology. See Hong, *Niulang*.

49. *SSB* 6, no. 9, p. 714; *SSB* 3, no. 26, pp. 637–638.
50. *SSB* 4, no. 40, p. 664; *SSB* 5, no. 44, pp. 693–694.
51. *SSB* 8, no. 66, pp. 789–790; *SSB* 9, no. 11, p. 796.
52. I take this phrase from Felicity Nussbaum's study of women writers in eighteenth-century England. She derives the term from Michel Foucault's analysis of the act of religious confession in Catholic ritual, a "way of regulating interiority," by placing the self as subject in the context of external power relations while at the same time bringing the self into consciousness as a writing/speaking subject. See Michel Foucault, *The History of Sexuality*, vol. 1, *An Introduction*, trans. Robert Hurley (New York: Vintage Books, 1980), pp. 58–65; Felicity Nussbaum, *The Autobiographical Subject: Gender and Ideology in Eighteenth-Century England* (Baltimore: Johns Hopkins University Press, 1989), pp. xiv–vi.
53. As I became pregnant.
54. A handkerchief was hung to the right of the door to announce the birth of a daughter; for a son, a hunting bow was hung outside the door.
55. Poem by Dai Lanying, *SNS* 5:21a.
56. Poem by Dai Lanying, *SNS* 5:22a. See also Xi Peilan's lament for her son, *SNS* 1:6b–8a.
57. The phrase "pure official" *(lian li)* refers here to Zhai's own father, a holder of the *juren* (provincial civil service examination) degree. Such degree holders were given the literary designation "filial and pure" *(xiao lian)*.
58. The poet uses "external" *(wai)* and "internal" *(nei)* in reference to the empire and military unrest, but she may also be using the terms to criticize the humiliation from outside the home *(wai)* and distress within the family *(nei)* that her son suffered because of his failures in scholarship. Thus these two lines could also read: "Humiliation from the outside world followed him back; Distress within his family gave him no reprieve."
59. Poem by Zhai Jingyi, in Xu Kuichen, comp., *Xiangke ji xuancun* (Collection of Selected "Fragrant Writings"), preface dated 1804, reprinted in *Xiangyan congshu* (Collection of Feminine Fragrance), printed 1901–1911, *ji* 8, *juan* 4:1a–40b; poem on p. 2a; hereafter *XJX*.
60. The pilgrim's companions.
61. She uses the term *laoren* (old person), not *laofu* (old woman), invoking her authority as the surrogate patriarch.
62. *XJX* 3a. Stories about Lady Zhang's life are collected in Hu Wenkai, *Lidai funü zhuzuo kao* (A Survey of Women's Writings through the Ages) (1966; rpt. Shanghai: Guji chubanshe, 1985), p. 533; and *QGSZ*, pp. 628–629.

63. Yun Zhu, comp. *Guochao guixiu zhengshi ji* (Correct Beginnings: Collected Women's Poetry of the Ruling Dynasty), preface dated 1829, first preface, p. 1a; hereafter *GGZJ*.

64. Cited in Yang Liansheng, preface to Yu Yingshi, *Zhongguo jinshi zongjiao lunli yu shangren jingshen* (Religious Ethics and the Entrepreneurial Spirit in Modern China) (Taipei: Lianjing chuban shiye gongsi, 1987), pp. 21–22. For the original text, see Yuan Shang et al., comp., Qian Xiao, ed., *Tingwei zalu* (Scattered Records of Our Home Life), first printed early seventeenth century (rpt. Changsha: Shangwu yinshu guan, 1939), pp. 12, 15, 18.

65. See Ann Waltner, "T'an-yang-tzu and Wang Shih-chen: Visionary and Bureaucrat in the Late Ming," *LIC* 8.1 (1987): 105–133.

66. *SS* 2, no. 53, p. 54.

67. Yun Zhu, *GGZJ*, first preface, p. 1a.

68. Wang Pan Suxin, *GGZJ*, second preface, p. 1a.

69. The title of the collection, *Guochao guixiu zhengshi ji*, takes the term *zhengshi* (correct beginnings) from the Little Preface *(Xiao xu)* to the first two books of the *Book of Odes* (the translation that follows slightly paraphrases the original translation by Legge, *Chinese Classics*, p. 37): "The Chou Nan and the Shao Nan show the Way of Correct Beginnings, the foundation of kingly transformation" *(Zhou Nan, Shao Nan, zhengshi zhi dao, wanghua zhi ji)*. See *Mao shi zhushu* 1:22a. In other words, the ruler's consort, in this case the consort of King Wen, presiding over the Inner Chambers, corrects the ruler. This is the source, or the beginning, of the king's capacity to extend his own moral sway over his realm.

2. From Daughter to Daughter-in-Law in the Women's Script of Southern Hunan

This essay is the first product of fieldwork conducted in August 1988 and October 1988–April 1989, primarily with Yi Nianhua, and more infrequently with Gao Yinxian (1902–1990), who at that time were the only known writers of *nüshu* still living. I am grateful to them, and the family of Lu Gaiqiang, Li Hui, Zhou Shuoqi, Zhou Huijuan, Ding Xiaoqi, and the Lingling District Women's Federation. I thank the many people who encouraged and commented on drafts, especially Lisa Rofel, Rubie Watson, and Margery Wolf, and Benedikta Dorer, for her gracious permission to cite her letters.

1. For examples of work that shows this tendency, see Cathy Silber, "A 1,000-Year-Old Secret," *Ms.* 3.2 (1992): 58–61; and Robin Morgan, *The Word of a Woman: Feminist Dispatches, 1968–1992* (New York: Norton, 1992), pp. 275–277. Lila Abu-Lughod points out that by romanticizing resistance, "we collapse distinctions between forms of resistance and foreclose certain

questions about the workings of power"; she asks how we might credit women with resistance "without . . . misattributing to them forms of consciousness or politics that are not part of their experience." See Lila Abu-Lughod, "The Romance of Resistance: Tracing Transformations of Power through Bedouin Women," *American Ethnologist* 17 (1989): 41–55.

2. This time period is an educated guess, an attempt to place largely undatable extant texts (though none earlier than late Qing) and the contexts of their production. The demise of *nüshu* is generally understood to have begun with the social changes of 1949, after which younger women no longer learned the script and the number of those who knew it decreased steadily. My account of these sociotextual practices cannot speak to whatever changes they may have undergone within this time period.

3. This list includes, but is far from limited to, the uterine family and women's community (Margery Wolf, *Women and the Family in Rural Taiwan* [Stanford: Stanford University Press, 1972]); delayed transfer marriage practices of the Pearl River delta (Marjorie Topley, "Marriage Resistance in Rural Kwangtung," in *Women in Chinese Society,* ed. Margery Wolf and Roxane Witke [Stanford: Stanford University Press, 1975]; Andrea Sankar, "The Evolution of the Sisterhood in Traditional Chinese Society: From Village Girls' Houses to Chai T'angs in Hong Kong" [Ph.D. diss., University of Michigan, 1978]; Janice Stockard, *Daughters of the Canton Delta: Marriage Patterns and Economic Strategies in South China, 1860–1930* [Stanford: Stanford University Press, 1989]; and Helen Siu, "Where Were the Women? Rethinking Marriage Resistance and Regional Culture in South China," *Late Imperial China* 11.2 [1990]: 32–62); women's expressive culture and communities (Rubie Watson, "Girls' Houses and Working Women: Expressive Culture in the Pearl River Delta, 1900–1941," in *Bondage, Rescue, and Escape among Chinese Women,* ed. Suzanne Miers and Maria Jaschok [Hong Kong: Hong Kong University Press, 1994]; and Watson, "Dutiful Daughters and Loyal Wives: Korean and Chinese Women," in *Korean Studies, Its Cross-Cultural Perspective,* vol. 2 [N.p.: The Academy of Korean Studies, 1990]); "post-marital dual residence for women and continuing ties between married women and their natal families" in Shandong (Ellen Judd, "*Niangjia:* Chinese Women and Their Natal Families," *Journal of Asian Studies* 48 [1989]: 525–544); and hundreds upon hundreds of women writers and their socioliterary networks existing by Ming and Qing times (Dorothy Ko, "Toward a Social History of Women in Seventeenth-Century China" [Ph.D. diss., Stanford University, 1989]; Ellen Widmer, "The Epistolary World of Female Talent in Seventeenth-Century China," *Late Imperial China* 10.2 [1989]: 1–43; Maureen Robertson, "Refiguring the Feminine: Self-Representation by Literary Women in Late Imperial China," paper presented at the Faculty Research Seminar, Center

for Chinese Studies, University of Michigan, March 10, 1992, and Robertson, "Voicing the Feminine: Constructions of the Gendered Subject in
Lyric Poetry by Women of Medieval and Late Imperial China," *Late Imperial China* 13.1 [1992]: 63–110).

4. William Chiang, "'We Two Know the Script; We Have Become Good
Friends': Linguistic and Social Aspects of the Women's Script Literacy in
Southern Hunan, China" (Ph.D. diss., Yale University, 1991), p. 61; cited
hereafter as Chiang.

5. I have taken pains to avoid using the term *fictive kin* to describe these
relationships because, as Kath Weston puts it in *Families We Choose: Lesbians, Gays, Kinship* (New York: Columbia University Press, 1991), p. 105:
"The concept of fictive kin lost credibility with the advent of symbolic
anthropology and the realization that all kinship is in some sense
fictional—that is, meaningfully constituted rather than 'out there' in a
positivist sense. Viewed in this light, genes and blood appear as symbols
implicated in one culturally specific way of demarcating and calculating
relationships."

6. For brotherhoods among males, see, for example, David Jordan, "Sworn
Brothers: A Study in Chinese Ritual Kinship," in *The Chinese Family and Its
Ritual Behavior,* ed. Hsieh Jih-Chang and Chuang Ying-Chang (Taipei:
Institute of Ethnology, Academia Sinica, 1985); for brotherhoods among
females (this, if nothing else, shows how similar social practices can have
quite different meanings and referents), see Thamora Fishel, "Social Con-
structionism and 'Lesbians' in Taiwan," *Historical Reflections/Réflexions His-
toriques* (1994); and Xiong Cunrui, "Sui-Tang Chang'an (A.D. 582–904)"
(Ph.D. diss., Australian National University, 1988), p. 269. For sisterhoods,
see Sankar, "Evolution of the Sisterhood"; Stockard, *Daughters;* and Emily
Honig, *Sisters and Strangers: Women in the Shanghai Cotton Mills, 1919–1949*
(Stanford: Stanford University Press, 1986). Stockard, *Daughters,* pp. 170–
171, provides a cursory review of the literature on delayed transfer–type
marriage practices among non-Han groups in the Lingnan region; see
also Siu, "Where Were the Women?"

7. Stockard, *Daughters;* Chiang; and Siu, "Where Were the Women?" discuss
a cultural complex in southern China produced by indigenous accommodation to incursions of Han patriarchy. While cultural similarities between
Han and many different non-Han peoples in South China is clearly an
issue for the *nüshu* area, much less is known about the non-Han layers of
the Han dialect that *nüshu* represents, and linguistic evidence would go
farther, I think, than cultural borrowing toward identifying the non-Han
aspects of *nüshu* culture. For descriptions of this dialect, see Huang
Xuezhen, "Hunan Jiangyong fangyan yinxi" (The Sound System of
Jiangyong Dialect in Hunan), *Fangyan* (Dialect), no. 3 (1988): 161–176;

Chiang, pp. 64–71; Zhao Liming, *Zhongguo nüshu jicheng* (Collection of Chinese *Nüshu*), translated and annotated by Zhou Shuoqi (Beijing: Qinghua daxue chubanshe, 1991), p. 21 (cited hereafter as Zhao); and Xie Zhimin, *Jiangyong "nüshu" zhi mi* (The Enigmatic Women's Script of Jiangyong), 3 vols., Women's Studies Series, ed. Li Xiaojiang (Henan: Henan People's Press, 1991), p. 1857 (hereafter cited as Xie). For descriptions of the script and its relation to dialect and *hanzi* (standard written Chinese), see Chiang, pp. 111–114, and Xie, pp. 5–11; for local legends and explanations concerning the origin of *nüshu*, which may never be known, see Chiang, pp. 105–111; Zhao, pp. 15–16; and Xie, pp. 4–5.

8. I agree with Victor Mair that passing "local cultures through an MSM [Modern Standard Mandarin] filter causes linguistic, social, and ideological distortions which may prevent us from gaining a true comprehension of their nature" ("Sound and Sense in the Study of Chinese Popular Culture," *Chinese Literature: Essays, Articles, Reviews* 12 (1990): 121), but technical constraints prevent me from transliterating dialect terms in any system but pinyin. Throughout this essay I indicate the few terms whose distortion is most probable by enclosing their romanization in quotation marks.

9. Xie, pp. 1868–69. *Laotong* relationships are not unique to the *nüshu* area. According to Shang Bi, *Yuefeng kaoshi* (The Annotated Songs of Yue) (Nanning: Guangxi minzu chubanshe, 1985), pp. 17–18, a variety of such practices is known among southern ethnic minorities such as the Zhuang, Bouyei, and Yao, as well as their Han neighbors in northern and southeastern Guizhou who assimilated their customs; Chiang, pp. 186–187, mentions a few non-Han age mate practices.

10. See, for example, the text collected in Zhao, p. 496.

11. Zhao, p. 17.

12. Chiang, pp. 62–63.

13. What connection, if any, this ideal of seven has with the Seven Sisters festival described in Sankar, "Evolution of the Sisterhood," pp. 23–25, and Stockard, *Daughters*, pp. 41–45, merits further study.

14. Published accounts conflict with one another and my own fieldnotes; the details are not the point. I think the ideal of seven combined with overlapping membership between sisterhoods was the source of the disagreement. At least part of this sisterhood was formed much later in the lives of its members than the sisterhoods I focus on in this paper—those of the unmarried or recently married.

15. This letter is collected in Zhao, p. 415, and this is the way Yi Nianhua explained the sixth couplet when I studied and translated the text with her in late 1988.

16. See Zhao, p. 409.

17. This seems to be a good example of "the assertion that language does not simply express or reflect extant social relations; it actually helps generate such relations in the first place." See Michael Gardiner, *The Dialogics of Critique: M. M. Bakhtin and the Theory of Ideology* (London: Routledge, 1992), p. 164.

18. Of course, the conventional relation of signifier to signified holds for all writing, but this point is especially salient for formulaic literature generally, and here, for those outside the *nüshu* literacy community who approach *nüshu* texts. *Nüshu* (the term can refer to both the script itself and writings in it) is a syllable-based, largely phonetic representation of the local dialect, which is mutually unintelligible with Mandarin, and contains a large number of expressions for which there are no *hanzi* (see note 8). Furthermore, many of the dialect expressions that *hanzi* can render (as opposed to transliterate) have markedly different (sometimes even opposite) meanings from their standard Chinese denotations. This is a case of the same words meaning different things in different speech communities. Translating *nüshu* into *hanzi* with Yi Nianhua, I found that it is sometimes hard to know whether what you come up with is a *hanzi* equivalent or just a transliteration. Some *nüshu* expressions are incomprehensible to dialect speakers now in their forties; speech differences are found not only between generations but between villages in the *nüshu* area, and these speech differences are reflected in *nüshu*. There are dialect usages specific to *nüshu* literacy, and I have begun to find puns in this writing.

19. I cannot treat them here, but the connection between Buddhism and sisterhoods, described in Sankar, "Evolution of the Sisterhood," and suggested by Honig, *Sisters and Strangers,* p. 215, merits further exploration.

20. All but two of the nine *laotong* letters examined here appear in at least one *nüshu* anthology, either Zhao or Xie, sometimes in slightly different versions (not at all uncommon for *nüshu*). The text translated in the appendix was penned for me by Yi Nianhua in 1989.

21. Zhao, p. 450. For the quotations that follow I provide one citation, though many of these conventional expressions can be found in more than one letter.

22. Silber 2, p. 15. This line is from an unpublished text; I refer to my own notebooks.

23. Xie, p. 481.

24. Zhao, p. 450.

25. Zhao, p. 409. It is difficult to know which aspects of the polysemous term *qin* (closeness, dearness, kin relation) are indicated here, or indeed what exactly the people of Shangjiangxu have in mind whenever they use this

term. This line appears in the letter mentioned earlier, to the daughter of the writer's mother's brother; it also appears in other letters that contain no such mention of a kin relationship.

26. Zhao, p. 420.
27. Zhao, p. 409.
28. Silber 4, pp. 38–39.
29. Zhao, pp. 449, 442.
30. Zhao, p. 419.
31. Xie, p. 481.
32. Zhao, p. 418.
33. Silber 2, p. 16. Yi Nianhua explained the second line of this couplet as "the farther you go, the deeper it gets."
34. Zhao, p. 416.
35. Zhao, p. 419.
36. Silber 2, p. 19.
37. Zhao, p. 419.
38. Zhao, pp. 421, 422. More often than not in these letters, *qing* denotes the one who experiences the feeling rather than feeling in any abstract sense. Zhao (p. 421) glosses it as *zhixinde pengyou*, literally, a friend who knows one's heart. Thus, in direct address it can act as a second-person singular pronoun of endearment. The sense I get from this line is, "We of such good affection don't break up," or perhaps, "You of good affection don't break up with me."
39. Zhao, pp. 422, 419, 450.
40. Xie, pp. 53–54.
41. Silber 2, p. 19.
42. Zhao, p. 416.
43. Zhao, p. 449. We might expect that the guest would wash first in fresh water and her host would then use the same water, indicating enough closeness to share her same's dirt, as she would with a sibling, but also the conservation of the female water-carrying labor for the household, thus marking a same as one of the fold.
44. Zhao, pp. 415, 418, 422.
45. Zhao, pp. 415, 418.
46. Zhao, p. 418.
47. Silber 2, p. 15.
48. Zhao, pp. 410, 419.
49. Zhao, pp. 422, 419.
50. This term has also been transliterated *"fangxiangnü."* I rely here on Yi Nianhua's explanation of the term (see note 8).
51. Zhao, p. 409.

52. My current understanding of this distinction has been sharpened by communications with Benedikta Dorer, who, during a month or so of fieldwork in Shangjiangxu in the fall of 1992, was able to follow up on issues raised in the conference presentation and discussion of the earlier version of this essay. Her M.A. thesis offers much new information on social practices in Shangjiangxu; see "Die Frauenschrift Nüshu und ihr sozialer Kontext (Arbeitstitel)" (The Women's Script *Nüshu* and Its Social Context [working title]) (M.A. thesis, Department of Sinology, University of Vienna, 1993).

53. Personal communication, November 23, 1992. Recognizing Yi's literacy bias, I wonder if she shaped her normative account of *laotong* matching practices to fit the texts she was teaching me, for most of what she told me came up in our reading of *laotong* letters.

54. Personal communication, May 4, 1993. To put 50 catties in perspective, explaining her foraging for stray rice at a hulling ground in August 1988, Tang Baozhen, at age seventy-six, said she needed 500 catties of rice a year; younger people probably eat more—perhaps 800 catties a year.

55. Xie, 1875–76.

56. I wonder if this signals a marriage resistance tactic.

57. When asked how many nights a bride would spend with her husband in their first year of marriage, Gao Yinxian came up with four or five: one night at the lunar new year, one or two nights during *chatian* (rice planting), one night on the birthday of her mother- or father-in-law, and one night on the ghost festival (the fifteenth of the seventh lunar month). Significantly, Gao noted that the bride always brought her own food from her natal home on these conjugal visits; see Stockard, *Daughters*, pp. 19–20, for a discussion of this practice elsewhere. According to Gao, it usually took two or three years to conceive, and if conception was not achieved in that time, the family would look down on the bride or marry in a second wife. In describing all phases of the wedding process "in the old days" in some detail, Xie (pp. 1877–88) provides a more complicated itinerary for the bride in the few days after the wedding; suffice it for now to say that it entailed obligatory overnight visits to various matrilateral kin and a return stopover cum gift delivery at her marital home before she returned to her natal home for an extended stay. Chiang (p. 61) describes how this marriage practice in recent years can entail far more time spent living virilocally than in days gone by.

58. I cannot speak to the historical processes that produced this form of marriage. In describing girls' unwillingness to marry, Xie (p. 1874) reports that "in order to prolong their girlhood and avoid the suffering and hardships of being a daughter-in-law, girls often got together to help one

another resist and avoid marriage. When they ran out of ways to resist, the sworn sisters would help tie the bride's pants at the waist with many tight knots" to keep the groom out. Elsewhere (p. 1769), Xie notes that "in the old days," girls were mostly unwilling to marry, and after becoming sworn sisters, they were even less willing: "Marriage avoidance [*taohun*, literally, 'fleeing the wedding'] happened frequently. Most parents, to prevent a daughter from organizing with her sworn sisters to avoid marriage, would not let her leave the house in the year before her wedding. The activities of sworn sisters were thus restricted." No evidence suggests that these girls posed actual flight risks; what exactly *taohun* entailed for them must await further research.

59. See Abu-Lughod, "The Romance of Resistance."

60. As Helen Siu, "Where Were the Women?," p. 39, points out, "The women were not acting on their own."

61. See Zhao, pp. 455 and 483, for examples of such tales.

62. Rubie Watson, "Dutiful Daughters," identifies this conflict between filiality and fertility and raises many of the issues I have been discussing in her treatment of marriage laments in Ha Tsuen. This conflict is represented in *nüshu* oral and written marriage discourses, perhaps best exemplified by the couplet, "If a daughter doesn't marry out, she's not valuable; if fire doesn't raze the mountain, the land will not be fertile." See Zhao, p. 543.

63. Space does not permit me to treat them fully here. Suffice it to say that in the year before her wedding, upstairs in the company of her close companions, a bride was fully occupied embroidering and sewing many a pair of cotton shoes (the dialect word for which puns with "child") for her male affines; for a month before her wedding (ten days nowadays), her close companions spent the night in her loft; the days before she left were marked by intensive singing sessions with her companions and village women, and the night before her departure was spent on what could become an exhaustive house-to-house group tour (or a more selective one) through her village to cry farewell lyrics, which were also sung to every member of her natal family and those of her mother's natal family in for the wedding. (See Zhao, pp. 541–578, and Xie, pp. 751–841, for texts of these farewell crying lyrics and other wedding songs; see Xie, pp. 1884–86, for a description of these practices.) Most of these songs, particularly the crying lyrics, were part of an oral tradition that came to be written in *nüshu* for the benefit of researchers.

64. Speaking of the "stylistic and generic origin" of *nüshu* literature generally, William Chiang identifies a mixture of Han and non-Han elements, and suggests that "perhaps because Shangjiangxu is more Sinicized, the felicitation and lament are commingled in marriage congratulation texts which

superimpose a framework of congratulation upon a content largely composed of lament," such that congratulations are implicitly associated with Han and laments with non-Han peoples. See Chiang, pp. 177–178.

65. The "discovery" of *nüshu* in the early 1980s prompted a hasty raid on the villages in and around Shangjiangxu for extant texts, most of which were *sanzhaoshu*. Elderly women parted with these treasures with the understanding that they would be returned or for the promise or payment of a couple of *yuan*. As far as I can tell, little attempt was made in the early days to keep track of the sources of these finds, let alone to inquire about their writers or recipients, some of whom were probably still living. Denied access to these original documents, I rely here on their anthologized versions in, primarily, Zhao, which offer few glimpses of the physical layout of these texts, which would provide a helpful clue for distinguishing writers in cases where this is difficult. Chiang (pp. 132–136) provides a detailed physical description of these books, in which he notes that successive writers would turn the book upside down and start writing on the next page or from the other end of the book or somewhere in the middle. Xie (p. 1862) notes that blank pages were left for a recipient to write a reply; his anthology contains one such reply.

66. For example, the dialect term that researchers commonly render "*lianjin*" (see note 8) is glossed by native speaker Zhou Shuoqi (see Zhao, p. 41) as "the relationship between siblings of the same parents," while Xie (p. 1747) describes this term as an appellation for siblings or sworn sisters, on the basis, I think, of the fact that the term also refers to sworn sisters in *nüshu*.

67. Zhao, pp. 68, 70.

68. Zhao, pp. 66, 86.

69. Zhao, pp. 73–74, 33, 91, 178.

70. Zhao, p. 36.

71. This reading of *sanzhaoshu* as a discourse on the disruption of girlhood relationships has done an injustice to the richness and complexity of the material by slighting other important themes. Metaphors for marriage (death among them) in these texts deserve further study, especially in light of the laments treated by C. Fred Blake, "Death and Abuse in Marriage Laments: The Curse of Chinese Brides," *Asian Folklore Studies* 37 (1978): 13–33; and Rubie Watson, "Dutiful Daughters." Also, *sanzhaoshu* often deploy contradictory statements about marriage within a single text in a way that highlights the overlap and simultaneity of competing discourses that are never purely dominant or purely resistant.

72. In August 1988, Li Hui and I spoke with an eighty-nine-year-old woman who earned money as a seamstress as a girl, became a vegetarian at nineteen, stayed in her natal home to help her mother care for a younger

brother who was born when she was in her twenties, and then in her thirties became one of three nuns in the Guanyin temple in the village of Jinjiang, roughly a three-hour walk from her natal home of Tongxiwei in Dao county. She could read scripture in *hanzi* but not *nüshu*. She had no sworn sisters; her explanation for not marrying was that she did not like what she saw of the suffering of wives. Twice in her life Yi Nianhua wished to become a nun, the first time at fifteen because she was afraid of ghosts and the second time right after liberation, at which point she had been struggling through widowhood for about fifteen years.

73. Another version appears in Zhao, p. 446.

74. See Zhao, p. 605.

75. This text, penned by Yi Nianhua, does not appear in any of the anthologies, but space does not permit me to include it here.

76. Personal communication, November 23, 1992.

77. A pun on the last syllable of this line, which can mean "bird" or "bottom," yields another reading: "like the bottom of the sea."

78. The text ends with an incomplete line that seems to be another complaint about protocol.

3. Out of the Traditional Halls of Academe

All notes for this chapter are provided by translator and editors.

1. Literally, "female same-sex love," or lesbianism.

2. These terms were originally used to refer to the import of Buddhist doctrines into China.

3. Household registrations in China fall into two general classes, rural and urban. In rural areas they confer eligibility to receive land for building or expanding a house, as well as the right to bid on local work contracts. In urban areas registration also provides access to housing and legal work opportunities. In both places registration was the historical basis for distribution of social welfare benefits such as rice, cloth, and other sundry rations. Demand for urban registration among rural residents has always been strong, and has been intensified by job creation and industrial development in small towns and cities stimulated by economic reforms. Overall, the household registration system limits social and geographic mobility.

4. "Leading cadres" here refers to women in social and economic positions of acknowledged seniority and responsibility.

5. Shenzhen is a Special Economic Zone (SEZ) on China's southern border with Hong Kong, and Dingxi is a village in the relatively remote and sparsely populated western province of Gansu.

6. "Guerrilla units" are groups of families that have fled their homes and

---

villages in order to avoid birth control limits and have additional children. These families sometimes converge on particular towns or districts that are known to be temporary havens for violators of the birth plan. The guerrilla units are supplemented by migrant worker households who take advantage of their migrant status to have additional, "illegal" children.

7. Lushan is a famous Chinese mountain. The Chinese reads, "Bu shi Lushan zhen mianmu, zhi yuan shen zai ci shan zhong."

8. Susan Faludi, *Backlash: The Undeclared War against American Women* (New York: Crown, 1991).

4. China's Modernization and Changes in the Social Status of Rural Women

1. "Nan zhu wai, nü zhu nei." [Translator.]

2. Huang Xiyi, *Zhongguo dangdai shehui bianqianzhong nongcun funü jingji shenfen de zhuanhuan* (Changes in Rural Women's Economic Status in the Course of China's Contemporary Social Transformation), in *Zhongguo funü fenceng yanjiu* (Research on Differentiation among Chinese Women) (Zhengzhou: Henan People's Press, 1991).

3. Work points recorded each person's work contribution to collective agriculture or other small industrial projects, and were periodically (or annually) distributed in the form of grain or cash. [Translator.]

4. "Paobu jinru gongchan zhuyi." [Translator.]

5. "Chounan huannü." [Translator.]

6. All-China Women's Federation, *Dangdai Zhongguo funü* (Contemporary Chinese Women), unpublished study.

7. This was the new agricultural production *(lianchan chengbaozhi)* structure begun in 1978, which contracted responsibility for certain pieces of production (specific fields, fish ponds, orchards, and so on) to individuals or households on a bidding system. Remuneration was linked directly to output; production decisions were thus often returned from the production team (a subset of the commune) to the household. [Translator.]

8. Huang Xiyi.

9. *Dangdai Zhongguo funü.*

10. They thus do not have the same access to grain and other commodities at subsidized prices as urban residents. [Translator.]

11. For details, see Gao Xiaoxian and Cui Zhiwei, *Shaanxi Guanzhong diqu baihu nongfu zhuangkuang diaocha* (An Investigation of Peasant Women in One Hundred Households, in Guanzhong, Shaanxi), pp. 50–60.

12. Here Gao uses the phrase "getihu shanghu." *Getihu* can be translated as "private," "entrepreneurial," or "self-employed." [Translator.]

13. Research Office of the Sichuan Provincial Women's Federation, *Funü diaocha wenxuan* (Collected Documents on Research on Women), vol. 3.

14. Shehui fazhan zonghe yanjiu ketizu (Task Force for the Study of Comprehensive Social Development), *Woguo zhuanxing shiqi shehui fazhan zhuangkuang de zonghe fenxi* (A Comprehensive Analysis of the State of Social Development in This Period of National Structural Transformation), *Shehuexue Yanjiu* (Sociological Research) 4 (1991).

15. For details, see Gao Xiaoxian, *Nüxing renkou qianyi yu chengzhenhua* (Urbanization and Women's Migration), *Nongcun jingji yu shehui* (Rural Society and Economy) 6 (1990), pp. 22–28.

16. "Lunhuan gong." [Translator.]

17. "Da gong mei." [Translator.]

18. "Xiao baomu." [Translator.]

19. *Zhongguo tongji zhaiyao* (China Statistical Summary) (1989), p. 16.

20. "Ren de xiandaihua." [Translator.]

21. This would mean approximately one radio for every ten rural residents, and one television set for every fifteen. [Translator.]

22. Shehui fazhan zonghe yanjiu ketizu. (By "popularization," Gao most likely means the percentage of households that have television sets, which would be in line with the number of sets she cites.) [Translator.]

23. Lu Xueyi, *Chongxin renshi nongmin wenti—shinianlai Zhongguo nongminde bianhua* (A Fresh Look at Peasant Problems—Ten Years of Change among China's Peasants), *Shehuixue Yanjiu* (Sociological Research), no. 6 (1989).

24. Gao Xiaoxian and Cui Zhiwei.

25. Shehui fazhan zonghe yanjiu ketizu.

26. By independent municipalities, Gao is referring to the three Chinese cities (Beijing, Shanghai, and Guangzhou) that fall administratively directly under the central government, not unlike the District of Columbia in the United States. The three categories of province, autonomous region, and independent municipality are administratively comparable units; China has altogether twenty-nine such units. [Translator.]

27. Jin Yihong, *Jingji gaigezhong nongcun funü de xianzhuang yu chulu* (Rural Women's Situation and Prospects in Economic Reform), *Zhongguo funü fenceng yanjiu*, p. 34.

28. This refers to work points awarded per full day of labor, when it was assumed that any man would do more than any woman. [Translator.]

29. Jin Yihong.

30. Equivalent at that time to approximately $65. [Translator.]

31. Equivalent at that time to approximately $250. [Translator.]

32. Gao Xiaoxian and Cui Zhiwei.

33. Shehui fazhan zonghe yanjiu ketizu.

34. Ibid.
35. Ibid.
36. Taken in 1987. [Translator.]
37. "Dunühu." [Translator.]
38. Periodic redistributions of land contracted for household production under the responsibility system is based on the number of people in the
household. [Translator.]

5. Desire, Danger, and the Body

I gratefully acknowledge a grant from the American Council of Learned Societies in 1987–88, which enabled me to begin the research on which this paper
is based. I also thank Lisa Rofel and Ann Waltner for extremely helpful comments on an earlier draft.

1. Qiu Jun (1420–1495), *Wu lun quan bei* (The Five Relationships Complete
and Perfected), Ming Dynasty Shi de tang edition, scene 19.

2. Yao Maoliang (15th century), *Shuang zhong ji* (Loyalty Redoubled), Ming
Dynasty Fu chun tang edition, scene 29.

3. Both stories are reproduced in Lü Kun (1536–1618), *Gui fan* (Female
Exemplars), 1618 Huizhou edition; and in the early seventeenth-century
compilation *Hui tu Lienü zhuan* (Illustrated Biographies of Notable
Women), 1779 Zhi bu zu zhai edition (rpt. Taipei: Cheng-chung shu-chü,
1971). Liu Cuige's story is in *Female Exemplars, juan* 3.46a–47a, and *Illustrated Biographies, juan* 13.35b–36b; the story of Zhou Di's wife is in *Female
Exemplars, juan* 3.37a–38a.

4. Jennifer Holmgren, "The Economic Foundations of Virtue: Widow-Re-
marriage in Early and Modern China," *Australian Journal of Chinese Affairs*
13 (1985): 1–27.

5. Susan Mann, "Widows in the Kinship, Class, and Community Structures
of Qing Dynasty China," *Journal of Asian Studies* 46.1 (1987): 37–56.

6. Jerry Dennerline, "Marriage, Adoption, and Charity in the Development
of Lineages in Wu-hsi from Sung to Ch'ing," in *Kinship Organization in Late
Imperial China, 1000–1940,* ed. Patricia Ebrey and James L. Watson
(Berkeley: University of California Press, 1986), pp. 188–194.

7. Mark Elvin, "Female Virtue and the State in China," *Past and Present* 104
(1984): 111–152.

8. T'ien Ju-k'ang, *Male Anxiety and Female Chastity: A Comparative Study of
Chinese Ethical Values in Ming-Ch'ing Times* (Leiden: E. J. Brill, 1988).

9. Elvin, "Female Virtue," p. 112.

10. For the story of the woman's hand, see *Ming shi* (Ming History) (Beijing:
Zhonghua shuju, 1974), *juan* 191 (*Lienü zhuan* 3), p. 7760 *(Tao shi); for*

that of the chicken skin, see *Ming History, juan* 191 (*Lienü zhuan* 3), p. 7716 *(Wang shi).*

11. Elvin, in "Female Virtue," and T'ien Ju-k'ang, in *Female Chastity,* both emphasize the dramatic *public* suicides that took place in Ming and Qing. But striking as their cited cases are, I find that the majority of suicides described in Ming sources I have consulted are private, almost surreptitious.

12. The complex emotion of *qing,* translated sometimes as "emotion" and elsewhere as "passion," is analyzed by Patrick Hanan in *The Vernacular Chinese Story* (Cambridge, Mass.: Harvard University Press, 1981), pp. 146–147; by Hua-yuan Li Mowry in *"Ch'ing-shih* and Feng Meng-lung" (Ph.D. diss., University of California at Berkeley, 1976), pp. 9–13; and by Kang-i Sun Chang in *The Late Ming Poet Ch'en Tzu-lung: Crises in Love and Loyalism* (New Haven: Yale University Press, 1991), pp. 3–9 (Chang discusses only one facet of *qing,* that of romantic love).

13. Katherine Carlitz, "The Social Uses of Female Virtue in Late Ming Editions of *Lienü zhuan," Late Imperial China* 12.2 (1991): 141.

14. Elvin, "Female Virtue," and T'ien, *Female Chastity,* both spell out the criteria for and content of these awards.

15. See T'ien, *Female Chastity,* pp. 2–6.

16. The composition of the Song history is described by Hok-lam Chan in "Chinese Official Historiography at the Yuan Court: The Composition of the Liao, Chin, and Sung Histories," in *China under Mongol Rule,* ed. John D. Langlois, Jr. (Princeton: Princeton University Press, 1981), pp. 56–106.

17. See especially Chen Dexiu (1178–1235), *Daxue yanyi* (An Explication of the Great Learning) (Taipei: Chung-kuo tzu-hsüeh ming-chu chi-ch'eng pien-hsin wei-yuan-hui, 1977), 2:1115.

18. Elvin ("Female Virtue," pp. 124, 132) notes that, despite the state's aim to honor only commoner women (since the desideratum was to elevate by example the morals of the common people), local notables kept slipping the wives of officials into the records.

19. T'ien, *Female Chastity,* p. 39.

20. T'ien, *Female Chastity,* pp. 70–89.

21. The pervasive culture of the examination system is described by Benjamin Elman in "Political, Social, and Cultural Reproduction in Civil Service Examinations in Late Imperial China," *Journal of Asian Studies* 50.1 (1991): 7–28.

22. This is markedly apparent by comparison with the highly variable format of extant Song and Yuan local histories, few of which contain biographies of virtuous women. Extant Song and Yuan gazetteers have been collected in *Song Yuan fangzhi congkan* (Collected Local Histories from Song and Yuan) (rpt. Beijing: Zhonghua shuju, 1990).

23. The phrase is Susan Mann's from "Widows," p. 43.
24. Elvin ("Female Virtue," p. 123) states that the upper age limit during the Ming was fifty *sui*, but T'ien Ju-k'ang (*Female Chastity*, p. 5) cites statutes showing that the upper age limit was sixty *sui*.
25. Mann, "Widows," and Dorothy Yin-yee Ko, "Toward a Social History of Women in Seventeenth-Century China" (Ph.D. diss., Stanford University, 1989), pp. 11–40. A widow would most likely be sold as a concubine, since widow marriage was a transaction, not an alliance.
26. Wang Tingna, *Ren jing yang qiu* (Bright Autumn Mirror for Mankind), 1600 Huan cui tang edition, Beijing Library. Wang was an official in the salt administration who retired with great wealth to his villa, Huan cui tang, where he wrote and published a number of plays and anthologies.
27. *The Anatomy of Love* is described at length in Hanan, *Vernacular Story*, pp. 95–97. Mowry, "*Ch'ing-shih*," is an analysis of *Ch'ing-shih*'s relationship to Feng Menglong and to other Ming vernacular fiction. See also Hua-yuan Li Mowry, *Chinese Love Stories from Ch'ing-shih* (Orinda, Calif.: Shoe-string Press, 1983). The Harvard-Yenching Library has a Ming edition of the *Green Window* collection, and the work is reprinted in the series *Ming Ch'ing shan-pen hsiao-shuo ts'ung-k'an*, 1st ser. (Taipei: T'ien-yi ch'u-pan she, n.d.).
28. See Fan Zhongyan, "Jun yi min wei ti fu" (Essay on the Sage Considering the People as His Own Body), in Fan's collected works, *Sibu congkan*, pt. 4, vol. 237, *bieji* (supplementary collection), *juan* 2.10b–11b.
29. See Gui Youguang, *Shi cheng An Wei su xing ru he* (How Will History Judge the Behavior of An and Wei), in his collected works, *Zhenchuan xiansheng ji* (The Collected Works of Master Zhenchuan (Shanghai: Guji chubanshe, 1981), 2:707.
30. *Illustrated Biographies*, *juan* 9.48b–49b; *Female Exemplars*, *juan* 3.58a–59a.
31. *Ming History*, *juan* 191 (*Lienü zhuan* 3), p. 7744 *(Chai shi)*.
32. T'ien, *Female Chastity*, gives a history of the practice on pp. 152–159.
33. *Ming History*, *juan* 189 (*Lienü zhuan* 1), p. 7691; and *Illustrated Biographies*, *juan* 15.1b–3a.
34. Both stories in *Ming History*, *juan* 190 (*Lienü zhuan* 2), pp. 7734–35.
35. *Illustrated Biographies*, *juan* 8.14b–16a; *Female Exemplars*, 3.19b–20b.
36. *Illustrated Biographies*, *juan* 9.33b–35b; *Female Exemplars*, *juan* 2.30a–32a.
37. *Ming History*, *juan* 189 (*Lienü zhuan* 1), p. 7693; and *Female Exemplars*, *juan* 2.33a–34a.
38. *Ming History*, *juan* 189 (*Lienü zhuan* 1), p. 7683.
39. He Liangjun (1506–1573), *Yu lin* (Forest of Words) (Shanghai: Guji chubanshe, 1983), *juan* 3.11b; and Wang Tingna, *Mirror*, *juan* 20.24b–25a.
40. For the story of the singing girl, see He Liangjun, *Forest of Words*, *juan* 3.26b; for the boatman's daughter, see Zheng Xuan (1631 *jinshi*), *Zuo fei*

an ri zuan, in *Lidai xiaoshuo biji xuan* (Memoirs Selected through the Ages) (Hong Kong: Commercial Press, 1976), p. 324.

41. *Illustrated Biographies, juan* 5.40b–42a.
42. *Illustrated Biographies, juan* 6.5b–7a.
43. *Illustrated Biographies, juan* 7.31b–33b.
44. *Kunshan xianzhi*, 1576, *juan* 12.
45. *Ming History, juan* 189 (*Lienü zhuan* 1), p. 7695.
46. *Ming History, juan* 190 (*Lienü zhuan* 2), p. 7732.
47. *Illustrated Biographies, juan* 15.11b–13a.
48. *Illustrated Biographies, juan* 6.22b–23b.
49. *Ming History, juan* 189 (*Lienü zhuan* 1), p. 7705.
50. For a Qing dynasty court case, see M. J. Meijer, "The Price of a P'ai-lou," *T'oung Pao* 67.3–5 (1981): 288–304. Information on fathers-in-law has been collected by Vivian Ng in an unpublished manuscript.
51. See Gui Youguang, "Shu Lijing Zhang shi fu shi" (A Record of the Incident Involving Zhang of Lijing), *Zhenchuan xiansheng ji*, p. 94.
52. Wang Tingna, *Mirror, juan* 16.1a–1b.
53. For example, *Illustrated Biographies, juan* 9.26b–27b.
54. *Illustrated Biographies, juan* 11.13b–14a.
55. *Illustrated Biographies, juan* 13.16b–17b.
56. *Illustrated Biographies, juan* 13.27b–28b.
57. *Illustrated Biographies, juan* 12.5b–6b.
58. *Illustrated Biographies, juan* 11.26b–27b.
59. *Kunshan xianzhi*, 1538, *juan* 12.3a.
60. *Jiading xianzhi*, 1605, *juan* 13.19a–19b.
61. *Female Exemplars, juan* 3.30a, commentary to the story of the consort of King Zhao of Chu.
62. Zheng Xuan, *Zuo fei an ri zuan*, in *Lidai biji xiaoshuo xuan*, p. 331.
63. *Jiading xianzhi*, 1605, *juan* 13.17b–18a.
64. *Illustrated Biographies, juan* 14.21b–22b.
65. Wang Tingna, *Mirror, juan* 16.43b–44b.
66. Wang Tingna, *Mirror, juan* 16.38b–39b; and *Illustrated Biographies, juan* 16.24b–25b.
67. Wang Daokun, *Tai han ji*, final entry in *juan* 49. A copy of Wang's 120-chapter *Tai han ji* is in the Library of Congress, Washington, D.C.
68. *Female Exemplars, juan* 1.12a–12b.
69. *Female Exemplars, juan* 1.13a–13b.
70. D. C. Lau translates this passage as: "The Master said, 'To return to the observance of the rites [*li*] through overcoming the self constitutes benevolence [*ren*].'" See Confucius, *The Analects*, trans. D. C. Lau (London: Penguin Books, 1979), bk. 12.1, p. 112.
71. Commentary to the story of Zhu Cai, a courtesan who married a literatus,

was stolen back by her procurer, remained faithful to her husband even in the brothel, and was reunited with him and bore him sons. See the Qing Kangxi reign period (1662–1723) edition of *Qing shi lei lüe* in the Harvard-Yenching Library.

72. *Green Window, juan* 1, opening lines to *Yue rong* section.

73. Mowry, *"Ch'ing-shih,"* p. 73.

74. *Female Exemplars, juan* 1.3a–4a.

75. *Green Window,* passage cited in n. 72.

76. The topos of the virtuous singing girl in early Ming drama is treated in Wilt Idema and Stephen West, *Chinese Theater, 1100–1450: A Source Book* (Wiesbaden: Steiner Verlag, 1982), pp. 344–423.

77. Aisheng's story reflects the close friendships between celebrated courtesans and men of letters in the late Ming. It is translated in Mowry, *"Ch'ing-shih,"* pp. 265–269.

78. Translated in Mowry, *"Ch'ing-shih,"* pp. 190–192.

79. Dorothy Ko has shown that *Peony Pavilion* had a wide and enthusiastic female readership in the late Ming. Perhaps Feng was uncomfortable with the idea of gentry women, rather than literati men, studying the notion of revivifying love. Catherine Swatek, in "Feng Menglong's Romantic Dream: Strategies of Containment in His Revision of 'The Peony Pavilion'" (Ph.D. diss., Columbia University, 1990), examines *Peony Pavilion,* its author Tang Xianzu, and Feng's revision.

80. *Qi lie zhuan,* Wang Daokun's biographies of seven Huizhou widows, to whose virtue he points with regional pride. They are contained in Wang's collected works, *Tai han ji, juan* 29. The stories often traveled as a group; they are included in *Illustrated Biographies.*

81. *Green Window,* first preface.

82. This is a work dating from the time of the Ming-Qing transition. The author went by a variety of sobriquets, among them "Qin hai yu ke" (Temporary Sojourner in Qin Hai). It was a popular book, reprinted under several different titles. A reliable modern typeset edition is *Nü caizi shu* (Liaoning: Chun feng wenyi chubanshe, 1983).

83. A late Ming edition of this work is in the Harvard-Yenching Library.

84. See Richard Von Glahn, "The Enchantment of Wealth: The God Wutong in the Social History of Jiangnan," *Harvard Journal of Asiatic Studies* 51.2 (December 1991): 651–714.

6. Rethinking Van Gulik

1. Wan Quan, *Wan shi jia zhuan guang si si yao* (The Wan Family Tradition on Essentials for Multiplying Descendants), ca. 1549. Wan's collected

works, *Wan Mizhai yixue quan shu* (Complete Medical Writings of Wan Mizhai), were published in successive editions of 1663, 1712, 1724, and 1778. References here are to a collated multivolume modern edition based on the holdings of the Public Health Bureau of Lotian county, Hubei, his native place, and published between 1983 and 1986 by the Hubei kexue zhishu chubanshe. See *juan* 5, pp. 25–26.

2. John D'Emilio and Estelle Freedman, *Intimate Matters: A History of Sexuality in America* (New York: Harper and Row, 1988). See "Introduction," pp. xi–xx.

3. R. H. Van Gulik, *Sexual Life in Ancient China: A Preliminary Survey of Chinese Sex and Society from ca. 1500 B.C. till 1644 A.D.* (Leiden: E. J. Brill, 1961, 1974); subsequent citations appear in the text.

4. The asterisk indicates that *fang shu*, "bedchamber manual," is a homophone for *fang shu*, "art of the bedchamber," terms referring to the literary genre and to its teachings, respectively.

5. As an anti-Victorian, Van Gulik avoids a heavily moralistic approach here, saying only that fellatio, cunnilingus, and anal sex "verge on perversity" (157), while suggesting that the textual tradition confirms a discreet toleration of homosexual practice in both sexes.

6. Jeffrey Weeks, *Sex, Politics, and Society: The Regulation of Sexuality since 1800* (London: Longman, 1981, 1989), pp. 141–152.

7. See D'Emilio and Freedman, *Intimate Matters*, pp. 266–268, for a discussion of the reorientation of marriage manuals in the United States in the 1930s on the model of Theodore Van de Velde's book *Ideal Marriage*. Van de Velde evoked the ars erotica of classical Rome as a prototype for his discussion of marital pleasure.

8. In fact, the modern term *sexuality* itself implies the construction of sex around an ideology of instincts and drives which fundamentally shape personality and find an outlet in a social space devoted to sexual pleasure. See Michel Foucault, *The History of Sexuality*, vol. 1, *An Introduction* (New York: Random House, 1978), p. 150.

9. Foucault uses this term to refer to the common assumption that European Victorian culture repressed the expression of a natural and healthy human "sexuality," a view he believes obscures the more fundamental fact that Victorian discursive practice elevated "sexuality" into a fundamental and controlling aspect of human personality and experience. See Foucault, *History of Sexuality*, pp. 10–12.

10. For Ye Dehui's biography, see Howard Boorman and Richard Howard, eds., *Biographical Dictionary of Republican China* (New York: Columbia University Press, 1967), 4:35–37.

11. *Ishinpo*, orig. comp. 984 C.E. by Tamba no Yasuyori; first printed in Japan

in 1854. My references are to the two-volume Chinese reprint (Beijing: Renmin weisheng chubanshe, 1955).

12. The titles of the texts reconstructed by Ye are *Su nü jing* (Plain Girl's Classic); *Su nü fang* (Plain Girl's Pharmacy); *Yu fang mi jue* (Secret Instructions of the Jade Bedchamber); *Yu fang zhi yao* (Essentials of the Jade Bedchamber); and *Tong xuan zi* (The Mystery-Penetrating Master). Of these, *Secret Instructions of the Jade Bedchamber* is the longest and most detailed, suggesting an original of about eight *juan* rather than a single *juan* compilation like the others.

13. Ye Dehui, *Shuang mei jingan congshu* (The Double Plum Sun and Shadow Anthology) (Changsha: Printed by the Ye family, 1903); see *juan* 1, preface to *Su nü jing*.

14. As broad categories, both Confucian and Daoist have only limited explanatory value. Here I take Confucianism as referring to a system of family ethics rather than any philosophical school of thought. Daoism is even more elusive, since both the longevity cult and the *fang shu* of medieval times were descended from the archaic *wu* traditions of shamanism. I understand Daoist here to refer to the cult of immortality, as opposed to simple longevity, as sought through spiritual and physical disciplines which included sexual arts. In medieval China not all believers in such practices understood them as Daoist. In the late imperial period sexual mysticism was identified by its detractors as a mark of Daoist degeneracy, leading to its suppression or concealment. My thanks to Nathan Sivin for his critical admonitions on this as on many other matters.

15. Okanishi Tameto, *Song yiqian yi ji kao* (Investigation of Records Concerning Pre-Song Medical Books), 1958. For discussion of surviving data concerning these works, see the *nü ke* and *fang zhong* sections.

16. Ibid., pp. 1396–98.

17. Ibid., p. 1399.

18. For a complete list, see ibid., pp. 1399–1402. See also *Ishinpo, juan* 28; Ye Dehui, *juan* 1. Douglas Wile, *The Chinese Sexual Yoga Classics, Including Women's Solo Meditation Texts* (Albany: State University of New York Press, 1992), includes translations and commentary on a number of these, as well as his own versions of Van Gulik's material.

19. Sun Simo, *Bei ji jian jin yao fang* (Essential Prescriptions Worth a Thousand), first compiled 652 c.e., 30 *juan*. See *juan* 27, *Yang xing*, sec. 8, *Fang zhong bu yi* (Replenishing Benefits of the Bedchamber).

20. The term *coitus reservatus* is explained by Joseph Needham in his discussion of Daoist sexual techniques in *Science and Civilization in China*, vol. 2 (Cambridge: Cambridge University Press, 1962). Unlike coitus interruptus, familiar in traditional Europe as a contraceptive technique, the Chi-

nese method involved both intromission without ejaculation and the specific strategy of "making the sperm return"; that is, "at the moment of ejaculation, pressure was exerted on the urethra between the scrotum and the anus, thus diverting the seminal secretion into the bladder" (p. 149).

21. See *Ishinpo*, vol. 2, *juan* 28.

22. In his earliest writings on the art of the bedchamber (*Erotic Color Prints of the Ming Dynasty*, published privately in Tokyo in 1951), Van Gulik was quite critical of the service role of the female in passages which he labeled "Daoist vampirism." In the introduction to *Sexual Life in Ancient China* he explains that he was persuaded to change his interpretation by Joseph Needham. My discussion of Van Gulik here is based on the widely circulated later publication rather than the earlier one, which is extremely rare. The larger issue of sexual mysticism in Daoism, which interested Needham as an authority on Chinese science, is complex, and later textual traditions concerning it are little known as yet. Douglas Wile *(The Chinese Sexual Yoga Classics),* in his chapter "Elixir Literature of Sexual Alchemy," introduces some Ming-Qing texts attributed to Lu Dongpin, Zhang Sanfen, and Lu Xixing, which were preserved in the early nineteenth-century collection of Daoist esoterica by Fu Jinquan.

23. *Ishinpo*, vol. 2, *juan* 28, p. 633; subsequent references appear in the text.

24. See Sun, *juan* 27, sec. 8.

25. For a general discussion of visualization techniques in medieval Daoist *nei dan*, see Isabelle Robinet, "Visualization and Ecstatic Flight in Shangqing Taoism," in *Taoist Meditation and Longevity Techniques*, ed. Livia Kohn (Ann Arbor: Michigan Monographs in Chinese Studies, 1989), pp. 159–191.

26. *Huangdi neijing: Su wen* (The Yellow Emperor's Inner Canon: Basic Questions), *juan* 2, *"Si qi tiao shen da lun"* (Discourse on the Regulation of the Psyche/Self in Accordance with the *Qi* of the Four Seasons); citation is from the edition published by Kexue zhishu chubanshe (Shanghai, 1983), pp. 11–18.

27. Again the term is Foucault's: if desire is not a drive of the "natural" body but a socially malleable array of wishes, needs, and experiences, then culturally generated erotic scripts in fact produce desire, and societies that give sex great cultural importance are stimulating and multiplying desire itself.

28. Van Gulik, *Sexual Life in Ancient China*, pp. 224–225, 253. He quotes two twelfth-century scholars, Wang Mou and Zeng Zao, and the Yuan-era literatus Tao Zongyi.

29. Wan Quan, *Wan shi jia zhuan yang sheng si yao* (The Wan Family Tradition of "Four Essentials for Nourishing Life"); see *juan* 1, p. 5.

30. Wan Quan, *Wan shi jia zhuan guang si si yao, juan* 2, pp. 5–6.

31. Ibid., *juan* 4, p. 17. According to the editors' note here, some texts said "desirous" rather than "envious."
32. Ibid., *juan* 4, p. 17.
33. Ibid., *juan* 2, p. 6.
34. Ibid., *juan* 2, p. 7.
35. Ibid., *juan* 2, pp. 5–6.
36. Ibid., *juan* 5, p. 29.
37. For a discussion of similar views in other Ming-Qing medical writings, see Charlotte Furth, "Concepts of Pregnancy, Childbirth, and Infancy in Ch'ing Dynasty China," *Journal of Asian Studies* 46.1 (February 1987): 7–35.

7. Modernizing Sex, Sexing Modernity

Substantial portions of this essay appeared in Gail Hershatter, "Courtesans and Streetwalkers: The Changing Discourses on Shanghai Prostitution, 1890–1949," *Journal of the History of Sexuality* 3.2 (1992): 245–269, © 1992 by the University of Chicago. All rights reserved. The author thanks Guo Xiaolin and Wang Xiangyun for invaluable research assistance. Critical readings and suggestions were provided by participants in the "Engendering China" conference, particularly Christina Gilmartin, Emily Honig, Lisa Rofel, Ann Waltner, and Marilyn Young, as well as by Wendy Brown, Judith Farquhar, Carla Freccero, Carma Hinton, and Angela Zito.

1. Judith R. Walkowitz, *Prostitution and Victorian Society: Women, Class, and the State* (Cambridge: Cambridge University Press, 1980); Alain Corbin, *Women for Hire: Prostitution and Sexuality in France after 1850,* trans. Alan Sheridan (Cambridge, Mass.: Harvard University Press, 1990).
2. See, for example, the very useful but interpretively limited work by Wang Shunu, *Zhongguo changji shi* (History of Prostitution in China) (1935; rpt. Shanghai: Sanlian shudian, 1988).
3. For an eloquent demand that historians attend to discursive constructions of gender and their historical effects, see Joan Wallach Scott, *Gender and the Politics of History* (New York: Columbia University Press, 1988).
4. Huang Renjing, *Huren baolan* (Precious Mirror of Shanghai), English title: "What the Chinese in Shanghai Ought to Know" (Shanghai: Huamei shuju [Methodist Publishing House], 1913); Wang Liaoweng, *Shanghai liushinian huajie shi* (A Sixty-Year History of the Shanghai Flower World) (Shanghai: Shixin shuju, 1922); Zhan Kai, *Rouxiang yunshi* (A History of the Charm of the Gentle Village), 3d ed., 1st ed. 1914, author's preface dated 1907 (Shanghai: Wenyi xiaoqian suo, 1917), 3 *juan;* Banchisheng (Half-Crazy One), *Haishang yeyou beilan* (A Complete Look at Shanghai Philandering) (1891), 4 *juan.*
5. Qi Xia and Da Ru, eds., *Haishang hua yinglu* (A Record in Images of

Shanghai Flowers), rev. ed. (Shanghai: Zhongguo tushuguan, 1917), vol. 1, unpaginated.

6. Joseph Levenson, *Confucian China and Its Modern Fate* (Berkeley: University of California Press, 1972).

7. Huayu xiaozhu zhuren (Master of the Flower Rain Villa), *Haishang qinglou tuji* (Records and Drawings of Shanghai Houses of Prostitution) (1892), 6 *juan, juan* 1, p. 1.

8. *Jingbao* (The Crystal), August 15, 1919, p. 3.

9. *Jingbao*, August 27, 1919, p. 3.

10. For examples of this kind of poetry, see Chi Zhizheng, *Huyou mengying* (Dream Images of Shanghai Travels), ed. Hu Zhusheng (March 1893), photocopy of edited version of unpublished manuscript *(chaoben)* in Wenzhou museum, pp. 4–8; Li chuang wo dusheng (Student Who Lies on the Goosefoot Bed), ed., *Huitu Shanghai zaji* (Miscellaneous Shanghai Notes, Illustrated) (Shanghai: Shanghai wenbao shuju shi yingben, 1905), *juan* 6, p. 7, and *juan* 7, p. 7.

11. On the elections, see Chan Qingshi (Attendant Who Repents Emotion), *Haishang chunfang pu* (An Album of Shanghai Ladies) (Shenbao guan, 1884), 4 *juan;* Ping Jinya, *Jiu Shanghaide changji* (Prostitution in Old Shanghai), in *Jiu Shanghaide yanduchang* (Opium, Gambling, and Prostitution in Old Shanghai) (Shanghai: Baijia chubanshe, 1988), pp. 166–167; Chen Rongguang (Chen Boxi), *Lao Shanghai* (Old Shanghai Hand) (Shanghai: Taidong tushuju, 1924), pp. 90–95; Huayu xiaozhu zhuren, *juan* 1, p. 2; Qi Xia and Da Ru, vol. 1, unpaginated, and vol. 2, unpaginated; Yu Muxia, *Shanghai linzhao* (Shanghai Tidbits) (Shanghai: Shanghai Hubaoguan chubanbu, 1935), *ji,* pp. 37–38; Zhou Shoujuan, *Lao Shanghai sanshi nian jianwen lu* (A Record of Things Seen by an Old Shanghai Hand in the Last Thirty Years) (Shanghai: Dadong shuju, 1928), 2:2–4, 38–51; Xu Ke, *Qingbai leichao* (Qing Unofficial Reference Book) (Shanghai: Shangwu yinshuguan, 1928), 38:1–4.

12. Stephen H. L. Cheng, "*Flowers of Shanghai* and the Late Ch'ing Courtesan Novel" (Ph.D. diss., Harvard University, 1979), p. 252.

13. For examples of this kind of writing, see Sun Yusheng (Haishang juewusheng), *Jinüde shenghuo* (The Life of Prostitutes) (Shanghai: Chunming shudian, 1939), p. 8; and *Jingbao*, November 30, 1919, p. 3.

14. Wu Hanchi, ed., *Quanguo gejie qiekou da cidian* (National Dictionary of Secret Language from All Walks of Life) (Shanghai: Donglu tushu gongsi, 1924), pp. 9, 13; Wang Houzhe, *Shanghai baojian* (Precious Mirror of Shanghai) (Shanghai: Shijie shuju, 1925), unpaginated; Ping Jinya, p. 160; Shuliu shanfang (pseud.), "Shanghai qinglou zhi jinxi guan" (A Look at Shanghai Brothels Present and Past), *Jingbao*, March 18, 1919, p. 3.

15. Wang Zhongxian, *Shanghai suyu tushuo* (An Illustrated Dictionary of

Shanghai Slang) (Shanghai: Shanghai shehui chubanshe, 1935; rpt. Hong Kong: Shenzhou tushu gongsi, n.d.), p. 42.

16. Wang Liaoweng, p. 135.

17. Sun Yusheng, pp. 68–69; Wang Houzhe, unpaginated.

18. On her career and her frequent ablutions, and those of some of her fellow courtesans, see *Jingbao*, September 21, 1919, p. 3; Wang Liaoweng, pp. 50–56; and Zhou Shoujuan, 1:172–177.

19. Qi Xia and Da Ru, n.p. For a list of forty-seven liaisons between prostitutes and actors, see Chen Rongguang, pp. 123–128.

20. Sun Yusheng, p. 159.

21. Wang Dingjiu, *Shanghai de menjing* (Key to Shanghai) (Shanghai: Zhongyang shudian, 1932), p. 25.

22. See, for example, Sun Yusheng, pp. 170–171.

23. Various explanations for this term can be found in the guidebooks. One article notes both their gaudy dress and their habit of "go[ing] about from place to place like wild birds." "The Demi-Monde of Shanghai," *China Medical Journal* 37 (1923): 785–786.

24. This type of story about prostitutes is analyzed more fully in Gail Hershatter, "Sex Work and Social Order: Prostitutes, Their Families, and the State in Twentieth-Century Shanghai," in *Family Process and Political Process in Modern Chinese History*, ed. Zhongyang yanjiuyuan jindaishi yanjiusuo (Taipei: Zhongyang yanjiuyuan, 1992), 2:1083–1123.

25. *Shenbao*, November 12, 1919, p. 11.

26. See, for example, *Shenbao*, May 7, 1919, p. 11.

27. For a discussion of this literature, see Christian Henriot, "Medicine, V.D., and Prostitution in Pre-Revolutionary China," *Social History of Medicine* 5.1 (April 1992): 95–120.

28. For a fuller discussion of these sources, see Gail Hershatter, "Regulating Sex in Shanghai: The Reform of Prostitution in 1920 and 1951," in *Shanghai Sojourners*, ed. Frederic Wakeman and Wen-hsin Yeh (Berkeley: Institute of East Asian Studies, 1992), pp. 145–185.

29. *Shenbao*, October 31–November 3, 1941.

30. Lin Chongwu, *Changji wenti zhi yanjiu* (Research on the Prostitution Problem), *Minzhong jikan* 2.2 (June 1936): 221. On the emergence of race as a prominent category of analysis during this period, see Frank Dikötter, *The Discourse of Race in Modern China* (Stanford: Stanford University Press, 1992).

31. Huang Renjing, pp. 134–135.

32. *Chinese Recorder* (August 1920): 579–80.

33. Bu Minghui, M.D., of the Shanghai Moral Welfare League, writing in *Shenbao*, May 19, 1919, p. 11.

34. *Shenbao,* May 19, 1919, p. 11.
35. *Jingbao,* March 27, 1920, p. 2.
36. Hu Huaichen, *Feichang wenti* (The Question of Eliminating Prostitution), *Funü zazhi* 6.6 (1920): 9–10.
37. *Shenbao,* November 10, 1920, p. 11.
38. Mu Hua, *Gongchang zhidude bihai qiji lunjude huangmiu* (The Harm of the Licensed Prostitution System and the Absurdity of Its Grounds of Argument), *Nüzi yuekan* 4.4 (April 1936): 22.
39. Mu Hua, p. 22.
40. Mu Hua uses Bebel to make this point, but other authors prefer Havelock Ellis, Ellen Key, Anton Gross-Hoffinger, Max Rubner, and Bertrand Russell. Whether the discourse cited is tied to political economy or sexology, the universalizing impulse is similar. See, for example, Guo Chongjie, *Lun suqing changji* (On Ridding the Country of Prostitution), *Shehui banyue kan* 1.6 (November 1936): 23–28; and Lin Chongwu, pp. 215–223.
41. Mu Hua, p. 23.
42. Mu Hua, p. 23.
43. Mu Hua, p. 25.
44. Lin Chongwu, p. 222.
45. Lin Chongwu, passim.
46. Individual cities sometimes undertook to ban prostitution, but their ordinances were effective only within city limits, usually with the result that prostitutes moved to neighboring cities. Article 288 of the 1923 Provisional Criminal Code of the Republic of China stipulated imprisonment and fines for "whoever for lucrative purposes induces any woman belonging to a respectable family to have illicit intercourse with any person for hire," with stiffer penalties for "whoever makes the commission of the offence under the last preceding section a profession." Anatol M. Kotenev, *Shanghai: Its Mixed Court and Council* (1925; rpt. Taipei: Ch'eng-wen Publishing, 1968), pp. 413–414. The 1935 Criminal Code, while omitting a specific reference to respectable families, likewise made it a crime to remove "any person who has not completed the twentieth year of his or her age" from family or other "supervisory authority." The punishment was more severe if the person was removed without his or her consent or if the person was taken away "for the purpose of gain or for the purpose of causing the person who has been taken away to submit to carnal knowledge or to do a lascivious act." Shanghai Municipal Council Legal Department, trans., *The Chinese Criminal Code* (Shanghai: Commercial Press, 1935), pp. 86–88.
47. For statements that kidnappings accounted for a minority of trafficking cases, see "The Prostitution Problem in Shanghai," *China Critic,* April 1,

1937, p. 7; *Shenbao,* November 1, 1941, p. 3. A 1951 survey of 501 prostitutes found that only forty-seven, or 9.4 percent, had been tricked or kidnapped. Yang Jiezeng and He Wannan, *Shanghai changji gaizao shihua* (A History of the Reform of Shanghai Prostitutes) (Shanghai: Shanghai sanlian shudian, 1988), p. 61.

48. According to a 1937 *China Critic* report, the relevant laws in the International Settlement were by-law no. 36 and article 43 of Police Punishments for Violation of Morals. In the French Concession, the relevant laws were consular ordinance no. 183 and the provisions of Chapter 16 (221 and subsequent articles) and Chapter 17 (237 and subsequent articles) of the Chinese Criminal Code, which was applied by Chinese courts in the Concession. "The Prostitution Problem in Shanghai," *China Critic,* April 1, 1937, p. 7. After the Second World War, the Shanghai municipal government issued regulations prohibiting inducing others to become prostitutes in order to make a profit, or having sexual relations with people for profit. It is unclear how these regulations squared with the municipal government's elaborate schemes to license brothels and prostitutes. The relevant police regulations were nos. 64 and 65. Shanghai shi dang'an guan (Shanghai Municipal Archives), *Qudi jiyuan an* (Cases of Banning Brothels), File 011-4-163, 1946–1948, case 4.

49. *Shibao,* July 15, 1929, p. 7.

50. Shanghai shi dang'an guan (Shanghai Municipal Archives), *Qudi jiyuan an* (Cases of Banning Brothels), File 011-4-163, 1946–1948, case 4, documents 2–6.

51. For details of this campaign, see Gail Hershatter, "Regulating Sex," pp. 167–185.

52. This sentence is from Hershatter, "Regulating Sex," p. 176.

8. Male Suffering and Male Desire

I thank Lauren Smith, Ruedolf Kuenzli, Lisa Rofel, and Gail Hershatter for their constructive and thoughtful comments and suggestions.

1. The English version of *Nanren de yiban shi nüren* used in this essay is *Half of Man Is Woman,* trans. Martha Avery (New York: W. W. Norton, 1986).

2. In the Chinese Communist party's discourse during and before the Cultural Revolution, the two words *nanren* (man/men) and *nüren* (woman/women) were replaced by *nantongzhi* (male comrade) and *nütongzhi* (female comrade), which supposedly have a less sexual or erotic connotation.

3. In her article "Wo kan *Nanren de yiban shi nüren* de xing xinli miaoxie" (My View on the Representation of Sexual Psychology in *Half of Man Is*

Woman), which appeared in *Wenyi Bao* (Literature and Art), December 28, 1985, Zhang Xinxin commented on the wording of the title.

4. Martha Avery, "Translator's Introduction," in *Half of Man Is Woman*, p. xi.

5. Wei Junyi, "Yiben changxiao shu yingqi de sikao" (Some Thoughts Triggered by a Best Seller), *Wenyi bao* (Literature and Art), December 28, 1985; reprinted in *Xin hua wenzhai* (New China Digest), no. 1 (1986): 122–123.

6. Josef Skvorecky, quoted on the cover of the English translation of *Half of Man Is Woman*.

7. Avery, "Translator's Introduction," p. xii.

8. Discussions of the notions of "site" or "space" can be found, for example, in Teresa De Lauretis, "Imaging" and "Desire in Narrative," in *Alice Doesn't: Feminism, Semiotics, Cinema* (Bloomington: Indiana University Press, 1984).

9. I presented the first part of this essay at a conference years ago. After the presentation, I received some written comments from a critic. Responding to my questioning of the representation of women in the story, the critic wrote, "So what? What about his body?" This forced me to think more about the "his body" argument, and I raise this issue here as a response to this argument.

10. Zhang Xianliang, *Half of Man Is Woman*, p. 28; hereafter cited by page in the text.

11. From the cover of the English translation of *Half of Man Is Woman*.

12. Linda Williams, "Something Else Besides a Mother: *Stella Dallas* and Maternal Melodrama," *Cinema Journal* 24.1 (Fall 1984): 6.

9. Gender, Political Culture, and Women's Mobilization in the Chinese Nationalist Revolution, 1924–1927

1. "Feminist" is used here to refer to an organized ideological and programmatic effort to transform gender relations in the Chinese polity, economy, and society. Significantly, in the revolutionary upsurge of the mid-1920s, women were encouraged to participate in the mass mobilization campaigns as agents of their own emancipation, rather than merely to promote the political interests of the revolution.

2. Most historical accounts of twentieth-century China attribute little importance to the National Revolution, even declining in some cases to call the series of events in the mid-1920s leading to the establishment of a republican government in Nanjing a revolution. See, for instance, Jonathan D. Spence, *The Search for Modern China* (New York: W. W. Norton & Co., 1991), pp. 334–360. For examples of works that look at the origins of the communist revolutionary strategy for mobilizing peasants in the National Revolution, see Fernando Galbiati, *P'eng P'ai and the Hai-lu-feng Soviet*

(Stanford: Stanford University Press, 1985); Roy Hofheinz, Jr., *The Broken Wave: The Chinese Communist Peasant Movement, 1922–1928* (Cambridge, Mass.: Harvard University Press, 1977); and Robert Marks, *Rural Revolution in South China: Peasants and the Making of History in Haifeng, 1570–1930* (Madison: University of Wisconsin Press, 1986).

3. For a discussion of gender issues in post-Mao China, see Emily Honig and Gail Hershatter, *Personal Voices: Chinese Women in the 1980s* (Stanford: Stanford University Press, 1988); and Xie Zhihong, "Violence against Women in China," unpublished paper, May 1992.

4. For an illuminating theoretical discussion of the centrality of gender in the revolutionary process, see Valentine M. Moghadam, "Revolution, Culture, and Gender: Notes on 'The Woman Question' in Revolutions," unpublished paper, 1990.

5. For a fuller discussion of the expendability of women in traditional China, as well as a conceptualization of lineages as a type of patricorporation, see Hill Gates, "The Commoditization of Chinese Women," *Signs* 14.4 (1989): 799–832.

6. Ono Kazuko, *Chinese Women in a Century of Revolution, 1850–1950* (Stanford: Stanford University Press, 1989), pp. 1–4; and Rubie S. Watson, "Girls' Houses and Working Women: Expressive Culture in the Pearl River Delta, 1900–1941" in *Bondage, Rescue, and Escape among Chinese Women,* ed. Suzanne Miers and Maria Jaschok (Hong Kong: Hong Kong University Press, 1994).

7. The Hakka are a Han people who were not indigenous to the region and were treated as an ethnic minority by the Cantonese-speaking population (known locally as Punti) ever since they migrated south from central China many centuries ago.

8. Wolfgang Franke, *A Century of Chinese Revolution, 1851–1949* (Cambridge: Oxford University Press, 1970).

9. For a full consideration of this issue, see Watson, "Girls' Houses and Working Women."

10. Chen Han-seng, *Landlord and Peasant in China: A Study of the Agrarian Crisis in South China* (New York: International Publishers, 1936).

11. Agnes Smedley, *The Great Road: The Life and Times of Chu Teh* (New York: Monthly Review Press, 1956), p. 206.

12. For a discussion of the history of outmigration from Guangdong, see Ta Chen, *Emigrant Communities in South China: A Study of Overseas Migration and Its Influence on Standards of Living and Social Change* (New York: Institute of Pacific Relations, 1940).

13. Hakka women from Guangdong province joined with their Guangxi neighbors to fight in the women's army, a force of more than ten thou-

sand, which was known for its ferocity in combat and for striking fear into the hearts of imperial (male) troops. Once the Taiping became successful on the battlefield, they initiated a series of radical gender policies, including issuing marriage licenses, giving women work in the public domain, discouraging arranged marriages, and prohibiting footbinding, polygamy, prostitution, and adultery. For an extensive discussion of the new gender codes of the Taiping Rebellion, see Kazuko, *Chinese Women*, pp. 5–22.

14. During the 1911 revolution women from Guangdong formed their own battalions and fought in the revolutionary battles. Shortly thereafter, thirteen women entered the Guangdong Provincial Assembly. In the May Fourth era Guangdong produced the most vigorous and pathbreaking independent women's movement, which by the time of the National Revolution included approximately sixty different groups. For more complete discussion of the women's movement in Guangdong, see Tan Sheying, *Zhongguo funü yundong shi* (A History of the Chinese Women's Movement) (Shanghai, 1936).

15. For a discussion of Bolshevik mobilization techniques in the 1920s, see Peter Kenez, *The Birth of the Propaganda State: Soviet Methods of Mass Mobilization, 1917–1929* (New York: Cambridge University Press, 1985).

16. For a discussion of feminist ideals of the May Fourth era, see Roxane Witke, "Transformation of Attitudes towards Women during the May Fourth Era of Modern China" (Ph.D. diss., University of California, Berkeley, 1970); and Elisabeth Croll, *Feminism and Socialism in China* (New York: Schocken, 1978), chap. 4. For a discussion of the impact of May Fourth ideas on Nationalist and Communist activists, see Lu Fangshang, *Geming zhi zaiqi—Zhongguo Guomindang gaizu qian de xin sichao (1914–1924)* (Resurgence of the Revolution—New Intellectual Trends before the Reorganization of the Chinese Nationalist Party [1914–1924]) (Taipei: Zhongyang yanjiuyuan jindaishi yanjiusuo, 1989); and Christina Gilmartin, "Gender in the Formation of the Chinese Communist Body Politic," *Modern China* 19:3 (July 1993): 299–329.

17. For a discussion of the extent of Russian financing of the National Revolution, see C. Martin Wilbur, *The Nationalist Revolution in China, 1923–1928* (Cambridge: Cambridge University Press, 1983), pp. 40–42.

18. After the university was closed down in the International Settlement, it was moved to another site in the Chinese section of Shanghai. Although it continued to function as an important center of communist activity, it did not regain its earlier prominence as a vibrant, exciting student center. After the suppression of communists in April 1927, the university was permanently shut down. See Huang Meizhen, Shi Yuanhua, and Zhang Yun, eds., *Shanghai Daxue shiliao* (Historical Materials on Shanghai Univer-

sity) (Shanghai: Fudan University Press, 1984), pp. 165–170. For an excellent discussion of the restrictions on public meetings and discourse in Beijing in this period, see David Strand, *Rickshaw Beijing: City People and Politics in the 1920s* (Berkeley: University of California Press, 1989).

19. For a discussion of this strike, see Jean Chesneaux, *The Chinese Labor Movement, 1919–1927* (Stanford: Stanford University Press, 1968), pp. 290–318.

20. Jean Chesneaux, François Le Barbier, and Marie-Claire Bergère, *China: From the 1911 Revolution to Liberation,* trans. Paul Auster and Lydia Davis (New York: Pantheon, 1977), p. 157.

21. For a discussion of the socialist-feminist tradition, see Jean Quataert, *Reluctant Feminists in German Social Democracy, 1885–1917* (Princeton: Princeton University Press, 1979); Richard Stites, *The Women's Liberation Movement in Russia* (Princeton: Princeton University Press, 1978); and Beatrice Farnsworth, "Communist Feminism: Its Synthesis and Demise," in *Women, War, and Revolution,* ed. Carol R. Berkin and Clara M. Lovett (New York: Holmes & Meier, 1980). Communists pledged their general commitment to nationalism as an important immediate goal for China in a number of documents, including the Sun-Joffe Declaration of 1923, the resolutions of the Third Party Congress of the Chinese Communist party, and the resolutions of the Nationalist Party Congress in 1924.

22. Even though Clara Zetkin is credited with establishing this holiday among socialists in 1910, the exact date for celebrating International Women's Day differed in Europe and the United States for more than a decade. A specific date was finally set in 1922, when Lenin proclaimed it on March 8 in honor of the women workers whose demonstration had precipitated the Bolshevik Revolution. For an account of the reasons for variations in the celebration of this festival among socialists, see Marilyn J. Boxer and Jean H. Quataert, *Connecting Spheres: Women in the Western World, 1500 to the Present* (New York: Oxford University Press, 1987), pp. 199, 252.

23. *Guoji funü ri yu Zhongguo funü jiefang, Guangzhou minguo ribao,* March 9, 1927, p. 2 of the supplement.

24. Slogans of March 8 found in Pi Yishu, *Zhongguo funü yundong* (Taipei: Fulian shukan she, 1973), p. 51. The number of participants at the 1926 March 8 celebrations was provided by [Yang] Zhihua, *Zhongguo sanba yundong shi* (The History of March 8 in China), *Chinü zazhi* (Red Women's Journal), no. 6 (March 1927), p. 23. The source for the number of people attending the 1927 March 8 rally is Croll, *Feminism and Socialism in China,* p. 124, citing as her source I. Dean, "The Women's Movement in China," *Chinese Recorder* 58.10 (1927): 658. General information on the festival can be found in *Guangzhou wenshi ziliao,* no. 30 (September 1983).

25. "Guomindang de zuzhi," *Tianjin funü ribao,* March 1, 1924, p. 2.

26. Vera Vladimirovna Vishnyakova-Akimova, *Two Years in Revolutionary China, 1925–1927,* trans. Steven Z. Levine (Cambridge, Mass.: East Asian Research Center, Harvard University, 1971), pp. 208–209.

27. No text was deemed necessary, for instance, by the editors of *Funü shenghuo,* a publication of the Guangdong Women's Liberation Association, when they ran Rosa Luxemburg's picture on the cover of their March 1, 1927, issue (no. 5) commemorating International Women's Day.

28. Wenshi ziliao yanjiu weiyuanhui, ed., *Guangdong wenshi ziliao,* no. 30 (Guangzhou: Guangdong renmin chubanshe, 1981), p. 243. Karl Liebknecht was a prominent leader of the German Spartakus League, who was arrested along with Rosa Luxemburg on January 15, 1919, and killed soon after. For a detailed account of his political role and his violent death, see Paul Frölich, *Rosa Luxemburg: Her Life and Work* (New York: Monthly Review Press, 1972), pp. 297–300.

29. *Guangdong wenshi ziliao,* p. 101.

30. Catherine Gipoulon, *Qiu Jin, Pierres de l'oiseau Jingwei: Femme et révolution-naire en Chine au XIX siècle* (Paris: des femmes, 1976), p. 9. In addition to the rhetorical emphasis placed on Qiu Jin in both the Nationalist and Communist press, her home in Shaoxing has been turned into a museum with much material highlighting her revolutionary activities.

31. Mary Backus Rankin, *Early Chinese Revolutionaries: Radical Intellectuals in Shanghai and Chekiang, 1902–1911* (Cambridge, Mass.: Harvard University Press, 1971), pp. 40–46; and Rankin, "The Emergence of Women at the End of the Ch'ing: The Case of Ch'iu Chin," in *Women in Chinese Society,* ed. Margery Wolf and Roxane Witke (Stanford: Stanford University Press, 1975), p. 52.

32. *Guangzhou minguo ribao,* March 8, 1927.

33. Qiu Jin's decision to join the Restoration Society was most likely made for pragmatic reasons, not as a veiled criticism of Sun Yatsen. But her involvement with Xu Xilin, a Restoration Society member who was well known for his repudiation of Sun Yatsen, in an uprising against the Manchu imperial government, established the basis for later assertions that she may have shared his feelings about Sun Yatsen. For a fuller discussion of Qiu Jin's political affiliations and the rivalry between the Restoration Society and the Tongmenghui, see Rankin, *Early Chinese Revolutionaries,* pp. 108–112, 154–155, and 210–211.

34. Qiu Canzhi, *Qiu Jin zhuan* (Taipei: Lianhe tushu gongsi, 1969), p. 155.

35. C. Martin Wilbur, *Sun Yatsen: Frustrated Patriot* (New York: Columbia University Press, 1976), p. 280.

36. This pledge was embedded in the "First Party Congress Proclamation," reprinted in *Shuangqing wenji* (Beijing: Renmin chubanshe, 1985), 2:461.

37. For a discussion of Borodin's role in reorganizing the Nationalist party,

see Wilbur, *Nationalist Revolution*, pp. 8–9. For a discussion of the impact of the May Fourth movement on the Nationalist party, see Lu Fangshang, *Geming zhi zaiqi.*

38. The assertion that she was the first woman to join the Revolutionary Alliance (Tongmenghui) is made in her article "When I Learned How to Cook," in *Chinese Women through Chinese Eyes*, ed. Li Yuning (Armonk, N.Y.: M. E. Sharpe, 1992). It is also contained in the permanent exhibition of the Memorial Hall for Liao Zhongkai and He Xiangning (located at the site of the Peasant-Worker School in Guangzhou). Other women who joined at about the same time were Tang Chunying, Qiu Jin, Wu Yanan, Wu Ruonan, Lin Zongsu, Zhang Hanying, Zhang Zhaohan, and Liao Bingjun. Ultimately fifty-nine women joined this organization. Liu Jucai, *Zhongguo jindai funü yundong shi* (Liaoning: Zhongguo funü chubanshe, 1989), p. 283. For an early example of He Xiangning's writings about the relationship of women's emancipation and nationalism, see *Jinggao wo tongbao dimei, Jiangsu*, no. 4 (June 1903): 1.

39. He Xiangning, "When I Learned How to Cook," pp. 133–143.

40. Women's International Secretariat, Russian Centre of Conservation and Study of Records of Modern History, Moscow (hereafter Russian Archives), collection 507, file 105, p. 87.

41. *Funü yundong xiuzhi* (Information on the Women's Movement), quoted in Zhonghua quanguo funü lianhehui, ed., *Zhongguo funü yundong shi* (Beijing: Chunqiu chubanshe, 1989), p. 160. These figures are to some extent impressionistic, as was the slightly smaller number of 1.5 million women that He Xiangning gave in an interview with an American reporter, Anna Louise Strong, in 1927. Nevertheless, they are indicative of the massive number of women who were mobilized for the revolution. See Anna Louise Strong, *China's Millions* (New York: Coward-McCann, 1928), p. 115.

42. Zeng Xing was the first woman selected to head the Central Women's Department of the Nationalist party. At that time she held the position of principal of the Zhixin School in Guangzhou and was also a veteran member of the Tongmenghui; she had studied in France and actually fought in the 1911 revolution. When she resigned from this position in August, Liao Bingjun, a cousin of Liao Zhongkai, was selected, but in a very short time she too resigned. Zhonghua quanguo funü lianhehui, *Zhongguo funü yundong shi* (Historical Materials on the Chinese Women's Movement) (Beijing: Renmin chubanshe, 1986) pp. 159–160.

43. He Xiangning, *Zhongguo Guomindang di'erci quanguo daibiao dahui zhongyang funübu funü yundong baogao*, in *Zhonghua quanguo funü lianhehui funü yundong lishi yanjiushi* (All-China Women's Federation, Research Department on the History of the Women's Movement in China), p. 503.

44. Russian Archives, collection 507, list 2, file 69, p. 45.

45. Interview with Lu Jingqing at her home in Shanghai, February 6, 1983.

46. Zhonghua quanguo funü lianhehui, *Zhongguo funü yundong shi*, p. 200.

47. [Deng] Yingchao, *Minguo shisi nian de funü yundong* (The Women's Movement in 1925), in *Funü zhi sheng huikan* (Guangzhou: Nationalist Women's Department, n.d. [ca. early 1926]), pp. 6–12.

48. Zhonghua quanguo funü lianhehui, *Zhongguo funü yundong shi*, p. 201.

49. For the complete text of Deng Yingchao's speech to the Congress, see *Deng Yingchao guanyu funü yundong de baogao* (Deng Yingchao's Report on the Women's Movement), in *Zhongguo funü yundong lishi ziliao, 1921–1927*, pp. 508–511.

50. See, for instance, [Deng] Yingchao, *Minguo shisi nian de funü yundong*, p. 9.

51. Ibid., p. 9.

52. Ibid., pp. 6–12.

53. Croll, *Feminism and Socialism in China*, pp. 124–125.

54. Helen Foster Snow, *Women in Modern China* (The Hague: Mouton, 1967), p. 99.

55. For a discussion of He Xiangning's role in establishing the People's Drama Society, see *Guangdong wenshi ziliao*, no. 34 (1982): 197–198.

56. *Di'erci guan Guomindang daibiao dahui funü yundong jueyi an, Zhengzhi zhoubao*, no. 6–7; reprinted in *Guangdong funü yundong shiliao, 1924–1927* (Guangdong: Guangdong sheng dang'an guan, 1983), pp. 105–109.

57. See, for instance, He Xiangning, *Guomin geming shi funü weiyi de shenglu, Funü zhi sheng huikan*, May 31, 1926; reprinted in *Zhongguo funü yundong lishi ziliao, 1921–1927*, pp. 285–286.

58. Xia Songyun, *Funü yundong he guomin geming* (The Women's Movement and the National Revolution), in *Guangming* (Light) (1926), pp. 14–16.

59. The term *funü jiefang* came to be preferred during the May Fourth era over *nüquan* (women's rights), which had been widely used in the 1911 revolution period. It signified a belief that much more was necessary for women to achieve emancipation from social constraints than just granting certain rights. In 1919 and 1920 various male feminists further publicized this term when they debated whether women could actually be liberated. See, for instance, Hu Shi et al., *Nüzi jiefang cong nali zuoqi?* (Where Does Women's Emancipation Start From?), in *Xingqi pinglun;* and Zhang Shenfu, *Nüzi jiefang da budang* (The Great Unfairness of Women's Emancipation), *Shaonian Zhongguo* (October 1919). The Guangxi mass women's associations in the Nationalist Revolution were closely connected with those in Guangdong; hence, the decision to adopt the same name for the organization. This linkage was also made in the Women's Bureau of the

Chinese Communist party, which oversaw the women's movement in these two provinces *(liangguang)* as if it were one closely interconnected unit.

60. *Guangdong funü jiefang xiehui xuanyan ji gangling,* in *Zhongguo funü yundong lishi ziliao, 1921–1927,* pp. 395–397.
61. Galbiati, *P'eng P'ai,* p. 198.
62. *Zhonggong zhongyang funü weiyuanhui gongzuo baogao,* in *Zhongguo funü yundong lishi ziliao, 1921–1927,* p. 697.
63. *Guangdong funü yundong shiliao, 1924–1927,* p. 171.
64. Ibid., p. 321.
65. Ibid. Later the program was formalized, the name of the school was changed to Laodong Funü Xuexiao, and Chen Tiejun became its head teacher.
66. Deng Yingchao, *Deng Yingchao guanyu funü yundong de baogao,* in *Zhongguo funü yundong lishi ziliao, 1921–1927,* p. 510.
67. *Zhonggong zhongyang funü weiyuanhui* (A Working Report of the CCP Women's Committee, June 1926–February 1927), in *Zhongguo funü yundong lishi ziliao, 1921–1927,* pp. 696–700.
68. *Guangdong funü yundong shiliao, 1924–1927,* p. 327.
69. For studies of these marriage practices, see Janice Stockard, *Daughters of the Canton Delta* (Stanford: Stanford University Press, 1989); Marjorie Topley, "Marriage Resistance in Rural Kwangtung," in Wolf and Witke, *Women in Chinese Society;* and Watson, "Girls' Houses and Working Women."
70. Robert Y. Eng, "Luddism and Labor Protest among Silk Artisans and Workers in Jiangnan and Guangdong, 1860–1930," *Late Imperial China* 11.2 (December 1990): 92.
71. *Guangdong funü yundong shiliao, 1924–1927,* pp. 173, 316.
72. They were Zhang Wei, Peng Keng, Chen Xin, Zhang Xing, Gao Yu, and Fang Shaoqiong. Ibid., p. 315.
73. The establishment of these associations was traced through the periodical literature, such as *Guangming, Funü zhi sheng, Guangzhou minguo ribao,* and clippings from various newspapers filed at the Guomindang party archives at Yangmingshan, particularly files 447/47 and 474/47. This list is similar but not identical to the ones provided in *Guangdong funü yundong shiliao, 1924–1927,* pp. 195, 209.
74. Tan Zhushan, *Huishu funü de wenhua yu shenghuo diaocha* (Investigations into the Education and Lives of Women in Huishu, Dongjiang), *Funü zhisheng,* no. 20 (n.d.): 3–8.
75. Ibid.
76. I was not able to locate this journal while in Guangdong, but several articles have been republished in *Guangdong funü yundong shiliao, 1924–*

1927, pp. 233, 235. Ultimately the reaction against this organization was so strong that the local magistrate was able to install a more conservative administration under Cheng Zhixing. When students protested, the police were sent in to quell the disturbance.

77. Liao Wang Editing Bureau, *Hongjun nüyingxiong zhuan* (Beijing: Xinhua Publishing House, 1986), pp. 55–56.

78. For a full account of social conditions and the struggle to establish a peasant association in Guangning in the mid-1920s, see Hofheinz, *The Broken Wave,* pp. 179–213.

79. *Zhonggong zhongyang funü weiyuanhui gongzuo baogao;* reprinted in *Zhongguo funü yundong lishi ziliao, 1921–1927,* p. 700.

80. *Guangdong funü yundong shiliao, 1924–1927,* pp. 330–331.

81. Huanan nongxueyuan maliezhuyi jiaoyanshi, comp., *Peng Pai zhuan* (Biography of Peng Pai) (Beijing: Renmin chubanshe, 1984), p. 9; Holfheinz, *The Broken Wave,* p. 143; Galbiati, *P'eng P'ai,* p. 225.

82. Croll, *Feminism and Socialism in China,* p. 126.

83. The figure of 30 percent comes from Snow, *Women in Modern China.* For a discussion of the female bondservant issue, see Galbiati, *P'eng P'ai,* p. 310.

84. *Peng Pai wenji* (Collected Works of Peng Pai) (Beijing: Renmin chubanshe, 1981), p. 119.

85. For a fuller discussion of Peng's role as director and teacher at the Peasant Movement Training Institute, see Galbiati, *P'eng P'ai,* pp. 240–248; and Hofheinz, *The Broken Wave,* pp. 85–86.

86. Hofheinz, *The Broken Wave,* p. 79.

87. Zhonghua quanguo funü lianhehui, ed., *Zhonghua nüyinglüe* (Chinese Women Martyrs) (Beijing: Wenwu chubanshe, 1988), p. 49.

88. *Peng Pai wenji,* p. 196.

89. Ibid., p. 196.

90. Ibid., p. 98.

91. Ibid.

92. *Litou zhoubao,* nos. 17–18 (1926): 37.

93. Hofheinz, *The Broken Wave,* p. 97.

94. For instance, just in the one Southeast Asian colony of British Malaysia, Meixian immigrants numbered 218,139 in 1921 and 318,739 in 1931. Chen, *Emigrant Communities in South China,* p. 269.

95. *Guangzhou minguo ribao,* August 25, 1926, p. 5.

96. *Peng Pai yanjiu shiliao* (Peng Pai Historical Research Materials) (Guangdong: Guangdong renmin chubanshe, 1981), pp. 33–34, 227–228.

97. Vishnyakova-Akimova, *Two Years in Revolutionary China,* p. 163.

98. Galbiati, *P'eng P'ai,* p. 205; *Peng Pai wenji,* p. 329.

99. For a discussion of one brief campaign by the Chinese Communist party to alter the marriage system, see Kay Ann Johnson, *Women, the Family, and Peasant Revolution in China* (Chicago: University of Chicago Press, 1983), chap. 5.
100. For a discussion of the Nationalist women's policy, see Norma Diamond, "Women under Kuomintang Rule: Variations on the Feminine Mystique," *Modern China* 1.1 (January 1975): esp. 8–18.

10. Liberation Nostalgia and a Yearning for Modernity

I thank the workers, managers, and state bureaucrats of the Hangzhou silk industry, who patiently taught me about their world(s); the Committee for Scholarly Communication with the People's Republic of China for research funds without which I would never have been able to enter that world; and the American Council of Learned Societies for the postdoctoral fellowship that made the writing of this essay possible. Earlier versions were presented on a panel, "Quandaries of Representation and Writing: Post-Ethnographic Texts," at the Eighty-Ninth Annual Meeting of the American Anthropological Association; to the Women's Studies Program, University of California, Santa Cruz; and at "Feminist Dilemmas in Fieldwork: Studying Ourselves/Studying Others," a conference at the University of California, Davis. I thank those at that conference who engaged so forcefully with my argument, as well as Jane Atkinson, Gail Hershatter, Dorinne Kondo, Beth Notar, Anna Tsing, and Sylvia Yanagisako. Portions of this essay were quoted in Lisa Rofel, "Where Feminism Lies: Field Encounters in China," *Frontiers: A Journal of Women's Studies* 14.1 (1993), *Frontiers* Editorial Collective. All rights reserved.

1. A prep worker is someone who prepares the silk thread for weaving.
2. Renato Rosaldo, *Culture and Truth: The Remaking of Social Analysis* (Boston: Beacon Press, 1989).
3. Dorinne K. Kondo, *Crafting Selves: Power, Gender, and Discourses of Identity in a Japanese Workplace* (Chicago: University of Chicago Press, 1990); Anna Lowenhaupt Tsing, *In the Realm of the Diamond Queen* (Princeton: Princeton University Press, 1993).
4. Teresa de Lauretis describes this process as one in which a person "perceives and comprehends as subjective (referring to, even originating in, oneself) those relations—material, economic, and interpersonal—which are in fact social and, in a larger perspective, historical." Teresa de Lauretis, *Alice Doesn't: Feminism, Semiotics, Cinema* (Bloomington: Indiana University Press, 1984), p. 159. See also Joan W. Scott, "Experience," in *Feminists Theorize the Political*, ed. Judith Butler and Joan W. Scott (New York: Routledge, Chapman and Hall, 1992), pp. 22–40. These articles reflect the

poststructuralist challenges to the Enlightenment assumption that man *(sic)* creates himself and his world. In the case of revolutionary China, however, the Communist party developed processes and practices of identification through which people such as Yu Shifu were made aware that the party was offering them the means to transform their lives and the language through which to describe it.

5. Donna Haraway, "Situated Knowledges: The Science Question in Feminism as a Site of Discourse on the Privilege of Partial Perspective," *Feminist Studies* 14.3 (1988): 575–599.

6. I distinguish between this delineation of historically situated generations and attention to life cycles, which still assumes a homogeneity of Chinese women as a group. The two approaches could, however, be usefully linked.

7. Stormy controversies have erupted in anthropology over self-reflexivity, colonial discourse, positioned knowledge, and the "literary-ness" of ethnography. These approaches have been characterized, in somewhat exaggerated fashion by those opposed to them, as creating an absolute dichotomy between self-critique and an exclusive emphasis on the Westerner as the primary actor in cultural encounters versus systematic knowledge of other people and a respect for their ability to strike back at the empire through cultural syncretism. See Marshall Sahlins, "Goodbye to Tristes Tropes: Ethnography in the Context of Modern World History," *Journal of Modern History* 65.1 (March 1993): 1–25. As I hope my essay demonstrates, I do not accept this dichotomy. I believe that reflecting on previous representations of other people is an enabling act, leading to new forms of knowledge about cultural difference.

8. Although I did not produce written texts on Chinese women during the height of these discussions, I was an avid student participant and activist who contributed to building these frameworks.

9. In later sections I interpret the changing meanings of "work" in the periods preceding and just after the 1949 socialist revolution. For the most thoroughly researched of texts from this period, see Elisabeth Croll, *Feminism and Socialism in China* (New York: Schocken Books, 1978); and Delia Davin, *Woman-Work: Women and the Party in Revolutionary China* (Oxford: Clarendon Press, 1976).

10. See Robert Young, *White Mythologies: Writing History and the West* (New York: Routledge, 1990); and Michael Taussig, "History as Commodity in Some Recent American (Anthropological) Literature," *Food and Foodways* 2 (1987): 151–169, for critiques of socialist and Marxist theories in terms of their teleological claims about world history. For a critique of world systems theory in light of its erasure of heterogeneity, see Edward Said, "Orientalism Reconsidered," *Cultural Critique* 1 (Fall 1985): 89–108.

11. The most influential texts in this vein were Phyllis Andors, *The Unfinished Liberation of Chinese Women: 1949–1980* (Bloomington: Indiana University Press, 1983); Kay Ann Johnson, *Women, the Family, and Peasant Revolution in China* (Chicago: University of Chicago Press, 1983); and Judith Stacey, *Patriarchy and Socialist Revolution in China* (Berkeley: University of California Press, 1983).

12. For the former argument, see Margery Wolf, *Revolution Postponed: Women in Contemporary China* (Stanford: Stanford University Press, 1985); for the latter, see Tani Barlow, "Theorizing Women: *Funü, Guojia, Jiating* [Chinese Women, Chinese State, Chinese Family]," *Genders* 10 (1991): 131–160.

13. Edward Said theorized the now classic critique of orientalism as a body of institutionalized expertise produced in Europe and in the United States which fabricated the "Orient" in terms of assumptions about foundational essences immune to historical change. The authoritative status of orientalism was both the result of and the enabling condition for colonialism (and neocolonialism). But in its creation of an absolute binary opposition between the West and the East and in its portrayal of "Orientals" as inert, timeless objects of culture, orientalism ironically made colonial dominance appear irrelevant to this production of knowledge. This intellectual operation, Said and others have argued, is essential to the ability of the West to dominate the third world. Edward Said, *Orientalism* (New York: Vintage, 1978). See also Abdul R. JanMohamed and David Lloyd, eds., *The Nature and Context of Minority Discourse* (Oxford: Oxford University Press, 1990). For arguments that Said recapitulates some of the very operations he unearths, see Young, *White Mythologies*. Gyan Prakash, in another vein, has called for the mapping of "post-Orientalist historiographies" through acknowledging that all knowledge about that which we call the third world is historical. Gyan Prakash, "Writing Post-Orientalist Histories of the Third World: Perspectives from Indian Historiography," *Comparative Studies in Society and History* 32.2 (1990): 383–408.

14. Chandra Talpade Mohanty, "Under Western Eyes: Feminist Scholarship and Colonial Discourses," *boundary* 2.12/13 (1984): 333–358; Gayatri Spivak, *In Other Worlds: Essays in Cultural Politics* (New York: Methuen, 1987); Trinh T. Minh-ha, *Woman, Native, Other: Writing Postcoloniality and Feminism* (Bloomington: Indiana University Press, 1989).

15. Aihwa Ong, "Colonialism and Modernity: Feminist Re-Presentations of Women in Non-Western Societies," *Inscriptions* 3/4 (1988): 79–93.

16. Lata Mani, "Multiple Mediations: Feminist Scholarship in the Age of Multinational Reception," *Feminist Review* 35 (1990): 24–42.

17. Wolf, *Revolution Postponed*, p. 12.

18. I am grateful to Beth Notar for reminding me to make this point explicit.

19. This interpretation of gendered spatial geographies of identity has been sparked by Sylvia Yanagisako's essay on gender and kinship domains and by Joan Scott's insights into the politics of discourses on work identities. See Sylvia Junko Yanagisako, "Mixed Metaphors: Native and Anthropological Models of Gender and Kinship Domains," in *Gender and Kinship: Essays toward a More Unified Analysis,* ed. Jane Fishburne Collier and Sylvia Junko Yanagisako (Stanford: Stanford University Press, 1987), pp. 86–118; Joan Scott, "Work Identities for Men and Women: The Politics of Work and Family in the Parisian Garment Trades in 1848," in *Gender and the Politics of History* (New York: Columbia University Press, 1988), pp. 93–112.

20. For an insightful analysis of this point, see Rey Chow, "Violence in the Other Country: China as Crisis, Spectacle, and Woman," in *Third World Women and the Politics of Feminism,* ed. Chandra Talpade Mohanty, Ann Russo, and Lourdes Torres (Bloomington: Indiana University Press, 1991), pp. 81–100.

21. Barlow, "Theorizing Women."

22. There is an ironic tale to be told here about the parallel images of "national woman" produced by the official discourse in China and the "Chinese woman" produced through American and British feminisms. In no small measure they are linked through a past reliance on official publications.

23. Maxine Hong Kingston, *The Woman Warrior: Memoirs of a Girlhood among Ghosts* (New York: Vintage, 1976).

24. For an insightful discussion of these changes, see Marilyn Young, "Chicken Little in China: Some Reflections on Women," in *Marxism and the Chinese Experience,* ed. Arif Dirlik and Maurice Meisner (Armonk, N.Y.: M. E. Sharpe, 1989), pp. 253–268.

25. For an elaborate discussion of this point, see Emily Honig and Gail Hershatter, *Personal Voices: Chinese Women in the 1980s* (Stanford: Stanford University Press, 1988).

26. The resistance to which I refer here is not meant to include all Chinese women or all the different ways Chinese women become mothers. I include only those women who work in the labor-intensive "women's industries" such as silk factories.

27. Mohanty, "Under Western Eyes."

28. The Engendering China conference on which this volume is based is one example. The November 1992 International Women's Studies conference in Beijing, to which the organizers of the Engendering China conference were invited, is another.

29. See Li Xiaojiang, "Economic Reform and the Awakening of Chinese Women's Collective Consciousness," in this volume.

11. The Origins of China's Birth Planning Policy

Research for this paper was supported by a sabbatical from Swarthmore College, a grant from the Swarthmore College Faculty Research Support Fund, and a postdoctoral fellowship from the John King Fairbank Center for East Asian Research, Harvard University. I thank my coeditors, especially Lisa Rofel, for comments on this essay. This chapter is adapted from the author's book manuscript, *Rationing the Children: China's One-Child Campaign in the Countryside*, and is published here with the permission of The University of California Press.

1. U.S. Department of State, *The China White Paper*, vols. 1 and 2 (Stanford: Stanford University Press, 1967).
2. Mao Tse-tung, "The Bankruptcy of the Idealist Conception of History," *Selected Works of Mao Tse-tung*, vol. 4 (Beijing: Foreign Languages Press, 1961).
3. Ding Ling, "Thoughts on March 8," trans. Mark Selden, in *The Yenan Way in Revolutionary China* (Cambridge, Mass.: Harvard University Press, 1971), pp. 165–166.
4. Shi Chengli, *Zhongguo jihua shengyu huodongshi* (A History of China's Birth Planning Activities) (Urumuchi: Xinjiang People's Publishing House, 1988), pp. 52–53; see also Liu Shaoqi, *Tichang jieyu* (Promote Birth Control), in Zhongguo shehui kexueyuan renkou yanjiu zhongxin, *Zhongguo renkou nianjian (1985)* (Population Yearbook of China, 1985) (Beijing: Chinese Academy of Social Sciences Publishing House, 1985), pp. 4–5.
5. Shi, *Zhongguo jihua shengyu*, pp. 50–51.
6. Ibid., p. 111.
7. The regulations were titled "Provisional Method for Limiting Birth Control Surgery and Abortion" *(Xianzhi jieyu ji rengong liuchan zanxing banfa)*. See Shi, *Zhongguo jihua shengyu*, p. 113.
8. Deng Lichun and Ma Hong, eds., *Dangdai zhongguode weisheng shiye (xia)* (Health Work in Contemporary China), vol. 2 (Beijing: Chinese Academy of Social Sciences Publishing House, 1986), p. 231.
9. Shi, *Zhongguo jihua shengyu*, p. 115.
10. For a draft of the 1950 Marriage Law and related documents, see *Zhongguo renkou nianjian (1985)*, pp. 65–72.
11. "Second All-China Women's Congress Opens," *New China News Agency* (hereafter *NCNA*), April 15, 1953, in *Survey of China Mainland Press* (hereafter *SCMP*), no. 553, April 17, 1953, pp. 8–9.
12. "Deng Yingzhao's Report to All-China Women's Congress," *NCNA*, April 23, 1953, in *SCMP*, no. 558, April 25–27, 1953, pp. 30–33.
13. On the encouragement of citizen participation in the three-anti campaign, see Harry Harding, *Organizing China: The Problem of Bureaucracy, 1949–1976* (Stanford: Stanford University Press, 1981), p. 83.

14. Deng and Ma, *Dangdai zhongguode weisheng,* p. 231; Shi, *Zhongguo jihua shengyu,* p. 117. For an oblique reference to the receipt of letters regarding marriage and public health, see "North China Organs Strengthen Measures in Dealing with Public Complaints," *NCNA,* January 30, 1953, in *SCMP,* no. 505, pp. 17–19.

15. Deng and Ma, *Dangdai zhongguode weisheng,* pp. 231–232. It is noteworthy that the Second All-China Labor Congress was held in late April 1954, overlapping with the Women's Congress. Zhou's survey may have been triggered by combined requests from women in both organizations. Of course, Deng Yingzhao, Zhou Enlai's wife, was well placed to bring this issue directly to Zhou's attention.

16. Ibid., pp. 231–232.

17. Zhou Enlai, *Jingji jianshede jige fangzhenxing wenti* (Several Policy Problems Related to Economic Construction), in *Zhou Enlai xuanji (xia)* (Selected Works of Zhou Enlai), vol. 2 (Beijing: People's Publishing House, 1984), p. 231.

18. Li Honggui, *Zhongguode renkou zhengce* (China's Population Policy), in *Zhongguo renkou nianjian (1985),* p. 217; editorial, *Yinggai shidangde jiezhi shengyu* (There Should Be Appropriate Birth Control), *Renmin ribao* (People's Daily), March 5, 1957; reprinted in *Zhongguo renkou nianjian (1985),* pp. 10–11.

19. Deng and Ma, *Dangdai zhongguode weisheng,* p. 232.

20. Shi, *Zhongguo jihua shengyu,* p. 119.

21. Audrey Donnithorne, *China's Economic System* (London: C. Hurst and Co., 1981), p. 458.

22. Shi, *Zhongguo jihua shengyu,* p. 114.

23. See Ma Qibin et al., eds., *Zhongguo gongchandang zhizheng sishinian (1949–1989)* (Forty Years of Rule of the Chinese Communist Party) (Beijing: Central Party History Materials Publishing House, 1989), p. 84.

24. On the problem of peasant migration, see Chen Yun, *Dongyuan chengshi renkou xiaxiang* (Mobilize the Urban Population to Go to the Countryside), in *Chen Yun wenxuan, 1956–1985* (Selected Works of Chen Yun, 1956–1985) (Beijing: People's Publishing House, 1986), pp. 152–154.

25. Ibid., p. 153; "GAC Directive on Dissuasion of Peasants from Blind Influx into the Cities," *NCNA,* April 17, 1953, in *SCMP,* no. 554, April 18–20, 1953, pp. 24–25.

26. On the implementation of the system of unified procurements, see Vivienne Shue, *Peasant China in Transition: The Dynamics of Development toward Socialism, 1949–1956* (Berkeley: University of California Press, 1980), chap. 5. See also Jean C. Oi, *State and Peasant in Contemporary China: The Political Economy of Village Government* (Berkeley: University of California Press, 1989), chap. 3.

27. On the 1955 crisis, see Thomas P. Bernstein, "Cadre and Peasant Behavior under Conditions of Insecurity and Deprivation: The Grain Supply Crisis of the Spring of 1955," in *Chinese Communist Politics in Action*, ed. A. Doak Barnett (Seattle: University of Washington Press, 1969), pp. 365–399.

28. Shi, *Zhongguo jihua shengyu*, p. 118.

29. Liu Shaoqi, *Tichang jieyu* (Promote Birth Control), in *Zhongguo renkou nianjian (1985)*, pp. 4–5.

30. To support his claim, he noted that party cadres were never encouraged to increase births. Ibid., p. 4.

31. Ibid., p. 4.

32. Ibid., pp. 4–5.

33. Ibid., p. 5.

34. Ma et al., *Zhongguo gongchandang*, p. 91.

35. Ibid., p. 91. See also Li Honggui, *Zhongguode renkou zhengce*, p. 217.

36. On these and subsequent policy debates, see David Bachman, *Bureaucracy, Economy, and Leadership in China: The Institutional Origins of the Great Leap Forward* (Cambridge: Cambridge University Press, 1991).

37. See Harding, *Organizing China*, chap. 4.

38. Shi, *Zhongguo jihua shengyu*, p. 119. For an example of this line of argument, see Shao Li-tzu, "Planned Parenthood," *Renmin ribao* (People's Daily), March 20, 1957; reprinted in *Current Background*, no. 445, April 5, 1957, pp. 9–13.

39. The plan originally was intended to guide the pace of collectivization and the direction of rural development between 1956 and 1967, but it was quickly rendered obsolete by the escalating pace of collectivization in 1955–56, followed by the Great Leap Forward of 1958–1960.

40. For the relevant excerpt from the draft plan, see *Zhongguo renkou nianjian (1985)*, p. 13.

41. *Zhongguo renkou* (Guangdong) (Beijing: Zhongguo caizheng jingji chubanshe, 1988), p. 399; *Zhongguo renkou* (Hebei) (Beijing: Zhongguo caizheng jingji chubanshe, 1987), p. 460; *Zhongguo renkou* (Hunan) (Beijing: Zhongguo caizheng jingji chubanshe, 1987), pp. 435–436; *Zhongguo renkou* (Sichuan) (Beijing: Zhongguo caizheng jingji chubanshe, 1988), p. 400.

42. *Zhongguo renkou* (Shanghai) (Beijing: Zhongguo caizheng jingji chubanshe, 1987), p. 360.

43. Zhou Enlai, *Guanyu fazhan guomin jingjide dierge wunian jihuade jianshede baogao* (Report on the Second Five-Year Construction Plan for the Development of the National Economy), September 27, 1956, in *Zhongguo renkou nianjian (1985)*, p. 9; Zhou Enlai, *Jingji jianshede jige fangzhenxing wenti* (Several Economic Construction Policy Questions), in *Zhou Enlai xuanji (xia)*, pp. 229–238.

44. Zhou Enlai, *Jingji jianshede*, p. 231.

45. Chen Yun, *Bixu tichang jiezhi shengyu* (We Must Promote Birth Control), in *Chen Yun Wenxuan, 1956–1985* (Selected Works of Chen Yun, 1956–1985) (Beijing: People's Publishing House, 1986), p. 59. This text dates these comments August 20, 1957, whereas the party administrative history gives the date as August 26. See Ma et al., *Zhongguo gongchandang*, p. 133.

46. The text can be found in Roderick MacFarquhar, Timothy Cheek, and Eugene Wu, *The Secret Speeches of Chairman Mao: From the Hundred Flowers to the Great Leap Forward* (Cambridge, Mass.: Council on East Asian Studies, Harvard University, 1989), pp. 131–189.

47. Ibid., pp. 159–160. The fact that Mao's comments elicited loud laughter should not be misinterpreted. Even in the early 1980s male party cadres were still prone to giggle and titter when the subject of family planning was raised. The high-level cadres who heard this speech were most likely moved to laughter by a combination of Mao's manner, their own embarrassment, and their generally dismissive attitude toward the subject. For high-level male cadres, birth control remained a highly controversial subject, which left them nervous and embarrassed when raised in public. Birth control might be an appropriate topic for the Women's Congress, but not for them.

48. Mao Zedong, *Zuo gemingde zujinpai*, in *Mao Zedong xuanji* (Selected Works of Mao Zedong), vol. 5 (Beijing: People's Publishing House, 1977), pp. 469, 471.

49. See Harding, *Organizing China*, pp. 167–177.

50. Mao Zedong, "Talks at the Beidaihe Conference" (August 17, 1958), in MacFarquhar et al., *Secret Speeches*, p. 403.

51. *Jihua shengyu jishu zhidao* (Family Planning Technical Guidance), in Deng and Ma, *Dangdai zhongguode weisheng*, p. 234; "Directive on Enthusiastically Promoting Planned Births," in Ma et al., *Zhongguo gongchandang*, p. 226; State Family Planning Commission, *Zhongguo jihua shengyu gongzuode sanshinian* (Thirty Years of China's Family Planning Work), in *Zhongguo renkou nianjian (1985)*, p. 921. An abbreviated text of the directive, *Zhonggong zhongyang, guowuyuan guanyu renzhen tichang jihua shengyude zhishi* (Central Committee and State Council Instructions on Enthusiastically Promoting Planned Birth), may also be found in this yearbook on p. 14.

52. "Directive on Enthusiastically Promoting Planned Births," *Zhongguo renkou nianjian (1985)*, p. 14.

53. Ibid., p. 14.

54. Deng and Ma, *Dangdai zhongguode weisheng*, p. 234; Fang Weizhong et al., eds., *Zhonghua renmin gongheguo jingji dashiji, 1949–1980* (Economic Chronicle of the People's Republic of China, 1949–1980) (Beijing: Chinese Academy of Social Sciences Publishing House, 1984), pp. 366–367.

55. Fang et al., *Jingji dashiji*, p. 367.

56. Ma et al., *Zhongguo gongchandang*, p. 264; Shi Chengli, *Wo guo jihua shengyu gongzuode fenqi* (An Analysis of Our Country's Birth Planning Work), *Xibei renkou* (Northwest Population) 1 (1988): 27–32.

57. Shi, *Zhongguo jihua shengyu*, p. 158.

12. Chinese Women Workers

1. Because China is developing rapidly into an urban industrial state, this chapter focuses primarily on women in urban industry.

2. Constitution of the People's Republic of China (1982), art. 48, trans. in *Laws of the PRC, 1979–1982* (Beijing: Foreign Languages Press, 1987), p. 14.

3. The law referred to as the Women's Rights Protection Law has commonly been translated as the Law Protecting Women's Rights and Interests (Draft). See *Foreign Broadcast Information Service, Daily Report: People's Republic of China* (hereafter *FBIS-CHI*), April 14, 1992, pp. 17–20; *China Daily*, March 28, 1992. A more accurate translation might be the Law to Guarantee Women's Rights and Interests, for the law is designed to guarantee, not to expand, rights by pulling together and coordinating provisions in existing regulations. This law went through ten drafts before its promulgation in 1992. Zhao Wen, *Nüfaxuejia tan funü quanli baozhang fa* (Woman Legal Specialist Discusses Women's Rights Protection Law), *Minzhu yu fazhi* (Democracy and Law), no. 4 (1991): 43. Most provinces have had a general provincial law "protecting women and children" since the early 1980s. *Difang xingfa gui xuanbian* (Compilation of Local Laws and Regulations) (Beijing: Zhongguo jingji chubanshe, 1991).

4. Women's Rights Protection Law, art. 25.

5. See, e.g., Provisional Regulations on the Implementation of the Contract Employment System in State Enterprises, arts. 14(iv) and 20, trans. in Hilary K. Josephs, *Labor Law in China: Choice and Responsibility* (Salem, N.H.: Butterworth Legal Publishers, 1990), p. 157. The regulations contain a provision prohibiting the discriminatory termination of a woman worker when the woman is pregnant, on maternity leave, or nursing a child. They also provide that a female contract worker is to receive the same maternity benefits as a permanent worker doing the same work in the enterprise.

6. Provisional Regulations on the Hiring of Workers in State Enterprises, art. 8, trans. in, Josephs, *Labor Law in China*, p. 161.

7. Labor Insurance Regulations of the People's Republic of China, arts. 15(a) and (b), trans. in Eng-Pao Wang, ed., *Selected Legal Documents of the*

People's Republic of China (Arlington, Va.: University Publications of America, 1976).

8. See Regulations Governing Labor Protection for Female Staff Members and Workers, trans. in *FBIS-CHI,* July 27, 1988, pp. 42–43; Regulations for Health Care for Women Employees (Trial Implementation), *Zhongguo falü nianjian 1987* (Law Yearbook of China) (Beijing: Falü chubanshe, 1988), pp. 407–409.

9. The 1988 regulations preempted the regulations governing special treatment in childbirth for female workers under the 1953 Regulations Governing Labor Insurance of the PRC and the 1955 Circular of the State Council on Female Workers' Maternity Leave. Whereas the 1986 Health Care Regulations focused primarily on the protection of a woman worker's health, the 1988 Labor Protection Regulations covered not only health but also wages, benefits, and other labor issues. *Zhongguo fazhi bao* (China Legal News), November 22, 1988.

10. 1986 Health Care Regulations, art. 3; 1988 Labor Protection Regulations, art. 1.

11. Interestingly, for no clear reason, the 1988 Labor Protection Regulations deleted menopause from its protected periods.

12. High altitude has been defined as two meters and above. *Zhongguo fazhi bao,* November 22, 1988.

13. 1988 Labor Protection Regulations, art. 10.

14. 1988 Labor Protection Regulations, art. 7.

15. 1986 Health Care Regulations, art. 10(7).

16. 1988 Labor Protection Regulations, art. 6; 1986 Health Care Regulations, art. 7(3).

17. 1988 Labor Protection Regulations, art. 7.

18. 1988 Labor Protection Regulations, art. 10.

19. Third-grade intensity refers to work that requires the exertion of 1,746 calories per eight-hour day, or strenuous exertion for 350 minutes or 73 percent of an eight-hour day. Fourth-grade labor refers to work requiring the exertion of 27,000 calories per eight-hour day, or strenuous exertion for 370 minutes or 77 percent of an eight-hour day. Zhou Minlin and Xie Liusheng, *Zhigong quanyi falü guwen* (Inquiries on Workers' Legal Rights) (Nanning: Guangxi renmin chubanshe, 1990), pp. 313–314.

20. There are eight grades of work in China, with grade one being paid the least and grade eight being paid the most. The grades are classified according to several variables including the level of exertion required, the role of the work in the economy, and the amount of skill involved. Jobs requiring complicated skills can be classified as high as eighth grade, while simpler work such as streetcleaning is limited to first or second

grade. Tong Zhehui, ed., *Shehui jingji tongji cidian* (Social and Economic Statistics Compilation) (Jilin: Jilin renmin chubanshe, 1987), pp. 736–737; see also Ma Hong, ed., *Xiandai Zhongguo jingji shidian* (Modern Chinese Economic Statistics) (Beijing: Zhongguo shehui kexue chubanshe, 1982), pp. 522–525.

21. 1988 Labor Protection Regulations, art. 8; 1986 Health Care Regulations, art. 10. Those who experience difficulty in labor are given an additional fifteen days of leave, and those who experience a multiple birth are given fifteen additional days of paid leave for each additional baby. Female workers who have a miscarriage are given leave on presentation of a medical certificate. See 1988 Labor Protection Regulations, art. 8.

22. 1988 Labor Protection Regulations, art. 7.

23. 1986 Health Care Regulations, art. 12. An appropriate extension may be considered. See 1988 Labor Protection Regulations, art. 10. In cases of multiple births, the regulations permit an additional thirty minutes for each additional nursing baby.

24. 1988 Labor Protection Regulations, art. 7.

25. 1986 Health Care Regulations, art. 7(1), 8. Premarital health care includes education, advice, and a health exam prior to marriage.

26. 1986 Health Care Regulations, art. 10.

27. Smaller units are required to set up sanitary washing facilities. See 1986 Health Care Regulations, art. 7(2).

28. 1988 Labor Protection Regulations, art. 11. The 1986 Health Care Regulations require units with five nursing mothers or more to set up a nursing room with hand-washing facilities.

29. 1986 Health Care Regulations, art. 7(1).

30. 1986 Health Care Regulations, art. 9.

31. For example, the Convention on the Elimination of All Forms of Discrimination against Women (CEDAW) encourages the provision of supporting social services and special protection for pregnant women against types of work proved to be harmful to them, and the right of women workers to social security, paid leave, and protection of health and safety in working conditions, including safeguarding reproductive functions. Convention on the Elimination of All Forms of Discrimination against Women, G.A. res. 34/180, 34 UN GOAR Supp. (no. 46) at 194, UN Doc. A/34/46 (1979), opened for signature March 1, 1980, entered into force September 3, 1981, reprinted in *Yale Journal of International Law* 10 (1985): 384.

32. After the establishment of the People's Republic in 1949, the new government acted to redress the horrible working conditions to which women had been subjected in the first half of the century. At that time, most women worked for low wages, while others were "sold" to factory owners

to work for a number of years without pay, and all worked long hours under unhygienic and unsafe conditions. For a good account of the working conditions of Chinese women around the turn of the century, see Ono Kazuko, *Chinese Women in a Century of Revolution, 1850–1950* (Palo Alto: Stanford University Press, 1989).

33. 1953 Labor Insurance Regulations, 1956 Regulation on Labor Conditions for Work Requiring Loading and Unloading, Moving and Lifting (Trial Implementation), discussed in Chen Wenyuan, *Shi lun dui nügong de teshu baohu* (A Preliminary Study of Special Protection for Women Workers), *Zhengfa luntan* (Tribune of Political Science and Law), no. 1 (1988): 58–59.

34. Other groups warranting protection include "the weak, the sick, and the disabled." *Funü de chulu* (Women's Way Out), *Zhongguo funü* (Chinese Women), no. 1 (1988): 5.

35. *Laodong faxue* (Studies in Labor Law) (Beijing: Qun Zhong chubanshe, 1985), pp. 205–207; see also Chen Wenguan, *Shilun dui nügong de teshu baohu* (A Preliminary Study of Special Protection for Women Workers), *Zhengfa luntan*, no. 1 (1988): 59.

36. Charlotte Furth and Ch'en Shu-yueh, "Chinese Medicine and the Anthropology of Menstruation in Contemporary Taiwan," *Medical Anthropology Quarterly* 6.1 (1992): 31.

37. Ibid.

38. Despite the literal translation of *zuo yuezi* as "resting for a month," the traditionally prescribed period of rest for a woman after delivery is about fifty days. Wang Yuchen and Zhao Yufeng, eds., *Laodong baohu gongzuo wenda* (Answers to Questions Relating to Labor Protection) (Beijing: Gongren chubanshe, 1984), p. 55.

39. Ibid., p. 52.

40. Following the socialist theory that gender equality was to be accomplished through the broader task of class revolution, gender equality as a state goal has fluctuated with changes in the government's economic and political campaigns. For critiques of the progress of Chinese women's liberation, *see* Phyllis Andors, *The Unfinished Liberation of Chinese Women, 1949–1980* (Bloomington: Indiana University Press, 1983); Judith Stacey, *Patriarchy and Socialist Revolution in China* (Berkeley: University of California Press, 1983); Margery Wolf, *Revolution Postponed: Women in Contemporary China* (Palo Alto: Stanford University Press, 1984).

41. Emily Honig and Gail Hershatter, *Personal Voices: Chinese Women in the 1980s* (Palo Alto: Stanford University Press, 1988), p. 243.

42. High unemployment has added to the large number of transient and unregistered persons, creating a "floating population" *(liudong renkou)*

problem for urban areas. Some newspapers estimate the total floating population at 50 million. *Dangdai da jiliu* (Flood of Modern Times), *Falü yu shenghuo* (Law and Living), no. 6 (1989): 12; *Jingdou, beifang liudong renkou dahuifang* (Beijing, the Floating Population Whirlpool), *Falü yu shenghuo* (Law and Living), no. 3 (1989): 12.

43. For an excellent account of women workers in China in the 1980s, see Honig and Hershatter, *Personal Voices*, pp. 243–263. For thorough research on urban women workers under Mao and Deng, see Elizabeth Hood, "Urban Chinese Women under Mao and Deng: The Gender Politics of Revolution and Reform in the People's Republic of China" (B.A. honors thesis, Radcliffe College, 1989). The author kindly shared her thesis with me, a copy of which is in my possession.

44. Honig and Hershatter, *Personal Voices*, pp. 252–253; Ding Juan, "Women in the Tide of Reform," *Beijing Review* 30.4 (September 1989): 30.

45. *Zhongguo funü*, no. 4 (1988): 10.

46. Zhou Minlin and Xie Liusheng, *Zhigong quanyi falü guwen*, p. 54.

47. For one woman's account of the difficulties she faced as a result of reduced income and status owing to the "return home" policy, see Li Jing, *Wo de chulu zai nali?* (Where Is My Way Out?), *Zhongguo funü*, no. 1 (1988): 6–7; see also *Cong yijia gongchang kan nüxing de chulu* (Examining the Issue of Women's Way Out by Looking at One Factory), *Zhongguo funü*, no. 8 (1988) 24.

48. In a 1988 survey of five hundred working women, 67 percent rejected the notion of a "return to the home," while 33 percent said they would quit work if their husband's wage could support the family. "Discussion on Women and Work," *Beijing Review* 31.33 (August 1988): 38. The Shenyang Women's Federation conducted a sample survey of twenty thousand women, 92 percent of whom responded. Those women who answered the survey reported feeling anxiety and discrimination in the optimization of labor organization. With regard to the redeployment of redundant personnel, only 35.4 percent agreed with the way it was being carried out, 25.3 percent held a contrary opinion, and 35.7 percent did not express any view. Ding Juan, "Women in the Tide of Reform," *Beijing Review* 30.36 (September 1989): 30.

49. Tyrene White, "Post-Revolutionary Mobilization in China: The One-Child Policy Reconsidered," *World Politics* 43.1 (October 1990): 53–76.

50. Zhou Minlin and Xie Liusheng, *Zhigong quanyi falü guwen*, p. 315.

51. Liu Ping, manager of the Guangzhou Automobile Corporation, said women have "many troubles" caused by their physiology and childbearing responsibilities which affect the economic benefits of a company. "Unless women can get compensation and the state can reduce the tax on women

workers, we heavy industrial factories prefer male workers," she said. See "A Woman's Place Is Certainly Not in the Kitchen," *FBIS-CHI,* September 7, 1988, p. 28.

52. Zhang Yigong, *Weishenma qiye bu yunyao nügong* (Why Are Enterprises Reluctant to Hire Women?), *Zhongguo funü,* no. 2 (1988): 6.

53. Department of State Report, *Country Reports on Human Rights Practices for 1989* (Washington, D.C.: U.S. Government Printing Office, 1990), pp. 820–821.

54. The three factories I visited were selected for size (one large, one medium-sized, and one small) and for their large number of women workers. Two of the factories were state enterprises (Wuhan no. 6 Textile Factory and Wuhan White-Flag Dolphin Steel and Wood Furniture Coalition Company), while the small third factory was a collective enterprise (the Wuhan 555 Instruments Factory). My assumption was that labor regulations were more likely to be fully implemented by state-owned or collective enterprises than by private enterprises. At every visit I toured the facilities and met with the leadership of the factory, the leadership of the women workers, and individual women workers.

55. Dong Qiyuan and Leng Mingzhu, *Pingdeng jingzheng—nüxing de huhuan* (Struggle for Equality: Women's Cry), *Minzhu yu fazhi* (Democracy and Law), no. 8 (1992): 32–33.

56. Both Wu Dalang and Mu Guiying are legendary figures. Wu Dalang traditionally symbolizes a weak man who cannot handle his wife's infidelity, while Mu Guiying is a strong woman who led her sisters into battle in place of her fallen husband.

57. Management in Enterprises in the Special Economic Zones in Guangdong Province, art. 13; Interim Regulations for Labor Management in the Economic and Technological Development Zone of Shandong Province, art. 13; Regulations for Labor Management of the Tianjin Economic and Technological Development Zones, art. 19. Almost all of the SEZs have a provision against firing "women workers who are over six months pregnant or on maternity leave." See Implementation Provisions of Ningbo Municipality on Labor Management for Sino-Foreign Joint Ventures, art. 10; Procedures for Labor and Wages Management in Enterprises in the Dalian Economic and Technological Development Zone, art. 11.

58. *Dangdai da jiliu,* pp. 14–15.

59. One woman tells of her escape back to Beijing, despite having been paid a monthly salary five times her salary in Beijing, to avoid advances made by her boss. Nicholas Kristof, "Free Market 'Dragon' Gains in the Fight for China's Soul," *New York Times,* March 26, 1992, pp. A1, A14.

60. The discussion began with the article by Zhang Jun and Ma Wenrong,

Daqiu Zhuang "funü huijia" de sisuo (Some Thoughts about Da Qiu Village's "Women Return Home" Policy), *Zhongguo funü*, no. 1 (1988): 8–9.

61. See, e.g., Zhang Yigong, *Weishenma qiye bu yunyao nügong* (Why Are Enterprises Reluctant to Hire Women?), *Zhongguo funü*, no. 2 (1988): 6. In addition, Zhang argues against the equal pay provision on the ground that women should be paid for actual work performed, in order to alleviate employers' reluctance to hire women.

62. This is in contrast to and in competition with the "natural role" concept, which focuses on differences between men and women and celebrates the "special attributes" of women, resulting in legislation ensuring different treatment of women and men. As Deborah Rhode puts it, "Feminists [have] sometimes demanded equal status on the basis of natural rights but they also claimed it on the ground of natural roles." Deborah Rhode, *Justice and Gender* (Palo Alto: Stanford University Press, 1989), p. 12.

63. "In the Confucian view, a man is born into society and cannot prosper alone: the individual depends on the harmony and strength of the group." Andrew Nathan, "Sources of Chinese Rights Thinking in Chinese Constitutions," in *Human Rights in Contemporary China*, ed. R. Randle Edwards, Louis Henkin, and Andrew Nathan (New York: Columbia University Press, 1986), p. 138. Self-interested individualism was not defended even during the revolutionary period, when rejection of Confucian values was widespread.

64. Ibid., p. 141.

65. Ibid., citing "Miscellany of Mao Tse-tung Thought (1949–1968)."

66. Qiu Ye, *Lun falü quanli he yiwu de tongyixing* (On the Unity of Rights and Duties in Law), *Faxue yanjiu* (Studies in Law), no. 3 (1990): 16.

67. The efforts of Chinese women may thus complement, from a different direction, the efforts of American feminists. For example, one U.S. feminist scholar, Lucinda Finley, suggests that there must be a new approach to differences between men and women, one that sees them as "relational and accepts them in a nonhierarchical and nonpejorative way . . . to integrate values and structures of both the public and home worlds accordingly" and "to supplement existing notions of rights as zones of noninterference." Lucinda Finley, "Transcending Equality Theory: A Way Out of the Maternity and the Workplace Debate," *Columbia Law Review* 86 (1986): 1118.

68. Guo Tong, "Study on the Relationship between Women Workers' Labor Protection and Women Employment," presentation delivered at the First Sino-American Conference on Women's Issues, Beijing, June 25–28, 1990.

69. Industrial workers log 1,951 hours annually in the United States, 1,603 hours in the former West Germany, and 2,155 hours in Japan. Between 1969 and 1989 the average American's yearly work schedule increased by

an average of 138 hours. See Juliet B. Schor, "Americans Work Too Hard," *New York Times*, July 25, 1991, p. A21.

70. Wei Shiqing, *Nüxing chulu yu Zhongguo de weilai mingyun* (Women's Way Out and China's Future Fate, part 2), *Zhongguo funü*, no. 6 (1988): 12.

71. Wu Kuogong, *Women de shidai xiagu yu xingbie xiagu* (Gap between the Generations and between the Sexes), *Zhongguo funü*, no. 5 (1988): 11.

72. Bao Yushu, "Health Care and Labor Protection for Working Women in China," presentation delivered at the First Sino-American Conference on Women's Issues, Beijing, June 25–28, 1990. Bao is a professor at the School of Public Health, Beijing Medical University, and is the vice director of the National Center for Research and Training in Maternity and Health Care. According to Bao, the physical makeup of women predetermines that they have less strength than men, are more sensitive to toxic and harmful substances, and retain such substances longer than men. According to Bao, when pregnant women work, growth of the embryo is bound to be impaired.

73. Dong Qiyuan and Leng Mingzhu, *Pingdeng jingzheng–nüxing de huan*, p. 33. About eight cities and seven counties have adopted the idea, which has helped to reduce the number of unemployed women workers.

74. Ibid.; Lun Yun, "New Challenges to Women's Employment," *Beijing Review*, 31.44 (October 31–November 6, 1988): 17.

75. *FBIS-CHI*, September 7, 1988, pp. 31–32.

76. Zhang Yigong, *Weishenma qiyie bu yunyao nügong?* p. 6. The Chinese regulations assume that a woman is married prior to pregnancy and childbirth. Unmarried women with children are entitled to maternity leave but not to other child care benefits provided under these regulations. Zhou Minlin, *Zhigong quanyi falü guwen*.

77. Finley, "Transcending Equality Theory," p. 1118.

78. "Survey Revealed Social, Economic Status of Women," *FBIS-CHI*, October 8, 1991, p. 29. The survey was distributed to 41,890 men and women from all walks of life and aged between eighteen and sixty-four. See also "Survey Analyzes Social Status of Women," *FBIS-CHI*, October 2, 1991, p. 20.

79. These are colloquially known as the "four selfs" *(si zi)*. See He Zhengshi, *Funü xueli lunti xi de gouxiang* (Thoughts on the Fundamental Principles of Women's Studies), *Zhongguo funü*, no. 3 (1987): 19–20; Li Hanshun, *Dangdai funü yinggai shi chao xianqi liangmu* (Modern Women Should Exceed the Image of Wife and Mother), *Zhongguo funü*, no. 7 (1987): 10; Wang Xuan, *Miandui wenhao de sisuo* (Some Thoughts about the Present Inquiry), *Zhongguo funü*, no. 4 (1988): 8 (urging women to be self-reliant and overcome dependency as a result of women's special status for the past several decades); Mi Puohua, *Duo nan de xuanze: miandui nüren de chulu de shensi* (How Difficult a Choice: Some Thoughts on Women's Way

Out), *Zhongguo funü*, no. 3 (1988): 10 (arguing against overreliance on the party).

80. See, e.g., Lei Yi, *Tupo liangji siwei moshi* (Break Through Dichotomous Thinking), *Zhongguo funü*, no. 6 (1988): 15–17.

81. This term comes from Lucinda Finley's suggestion that U.S. women supplement U.S. notions of rights as "zones of non-interference" in order to achieve equality. Finley, "Transcending Equality Theory," p. 1118.

82. Jack Donnelly, "Cultural Relativism and Universal Human Rights," *Human Rights Quarterly*, no. 6 (1984): 418–419.

83. Ibid., citing Rhoda Howard, "Women's Rights in English Speaking Sub-Saharan Africa," in *Human Rights and Development in Africa*, ed. Claude E. Welch, Jr., and Ronald I. Meltzer (Albany, N.Y.: State University of New York Press, 1984), pp. 66–68.

84. Whereas in the past the All-China Trade Union has had offices representing women workers, a Women Worker's Committee was not formally established until February 5, 1991. See *Fazhi ribao* (Legal News Daily), February 8, 1991, p. 1. The Chinese Communist party reasserted its leadership over mass organizations after the prodemocracy movement of 1989. "Circular of the CCP Central Committee on Strengthening and Improving Party Leadership over the Work of Trade Unions, Communist Youth League, and Women's Federations," *Fazhi ribao*, February 1, 1990, p. 1.

85. For example, Li Xiaojiang, one of China's foremost experts on women's studies, has established the Center for Women's Studies at Zhengzhou University in Henan Province.

14. Women, Illness, and Hospitalization

1. Sigrid McLaughlin, ed., *The Image of Women in Contemporary Soviet Fiction* (New York: St. Martin's Press, 1989), p. 10.

2. Li Ziyun, *Dangdai nüzuojia sanlun* (Essays on Contemporary Women Writers) (Hong Kong: Joint Publishing Co., 1984), pp. 124–128.

3. Virginia Woolf, "Women and Fiction" (1929), in *Collected Essays*, vol. 2 (New York: Harcourt Brace, 1967), p. 146.

4. Cao Wenxuan, *Bashi niandai wenxue xianxiang yanjiu* (Studies in the Literature of the Eighties) (Beijing: Peking University Press, 1988), p. 252.

5. Ibid., p. 255.

6. *New York Times*, February 1, 1991, p. A4.

7. *People's Daily*, overseas edition, March 8, 1991, p. 6.

8. Robert Hegel, *Expressions of Self in Chinese Literature* (New York: Columbia University Press, 1985), p. 14.

9. Sandra Gilbert and Susan Gubar, *The Madwoman in the Attic* (New Haven: Yale University Press, 1979), p. 17.

10. Patricia Meyer Spacks, *The Female Imagination* (New York: Alfred A. Knopf, 1975), p. 35.

11. Gilbert and Gubar, *The Madwoman in the Attic,* p. 25.

12. Elaine Showalter, "Feminist Criticism in the Wilderness," in *The New Feminism,* ed. Elaine Showalter (New York: Pantheon, 1985), p. 252.

13. Zhang Jie, "What's Wrong with Him?" in *As Long as Nothing Happens, Nothing Will,* trans. Gladys Yang (New York: Grove & Weidenfeld, 1984), p. 4.

14. This view is quite different from the punitive notion of cancer mentioned in Susan Sontag's *Illness as Metaphor* (New York: Farrar, Straus and Giroux, 1977). Another well-known story relying on cancer as a metaphor for victimization of the innocent is Dai Qing's "Anticipation," in *Roses and Thorns,* ed. Perry Link (Los Angeles, Calif.: University of California Press, 1984).

15. *Boston Globe,* October 6, 1991, p. 10.

16. Phyllis Chesler, *About Men* (New York: Simon & Schuster, 1978), pp. 211–212.

17. *China Now,* no. 128 (1989): 28.

18. Afterword to *Zhang Jie ji* (Zhang Jie Anthology) (Fujian: Haixia, 1986), p. 322.

15. Politics and Protocols of *Funü*

1. I situate myself in scholarship that excites my best effort. I have been stimulated over the years by the work of several scholars, and I thank them once again for their contributions to my thinking: Angela Zito, Jing Wang, Donald M. Lowe, Lydia Liu, James Hevia, Inderpal Grewal, Judith Farquhar, and Ann Anagnost. The editors of this volume suggested various improvements and thus contributed to the shape of the final version.

2. See my *Imagining Woman* (Durham: Duke University Press, forthcoming).

3. See Denise Riley, *"Am I That Name?" Feminism and the Category of Woman* (Minneapolis: University of Minnesota Press, 1988).

4. I do not read directly through words to ascertain the "real historical conditions" beyond words that contemporaries were either too close to see or too ignorant of their effects to understand. Such real conditions can never be recovered.

5. Fulian, ed., *"Sida" yilai funü yundong wenxuan* (Women's Movement Documents since the Fourth All-China Women's Congress [of 1978]), hereafter *FYW,* p. 1 *Qunzhong tuanti shi guangda qunzhong di zhongyao daibiaozhe* (Mass Organizations Are Important Representatives of the Great Masses) (Beijing: Renmin chubanshe, 1982). Or to reverse the logic, it seems historically more accurate to say that Fulian tended to "construct the interests

that it represents." Ernesto Laclau and Chantal Mouffe, *Hegemony and Socialist Strategy* (London: Verso, 1985), p. 120.

6. Many of the documents I consulted are national media articles reprinted in a resources collection published by the People's University and titled *Funü zuzhi yu huodong: yinshua baokan ziliao* (Women's Organizations and Activities: Published Press Materials Reader), hereafter cited as *ZH*. See Tan Xiangbei, *ZH* 2 (1986): 5–9.

7. See, for instance, *Ba shixian yuan da lixiang tong gaohao benzhi gongzuo jieheqilai* (Coordinate Realizing Great Aspirations with Doing Basic Work: Remembering March 8, International Working Women's Day), *ZH* 2 (1986): 7.

8. See, for instance, the Taiwan reprint, T'an Man-ni, *Chung-kuo talu ch'i-shih chih-ye fu-nü ma?* (Are Women Professionals Discriminated against on the Chinese Mainland?), *ZH* 5 (1986): 33–35; and Liu Li, *Xianshi funü jiefang de xin mubiao* (Put into Practice Women's Liberation's New Objectives), *ZH* 4 (1987): 19–22.

9. *Funü yaoqiu gaige, gaige xuyao funü* (Women Demand Reform, the Reforms Need Women), *ZH* 2 (1985): 29.

10. *Zhonggong zhongyang bangongting zhuanfa quanguo Fulian dangzu "Guanyu peiyang tiba nü ganbu wenti xiang zhongyang de qinshi baogao"* (The CCP Central Committee Work Group Changes the Organization [of the All-China Women's Federation] with the Resolution "On Nurturing and Promoting Resolution of the Female Cadre Question"), in *FYW*, p. 11. For examples of this campaign rhetoric, broadly represented in my sources, see *ZH* 4 (1987): 37–40, and 5 (1987): 5–6. See also Kang Keqing, *Fenfa ziqiang, kaizhuan funü yundong xin jumian* (Arouse Self-Strengthening, Begin Creating a New Situation for the Women's Movement), in Cai Chang, Deng Yingchao, and Kang Keqing, *Funü jiefang wenti wenxuan* (Collection of the Problems of Women's Liberation) (Beijing: Renmin chubanshe, 1988), pp. 450–474 (hereafter cited CDK), for a discussion of future campaigns and current achievements.

11. See *ZH* 3 (1986): 5–12, calling for protecting women from illegal discrimination in hiring, and 3 (1986): 26–30, which argued that the mandatory retirement age for women set at sixty-six years was discriminatory. *Quandang quanshehui yao wo funü yundong qianjiang er fendou* (The Whole Party and Society Want to Fight for Our Women's Movement), *FYW* 1983, pp. 182–186. See also Elisabeth Croll, *Feminism and Socialism in China* (London: Routledge and Kegan Paul, 1978), pp. 260–333.

12. *Guanyu shunru xuanzhuan hunyinfa de tongzhi* (Official Notice on Getting Deeply into Propagandizing the Marriage Law), in *FYW*, pp. 124–131. See

also Peng Jianming and Zhu Kefen, eds., *Funü, ertong fagui zhengci xuanpian* (Selected Policy Regulations on Women and Children) (Shanghai: Shanghai shi zonggonghui nügongbu, 1988).

13. For instance, hopelessly old-fashioned sloganeering for the "Four-self" *(si zi)* movement beginning in 1983 urged *funü* to love and respect themselves, and was couched in venerable political vernacular. See *ZH* 2 (1985): 43–46 for a history of the campaign. See also *ZH* 5 (1988): 15–21 and 4 (1989): 23–28 for later discussions of its prosecution. Not every Fulian offensive echoed past "Maoist" lines. For instance, officials endorsed the "socialization of housework" agenda calling for an end to women's double burden under the reforms, and argued that unremunerated housework should count as social labor. This formulation tends to be associated with the so-called liberal CCP line rather than with Maoist practice. See *ZH* 4 (1986): 12–14, 4 (1986): 15–19, and 5 (1986): 31–32, for good examples of this argument.

14. Meng Qiong, *Fulian gongzuo baogao* (Report on Federation Work), *FYW* 1979, p. 219.

15. Deng Weizhi and Wu Liangrong, *Zhongguo funü lilun yanjiu shinian huigu* (A Ten-Year Retrospective of Chinese Woman Theory), *ZH* 3 (1990): 7.

16. Deng Yingchao, *Bianzhuan Zhongguo funü yundong shi de zhuxian* (Compiling the History of the Chinese Women's Movement), in CDK, pp. 366–368; and *Jingshen, zuohao fuyunshi gongzuo* (Enliven Revolutionary Spirit, Do Good Work on the History of the Women's Movement), in CDK, pp. 413–420. See also Deng Yingchao, *Zhongguo nüxianfeng Xiang Jingyu* (China's Woman Pioneer Xiang Jingyu), in CDK, pp. 427–432; and Kang Keqing, *Li Dequan*, in CDK, p. 433.

17. I speak of *funü's* production as a matter of protocol and enactment because I want to distinguish between anatomical women, who may or may not identify as "woman," and the *funü* who enacts a protocol, thereby becoming a subject within the discourses of the state. A protocol is a blueprint for "gender." A fuller discussion of protocol and gendering appears in my essay "Theorizing Woman," in *Body, Subject, and Power in China*, ed. Angela Zito and Tani Barlow (Chicago: University of Chicago Press, 1994).

18. See Cai Chang, *Zhongguo gongchandang yu Zhongguo funü* (The Chinese Communist Party and Chinese Women), in CDK, pp. 220–223.

19. Deng Yingchao, *Yanzhe zuguo qianjin, wei shehui zhuyi gongxian liliang* (Go Forward with the Fatherland, Powerfully Contribute to Socialism), in CDK, p. 262.

20. See Kang Keqing, *Mao Zhuxi shuailing women zou funü chedi jiefang de daolu*

(Chairman Mao Led Us onto the Path of Complete Women's Liberation), and *Meiyou Zhongguo gongchangdang jiu meiyou Zhongguo funü de jiefang* (Without the Chinese Communist Party, There Would Be No Chinese Women's Liberation), in CDK, pp. 404–412.

21. For more on Li's position in disputes over woman theory and female subjects, see Li Xiaojiang, *Gaige he Zhongguo nüxing qunti yishi de juexing* (Economic Reform and the Awakening of Chinese Women's Collective Consciousness), *ZH* 2 (1989): 17–27. This article is translated in Chapter 16 of this volume. The quote is on p. 21 of the original.

22. Pan Suiming, *Fulian yinggai you duli de yizhi* (Fulian Should Have Its Independent Will), *ZH* 3 (1988): 44.

23. Ibid., p. 44. Fulian did undertake a structural reform in late 1988. But never, even under tremendous criticism, did it relinquish the national woman, *funü. Zhongyang shuji chu yuanze pizhun "Guanyu Fulian tizhi gaige di shexiang"* (Central Committee Secretariat Approves in Principle "Concerning the Organizational Structural Reform of the Women's Association"), *ZH* 5 (1988): 5–7.

24. My sources are full of this argument. See *ZH* 1 (1985): 9–10, and 1 (1985): 27–29, for very good examples. It received its most thorough elucidation in 1980s women's fiction. For an interesting view of how the recent women's studies/theory frame has affected the views of writers, see Wang Zheng, "Three Interviews: Wang Anyi, Zhu Lin, Dai Qing," in *Gender Politics in Modern China: Writing and Feminism*, ed. Tani Barlow (Durham: Duke University Press, 1994).

25. Ruo Shui and Feng Yuan, *Nüxing lixiang di fansi yu qiuzheng* (Seeking and Reflecting on Women's Ideals), *ZH* 2 (1987): 29–33.

26. "Women's liberation does not mean obliterating women's special characteristics, does not require forcing women not to be female but rather wants them to be women and also to be persons." Ibid., p. 31.

27. Wang Jinling, *Shehui kongzhi: tade qidian yu zhongdian—lun xingbie wenhua* (Social Controls: Their Beginning and Their End, a Discussion of "Gender Culture") *ZH* 6 (1987): 15–618.

28. See Huang Hongyu, *Nüxing zhuti yishi ji qi jianguo tujing* (Essential Female Consciousness and the Constructed Path), *ZH* 3 (1988): 21–23. The problematic of woman culture commanded enough interest that a Women's Culture Study and Discussion Association formed in 1989, and evaluative essays appeared in the press. When they met for the first time, participants expressed ambivalence over what "women's culture" meant. Jin Jong had reservations about the claim that it could resolve the crisis that Fulian's passivity had raised. But she did endorse it as one of the weapons available

in the academic study of women that would eventually lead to women's self-liberation.

29. Why not simply call *nüxing* critics feminists? Because a word for "feminist" *(nüquanzhuyi)* exists in Chinese but does not appear in these texts. The *nüxing* critique of *funü* positioned itself between feminism in other countries and Fulian officialdom through an exposition of problems, a discourse I call simply *nüxingist*. There are three explanations for the absence of feminism in this discourse, listed here in what I judge to be their ascending order of importance. First, theorists did not wish to provoke charges of bourgeois feminism, and thus preferred to keep western feminism to their right as a means of centering their own "Chinese" project within a sphere of women's politics. Second, they had access to feminism through the May Fourth period. Third, the issues that theorists raised as a consequence of taking *nüxing* positions had experiential roots in personal identity, and since the rhetoric of liberation had long been part of contemporary life, no one needed to go outside China for intellectual ammunition.

30. Li Xiaojiang, *Zouxiang nüren* (Toward Woman), in Gu Yanling, *Cong "ren" dao "nüren"* (From Person/Man to Female/Woman), *Nüxingren* 4.9 (1990): Special issue, *Shei kongzhi wode shenti?* (Who Controls My Body?), p. 256.

31. These theories are discussed later in this essay, along with the theorists who forwarded them.

32. To this point the *nüxing* critique of role owed an obvious debt to earlier May Fourth feminist *(nüquanzhuyi)* attacks on *lijiao*, or ritual etiquette. Space does not allow me to lay out the connection here, but it can be found in my book *Imagining Woman*. It is enough to say here that the entire line of argument probably developed out of the post-Maoist intellectuals' effort to recuperate the May Fourth discursive frame and reinvent the "Chinese Enlightenment," thus inscribing themselves as central to the immediate tasks of Chinese history.

33. Ruo Shui and Feng Yuan, *Nüxing lixiang*, p. 30. The object is to accept a multiplicity of roles that nurture female *renge* while refusing the extremes of accepting only male roles or accepting old-fashioned female roles such as "virtuous wife, good mother" which suppress female individuality.

34. Wei Bingjie, *Nüxing renge*; Li Ying, *Lun nüxing yishi* (On Female Consciousness), *ZH* 3 (1987): 23–29.

35. See *ZH* 4 (1988): 31.

36. Deng Weizhi, *Yingjie funüxue di huangjin shidai* (Welcome the Golden Age of Women's Studies), *ZH* 2 (1986): 31–32.

37. Ibid., p. 23.

38. Li Xiaojiang, *Xiaowa de tansuo* (Eve's Exploration) (Changsha: Hunan renmin chubanshe, 1988).

39. Ibid., p. 22. For a full discussion, see Li's amusing critique of the "three off-limits areas" of sex, class, and feminism. It is ridiculous, she argues, to ban these topics, particularly in a body of thought as potentially useful as feminism.

40. Ibid., pp. 21–22.

41. For a discussion of the problem of category in determining how to judge women's liberation, see also Li Xiaojiang, *Gaige yu Zhongguo nüxing qunti yishi de juexing* (Economic Reform and the Awakening of Chinese Women's Collective Consciousness), *ZH* 2 (1989): 17–27.

42. Li Xiaojiang, *Xiaowa*, pp. 42–43.

43. Indeed, alternate subjectivities appeared in 1980s literature, which dismantled stereotypes common in the texts of the immediate postliberation decades. Here one need only mention writers such as Cheng Naishan, Dai Qing, Dai Houying, Fen Xiaoyu, Shen Rong, Wang Anyi, Zhu Lin, Zhang Jie, Zhang Kangkang, Zhang Xinxin, and Zong Pu. See Lydia H. Liu, "Invention and Tradition," and Wang Zheng, "Three Interviews," in Barlow, *Gender Politics*.

44. Wan Shanping, "The Emergence of Women's Studies in China," *Women's Studies International Forum* 11.5: 458–459.

45. Deng Weizhi, *Funü wenti: wanshan he fazhan* (Women's Studies Questions: Excellence and Progress), *ZH* 2 (1985): 10; and Deng Weizhi, *Yingjie funüxue*.

46. Deng Weizhi, *Yingjie funüxue*, p. 31. Excluded is the academic study of women's sexuality, which it is best to leave to western feminism, as Deng points out elsewhere.

47. See Li Min and Wang Fukang, *Zhongguo funü xue* (Chinese Women's Studies) (Nanchang: Jianqxi renmin chubanshe, 1988), pp. 33–34. Li Xiaojiang tends to argue for more interventionist objectives. Although she shares the notion that women's studies is a social science, she stresses historical factors when she explains the development of women's studies in China. "Just as in the West women's studies was derived from the sixties decade of the women's rights movement, the present Chinese women's studies is a direct product of China's 'women's liberation question,'" which reform abuses instigated. See Li Xiaojiang, *Zenyang kan dangqian funü wenti he funü yanjiu* (How to Look at the Present Woman Question and Women's Research), *ZH* 1 (1989): 5–9.

48. *Nannü tongbu shidai de lilun tanqiu* (Theory and Investigation of the Period of Women's and Men's Collaboration), *ZH* 6 (1987): 12–14.

49. Li Min, *Funüxue*, chap. 3.

50. Ibid., pp. 125–146.
51. Xiao Li and Xiao Yu, *Zhongguo jindaishi shang guanyu funü jiefang de sanci lunzheng* (Chinese Modernity's Three Debates over Women's Liberation), *ZH* 3 (1986): 53–54.
52. Chen Dongyuan, *Zhongshi he jiangqing funüshi yanjiu* (Take Seriously and Strengthen the Study of Women's History), *ZH* 3 (1987): 52–54.
53. Chang Ying, *Zhongguo jindai funü yundongshi xueshu taolunhui zongshu* (Summary of Scholarly Discussion Meeting on the History of the Modern Chinese Women's Movement), *ZH* (1988): 39–40. These are notes from the September 1987 meeting at Henan University attended by historians from all over China.
54. *Nannü tongbu shidai de lilun tanqiu.*
55. Qing Ren, *Funü wenti yanjiu zongshu* (Summary of Research into the Woman Question), *ZH* 4 (1989): 11–14. This, like several others, is a direct response to Wei Shiqing's key article on the path of women's future, published in 1988.
56. Li Xiaojiang, *Xiaowa,* p. 8.
57. See Wan Shanping, "Emergence," for lists.
58. See Li Xiaojiang's "Open Letter to Su Shaozhi," *POSITIONS: east asia cultures critique* 1.1 (Spring 1993): 268–279, which, though a critique of China studies generally, applies equally well to women's studies.
59. This maneuver would coincide with what Judith Butler has called "strategic provisionality," as opposed to the so-called strategic essentialism Gayatri Spivak has sporadically promoted. See Judith Butler's comments in the special issue on identity, *October* 61 (1992): 110.
60. For an example of how one particularly good historian has handled this issue, see Antoinette M. Burton, "The White Woman's Burden: British Feminists and 'The Indian Woman,' 1865–1945," in *Western Women and Imperialism: Complicity and Resistance,* ed. Nupur Chaudhuri and Margaret Strobel (Bloomington: Indiana University Press, 1992), pp. 137–158.
61. The differences between the two constructions of woman are local, contextual, and obvious. The politics of sexuality in contemporary Chinese women's theory do not directly translate into anglophone feminist preoccupations. The critiques of racism and imperialism as the constituting frame of Essential Woman (and therefore of white feminisms), though probably interesting and useful to Chinese scholars, do not apparently bear on questions of economic and social reforms that have occupied Chinese theorists and politicians for the last decade or so. My point is simply that while an analogy exists and can be useful hermeneutically, local practices determine value because that is where political actions take place.

16. Economic Reform and the Awakening of Chinese Women's Collective Consciousness

This article was originally published as *Gaige yu Zhongguo nüxing qunti yishi de juexing, Shehui kexue zhanxian* (Social Science Battlefront) 4 (1988): 300–310. Notes are provided by the translator.

1. Published in 1988.
2. The phrase "iron rice bowl" refers to the comprehensive social welfare system in place up until 1978 in rural areas and 1984 in urban areas. It ensured, at the very least, a job and a grain ration for all, regardless of work performance.
3. Zhang Juan and Ma Wenrong, *Daqiu Zhuang "funü huijia" de sisuo* (An In-Depth Discussion of Daqiu Village's "Women Returning to the Home"), *Zhongguo funü* (Women of China) 1 (January 1988): 8–9.
4. Li Jing, *Wo de chulu zai nali?* (Where Is My Way Out?), *Zhongguo funü* 1 (January 1988): 6–7.
5. That is, 1987.
6. Zhou Lang and Feng Kewei, *Nü daxüe biyesheng mianlin de xin tiaozhan* (New Challenge for Female College Graduates), *Renmin ribao* (People's Daily), December 26, 1987, p. 5.
7. Held in 1987.
8. In 1988.
9. Empress Wu enthroned herself as empress and later as sovereign early in the Tang dynasty; she ruled from 655 to 705.
10. Queen Victoria ruled the United Kingdom from 1837 to 1901.
11. Catherine the Great of Russia staged a successful coup to take power and the imperial title from her husband, Peter. She ruled from 1762 to 1796.
12. That is, decollectivization.
13. Qin Xianglian was a woman in the Song dynasty (906–1158) who persisted in seeking government aid and redress after being abandoned by her husband, Chen Shimei, who had left her to marry a younger woman who gave him a powerful connection to the imperial family. By invoking Qin Xianglian's name, Li Xiaojiang seems to be reiterating her accusation that the Women's Federation is not really supporting women's right to divorce, which was reaffirmed by the new marriage law in 1981.
14. A phrase naming ideal traditional characteristics of femininity.
15. This is a reference to the May Fourth movement of 1919.
16. Here Li appears to be arguing that equal pay (including benefits) for equal work will eliminate consideration of women's different needs on the job, especially during their childbearing years.
17. That is, the establishment of the People's Republic of China in 1949.

Contributors

Tani E. Barlow is Associate Professor of History at San Francisco State University, and senior editor of *positions: east asia cultures critique.* With Angela Zito she has coedited *Body, Subject, and Power in China* (University of Chicago Press).

S. Katherine Campbell lived and studied in China for two years in the early 1980s. Her graduate work in anthropology focused on gender and economics. She lives and works in the San Francisco Bay area.

Katherine Carlitz is affiliated with the Department of East Asian Languages and Literatures at the University of Pittsburgh. She is the author of *The Rhetoric of Chin P'ing Mei* (University of Indiana Press). She has been studying the transformation of women's ordeals into paradigms of virtue for both men and women in late imperial China.

Chen Yiyun is a senior researcher at the Institute of Sociology of the Chinese Academy of Social Sciences in Beijing. She has been working in the area of family-centered social work and women's issues for several years. Her monographs include *Psychology and Ethics of Marriage and Family* and *Education and Training before Marriage.* In addition, she is a regular columnist in five women's magazines, a featured speaker on Beijing Radio's "Life Hotline," and the editor of a series on marriage and family education. She also researches prostitution and sexually transmitted diseases.

Charlotte Furth is the author of *Ting Wen-Chiang: Science and China's New Culture* and numerous articles on modern Chinese intellectual history. Currently she is writing a book on medicine and gender in Ming-Qing China. She is Professor of History at the University of Southern California in Los Angeles.

Gao Xiaoxian graduated with a degree in history from Xibei University in Xian. She directs the Research Office of the Shaanxi Provincial Women's Federation. Her articles include "Reflections on Modernization and Women's Liberation," "An Investigation of Peasant Women in One Hundred Households in Guanzhong, Shaanxi," and "Women's Migration and Urbanization." She edited *Statistical Reference on Chinese Women (1949–1989)* and *Contemporary Reflections on Women's Issues.*

Christina K. Gilmartin is Assistant Professor of History at Northeastern University. She has published several articles on Chinese gender issues and is finishing a book, *Gender and Revolution in China's Roaring Twenties.*

Gail Hershatter, Professor of History at the University of California, Santa Cruz, is the author of *The Workers of Tianjin* (Stanford University Press) and coauthor with Emily Honig of *Personal Voices: Chinese Women in the 1980s* (Stanford University Press). She is writing a book, *Shanghai Prostitutes: Sex, Gender, and Modernity in a Chinese City, 1890–1993.*

Li Xiaojiang is a professor in the Department of Chinese at Zhengzhou University, where she also chairs the Women's Studies Research Center. Her major works include *Women's Way Out* (Liaoning renmin chubanshe), *An Exploration of Female Aesthetic Consciousness* (Henan renmin chubanshe), and *Gender Gap* (Sanlian shudian). She is general editor of the Women's Studies Research series.

Li Ziyun was for many years editor of the literary magazine *Shanghai Literature.* She began publishing literary criticism in the 1960s, and is the author of *On Contemporary Women Writers* (Hong Kong Joint Publishers), *The Meandering Stream* (Sichuan Literature Publishing House), and

The Scenes of Yesterday (Zhejiang Literature Publishing House). She is best known for her studies of Chinese women writers.

Susan Mann is Professor of History at the University of California, Davis. Author of *Local Merchants and the Chinese Bureaucracy, 1750–1950* (Stanford University Press) and "Widows in the Kinship, Class, and Community Structures of Qing Dynasty China" (*Journal of Asian Studies* 46.1 [February 1987]), she is currently completing a book on women in eighteenth-century China.

Lisa Rofel is Assistant Professor of Anthropology at the University of California, Santa Cruz. She is completing a book on gender, labor, and modernity in post-Mao China.

Cathy Silber is a doctoral candidate in Chinese literature at the University of Michigan, writing a dissertation on *nüshu*. She has published two co-translated books: *Selected Works of Wang Meng*, vol. 2, and *Maidenhome and Other Stories* by Ding Xiaoqi. She has also published an article in *Ms.* magazine and translations in *Mother Jones, The Literary Review,* and *Australian Short Stories.* She is contributing translations to *An Anthology of Chinese Women Poets*, ed. Kang-i Sun Chang (Yale University Press), and completing a book of translations of Wu Zao's lyrics.

Tyrene White is Associate Professor of Political Science at Swarthmore College. She is author of *Rationing the Children: China's One-Child Campaign in the Countryside* (University of California Press). Her current research is on rural government and institutional development in China.

Margaret Y. K. Woo is Associate Professor at Northeastern University School of Law, where her research focuses on Chinese law. She is also a research fellow of the East Asian Legal Studies Center of Harvard Law School and of the Fairbank Center for East Asian Research. Her writings have included pieces on criminal law, judicial procedure, human rights, and legal reform in China.

Zhong Xueping is Assistant Professor of Chinese Language and Literature at Tufts University.

Zhu Hong is affiliated with the Institute of Foreign Literature of the Chinese Academy of Social Sciences in Beijing. She is currently teaching at Boston University. She has published widely on English and American literature, and has translated two volumes of contemporary Chinese fiction into English: *The Chinese Western* (Ballantine), and *The Serenity of Whiteness* (Ballantine).

Harvard Contemporary China Series

After Mao: Chinese Literature and Society, 1978–1981
Edited and with an Introduction by Jeffrey C. Kinkley

The Political Economy of Reform in Post-Mao China
Edited and with an Introduction by
Elizabeth J. Perry and Christine Wong

China's Intellectuals and the State: In Search of a
New Relationship
Edited by Merle Goldman, with
Timothy Cheek and Carol Lee Hamrin

Ai Ssu-Chi's Contribution to the Development of
Chinese Marxism
by Joshua A. Fogel

Science and Technology in Post-Mao China
Edited by Denis Fred Simon and Merle Goldman

The Secret Speeches of Chairman Mao
Edited by Roderick MacFarquhar, Timothy Cheek,
and Eugene Wu

Chinese Society on the Eve of Tiananmen:
The Impact of Reform
Edited and with an Introduction by Deborah Davis
and Ezra F. Vogel

New Perspectives on the Cultural Revolution
Edited and with an Introduction by William A. Joseph,
Christine P. W. Wong, and David Zweig

From May Fourth to June Fourth:
Fiction and Film in Twentieth-Century China
Edited by Ellen Widmer and David Der-Wei Wang